Tafsīr al-Qurṭubī
Vol. 4
Juz' 4: Sūrah Āli 'Imrān 96 – 200
& Sūrat an-Nisā' 1 – 23

Tafsīr al-Qurṭubī

The General Judgments of the Qur'an and Clarification of what it contains of the Sunnah and *Āyah*s of Discrimination

Abū 'Abdullāh Muḥammad ibn Aḥmad ibn Abī Bakr ibn Farḥ al-Anṣārī al-Khazrajī al-Andalusī al-Qurṭubī

Vol. 4

Juz' 4: Sūrah Āli 'Imrān 96 – 200
& Sūrat an-Nisā' 1 – 23

translated by
Aisha Bewley

DIWAN PRESS
Classical and Contemporary Books on Islam and Sufism

Published by: Diwan Press Ltd.

Website: www.diwanpress.com
E-mail: info@diwanpress.com

By: Abu 'Abdullah Muhammad ibn Ahmad al-Qurtubi
Translated by: Aisha Abdarrahman Bewley
Edited by:Abdalhaqq Bewley

A catalogue record of this book is available from the British Library.

ISBN13: 978-1-908892-96-6 (Paperback)
978-1-908892-97-3 (Casebound)
978-1-908892-98-0 (ePub & Kindle)

Contents

Translator's note	vii
2. Sūrah Āli 'Imrān – The Family of 'Imrān 96 – 200	1
3. Sūrat an-Nisā' – Women 1 – 23	188
Table of Contents for *Āyat*s	285
Glossary	288

Table of Transliterations

ء	’	ض	ḍ
ا	a	ط	ṭ
ب	b	ظ	ẓ
ت	t	ع	‘
ث	th	غ	gh
ج	j	ف	f
ح	ḥ	ق	q
خ	kh	ك	k
د	d	ل	l
ذ	dh	م	m
ر	r	ن	n
ز	z	ه	h
س	s	و	w
ش	sh	ي	y
ص	ṣ		

Long vowel		Short vowel	
ا	ā	ـَ	a [*fatḥah*]
و	ū	ـُ	u [*ḍammah*]
ي	ī	ـِ	i [*kasrah*]
أَوْ	aw		
أَيْ	ay		

Translator's note

The Arabic for the *āyat*s is from the Algerian State edition of the *riwāyah* of Imam Warsh from the *qirā'ah* of Imam Nāfi' of Madina, whose recitation is one of the ten *mutawātir* recitations that are mass-transmitted from the time of the Prophet ﷺ.

There are minor omissions in the text. Some poems have been omitted which the author quotes to illustrate a point of grammatical usage or as an example of orthography or the usage of a word, often a derivative of the root of the word used in the *āyah*, but not the actual word used. Often it is difficult to convey the sense in English. Occasionally the author explores a grammatical matter or a tangential issue, and some of these may have been shortened. English grammatical terms used to translate Arabic grammatical terms do not have exactly the same meaning, sometimes rendering a precise translation of them problematic and often obscure.

The end of a *juz'* may vary by an *āyah* or two in order to preserve relevant passages.

3. Sūrah *Āl 'Imrān* – The Family of 'Imrān 96 – 200

إِنَّ أَوَّلَ بَيْتٍ وُضِعَ لِلنَّاسِ لَلَّذِي بِبَكَّةَ مُبَارَكًا وَهُدًى لِّلْعَٰلَمِينَ ﴿٩٦﴾ فِيهِ
ءَايَٰتٌۢ بَيِّنَٰتٌ مَّقَامُ إِبْرَٰهِيمَ وَمَن دَخَلَهُۥ كَانَ ءَامِنًا وَلِلَّهِ عَلَى ٱلنَّاسِ
حِجُّ ٱلْبَيْتِ مَنِ ٱسْتَطَاعَ إِلَيْهِ سَبِيلًا وَمَن كَفَرَ فَإِنَّ ٱللَّهَ غَنِىٌّ عَنِ
ٱلْعَٰلَمِينَ ﴿٩٧﴾

96 The first House established for mankind was that at Bakkah, a place of blessing and a guidance for all beings. 97 In it are Clear Signs – the Maqām of Ibrāhīm. All who enter it are safe. Ḥajj to the House is a duty owed to Allah by all mankind – those who can find a way to do it. But if anyone disbelieves, Allah is Rich Beyond Need of any being.

It is confirmed in *Ṣaḥīḥ Muslim* that Abū Dharr said, 'I asked the Messenger of Allah ﷺ about the first mosque established on the earth and he answered, "The *Masjid al-Ḥarām.*" I asked, "And then?" He said, "*Al-Aqsa.*" I asked, "How long was there between them?" "Forty years," he replied, "and then the whole earth became a mosque for you, so pray wherever you are when the time for prayer comes."'

Mujāhid and Qatādah said, 'There was no house before it.' 'Alī said, 'There were many houses before it. What is meant is that it is the first house established for worship.' Mujāhid said, 'The Muslims and Jews boasted and the Jews said, "The temple of Jerusalem is better and greater than the Ka'bah because it was the place of the emigration of Prophets and is in the Holy Land." The Muslims said, "The Ka'bah is better." Allah then revealed this *āyah*.' How the House was built has already been dealt with in *al-Baqarah*. Mujāhid said, 'Allah created the site of this house two thousand years before He created any of the earth, and its foundations are in the seventh and lowest earth. As for *Al-Aqṣā*, Sulaymān built it.' An-Nasā'ī transmitted this with a sound *isnād* from 'Abdullāh ibn 'Amr. The Prophet ﷺ said, 'When Sulaymān ibn Dāwūd built the temple in Jerusalem, he asked Allah for three things. He asked Allah for judgment corresponding to His judgment and he was given it. He asked Allah for a kingdom which no one after him would have and he was given that. He asked Allah, when he finished building the temple, that anyone who approached it for the sole reason of praying in it would have his errors fall from him so that he would be like he was on the day he was born, and this was granted.' There is some equivocation between the two hadiths because there was a long period of time between Ibrāhīm and Sulaymān. Historians say that there was more than a thousand years between them. It is said that Ibrāhīm and Sulaymān were the predecessors for what others built after them.

It is related that Ādam was the first to build the House, as was already mentioned. Then it is possible that one of his sons built *al-Aqṣā* forty years later. It is also possible that the angels built it with Allah's permission. All of this is possible, and Allah knows best. 'Alī ibn Abī Ṭālib said, 'Allah commanded the angels to build a house on the earth and to do *ṭawāf* of it before Ādam was created. Then Ādam built what he built of it and did *ṭawāf* of it and then the Prophets after him, and then Ibrāhīm completed its construction.'

...that at Bakkah,

Bakkah is the actual site of the House and Makkah is the rest of the town according to Mālik ibn Anas. Muḥammad ibn Shihāb said that Bakkah is the mosque and Makkah is all the Ḥaram, including the houses. Mujāhid said that Bakkah is Makkah. The *bā'* is replaced by the *mīm* as done in the word for 'sticking': *lāzim* for *lāzib*. Aḍ-Ḍaḥḥāk and al-Mu'arrij said that.

Then it is also said that Bakkah is derived from the word *bakk*, which means crowding and Bakkah takes its name from the fact that the people crowd together in it during *ṭawāf*. *Bakka* means 'to throttle' and it is said that it is called that because it crushes the necks of any tyrants if they act unjustly towards it. 'Abdullāh ibn az-Zubayr said, 'No tyrant has ever directed evil at it without Allah breaking his neck.'

It is said that the name Makkah comes from its lack of water, and it is said that it is because it sucks (*makka*) the marrow from the bones through the hardship involved in reaching it. The verb *makka* is used for a foal suckling from its mother. A poet said:

It suckled (*makkat*) and no milk remained inside her.

It is said that it is called that because it sucks the one who does injustice in it, in other words destroys him. It is said that it is called that because people used to whistle (*makkā*) and laugh in it as in Allah's words: *'Their prayer at the House is nothing but whistling and clapping.'* (8:35)

a place of blessing and a guidance for all beings.

Allah made it blessed by multiplying the reward of action in it. *Barakah* is abundant good. It is in the accusative for the *ḥāl* modifying what is implied by 'established', or an adverb of Bakkah. It is a guidance for all.

In it are Clear Signs – the Maqām of Ibrāhīm

The people of Makkah, Ibn 'Abbās, Mujāhid and Sa'īd ibn Jubayr read this as 'a Clear Sign' in the singular, meaning a Sign of *tawḥīd*, referring to the Maqām of Ibrāhīm alone. They said, 'The mark of his feet in the Maqām is a Clear Sign.' Mujāhid explained it as referring to the entire Ḥaram and believed that its Signs include Ṣafā and Marwah, the Corner and the Maqām. The others read it in the plural, meaning the Maqām of Ibrāhīm, the Black Stone, the Ḥaṭīm, Zamzam and all the sacred hallmarks. Abū Ja'far an-Naḥḥās said the reading with the plural is clearer because the Signs certainly include Ṣafā and Marwah.

Another sign is that the birds do not fly over it when they are healthy and another sign is that when someone is hunting and the game enters the Ḥaram, he leaves it be. Another sign is that when there is abundant rain at the Yemeni Corner, there is plenty in Yemen, and when it is at the Syrian corner, there is plenty in Syria. When rain covers all of the House, there is plenty in all lands. Another aspect of it is that the *jamrah*s, in spite of what is added to them, remain the same size.

The word Maqām comes from the verb *qāma*, to stand, and so it is the place where one stands. The Maqām was dealt with in *al-Baqarah* along with the disagreement about it. It implies: 'one of them is the Maqām of Ibrāhīm', as al-Akhfash said. It is related that Muḥammad ibn Yazīd said that *'Maqām'* is an appositive for 'Signs'. A third view is that it means: 'They are the Maqām of Ibrāhīm' based on a known Arabic usage. [POEM] Abu-l-'Abbās said that the word *'maqām'* actually indicates the plural *'maqāmāt'* because it is a verbal noun. We see in the Qur'an: *'Allah has sealed up their hearts and hearing'* (92:8) where 'hearing' is in the singular. This is strengthened by the hadith which states: 'Ḥajj is all the Maqām of Ibrāhīm.'

All who enter it are safe.

Qatādah said, 'That is also one of the signs of the Ḥaram.' An-Naḥḥās says that is a good opinion because people are swept away all around it and no tyrant reaches it. They reached Jerusalem and destroyed it but never reached the Ḥaram.' Allah says: *'Do you not see what your Lord did with the Companions of the Elephant?'* (105:1) One of the people of meanings said, 'The form of the *āyah* is a report while its meaning is a command. It means: "Give security to whoever enters it."' The same usage is seen in 2:197. Along these lines, an-Nu'mān ibn Thābit said, 'Anyone who commits a wrong action and merits a *ḥadd* punishment and then takes refuge in the *Ḥaram* is safe,' based on this *āyah*. Allah made security mandatory for those who enter it. That is related from a group of the early generations, including Ibn Abbās and others.

Ibn al-'Arabī said, 'There is weakness in the statements of all who say this for two reasons. One is that they do not understand that the *āyah* is about the past and does not involve the establishment of a future ruling. The second is that they do not acknowledge that its security has been violated and killing and fighting occurred after that. What Allah states cannot occur differently to that statement. So that indicates that this must have been referring to the past.' Abū Ḥanīfah disagreed and said, 'Anyone who seeks refuge in the Ḥaram is not given food or water nor is any business done with him nor is he spoken to until he leaves.' His being forced to leave is not consonant with security. It is related that he said, 'Retaliation for limbs takes place in the Ḥaram. There is also no security in this case.' The majority of scholars say that *ḥudūd* punishments may be carried out in the Ḥaram. It is reported that the Prophet ﷺ ordered the killing of Ibn Khaṭal while he was clinging to the drapes of the Ka'bah.

Ath-Thawrī related that Ibn 'Abbās said, 'If someone commits a crime that merits a *ḥadd* punishment in the Ḥaram, it is carried out on him. If he commits it outside of the Ḥaram and then seeks refuge in it, he is not spoken to nor is business carried out with him until he leaves the Ḥaram and then the *ḥadd* is carried out on him.' This is the position of ash-Sha'bī. This is also the argument of Kufans. Ibn 'Abbās understands that this is what the *āyah* means. He was the scholar of the Community.

What is sound is that by saying that Allah is referring to the many blessings granted to anyone who is there, whoever they are, as Allah also says: *'Do they not see that We have established a safe haven while people all round them are violently dispossessed?'* (29:67) In the Jāhiliyyah, those who entered it and sought sanctuary were safe from attack and killing as will be explained in *al-Mā'idah*. Qatādah said, 'In the Jāhiliyyah, whoever entered it was safe.'

This is good. It is related that an atheist said to one of the scholars, 'Does the Qur'an not say: *"All who enter it are safe"*? We have entered it and we have done such-and-such. Is not the one who enters it safe?' He said to him, 'Are you not one of the Arabs? What does someone mean when he says that whoever enters his house is safe? Does he not say to those who obey him, "Leave him be. I have granted him security." Will he leave him be?' 'Yes, of course,' he replied. He said, 'That is how it is with His words: *"All who enter it are safe"*' Yaḥyā ibn Ja'dah said that it means he is safe from the Fire.

This is not universal because we find in *Ṣaḥīḥ Muslim* in the hadith of intercession reported by Abū Sa'īd al-Khudrī: 'By the One Who has my soul in his hand, none of you can be more insistent in asking Allah for his rights than the believers on the Day of Rising who will ask Allah for their brothers who are in the Fire. They will say, "Our Lord, they used to fast with us, pray and perform *ḥajj*!" They will be told, "Bring out those you recognise."' The one who enters it is safe from the Fire by performing the practices connected with it, respecting it, acknowledging its right, and seeking to draw near to Allah Almighty.

Ja'far aṣ-Ṣādiq said, 'Whoever enters it with purity, as the Prophets and *awliyā'* entered it, is safe from Allah's punishment.' This is what is meant by his words ﷺ, 'Anyone who makes *ḥajj* to this House and does not engage in sexual activity or wrongdoing emerges from his errors like the day his mother bore him. An accepted *ḥajj* has no reward but the Garden.' Al-Ḥasan said, 'An accepted *ḥajj* is that he returns abstinent in this world, desiring the Next World.' He recited:

O Ka'bah of Allah! The supplication of the one who seeks refuge
is the supplication of one calling, in need.

He has bade farewell to those he loves and his home
and come hovering between fear and hope.

If Allah generously accepts his striving,
he is saved. Otherwise he is not saved.

You are one of those whose intercession is hoped for.
Be kind to Wāfid ibn Ḥajjāj!

It is also said that it means whoever entered it in the year of the Fulfilled 'Umrah with Muḥammad ﷺ is safe. The evidence is found in the words of the Almighty: *'You will enter the Masjid al-Ḥarām in safety, Allah willing.'* (48:27)

It is said that the word *'man'* (tr. as 'all') here refers to the non-sentient and the *āyah* is about the safety of game. This is odd. We see in the Revelation: *'Some of them* (minhum) *go on their bellies.'* (24:45)

Ḥajj to the House is a duty owed to Allah by all mankind

In the phrase *'owed to Allah'* Allah uses the *lām* of the obligation and then reinforces it with *''alā'* which is the strongest preposition in Arabic for making something obligatory. Allah uses the most comprehensive of the expressions of obligation to stress the right it has over us and the esteem owed to it. There is no disagreement about its obligatory nature. It is one of the pillars of Islam and is only obliged once in a lifetime. Some people said that it is obliged once every five years and relate about that a hadith which they trace back to the Prophet ﷺ. The hadith is false and not sound. The consensus invalidates their position.

'Abd ar-Razzāq related from Sufyān ath-Thawrī from al-'Alā' ibn al-Musayyab from his father from Abū Sa'īd al-Khudrī that the Prophet ﷺ said, 'The Lord says, "I have expanded my slave's provision and yet he does not visit me in *iḥrām* every four years."' It is famous from al-'Alā' ibn al-Musayyab ibn Rāfi' al-Kāhilī al-Kūfī from the children of hadith scholars. More than one related it from him. They include those who said 'every five years'. Some said: from al-'Alā' from Yūnus ibn Khabbāb from Abū Sa'īd. There is disagreement about all of that.

The atheists deny the *ḥajj* and say that it involves removing garments, which is contrary to modesty, running, which is contrary to gravity, and stoning the *jamrah*s for no purpose, which is contrary to logic. They say that all these actions are baseless because they do not recognise their wisdom or cause. They are ignorant of the fact that it is not necessary for the Lord to make His slave understand all that He commands him to do nor to acquaint him with the point of the actions He requires of him. It is incumbent on him to obey, and he must obey without seeking benefit nor asking about the goal. This is the meaning of what the Prophet ﷺ used to say in his *talbīyah*: 'At Your service, truly, truly in worship and slavehood. At Your service, God of the Truth.'

The imāms related that Abū Hurayrah said, 'The Messenger of Allah ﷺ addressed us and said, "People! The Ḥajj has been made obligatory for you, so perform it!" A man asked, "Every year, Messenger of Allah?" He was silent until the man had asked that three times. Then the Messenger of Allah ﷺ said, "If I had said yes, it would have become obligatory and you would not be able to do it." Then he said, "Leave me with what I have left you. Those before you were destroyed for asking too many questions and differing from their Prophets. If I command you to do something, do what you can of it. If I forbid you from doing something, then leave it.'" (Muslim)

This hadith makes it clear that when an obligation is directed to those responsible for doing it, it is enough that they do it once and it does need to be repeated. This differs from the position of Abū Isḥāq al-Isfarāyīnī. It is confirmed that his Companions said to the Prophet ﷺ, 'Messenger of Allah, is this *ḥajj* of ours for just this year or for all time?' He answered, 'It is for all time.' This is a text refuting those who say that it is obligatory once every five years. The *ḥajj* was well known among the Arabs. It was part of what they desired because of its markets, social acceptability and being part of the Ḥanīfiyyah. When Islam came, they were told to do what they knew and to hold to what they recognised. The Prophet ﷺ performed *ḥajj* before the obligatory *ḥajj*. He had stood at 'Arafah and did not change the Law of Ibrāhīm that had been changed by Quraysh when they stood at the Mash'ar al-Ḥarām, saying, 'We are the people of the Ḥaram and do not leave it. We are the Ḥums.' This was already explained in *al-Baqarah*.

One of the oddest claims that I have seen made is that the Prophet ﷺ performed *ḥajj* twice before the Hijrah and by that the obligation was cancelled for him because he had responded to the summons of Ibrāhīm when it was said: *'Announce the Ḥajj to mankind.'* (22:27) Aṭ-Ṭabarī said, 'This is unlikely. When it was announced as part of his Sharī'ah: *"Ḥajj to the House is a duty owed to Allah by all mankind,"* then it must also have been a duty for him according to that injunction. If it is said that it is only addressed to those who have not yet performed *ḥajj*, that is arbitrary and specific and there is no evidence for it. If someone claims that those who performed *ḥajj* in the religion of Ibrāhīm are not addressed by this, it is extremely unlikely.'

The Book and the *Sunnah* indicate that the *ḥajj* should be performed in a person's own good time, not immediately. That is the final position in the school of Mālik as Ibn Khuwayzimandād mentioned, and it is the position of ash-Shāfi'ī, Muḥammad ibn al-Ḥasan ash-Shaybānī, and Abū Yūsuf in one transmission. Some later Baghdadi Mālikīs believed that the obligation is immediate and it is not permitted to delay it when the ability to perform it exists. That is the position of Dāwūd. The sound view is the first one because Allah says in *Sūrat al-Ḥajj: 'Announce the Ḥajj to mankind'* (22:27) and *al-Ḥajj* is Makkan. He says: *'Ḥajj to the House is a duty owed to Allah by people.'* This *sūrah* was revealed in the year of Uḥud in Madīnah in 3 AH and the Prophet ﷺ did not perform *ḥajj* until 10 AH.

As for the *Sunnah*, there is the hadith of Ḍimām ibn Tha'laba as-Sa'dī of the Banū Sa'd ibn Bakr who came to the Prophet ﷺ and asked him about Islam and he mentioned the *shahādah*, prayer, *zakāt*, fasting and *ḥajj*. Ibn 'Abbās, Abū Hurayrah and Anas related it. There is a lot of mention of the *ḥajj* in the *Sunnah*. It is clearly obligatory. The hadith of Anas is better and more complete. There is disagreement about the date of this hadith. It is said that is 5 AH, 7 AH and 9 AH. Ibn Hishām mentioned from Abū 'Ubaydah al-Wāqidī that it was in the year of the Ditch after the Confederates left.

Ibn 'Abd al-Barr said, 'Part of the evidence that the *ḥajj* can be delayed is the consensus of scholars that if someone able to go on *ḥajj* delays it for a year or two, and then performs the *ḥajj* some years after his ability to perform it exists, then he has performed the obligatory *ḥajj* in its time. All agree that he is not like someone who misses the prayer until its time has passed and makes it up after its time, or someone who misses fasting Ramaḍān due to illness or travel and then makes it up, or like someone who invalidates his *ḥajj* and then makes it up. It is agreed that if someone performs the *ḥajj* years after he is able to do so, he is not said to be "making it up". From this we know that there is wide scope for the time of *ḥajj* and that it is not immediate.'

Abū 'Umar said, 'All who say that *ḥajj* can be delayed put no time limit on that except what is related from Saḥnūn who was asked about a man who had the wherewithal to make *ḥajj* and delayed it for some years while he was able to do it and whether that meant that he became *fāsiq* by delaying the *ḥajj*, causing his testimony to be rejected. He said it did not, even if that delay was up to sixty years. If it was more than sixty years, he was considered *fāsiq* and his testimony rejected.' So he made sixty years the limit. Limits are only stipulated in the Sharī'ah by someone who can legislate.

Ibn al-Khuwayzimandād related this from Ibn al-Qāsim. Ibn al-Qāsim and others said, 'If he delays it for sixty years, his character is not impaired. If he delays it beyond sixty years, his character is impaired because the Prophet ﷺ said, "The lifespan of my community is between sixty and seventy. Few exceed it." It is as if the requirement is made urgent for him in these ten years.

Abu 'Umar said, 'Some people, like Saḥnūn, cite as evidence the words of the Prophet ﷺ: "The lifespan of my community is between sixty and seventy. Few exceed that." There is no proof in that because the words deal with the majority of the ages of the community, if the hadith is sound. It contains evidence for scope for this up to the age of seventy because that is still within the lifespan of the majority. It is not proper to call someone of good character and trustworthiness impious through such a weak interpretation.' Success is by Allah.

Scholars agree that all are addressed in general. Ibn al-'Arabī said, 'Even if people disagree about the application of general terms, they agree that this *āyah* applies to all people, male and female, except children, who are excluded by the consensus that they are excluded from the obligations of responsibility. The same applies to slaves who are also not included. They are excluded from it by the words: *"those who can find a way to do it."* A slave lacks the ability because his master can prevent him from doing it by his right of ownership and Allah put the right of the master before His right out of kindness to His slaves. There is no disagreement about this either in the community as a whole or between the imams. We do not hasten to affirm what we do not actually know. The only evidence regarding it is the accepted consensus.' Ibn al-Mundhir said that most of the people of knowledge agree, with the exception of the odd person whose disagreement is not considered, that if a child or slave has made *ḥajj* and then the child becomes an adult or the slave is freed, they still owe the *ḥajj* if they can find a way to do it.

Abū 'Umar said, 'Dāwūd disagreed with most of the *fuqahā'* of the cities and leaders of tradition about slaves and said that they are required to perform *ḥajj*. According to the majority of scholars, however, slaves are not among those addressed by this command. That is because they do not possess freedom of action and cannot perform *ḥajj* without their master's permission. That is the same as slaves not being addressed by the requirement to attend Jumu'ah in 62:9. It is the position of most scholars except for rare exceptions. Slaves are also excluded from the obligation of giving testimony in 2:282. They are not included in that. It is also possible that children are excluded from the command to perform *ḥajj* in this *āyah* even though they are included in "mankind" since the pen [recording responsibility] has been lifted from them. Women are excluded from the words: *"You who believe, when the prayer is called…"*, despite the fact that they are among those who believe, just as slaves are excluded from this. That is the position of the *fuqahā'* of the Hijaz, Iraq, Syria and the Maghrib. It is not permitted for them to deviate in the interpretation of the Book.'

If it is asked, 'If the slave lives in the vicinity of the Masjid al-Ḥarām and his master gives him permission, why is it not necessary for him to perform *ḥajj*?' The answer is that this question is based on consensus and it may be that there is no reason for that. But since it is confirmed that this ruling is based on consensus, we use it as evidence for the fact that any *ḥajj* he performs while still a slave is not counted as the obligatory *ḥajj*. It is related from Ibn 'Abbās that the Prophet ﷺ said, 'If a child performs *ḥajj* and then reaches adulthood, he must perform another *ḥajj*. If a desert Arab performs *ḥajj* and then emigrates, he must perform another *ḥajj*. If a slave performs *ḥajj* and then is freed, he must perform another *ḥajj*.'

Ibn al-'Arabī said, 'Some of our scholars are careless and have said, "The *ḥajj* is not confirmed for a slave, even if his master has given permission, because originally he was an unbeliever and the *ḥajj* of an unbeliever is not counted. When he became a slave perpetually, he was not instructed to perform *ḥajj*." This is unsound in three ways. The first is that we believe that the secondary rulings of the Sharī'ah are also directed at unbelievers, and there is no disagreement that that is the view of Mālik. The second is that all acts of worship are obliged for him with respect to the prayer and fasting while he is a slave. If he had done them while an unbeliever, they would not be counted. The third is that unbelief is removed by Islam, so its ruling must also be removed.' Success is by Allah.

those who can find a way to do it.

Ad-Dāraquṭnī reported that Ibn 'Abbās said, 'It was asked, "Messenger of Allah, should *ḥajj* be done every year?" "Rather it is one *ḥajj*," he replied ﷺ. He was asked, "What is '*a way*'" He said, "Provision and a mount."' That is related from Anas, Ibn Mas'ūd, Ibn 'Umar, Jābir, 'Ā'ishah, and 'Amr ibn Shu'ayb from his father from his grandfather. 'Alī ibn Abī Ṭālib related that the Prophet ﷺ said: '*Ḥajj to the House is a duty owed to Allah by all mankind – those who can find a way to do it.*' He said that he was asked about that and the Prophet ﷺ said that it meant, 'That you have the use of a camel.'

Ibn Mājah also transmitted the hadith of Ibn 'Umar in the *Sunan* as did Abū 'Īsā at-Tirmidhī in the *Jāmi'*. He said that it is a good hadith. According to the people of knowledge, the practice is that when a man has provision and transport, he must perform *ḥajj*. Things are said by the people of hadith about the memory of Ibrāhīm ibn Yazīd al-Khūzī al-Makkī. They transmitted from Wakī' and ad-Dāraquṭnī from Sufyān ibn Sa'īd from Ibrāhīm ibn Yazīd from Muḥammad ibn 'Abbād that Ibn 'Umar said, 'A man went to the Prophet ﷺ and asked, "Messenger of Allah, what makes *ḥajj* mandatory?" He answered, "Provision and a mount." He asked, "Messenger of Allah, what is the state of the *ḥājjī*?" He replied, "Dishevelled, ill-smelling." Another rose and asked, "What is *ḥajj*?" He answered, "Clamour and shedding blood."' Wakī' said that 'clamour' is raising the voice with the *talbīyah* and 'shedding blood' is making the sacrifices.

Among those who said that provision and a mount are preconditions for the *ḥajj* were 'Umar ibn al-Khaṭṭāb, his son 'Abdullāh, 'Abdullāh ibn 'Abbās, al-Ḥasan al-Baṣrī, Sa'īd ibn Jubayr, 'Aṭā' and Mujāhid. That is the position of ash-Shāfi'ī, ath-Thawrī, Abū Ḥanīfah and his people, Aḥmad, Isḥāq, 'Abd al-'Azīz ibn Abī Salamah, and Ibn Ḥabīb. 'Abdūs mentioned something similar from Saḥnūn.

Ash-Shāfi'ī says, 'Ability has two aspects. One is that a person is physically able to do it and has enough money to achieve the *ḥajj*. The second is that someone is disabled in his body and unable to ride, but is able to have someone perform *ḥajj* on his behalf for a wage or without a wage. This will be explained. The one who is physically able is obliged by Allah's Book to perform *ḥajj* by Allah's words: *"those who can find a way to do it."* The one who is financially able to do it is obliged to perform the *ḥajj* by the *Sunnah* on the basis of the hadith related about the Khath'amī woman. As for the one who is able to do it himself, he is the strong person who incurs, in riding a mount, no hardship beyond his ability to bear it. If this is the case at a time when he possesses provision and a mount, he is obliged to make *ḥajj* himself. If he lacks provision and transport, or either one of them, then the obligation of *ḥajj* is cancelled for him. If someone is able to walk and has provision or the ability to earn provision on the way through their skill, such as leather work, cupping or a similar trade, it is recommended that they make *ḥajj* on foot, whether man or woman.' Ash-Shāfi'ī added, 'The man has less of an excuse than a woman because he is stronger.' They consider this to be recommended, not mandatory. If the only way he is able to get provision is by begging from people on the way, it is disliked for him to perform *ḥajj* because he becomes a burden on people.

Mālik ibn Anas said, 'If he is both able to walk and also has provision, he must perform *ḥajj*. If he has no mount but is able to walk, there is some question. If he possesses the necessary provision, he is obliged to perform *ḥajj*. If he does not possess it, but is able to obtain what he needs on the way, there is also some question about that. For those who do not themselves work, it is not obliged, but in the case of those who earn their living by a trade or craft, it is obliged. It is the same if it is someone's custom to beg. He must perform *ḥajj*.' Mālik made it obligatory for someone able to walk, even if he does not have provision or mount. That is the position of 'Abdullāh ibn az-Zubayr, ash-Sha'bī and 'Ikrimah.

Aḍ-Ḍaḥḥāk said, 'If a person is strong, young and healthy but has no money, he should hire himself out in exchange for food or its equivalent until he completes his *ḥajj*.' Muqātil said to him, 'So Allah has obliged people to walk to the House?' He answered, 'If someone were to have a legacy for him in Makkah, would he then abandon it? No, he would go to it, even crawling. It is on that basis that the *ḥajj* is obliged for him.'

These scholars cite as evidence the words of the Almighty: *'Announce the ḥajj to mankind. They will come to you on foot.'* (22:27) They said, 'That is because the *ḥajj* is one of the physical acts of worship which are individual obligations. For that reason neither provision nor a mount are obligatory preconditions for its being obligatory, any more than is the case with the prayer and fasting.' They said that if the hadith of al-Khūzī about provision and a mount is sound, then we would apply it to all people, most of whom live at a great distance. The generality of the words which apply to the most usual circumstances occurs frequently in the Sharī'ah, the words of the Arabs and their poetry.

Ibn Wahb, Ibn al-Qāsim and Ashhab reported that Mālik was asked about this *āyah* and said, 'With respect to that people are judged according to their ability, wealth and resilience.' Ashhab asked Mālik, 'Is it a matter of provision and a mount?' 'No,' he replied, 'By Allah, it is only according to the ability of people. Someone may have provision and a mount and still not be able to go whereas another may be able to go on foot.'

If someone has the ability and sets out to perform the obligatory *ḥajj*, and then something stops him, such as a creditor who prevents him from going until he settles his debt, there is no disagreement about that. If someone has a family who need support, he is not obliged to perform *ḥajj* until they have sufficient to maintain them for the time he is absent, because maintenance is an immediate obligation while *ḥajj* can be done later, and so the family is put first. The Prophet ﷺ said, 'It is enough of a wrong action for a man to let those he feeds perish.'

The same applies if someone fears his parents will perish and there are none to attend to them. There is no way for him to perform *ḥajj*. If they forbid him because of over-fondness and loneliness, however, he should not pay any attention to that. A woman can be prevented by her husband, but it is also said that he cannot prevent her. What is sound is that he can stop her from going, especially since we say that it is not necessary to perform *ḥajj* immediately.

The sea does not annul the obligation to do *ḥajj* when it is generally considered safe, as we mentioned in *al-Baqarah*, when someone knows he will not be adversely affected. If there is real probability of shipwreck or sea-sickness or inability to do the prayer, then people should not go. If there is no place to prostrate because of the crowd and narrowness of the place, Mālik said, 'If someone cannot bow and prostrate except on their brother's back, they should not go.' Then he said, 'Is someone going to embark when they are not going to be able to pray! Woe to anyone who abandons the prayer!'

The obligation of Ḥajj is cancelled if, on the route, there is an enemy taking lives or someone demanding money, if it is an unspecified or exorbitant amount. There is disagreement on whether the obligation is cancelled when the amount demanded is not exorbitant. Ash-Shāfi'ī said, 'He should not pay even a single grain, and the obligation of *ḥajj* is cancelled.' *Ḥajj* is obligatory for someone whose usual income is gained through begging and thinks that it is probable he will find someone to give what he needs, as we mentioned when we discussed possessing the means.

If the impediments preventing someone going on *ḥajj* are removed and he has insufficient ready funds to make *ḥajj* but possesses saleable goods, he must sell some of his goods to give himself enough money to fulfil the obligation. Ibn al-Qāsim was asked about a man who had a water-skin and nothing else. Should he sell it to enable himself to go on *ḥajj* and leave his children with nothing to live on? He said, 'Yes, he must do that and leave his children dependent on *ṣadaqah*.' The first position, however, is the correct one, based on the hadith: 'It is enough of a wrong action for a man to let those he feeds perish.' That is the view of ash-Shāfi'ī. The apparent position of his school is that *ḥajj* is only mandatory for someone with no family or children if he has sufficient money to cover the entire journey. One of them said that the return journey is not taken into account because the fact that someone has no wife or dependants there means that it is no great hardship for him to stay in other than his homeland and so, in fact, all lands can be his homeland. The first position is more correct because a person feels alienated when parted from his homeland. Do you not see that when an unmarried man commits fornication, he is flogged and exiled from his home, whether he has family there or not.

In *al-Umm*, ash-Shāfi'ī said, 'If someone has a residence, a servant and can provide maintenance for his family during his absence, then he is obliged to perform *ḥajj*.' The apparent meaning of this is that he considers the expense of *ḥajj* to be over and above that of a servant and a residence because he mentions that before maintenance of the family. It is as if he was saying that the obligation to go on *Ḥajj* only comes into force after all these have been taken into account. His people said that he is obliged to sell the house and servant and rent a house and servant for his family. If he has goods, he should trade in them and earn a sufficient profit to support his dependants during the whole of his absence. If he has to spend from the goods themselves, so that the profits from them are reduced and there is not enough to cover his costs, is he then obliged to perform *ḥajj* from the sale of the goods or not? There are two views. The first is the view of the majority, and it is sound and well known, which is that there is no disagreement that if someone has an estate whose revenue covers his needs, he must sell that estate to enable him to perform *ḥajj*, and so the same must be true of goods. Ibn Shurayḥ said, 'That is not the case. The goods should not be sold and the person does not perform *ḥajj* from their proceeds because the *ḥajj* is not obligatory if a person's sufficient needs are not met. This discussion is about ability both physically and in terms of wealth.'

As for someone who is ill and sickly (*ma'ḍūb*), *'aḍb* is cutting and that term is used of a sword. It is as if someone who reaches the point where they cannot stay on a mount or be firm on it is the same as someone whose limbs are severed and thus unable to do anything. Scholars disagree about the ruling governing such a person since there is a consensus that they are not obliged to travel on *ḥajj* on the basis that the *ḥajj* is only obligatory for someone who is able to do it. Someone ill or sickly does not have the ability to do it. Mālik said, 'When someone is sickly, the obligation of *ḥajj* is completely cancelled for him. No one should perform *ḥajj* on his behalf, even if he is in a position to enable them to do so, either with or without a wage. The *ḥajj* is not an obligation for him. If someone becomes chronically ill, the obligation of *ḥajj* is cancelled for him. It is not permitted for anyone to perform *ḥajj* on his behalf in any case. If he states in his will that someone should perform *ḥajj* on his behalf, that is taken from the third of the estate [allowed to be left as bequests] and it is a voluntary action.' His evidence is Allah's words: *'Man will have nothing but what he strives for.'* (53:39) He reported that he only has that for which he strives, so if someone says that he is striving on behalf of someone else, that is contrary to the literal meaning of the *āyah* and to Allah's words: *'Ḥajj to the house is a duty owed to Allah by all mankind...'* This person lacked the ability because the *ḥajj* is enjoined on those responsible for reaching the House themselves and because it is an act of worship which cannot be delegated when the ability is lacking, just as is the case with the prayer.

Muḥammad ibn al-Munkadir related from Jābir that the Messenger of Allah ﷺ said, 'By means of one *ḥajj*, Allah will admit three to the Garden: the deceased, the one who takes on *ḥajj* for him and the one who carries that out.' Abu-l-Qāsim Sulaymān ibn Aḥmad ad-Dāraquṭnī transmitted this from 'Amr ibn Ḥuṣayn as-Sadūsī from Abū Ma'shar from Muḥammad ibn al-Munkadir. The name of Abū Ma'shar was Najīḥ. They considered him to be weak.

Ash-Shāfi'ī said, 'Regarding someone who is chronically ill, very sickly or very old, who finds someone able to perform the *ḥajj* on his behalf, he possesses a certain type of ability. There are two forms of it. One is that he is able to pay someone to perform *ḥajj* on his behalf. That person performs his obligatory *ḥajj*. This is the view of 'Alī ibn Abī Ṭālib. It is related that he told a very old man who had not performed *ḥajj*, 'Equip a man to perform *ḥajj* on your behalf.' This position was taken by ath-Thawrī, Abū Ḥanīfah and his people, Ibn al-Mubārak, Aḥmad and Isḥāq. The second is that he is able to find someone to pay on his behalf and represent him in performing *ḥajj* on his behalf. According to ash-Shāfi'ī, Aḥmad and Ibn Rāhawayh, *ḥajj* is also an obligation for such a person. Abū Ḥanīfah said that the *ḥajj* is not obligatory for them. Ash-Shāfi'ī cited as evidence what Ibn 'Abbās related about the woman of Khath'am who asked the Prophet ﷺ, 'Messenger of Allah, Allah has obliged His slaves to perform *ḥajj*. My father is a very old man who cannot remain firm on a mount. Can I perform *ḥajj* on his behalf?' 'Yes,' he answered. That was during the Farewell Ḥajj. One variant has: 'He cannot remain upright on a camel.' The Prophet ﷺ said, 'Perform *ḥajj* for him. Do you think that if your father owed a debt, you would not settle it for him?' 'Yes,' she answered. He said, 'It is more fitting to settle a debt owed to Allah.' So the Prophet ﷺ said that his obligation to do *ḥajj* was fulfilled by his daughter voluntarily performing it and spending on it herself on his behalf. His indication that a father's obligation to do *ḥajj* could be fulfilled by the voluntary action of his daughter, suggests that it is even more appropriate to for someone to fulfil their *ḥajj* obligation by hiring someone to do it on their behalf on the basis of their ability to pay for it from their own wealth. As for someone having to give out wealth beyond what they are able to afford, what is sound is that it is not obliged for them to do so.

Our scholars have said the aim of the hadith about the Khath'amī woman is not to make *ḥajj* obligatory in that situation. Its aim is to encourage being good to parents and seeing to their best interests in this world and the Next and to accrue benefit for them naturally and in the Sharī'ah. When he saw in the woman reaction and obedience and true filial piety and eagerness to bring her father good and reward, and her sorrow at his missing the blessing of *ḥajj*, he responded to that in the same way that he said to another woman who said, 'My mother made a vow to perform *ḥajj* but did not perform *ḥajj* before her death. Can I perform *ḥajj* on her behalf?' 'Perform *ḥajj* on her behalf. Do you think that if your mother owed a debt you would not pay it?' 'Yes,' she answered. This indicates that it is about obedience and bringing good and blessings to dead people. Do you not see that he ﷺ likened the *ḥajj* to a debt?

The consensus is that if someone dies while owing a debt, his relative is not obliged to settle it from his money. He may do that voluntarily and thereby settle the debt for him. Part of the evidence in this hadith that it was not an obligation for her father is this woman's explicit statement: 'he was unable.' *Ḥajj* is not obligatory for someone who is unable. This is a clear statement denying the obligation and preventing the duty. So it is not permitted for what is definitively negative at the beginning of the hadith to become affirmative by supposition at the end of it. This is confirmed by the words: 'it is more fitting to settle Allah's debt.' Taking this literally, it is not a consensus. It is, in fact, more fitting to settle a debt to a person and the consensus is that one begins with that on account of the poverty of the human being and the wealth of Allah Almighty. Ibn al-'Arabī said that.

Abū 'Umar ibn 'Abd al-Barr mentioned that the hadith of the Khath'amī woman, in the view of Mālik and his people, was specific to her. Others said that there is some disturbance in it. Ibn Wahb and Abū Muṣ'ab said that it is specific to the right of the child. Ibn Habīb said, 'The indulgence comes about the *ḥajj* on behalf of an elderly person. There is no encouragement to do it if he has not yet performed *ḥajj* or, for someone who has died without performing *ḥajj*, that his child should perform it on his behalf, even if he has not left instructions about that and, Allah willing, it satisfies it. This discussion is about those who are sickly and the like. The hadith of the Khath'amī woman was transmitted by the imams. It refutes the statement of al-Hasan that a woman is not permitted to perform *ḥajj* on behalf of a man.'

Scholars agree that if someone does not have adequate provision for the journey, they are not obliged to perform *ḥajj*. Even if a non-relative gives them money with which to make *ḥajj*, there is consensus that they do not have to accept it since a favour is attached to it. If a man gives his father money, ash-Shāfi'ī said that he must accept it because a man's son is part of his earning and there is no favour attached to that. Mālik and Abū Ḥanīfah said that he is not obliged to accept it because it entails a lowering of respect for his parents. He can satisfy it when they have died. Allah knows best.

But if anyone disbelieves, Allah is Rich Beyond Need of any being.

Ibn 'Abbās and others said, 'This refers to anyone who rejects the obligatory nature of *ḥajj* and does not think that it is obligatory.' Al-Ḥasan al-Baṣrī and others said, 'Anyone who abandons the *ḥajj* when he is able to do it is an unbeliever.' At-Tirmidhī related from al-Ḥārith that 'Alī reported that the Messenger of Allah ﷺ said, 'When someone possesses provision and a mount with which to reach the House of Allah and does not perform *ḥajj*, he can die a Jew or a Christian. That is because Allah says in His Book: "*Hajj to the House is a duty owed to Allah by all mankind, those who can find a way to do it.*"' Abū 'Īsā said, 'This hadith, however, is *gharīb*. We only know it from this path. Its *isnād* is questionable. Hilāl ibn 'Abdullāh is unknown and al-Ḥārith is considered to be weak.' Something similar is related from Abū Umāmah and 'Umar ibn al-Khaṭṭāb.

It is related from 'Abd Khayr ibn Yazīd from 'Alī ibn Abī Ṭālib that the Messenger of Allah ﷺ said in a *khuṭbah* of his, 'O people! Allah has obliged *ḥajj* on those of you who are able to find a way to it. If someone does not do it, he can die however he wishes. If he wishes, as a Jew, a Christian or a Magian, unless he is excused by reason of illness, or a tyrant. He has no portion in my intercession nor will he come to My Basin.'

Ibn 'Abbās said that the Messenger of Allah ﷺ said, 'If someone has enough money to enable him to perform *ḥajj* but he does not perform *ḥajj*, or property on which *zakāt* is due but he does not pay *zakāt*, he will be questioned at death and the Resurrection.' It was said, 'Ibn 'Abbās, we think that this is about the unbelievers!' He said, 'I recite to you the Qur'an: *"O you who believe! do not let your wealth or your children divert you from the remembrance of Allah. Whoever does that is lost. Give from what We have provided for you before death comes to one of you and he says, 'My Lord, if only You would give me a little more time so that I might give ṣadaqah and be one of the righteous!'"'* (63:9-10) Al-Ḥasan ibn Ṣāliḥ said in his commentary, 'and give *zakāt* and perform *ḥajj*.'

It is reported that a man asked the Prophet ﷺ about this *āyah* and he said, 'Anyone who performs *ḥajj* not hoping for a reward, or remains behind not fearing punishment, has disbelieved in Him.' Qatādah related that al-Ḥasan said that 'Umar said, 'I thought about sending some men to the cities to look into those who had wealth but did not perform *ḥajj* and imposing the *jizyah* on them. That is on account of Allah's words: *"But if anyone disbelieves, Allah is Rich Beyond Need of any being."*' This is to demonstrate severity. That is why our scholars have said that the *āyah* implies that if someone dies without performing *ḥajj* when he was able to do so, the threat is aimed at him directly. It cannot be satisfied by someone performing *ḥajj* on his behalf because a *ḥajj* performed by someone else does not remove the obligation to do *ḥajj* from him and so the threat is not removed from him. Allah knows best. Sa'īd ibn Jubayr said, 'If my neighbour dies and possesses wealth, but has not performed *ḥajj*, I will not pray over him.'

قُلْ يَٰٓأَهْلَ ٱلْكِتَٰبِ لِمَ تَكْفُرُونَ بِـَٔايَٰتِ ٱللَّهِ وَٱللَّهُ شَهِيدٌ عَلَىٰ مَا تَعْمَلُونَ ﴿٩٨﴾ قُلْ
يَٰٓأَهْلَ ٱلْكِتَٰبِ لِمَ تَصُدُّونَ عَن سَبِيلِ ٱللَّهِ مَنْ ءَامَنَ تَبْغُونَهَا عِوَجًا وَأَنتُمْ
شُهَدَآءُ وَمَا ٱللَّهُ بِغَٰفِلٍ عَمَّا تَعْمَلُونَ ﴿٩٩﴾

98 Say, 'People of the Book, why do you reject Allah's Signs when Allah is witness of everything you do?' 99 Say, 'People of the Book, why do you bar those who believe from the Way of Allah, desiring to make it crooked, when you yourselves are witnesses to it? Allah is not unaware of what you do.'

'Why do you bar from the Way of Allah?'

It means to turn people away from the *dīn* of Allah. Al-Ḥasan recited '*tuṣiddūna*' [instead of '*taṣuddūna*']. They are two dialectical forms from *ṣadda, aṣadda.* 'Crookedness' denotes bias and deviation in the *dīn*, words and actions, and what will divert someone from the straight path or what is upright, as Abū 'Ubaydah and others said. We see the same meaning in His words: *'they will follow the Summoner who has no crookedness in him at all.'* (20:108) It means that they will not deviate if they respond to his summons. The verb *'āja* means to stop in a place and stand. *'Ā'ij* is someone standing. [POEM] A man who is *a'raj* has bad character and *'awaj* is clear bad character. In respect of a horse, *'ūj* refers to the curving of the sinews in the back leg. It is praised. The term *a'awjīyah* was used of certain horses in the Jāhilyyah whose legs were far apart.

you yourselves are witnesses to it.

It means: you understand it. It is said: 'You witness that it is written in the Torah that the *dīn* of Allah that is accepted is Islam alone by reason of the fact that it contains the description of Muḥammad ﷺ.'

يَٰٓأَيُّهَا ٱلَّذِينَ ءَامَنُوٓاْ إِن تُطِيعُواْ فَرِيقًا مِّنَ ٱلَّذِينَ أُوتُواْ ٱلْكِتَٰبَ
يَرُدُّوكُم بَعْدَ إِيمَٰنِكُمْ كَٰفِرِينَ ﴿١٠٠﴾

100 You who believe! if you obey a group of those given the Book, they will make you revert to unbelievers after you have believed.

This was revealed about a Jew who wanted to rekindle the civil war between Aws and Khazraj after it had been stopped by the Prophet ﷺ. He sat among them and recited some poetry to them which one of the tribes had recited about their wars. The other tribe said, 'But our poet said this and that about such-and-such a day.' Some of that provoked them and they said, 'Come on! Let us start the war again!' Aws shouted, 'People of Aws!' and Khazraj shouted, 'People of Khazraj!' They met and took up their weapons and formed ranks for fighting and then this *āyah* was revealed. The Prophet ﷺ came and stood between the ranks and recited it in a loud voice. When they heard his voice, they listened to him, and when he finished, they threw their weapons aside and embraced one another, weeping. 'Ikrimah, Ibn Zayd and Ibn 'Abbās reported the story.

The one who did this was Shās ibn Qays the Jew. He introduced into Aws and Khazraj someone who would recall to them the wars that had taken place between them. The Prophet ﷺ came and reminded them and people recognised that it was a provocation from Shayṭān and a machination on the part of their enemy. So they threw down their weapons, wept and embraced one another and then left with the Prophet ﷺ in obedience to him. Then Allah revealed this. *'You who believe'* are Aws and Khazraj and the words *'a group of those given the Book'* refer to Shās and his people.

they will make you revert to unbelievers after you have believed.

Jābir ibn 'Abdullāh said, 'There was no arrival that day more hateful to us than that of the Messenger of Allah ﷺ. Then he indicated to us with his hand and we refrained and Allah Almighty made peace between us. Then there was no one we loved more than the Messenger of Allah ﷺ. I have not experienced a day whose start was uglier or more repulsive and whose end had a greater reward than that day.'

وَكَيْفَ تَكْفُرُونَ وَأَنتُمْ تُتْلَىٰ عَلَيْكُمْ ءَايَٰتُ ٱللَّهِ وَفِيكُمْ رَسُولُهُۥ ۗ وَمَن
يَعْتَصِم بِٱللَّهِ فَقَدْ هُدِىَ إِلَىٰ صِرَٰطٍ مُّسْتَقِيمٍ ﴿١٠١﴾

101 How can you disbelieve, when Allah's Signs are recited to you and the Messenger is there among you? Whoever holds fast to Allah has been guided to a straight path.

The Almighty asks this with amazement. The words *'Allah's Signs'* refer to the Qur'an and *'the Messenger'* is Muḥammad ﷺ. Ibn 'Abbās said, 'There was fighting and bad feeling between Aws and Khazraj in the Jāhiliyyah. They mentioned what had happened between them and it provoked them to pick up swords against one another. They went to the Prophet ﷺ and mentioned that to him and he went to them. Then this *āyah* was revealed.'

The *āyah* includes those who did not see the Prophet ﷺ because the establishment of his Sunnah took the place of actually seeing him. Az-Zajjāj says that it is possible that this *āyah* was directed only to the Companions of Muḥammad ﷺ because the Messenger of Allah ﷺ was among them and they saw him. It is also possible that this is addressed to the entire Community because His traces and signs and the Qur'an which he was given are among us in the place of the Messenger ﷺ, even if we did not see him.

Qatādah said, 'There are two clear signs in this *āyah:* the Book of Allah and the Prophet of Allah. The Prophet of Allah has passed, and the Book of Allah remains among them as a mercy and a blessing. It contains its lawful and unlawful, and obedience and disobedience.'

The phrase *'Whoever holds fast'* means someone who is patient and holds to Allah's *dīn* and obeys Him. Then he is given success and rightly guided. Ibn Jurayj says that it means he believes in Him. It is said that it means, 'Whoever holds to the rope of Allah,' which is the Qur'an. The verbs *a'ṣama* and *i'taṣama* mean to hold to something to the exclusion of anything else. Anyone who clings to something is called *'mu'ṣim'* and *'mu'taṣim'*. Someone who defends something is called *'āṣim*. Al-Farazdaq said:

I am the son of the defenders (*'āṣimīn*) of the Banū Tamīm.

[POEMS] Food is described as defending (*'aṣama*) someone from being hungry. The Arabs say, 'the food kept him (*'aṣama*) from being hungry. That is why they call pottage (*sawīq*) 'Abū 'Āṣim.' Aḥmad ibn Yaḥyā said, 'The Arabs called bread *'āṣim* and *jābir*, and they also called it *'āmir*. [POEMS]

يَٰٓأَيُّهَا ٱلَّذِينَ ءَامَنُوا۟ ٱتَّقُوا۟ ٱللَّهَ حَقَّ تُقَاتِهِۦ وَلَا تَمُوتُنَّ إِلَّا وَأَنتُم مُّسْلِمُونَ ١٠٢

102 You who believe! have *taqwā* of Allah with the *taqwā* due to Him and do not die except as Muslims.

An-Naḥḥās related from Murrah ibn 'Abdullāh that the Messenger of Allah ﷺ said, 'The *taqwā* due to Him is that He be obeyed and not disobeyed, remembered and not forgotten, thanked and not shown ingratitude.' Ibn 'Abbās said, 'It means not disobeying Him for the blink of an eye.' The commentators mentioned that when this *āyah* was revealed, they asked, 'Messenger of Allah, who is strong enough for this?' It was hard for them and then Allah revealed: *'So show fear of Allah as much as you are able to'* (64:16), and this *āyah* was abrogated as Qatādah, ar-Rabī' and Ibn Zayd said. Muqātil said, 'Nothing in *Āl 'Imrān* is abrogated except this *āyah*.'

It is also said that the words: *'So show fear of Allah as much as you are able to'* is clarification of this *āyah*. The meaning is: 'Fear Allah with the *taqwā* due to Him as much you are able to.' This is more correct because when there is a choice between reconciling and abrogation, reconciling is more appropriate. 'Alī ibn Abī Ṭalḥah reported that Ibn 'Abbās said, 'The words of Allah: *"You who believe, have taqwā of Allah with the taqwā due to Him,"* are not abrogated. *"The taqwā due to Him"* is that one fights to the utmost in the Way of Allah and does not fear the blame of any blamer for Allah's sake, and establishes justice, even against oneself and one's children.' An-Naḥḥās said, 'Whenever an obligation is mentioned in an *āyah*, it is mandatory for the Muslims to implement it and there is no abrogation in it.' This was already mentioned in *al-Baqarah*.

وَاعْتَصِمُوا بِحَبْلِ اللَّهِ جَمِيعًا وَلَا تَفَرَّقُوا ۚ وَاذْكُرُوا نِعْمَتَ اللَّهِ عَلَيْكُمْ إِذْ كُنتُمْ
أَعْدَاءً فَأَلَّفَ بَيْنَ قُلُوبِكُمْ فَأَصْبَحْتُم بِنِعْمَتِهِ إِخْوَانًا وَكُنتُمْ عَلَىٰ شَفَا حُفْرَةٍ مِّنَ
النَّارِ فَأَنقَذَكُم مِّنْهَا ۗ كَذَٰلِكَ يُبَيِّنُ اللَّهُ لَكُمْ آيَاتِهِ لَعَلَّكُمْ تَهْتَدُونَ ﴿١٠٣﴾

103 Hold fast to the rope of Allah all together, and do not separate. Remember Allah's blessing to you when you were enemies and He joined your hearts together so that you became brothers by His blessing. You were on the very brink of a pit of the Fire and He rescued you from it. In this way Allah makes His Signs clear to you, so that hopefully you will be guided.

Hold fast to the rope of Allah all together, and do not separate.

'Hold fast' (*i'taṣimū*) comes from *'iṣmah*, which is defence, and it is also used for the guards (*badhraqah*) of a caravan. That is because they organise those who would defend it against those who would harm it. Ibn Khāluwayh said that *badhraqah* is not Arabic, but a Persian word that has been Arabicised.

'*Ḥabl*' (rope) is a word with multiple meanings. Its linguistic root is the means by one which one reaches a need and desire. It is a ligament in the neck and a long track of sand. That usage is found in hadith. It is a halter and a covenant. Al-A'shā said:

When the covenants (*ḥibāl*) of the tribe seceded it,
    they took their contracts from another for you.

He means security. It is also cunning, and *hibālah* is a snare. [POEM]

None of these meanings is meant in the *āyah* except that of 'covenant', as Ibn 'Abbās said. Ibn Mas'ūd said that the rope of Allah is the Qur'an. 'Alī and Abū Sa'īd al-Khudrī related this from the Prophet ﷺ, and the same is reported from Mujāhid and Qatādah. Abū Mu'āqiyah related from al-Hijrī from Abu-l-Aḥwaṣ from 'Abdullāh that the Messenger of Allah ﷺ said, 'This Qur'an is the rope of Allah.'

Taqiyy ibn Mukhallad related from Yaḥyā ibn al-Ḥamīd from Hushaym from al-'Awwām ibn Ḥawshab from ash-Sha'bī that 'Abdullāh ibn Mas'ūd said that it refers to the Community. It is related from him and others by various paths of transmission. All the meanings are similar because Allah commanded friendship and forbade separation. Separation is destruction and the group is salvation. Ibn al-Mubarāk said:

The community is the rope of Allah, so hold fast to
the firmest handhold of it for the one who draws near.

and do not separate.

This means in respect of your *dīn,* in the way the Jews and Christians separated in their respective religions, as Ibn Mas'ūd and others said. It is permitted for it to mean: 'Do not separate by following your individual passions and desires. Be brothers in the *dīn* of Allah.' So that should prevent them cutting off one another and plotting against one another. This is indicated by what follows it:

Remember Allah's blessing to you when you were enemies and He joined your hearts together so that you became brothers by His blessing.

There is no evidence in the *āyah* for the prohibition of disagreement concerning secondary rulings. That is not true disagreement. The disagreement intended here is that which makes harmony and joining together impossible. As for rulings in matters of *ijtihād*, disagreement regarding them is due to the deduction of precepts and fine meanings of the Sharī'ah. The Companions continued to disagree in respect of judgments about different matters. In spite of that, they were in complete harmony. The Messenger of Allah ﷺ said, 'The disagreements of my Community are a mercy.' Allah is forbidding any sort of disagreement that results in discord.

At-Tirmidhī reported from Abū Hurayrah that the Prophet ﷺ said, 'The Jews divided into seventy-one or seventy-two sects and the Christians into the like of that. My community will divide into seventy-three sects.' At-Tirmidhī said that it is a sound hadith. Ibn 'Umar also transmitted that the Messenger of Allah ﷺ said, 'What happened to the tribe of Israel will happen to my community, step by step, so that if one of them were to come to his mother openly, my community would also have those who do that. The tribe of Israel divided into seventy-two sects and my community will divide into seventy-three. All of them will be in the Fire except for one.' 'Who are they, Messenger of Allah?' they asked. He replied, 'What I and My Companions follow.' He transmitted it from 'Abdullāh ibn Ziyād al-Ifrīqī from 'Abdullāh ibn Yazīd from Ibn 'Umar. He said, 'This hadith is *ḥasan gharīb*. We only know it from this path.' Abū 'Umar said, "Abdullāh al-Ifrīqī is trustworthy. His people trusted him and praised him while others said that he was weak.'

In his *Sunan* Abū Dāwūd transmitted from Mu'āwiyah ibn Abī Sufyān that the Prophet ﷺ said, 'Before you the People of the Book divided into seventy-two sects and this community will divide into seventy-three. Seventy-two will be in the Fire and one in the Garden: it is the *Jama'āh*. Some people will emerge from my Community and those passions will move them as rabies moves its sufferer. There is no vein or joint of them which that will not enter.'

In the *Sunan* of Ibn Mājah, Anas ibn Mālik reported that the Messenger of Allah ﷺ said, 'Anyone who leaves this world sincerely believing in Allah alone and being sincere in worshipping Him with no partner, establishing the prayer and paying the *zakāt*, dies with Allah pleased with him.' Anas said, 'It is the *dīn* of Allah which the Messengers brought and conveyed from their Lord before the muddling of hadiths and different sects.' The confirmation of that is at the end of what Allah revealed. He says: *"If they repent..."* in other words 'if they abandon idols and worship of them', *"...and establish the prayer and pay zakāt, they are your brothers in the dīn."'* (9:11) It is transmitted from Naṣr ibn 'Alī al-Jahḍamī from Abū Aḥmad from Abū Ja'far ar-Rāzī from ar-Rabī' ibn Anas from Anas.

Abu-l-Faraj al-Jawzī said, 'If it is said that these sects are known, the answer is that we know the differences and the roots of sects and each of the sects is subdivided into further sects, even if we do not know all the names of those sects and schools. It is clear to us that the roots of sects are the Ḥarūriyyah (Khārijites), the Qadariyyah, the Jahmiyyah, the Murji'ites, the Rāfiḍites and the Jabriyyah.' One of the people of knowledge said, 'There are six sects that form the basis of these misguided sects and each of them divided into twelve sub-sects so they became seventy-two.'

There are twelve sects of the Ḥarūriyyah. The first are the Azraqiyyah who say, 'We do not know anyone to be a believer,' and they say that all the people of the *qiblah* are unbelievers except for those who espouse the same view as them. There are the Ibāḍiyyah who say, 'Whoever takes our view is a believer and whoever turns away from it is a hypocrite.' There are the Tha'labiyyah who say that Allah does not decree; the Khāzimiyyah who say that they do not know what faith is and all creatures are excused; the Khalafiyyah who claim that anyone who abandons *jihād*, male or female, is an unbeliever; and the Kūziyyah who said that no one should touch another person because he does not know whether he is pure or impure and should not eat with him until he repents and has a *ghusl*. There are the Kanziyyah who say that no one is allowed to give another person his wealth because he might not deserve it and so he should store it (*kanz*) in the earth until the people of the truth appear. There are the Shamrākhiyyah who say there is nothing wrong in touching women who are not relatives. There are the Akhnasiyyah who said that the dead find neither good nor evil after death. There are the Ḥakamiyyah who say that anyone who asks for the judgment of a creature is an unbeliever. There are the Mu'taziliyyah [of the Ḥarūriyyah] who say that the business of 'Alī and Mu'āwiyah is unclear and so they are free of both parties. And there are the Maymūniyyah who say that there is no ruler except with the consent of those we love.

There are also twelve sects of Qadariyyah. There are the Aḥmariyyah who stipulate about Allah's justice that He must give people charge of their affairs and come between them and acts of disobedience. There are the Thanawiyyah who claim that good is from Allah and evil is from Shayṭān. There are the Mu'tazilites who say that the Qur'an is created and deny the Attributes of Divine Lordship. There are the Kaysāniyyah who say, 'We do not know whether actions are from Allah or from people. We do not know whether people will be rewarded or punished.' There are the Shayṭāniyyah who say that Allah did not create Shayṭān. There are the Sharīkiyyah who say that all evil actions are decreed except for disbelief. There are the Wahmiyyah who say that the actions and words of people have no essence and they do neither good nor evil actions. There are the Zabriyyah who say that it is a duty to act by every revealed Book, whether abrogated or abrogating. There are the Mas'adiyyah who claim that if someone disobeys and then repents, his repentance is not accepted. There are the Nākithiyyah who claim that someone who breaks his allegiance to the Messenger of Allah ﷺ does not sin. There are the Qāsiṭiyyah who [preferred seeking the world to doing-without, and the Naẓẓāmiyyah who] followed Ibrāhīm ibn an-Naẓẓām in saying that someone who claims that Allah is a thing is an unbeliever.

The Jahmiyyah likewise make up twelve sects. There are the Mu'attilah who claim that everything a human being thinks of is created and if someone claims that Allah can be seen, he is an unbeliever. There are Marīsiyyah who say that most of the attributes of Allah are created. There are the Multaziqah who say that the Creator is everywhere. There are the Wāridiyyah who say that no one who recognises his Lord will enter the Fire and no one who enters it will ever emerge from it. There are the Zanādiqah who say that no one can establish a Lord for himself because affirmation can only occur after perception by the senses and what is not perceived cannot be confirmed. There are the Ḥarqiyyah who claim that the Fire will burn the unbeliever once and he will remain burned forever but not feel the heat of the Fire. There are the Makhlūqiyyah who claim that the Qur'an is created. There are the Fāniyyah who claim that the Fire and Garden will vanish. Some of them say that they are not created. There are the Qabriyyah who deny the punishment of the grave and intercession. There are the Lazfiyyah who say that our articulation of the Qur'an is created.

The twelve sects of the Murji'ah are the Tārikiyyah who say that Allah did not impose any obligation on His creation other than believing in Him and whoever believes in Him can do whatever he wishes. There are the Sā'ibiyyah who say that Allah left His creation to do whatever they wish. There are the Rājiyyah who say that someone obedient is not called obedient nor someone disobedient called disobedient because we do not know what Allah has in store for him. There are the Sālibiyyah who say that obedience is not part of faith. There are the Bahīshiyyah who say that faith is knowledge and whoever does not know the truth from the false or the lawful from the unlawful is an unbeliever. The 'Amaliyyah say that faith is action. The Manqūṣiyyah say that faith does not increase or decrease. The Mustathniyyah say that 'if Allah wills' is part of faith. The Mushabbihah say that His sight is like our sight and His hand like our hands. The Ḥashawiyyah said that ruling of all hadiths is the same and someone who omits the *nāfilah* is like someone who omits the obligatory. The Zāhiriyyah forbid analogy. The Bid'iyah were the first to innovate these things in this community.

The Rāfiḍites also have twelve sects. There are the 'Alawiyyah who say that the Message was really sent to 'Alī but Jibrīl made a mistake. The Amriyyah said that 'Alī and Muḥammad shared in Prophethood. The Shi'ah said that 'Alī was the executor of the Messenger of Allah ﷺ and his heir after him and the community fell into disbelief by giving allegiance to someone else. The Isḥāqiyyah said that Prophethood will continue until the Day of Rising and whoever has the knowledge of the People of the House is a Prophet. The Nāwūsiyyah say that 'Alī is the best of the community and anyone who prefers someone to him has disbelieved. The Imāmiyyah said that it is not possible for this world to be without an imām from the descendants of Ḥusayn. The imām is taught by Jibrīl and if he dies, another takes his place. The Zaydiyyah said that all the descendants of Ḥusayn have the right to be imāms in the prayer. If one of them is present, the prayer is not permitted behind someone else. It makes no difference whether they are pious or impious. The 'Abbāsiyyah claimed that al-'Abbās was the most entitled to be caliph. The Tanāsukhiyyah believed in transmigration of souls. If someone was a good-doer, his soul leaves and enters into someone who will have a happy life. The Raj'iyyah claim that 'Alī and his companions will return to this world and take revenge on their enemies. The Lā'inah curse 'Uthmān, Ṭalḥah, az-Zubayr, Mu'āwiyah, Abū Mūsā, 'Ā'ishah and others. The Mutarabbiṣah resemble those performing the *ḥajj* practices and in every age set up a man whom they put in charge, claiming that he is the *mahdī* of the community. When he dies, they set up another.

The Jabriyyah have twelve sects. There are the Muḍṭariyyah who say that the human being has no action: it is Allah who does everything. The Af'āliyyah say that we have actions but no capacity to do them. We are like beasts led by ropes. The Mafrūghiyyah said that all things were created in the past and now nothing is created. The Najjāriyyah claimed that Allah Almighty punishes people for His actions, not for their actions. The Mannāniyyah said that you are responsible for what occurs to your heart, so do whatever you deem to be good. The Kasbiyyah said that the slave of Allah earns neither reward nor punishment. The Sābiqiyyah said you may act as you wish. The fortunate will not be harmed by their wrong actions and the wretched will not be helped by their piety. The Ḥibbiyyah said that if someone drinks a cup of the love of Allah, the pillars of worship are cancelled for him. The Khawfiyyah said that if someone loves Allah, he cannot fear Him because the lover does not fear his Beloved. The Fikriyyah said that if someone increases his knowledge, worship is no longer binding on him. The Khashabiyyah said that this world is shared equally among people and there is no superiority between them in their legacy from their father Ādam. The Manniyyah say that we have no action, only ability.

Further discussion of sects in this Community will come at the end of *Sūrat al-An'ām* Allah willing.

Ibn 'Abbās said to Simāk al-Ḥanafī: 'Ḥanafī, the Community (*Jamā'ah*)! The Community! Past nations were destroyed when they split into sects. Did you not hear the words of the Almighty, *"Hold fast to the rope of Allah altogether and do not separate"*?'

Abū Hurayrah reports in *Ṣaḥīḥ Muslim* that the Messenger of Allah ﷺ said, 'Allah is pleased with three things for you and dislikes three things for you. He is pleased that you worship Him and do not associate anything with Him, that you hold all together to the rope of Allah, and that you do not split up. He dislikes three things for you: chitchat, asking too many questions and wasting wealth.' So Allah obliged us to hold to His Book and the *Sunnah* of His Prophet ﷺ and to consult them in cases of disagreement. He commanded us to join together in holding fast to the Book and *Sunnah* in terms of belief and action. That is the means to unity and the remedy for disunity and assures the best interests of of the community in this world and the *dīn* and safety from discord. He commanded togetherness and forbade us falling into the schisms which have occurred to the people of the two Books. This is the complete sense of the *āyah* and is evidence for the validity of consensus as one of the fundamental principles of *fiqh*. Allah knows best.

Remember Allah's blessing to you when you were enemies

Allah commanded them to remember His blessings, the greatest of which is Islam and following His Prophet ﷺ. By it enmity and division are removed and love and harmony are brought about. It is Aws and Khazraj who are meant although the *āyah* is of general import.

so that you became brothers by His blessing.

This means you became brothers in the *dīn* by the blessing of Islam. In the Qur'an *aṣbaḥa* always means 'become' as is seen elsewhere. *Ikhwān* (brothers) is the plural of *akh*. Someone is called a 'brother' because he aims to follow the path of his brother.

You were on the very brink of a pit of the Fire

'*Shafā*' is the edge of anything. Allah also uses the term in *'on the brink* (shafā) *of a crumbling precipice.'* (9:109) A poet said:

We dug (*ḥafarnā*) [the well] Sajlah for the *ḥājjīs*,
    growing above its edge (*shifāhā*) is a plant.

The verb *ashfā 'alā* means to be on the brink of something. The verb is used of a sick person on the brink of death. All that remains of it is *shafā*, a little. Ibn as-Sikkīt said, 'It is said of a dying man or waning moon or setting sun, "Only a little (*shafā*) remains of it."' Al-'Ajjāj said:

Many an elevated place is high for the one who ascends it.
    I ascended it when the sun had set or was close (*shafā*) to it.

'Had set' is '*bilā shafā*' and '*bi-shafā* means that a little remains of it. It is a weak verb with *yā'*. One dialect has it as being one of those words with a *wāw*. An-Naḥḥās said, 'The root of *shafā* is *shafawa* which is why it is written with an *alif* and without *imālah*.' Al-Akhfash said, 'When *imālah* is not permitted in it, it is known that there was originally a *wāw* there. *Imālah* comes from the *yā'*. The dual is *shafawān*.'

Al-Mahdawī said that being on the brink of a fire is a metaphor for them leaving disbelief for belief.

وَلْتَكُن مِّنكُمْ أُمَّةٌ يَدْعُونَ إِلَى الْخَيْرِ وَيَأْمُرُونَ بِالْمَعْرُوفِ وَيَنْهَوْنَ عَنِ
الْمُنكَرِ ۚ وَأُولَٰئِكَ هُمُ الْمُفْلِحُونَ ﴿١٠٤﴾

104 Let there be a community among you who call to the good, and enjoin the right, and forbid the wrong. They are the ones who have success.

We have already discussed what enjoining the right and forbidding the wrong entails. '*Min*' (among) here is partitive. It means that those who enjoin must be people with knowledge, and not all people have knowledge. It is also said that it is generic, and the command is general for everyone. The first position is sounder and indicates that enjoining the right and forbidding the wrong is a *farḍ kifāyah*. Allah made it specific when He says: *'Those who, if We establish them firmly on the earth, will establish the prayer…'* (22:41). This is not all people. Ibn az-Zubayr recited: 'Let there be a community among you who call to the good, and enjoin the right and forbid the wrong, and seek Allah's help in what befalls them.' Abū Bakr al-Anbārī said, 'This addition is, in fact, commentary on the part of Ibn az-Zubayr. It is an error on the part of some transmitters to add it to the words of the Qur'an. It indicates the soundness of the description in the hadith related from my father from Ḥasan ibn 'Arafah from Wakī' from Abū 'Āṣim from Abū 'Awn from Ṣubayḥ who said that he heard 'Uthmān ibn 'Affān recite, "Let there be a community among you who call to the good, and enjoin the right and forbid the wrong, and seek Allah's help in what befalls them." No intelligent person doubts the fact that 'Uthmān did not consider this addition to be part of the Qur'an since he did not include it in the text of his copy of the Qur'an when he was the leader of the Muslims. He mentioned it as an admonition and to stress the prior words of the Lord.'

وَلَا تَكُونُوا كَالَّذِينَ تَفَرَّقُوا وَاخْتَلَفُوا مِن بَعْدِ مَا جَاءَهُمُ الْبَيِّنَاتُ ۚ وَأُولَٰئِكَ
لَهُمْ عَذَابٌ عَظِيمٌ ﴿١٠٥﴾

105 Do not be like those who split up and differed after the Clear Signs came to them. They will have a terrible punishment

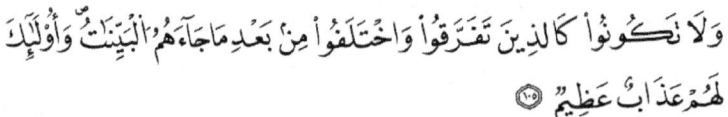

This means the Jews and the Christians, according to most commentators. One of them said that it refers to the innovators of this community. Abū Umāmah, reciting this *āyah,* said that it is about the Ḥarūriyyah. Jābir ibn 'Abdullāh said that it means the Jews and Christians. The verb *'came'* is in the masculine for the plural. If the verb had been in the feminine, it would refer to the group.

يَوْمَ تَبْيَضُّ وُجُوهٌ وَتَسْوَدُّ وُجُوهٌ فَأَمَّا الَّذِينَ اسْوَدَّتْ وُجُوهُهُمْ أَكَفَرْتُم
بَعْدَ إِيمَانِكُمْ فَذُوقُوا الْعَذَابَ بِمَا كُنتُمْ تَكْفُرُونَ ﴿١٠٦﴾ وَأَمَّا الَّذِينَ
ابْيَضَّتْ وُجُوهُهُمْ فَفِي رَحْمَةِ اللَّهِ هُمْ فِيهَا خَالِدُونَ ﴿١٠٧﴾

106 on the Day when faces are whitened and faces are blackened. As for those whose faces are blackened: 'What! Did you disbelieve after having believed? Taste the punishment for your unbelief!' 107 As for those whose faces are whitened, they are in Allah's mercy, remaining in it timelessly, for ever.

On the Day when faces are whitened and faces are blackened.

This is a reference to the Day of Rising when people are resurrected from their graves. The faces of the believers will be whitened and those of the unbelievers blackened. It is said that that occurs when the books are read out. When the book of the believer is read out and he sees his good actions in it, he will rejoice and his face will be brightened. When the unbeliever and hypocrite read their books and see their evil deeds, their faces will be darkened. It is said that this occurs when the scales are set up. It is said that it is when the Almighty says: *'Keep yourselves apart today, O evildoers.'* (36:59)

It is also said that it happens on the Day of Rising when every group is commanded to join what they worshipped. When they do that they will be wretched and their faces darkened. The believers, People of the Book and hypocrites will stay where they are. Allah will ask the believers, 'Who is your Lord?' and they will reply, 'Our Lord is Allah Almighty.' He will ask them, 'Will you recognise Him if you see Him?' They will reply, 'Glory be to Him! When He shows Himself, we will recognise Him.' They will see Allah in the way He wishes them to and the believers will prostrate and their faces will become as white as snow. The hypocrites and People of Book will be unable to prostrate and they will be miserable and their faces dark. The whitening of faces is their shining with bliss and the darkening is their being covered by the painful punishment.

It is also read as *'tibyaḍḍu'* and *'tiswaddu'* which is the dialect of Tamīm. Yayhyā ibn Waththāb recited it this way. Az-Zuhrī recited *'tabyāḍḍu'* and *'taswāddu.'* It is also permitted for the *tā'* to have a *kasrah* and to have *'yabyaḍḍu'* in the masculine plural. The whitening of the faces is their shining with blessing and their darkening is from the painful punishment that oppresses them.

There is disagreement about who specifically is being referred to here. Ibn 'Abbās said that the faces of the people of the *Sunnah* are white and those of innovation dark. This statement of Ibn 'Abbās is related by Mālik ibn Sulaymān al-Harawī, the brother of Ghassān, from Mālik ibn Anas from Nāfi' from Ibn 'Umar who reported that the Messenger of Allah ﷺ said about these words: 'It means that the faces of the people of the *Sunnah* will be whitened and the faces of the people of innovation will be blackened.' Abū Bakr Aḥmad ibn 'Alī ibn Thābit al-Khaṭīb mentioned it. It is said that this is *munkar* from Mālik.

'Aṭā' said, 'The faces of the Muhājirūn and Anṣār will be whitened and the faces of the Banū Qurayẓah and an-Naḍīr blackened.' Ubayy ibn Ka'b said, 'Those whose faces are blackened are the unbelievers and they will be asked, "Do you disbelieve after your affirmation of belief when you were brought forth from the back of Ādam like atoms?"' This is what aṭ-Ṭabarī preferred. Al-Ḥasan says that the *āyah* is about the hypocrites. Qatādah says that it is about the apostates. 'Ikrimah said, 'They are the people from the People of the Book who confirmed their Prophets and affirmed Muḥammad ﷺ before he was sent and then, when he was sent, rejected him. That is what is meant by the words of the Almighty: *"What! Did you disbelieve after having believed?"*' That is preferred by az-Zajjāj.

Mālik ibn Anas said, 'It is about the people of sects.' Abū Umāmah al-Bāhilī reported that it is about the Khārijites. Another report says that it is about the Qadariyyah. At-Tirmidhī reported that Abū Ghālib said, 'Abū Umāmah saw heads set up at the gate of Damascus. He remarked, 'The dogs of the Fire! The worst to be slain under heaven and the best is the one they killed.' Then he recited the *āyah*: *"On the Day when faces are whitened and faces are blackened...."* I said to Abū Umāmah, "Did you hear that from the Messenger of Allah ﷺ?" He answered, "If I had not heard it from the Messenger of Allah ﷺ once, two times, three times (and he went on to 'seven times'), I would not have related it to you."' He said that it is a *ḥasan* hadith.

We find in *Ṣaḥīḥ Bukhārī* that Sahl ibn Sa'd said, 'The Messenger of Allah ﷺ said, "I will reach the Basin before you. Whoever passes by me will drink, and whoever drinks will never be thirsty again. Some people will come whom I recognise and who recognise me but a barrier will be put between me and them."' Abū Ḥāzim said, 'An-Nu'mān ibn Abī 'Ayyāsh asked, "Is that how you heard it from Sahl ibn Sa'd?" "Yes," I answered. He said, "I testify that I heard it from Abū Sa'īd al-Khudrī and he added, 'I will say, "They are from me!" It will be said, "You do not know what they innovated after you." I will say, "Away! Away with those who altered things after me!"'"'

Abū Hurayrah related that the Messenger of Allah ﷺ said, 'On the Day of Rising, a group of my Companions will come to the Basin and be kept away from it. I will say, "O Lord, my Companions!" He will say, "You do not know what they innovated after you! They turned their backs in retreat."'

There are many hadiths that talk about this. Anyone who alters, changes or innovates in the *dīn* of Allah anything not pleasing to Allah and for which Allah has not given permission will be among those who are driven far from the Basin and whose faces are blackened. Those who are driven farthest away are those who opposed the Muslim Community and caused splits among them, such as the Kharijites and their different sects, the Rāfiḍites with their clear misguidance, and the Mu'tazilites with their various sects. All of these altered and innovated. That is also the case with the extravagant wrongdoers who commit injustice and tyranny and blot out the truth and kill and humiliate its people, as well as those who publicly commit major wrong actions and who treat acts of disobedience lightly, and the group of the people of deviation, sects and innovations. It is feared that all of those are meant by the *āyah*. As we made clear, only a denying unbeliever who does not have the weight of a mustard seed of faith in his heart will remain in the Fire forever. Ibn al-Qāsim said, 'There may be from other than the people of sects, those who are worse than the people of sects.' It used to be said, 'Full sincerity is avoiding acts of disobedience.'

As for those whose faces are blackened,

There is some elision here, like 'They were asked, "What! Did you disbelieve after having believed?"' on the Day of the Covenant when they said, 'Yes, indeed.' It is also said that these are the Jews who believed in Muḥammad ﷺ before he was sent and rejected him after he was sent. Abu-l-'Āliyah said that this is directed at the hypocrites: 'Do you reject secretly after affirming openly?' The people who know Arabic agree that there must be a *fā'* in the apodosis of *ammā* since it means: 'As for Zayd, he is happy.'

Those whose faces are whitened are those who obeyed Allah and fulfilled His covenant. *'In Allah's mercy'* is in His Garden and the Abode of His generosity. May Allah place us among them and make us avoid the paths of innovation and misguidance and guide us to the path of those who believed and did good deeds! Amīn.

تِلْكَ ءَايَٰتُ ٱللَّهِ نَتْلُوهَا عَلَيْكَ بِٱلْحَقِّ ۗ وَمَا ٱللَّهُ يُرِيدُ ظُلْمًا لِّلْعَٰلَمِينَ ﴿١٠٨﴾
وَلِلَّهِ مَا فِى ٱلسَّمَٰوَٰتِ وَمَا فِى ٱلْأَرْضِ ۚ وَإِلَى ٱللَّهِ تُرْجَعُ ٱلْأُمُورُ ﴿١٠٩﴾

108 These are Allah's Signs which We recite to you with truth. Allah desires no wrong for any being. 109 Everything in the heavens and everything in the earth belongs to Allah. All matters return to Allah.

'Allah's Signs' are the Qur'an. '*We recite to you*' means 'Jibrīl brought them down to you and recited them to you.' '*Truth*' is truthfulness. Az-Zajjāj said that the words '*These are Allah's signs*' mean that they are the proofs and evidence of Allah. It is said that '*tilka*', which normally means 'those', here means 'these', but when they came to an end, it becomes as if they are far and so 'those' is used. Also, 'Allah's Signs' can be an appositive for 'these' rather than an adjective. *'Allah desires no wrong for any being'* means that He will not punish them without wrong action on their part.

Everything in the heavens and everything in the earth belongs to Allah.

Al-Mahdawī says that the manner in which this is connected to what is before it is that, after Allah mentions the states of the believers and unbelievers and the fact that He does not desire wrong for any being, He then mentions the vast extent of His power and His absolute freedom from any hint of injustice, since everything in the heavens and the earth is in His hand. It is also said that it is the beginning of a new sentence: Allah is making it clear to His slaves that everything in the heavens and the earth belongs to Him so that they should ask of Him and worship Him and not worship other than Him.

كُنتُمْ خَيْرَ أُمَّةٍ أُخْرِجَتْ لِلنَّاسِ تَأْمُرُونَ بِٱلْمَعْرُوفِ وَتَنْهَوْنَ عَنِ
ٱلْمُنكَرِ وَتُؤْمِنُونَ بِٱللَّهِ ۗ وَلَوْ ءَامَنَ أَهْلُ ٱلْكِتَٰبِ لَكَانَ خَيْرًا لَّهُم ۚ مِّنْهُمُ
ٱلْمُؤْمِنُونَ وَأَكْثَرُهُمُ ٱلْفَٰسِقُونَ ﴿١١٠﴾

110 You are the best nation ever to be produced before mankind. You enjoin the right, forbid the wrong and believe in Allah. If the People of the Book were to believe, it would be better for them. Some of them are believers but most of them are deviators.

You are the best nation ever to be produced before mankind.

At-Tirmidhī related from Bahz ibn Ḥakīm that his grandfather heard the Messenger of Allah ﷺ say about these words: 'You are the culmination of seventy communities. You are the best and noblest of them in the sight of Allah.' He said that it is a *ḥasan* hadith.

Abū Hurayrah said, 'We are the best of people for people. We drag them in chains to Islam.' Ibn 'Abbās said, 'They are those who emigrated from Makkah to Madīnah and were present at Badr and Ḥudaybīyah.' 'Umar ibn al-Khaṭṭāb said, 'Whoever does what they did is like them.'

It is said that it is the Community of Muḥammad ﷺ, specifically the righteous among them and the people of excellence. They will be the witnesses against other people on the Day of Rising as mentioned in *al-Baqarah.* Mujāhid said that this is according to the preconditions mentioned in the *āyah.* It is said that it means: 'You are in the Preserved Tablet.' It is said, 'Since you believed, you were made the best nation.' It is said that it is good news for the Prophet ﷺ and His community. Al-Afkhash points out that it means the best people of a *dīn.* [POETRY]

It is said that the verb '*kāna*' here is in the perfect tense and it means: 'You have been created and brought into existence' and 'the best nation' is descriptive. It is also said that '*kāna*' is redundant and it simply means: 'you are the best nation.' Similar examples of this usage are found in 19:29 and 2:86.

Sufyān related from Maysarah al-Ashja'ī from Abū Ḥāzim that Abū Hurayrah said about this *āyah,* 'You drag people in chains to Islam.' An-Naḥḥās said, 'According to this, it implies; "you are the best nation for people."' Mujāhid said, 'You are the best nation when you enjoin the right and forbid the wrong.' It is also said that the nation of Muḥammad ﷺ will become the best nation because the Muslims will be the most numerous and enjoining the right and forbidding the wrong is widespread among them. It is also said that it is the Companions of the Messenger of Allah ﷺ who are being referred to as he said, 'The best of people are my generation...', meaning those among whom he was sent.

Since it is confirmed in Revelation that this nation is the best of nations and the Imāms report that the Prophet ﷺ said, 'The best of my community are my generation, then the one after them and then the one after them,' this indicates that those at the beginning of this community are better than those after them, and the majority of scholars believe that. Those who were Companions of the Prophet ﷺ and saw him, even once, are better than those who came after him. No action is equivalent to that of the company of the Prophet ﷺ.

Abū Umar Ibn 'Abd al-Barr believed that it was possible for there to exist after the Companions those who were better, owing to the fact that the statement of the Prophet ﷺ was not universal, since a generation inevitably contains both the excellent and less excellent. His generation contained hypocrites who opposed faith and people of major wrong actions who had the *ḥudūd* carried out on them. He said to them, 'What do you say about a thief, a drinker and a fornicator?' He said about those in his generation, 'Do not curse my Companions.' He said to Khālid ibn al-Walīd about 'Ammār, 'Do not insult someone who is better than you.'

Abū Umāmah reported that the Prophet ﷺ said, 'Bliss to the one who sees me and believes in me, and bliss seven times over to the one who did not see me but believes in me.' We find in the *Musnad* of Abū Dāwūd aṭ-Ṭayālisī from Muḥammad ibn Abī Ḥumayd from Zayd ibn Aslam from his father that 'Umar said, 'I was sitting with the Prophet ﷺ when he asked, "Do you know which of creation are best in faith?" We replied, "The angels." He said, "That is true of them, but other than them." We said, "The Prophets." He said, "It is true of them, but others." Then the Messenger of Allah ﷺ went on, "The best of creatures in faith are a people in the loins of men who will believe without seeing me. They will find a page and act by what is in it. They are the best of creatures in faith."' Ṣāliḥ ibn Jubayr related that Abū Jum'ah said, 'We asked, "Messenger of Allah, is there anyone better than us?" "Yes," he replied, "A people will come after you who will find a Book between two covers and believe in what is in it and believe in me without seeing me."' Abū 'Umar said that Abū Jum'ah was a Companion and his name was Ḥabīb ibn Sibā'. Ṣāliḥ ibn Jubayr was one of the trustworthy Tābi'ūn.

Abū Tha'labah al-Khashanī related that the Prophet ﷺ said, 'Ahead of you lie days requiring steadfastness, and steadfastness in those days will be like grasping live coals. The one who acts in those days will have the reward of fifty men who do the same action as he does now.' It was asked, "Messenger of Allah, of their men?" He replied, "Rather of your men."' Abū 'Umar said that some transmitters omit 'Rather your men'. 'Umar said in explanation of this *āyah,* 'Any who does the like of your actions is like you.' The hadiths are not contradictory because the first is particular, and success is by Allah.

It is said about what is conveyed by the hadiths regarding this matter that his generation ﷺ is preferred because they were strangers in respect of their faith because of the great number of unbelievers around them, their steadfastness in the face of the persecution they faced and their holding to their *dīn.* As for the later members of this community, they will be strangers when they establish the *dīn* and hold to it and are steadfast in obeying their Lord at the time of the appearance of evil, impiety, bloodshed, acts of disobedience and major wrong actions, and then, at that time, their actions will be pure just as the actions of the first ones were pure. Part of what attests to this are the words of the Prophet: 'Islam began as a stranger and will become as it began. Blessed be the strangers!' There is also the hadith reported by Abu Tha'labah that the Prophet ﷺ said, 'My Community is like the rain. It is not known whether the beginning or end of it is best.' Abū Dāwūd aṭ-Ṭayālisī and Abū 'Īsā at-Tirmidhī mentioned it. Hishām ibn 'Ubaydullāh ar-Rāzī mentioned from Mālik from az-Zuhrī that Anas said that the Messenger of Allah ﷺ said, 'The metaphor of my Community is like the rain. It is not known whether the beginning or end of it is best.' Ad-Dāraquṭnī mentioned it from Mālik. Abū 'Umar said that there is no disagreement that Hishām ibn 'Ubaydullāh is trustworthy.

It is related that when 'Umar ibn 'Abd al-'Azīz was appointed caliph, he wrote to Sālim ibn 'Abdullāh, 'Write to me informing me of the behaviour of 'Umar ibn al-Khaṭṭāb so I can act on it.' Sālim wrote to him, 'If you act on the behaviour of 'Umar, then you are better than 'Umar because your time is not like the time of 'Umar and your men are not like the men of 'Umar.' He wrote to the *fuqahā'* of his time and they wrote to him the same as Sālim told him.

Some counter the hadith, 'The best of people are my generation,' with the words of the Prophet ﷺ, 'The best of people is the one who has a long life and good actions and the worst of people is the one who has a long life and bad actions.' Abū 'Umar said that these hadiths mean that the first and the last are equal in faith and righteous action in a corrupt time when the people of knowledge and the *dīn* are few and there is a lot of corruption and bloodshed, and when the believers are abased and the deviants exalted and the *dīn* becomes a stranger again in the same way it began as a stranger, and the one who stands by it is like someone who holds on to hot coals. The two are equal, except for the people of Badr and al-Ḥudaybīyah. If someone reflects on the reports regarding this matter, what is correct will be clear to him. Allah gives His bounty to whomever He will.

You enjoin the right and forbid the wrong

This is praise for this community when they understand this and act by it. If they do not, praise is removed from them and censure attached to them. That is a reason for their destruction. We have already discussed what is meant by enjoining the right and forbidding the wrong at the beginning of this *sūrah.*

If the People of the Book were to believe, it would be better for them.

It would be better for the People of the Book to believe in the Prophet ﷺ. Then

Allah tells us that some of them are believers and some are deviants, but that the majority are deviants.

لَن يَضُرُّوكُمْ إِلَّآ أَذًى ۖ وَإِن يُقَٰتِلُوكُمْ يُوَلُّوكُمُ ٱلْأَدْبَارَ ثُمَّ
لَا يُنصَرُونَ ﴿١١١﴾

111 They will not harm you except with abusive words. If they fight you, they will turn their backs on you. Then they will not be helped.

This means that they deny you with their twisting and lies. They will not be victorious, as al-Ḥasan and Qatādah said. The exception here can be connective, meaning they will not harm you except for a little. So *'abusive words'* is a verbal noun. The *āyah* is a promise from Allah to His Messenger ﷺ and to the believers that the People of the Book will not overcome them and they will be helped against them and not be uprooted or harmed by their lies and twisting and that the ultimate victory will be for the believers. It is also said that the exception is one of separation, and the meaning is that they will not harm you at all, but you hear from them what vexes you. Muqātil said, 'The leaders of the Jews, Ka'b, 'Adī, an-Nu'mān, Abū Rāfi', Abū Yāsir, Kinānah and Ibn Ṣūriyā went to those of their people who were believers, such as 'Abdullāh ibn Salām and his people, and abused them for becoming Muslims, and Allah revealed this.' It means verbal abuse. *'If they fight you…'* refers to the fact that they will be defeated. *'Then they will not be helped'* is a new sentence. This *āyah* contains a miracle for the Prophet ﷺ because those Jews who fought him did turn their backs.

ضُرِبَتْ عَلَيْهِمُ ٱلذِّلَّةُ أَيْنَ مَا ثُقِفُوٓا۟ إِلَّا بِحَبْلٍ مِّنَ ٱللَّهِ وَحَبْلٍ مِّنَ ٱلنَّاسِ
وَبَآءُو بِغَضَبٍ مِّنَ ٱللَّهِ وَضُرِبَتْ عَلَيْهِمُ ٱلْمَسْكَنَةُ ۚ ذَٰلِكَ بِأَنَّهُمْ كَانُوا۟
يَكْفُرُونَ بِـَٔايَٰتِ ٱللَّهِ وَيَقْتُلُونَ ٱلْأَنۢبِيَآءَ بِغَيْرِ حَقٍّ ۚ ذَٰلِكَ بِمَا عَصَوا۟
وَّكَانُوا۟ يَعْتَدُونَ ﴿١١٢﴾ لَيْسُوا۟ سَوَآءً ۗ مِّنْ أَهْلِ ٱلْكِتَٰبِ أُمَّةٌ قَآئِمَةٌ يَتْلُونَ ءَايَٰتِ ٱللَّهِ
ءَانَآءَ ٱلَّيْلِ وَهُمْ يَسْجُدُونَ ﴿١١٣﴾ يُؤْمِنُونَ بِٱللَّهِ وَٱلْيَوْمِ ٱلْءَاخِرِ وَيَأْمُرُونَ
بِٱلْمَعْرُوفِ وَيَنْهَوْنَ عَنِ ٱلْمُنكَرِ وَيُسَٰرِعُونَ فِى ٱلْخَيْرَٰتِ
وَأُو۟لَٰٓئِكَ مِنَ ٱلصَّٰلِحِينَ ﴿١١٤﴾ وَمَا تَفْعَلُوا۟ مِنْ خَيْرٍ فَلَن تُكْفَرُوهُ ۗ وَٱللَّهُ
عَلِيمٌۢ بِٱلْمُتَّقِينَ ﴿١١٥﴾

112 They will be plunged into abasement wherever they are found, unless they have a treaty with Allah and with the people. They have brought down anger from Allah upon themselves, and they have been plunged into destitution. That was because they rejected Allah's Signs and killed the Prophets without any right to do so. That was because they disobeyed and went beyond the limits. 113 They are not all the same. There is a community among the People of the Book who are upright. They recite Allah's Signs throughout the night, and they prostrate. 114 They believe in Allah and the Last Day, and enjoin the right and forbid the wrong, and compete in doing good. They are among the righteous. 115 You will not be denied the reward for any good thing you do. Allah knows those who have *taqwā*.

They will be plunged into abasement wherever they are found,

This refers to the Jews. '*Wherever they are found*' means wherever they are encountered. This abasement was already mentioned in *al-Baqarah*. Then follows an absolute exception: '*unless they have a treaty* (literally, rope) *with Allah and the people*'. A treaty (rope) with the people means the *dhimmah* status which they have. '*The people*' here means Muḥammad ﷺ and the believers to whom they pay the *jizyah* and so they are protected. There is some elision here, meaning 'They are protected by a contract from Allah.' Al-Farrā' said that.

They have brought down anger from Allah upon themselves,

'*Brought down*' either means 'returned' or 'endured'. The linguistic root means that it is obliged for them, and this was discussed in *al-Baqarah*. Then Allah tells about the reason for that, and this was also discussed in *al-Baqarah*.

They are not all the same.

This is the conclusion of the statement. Ibn Mas'ūd said that it means that the People of the Book and the community of Muḥammad ﷺ are not the same. It is said that it means: the believers and unbelievers of the People of the Book are not the same. Abū Khaythamah Zuhayr ibn Ḥarb related from Hāshim ibn al-Qāsim from Shaybān from 'Āṣim from Zirr that Ibn Mas'ūd said, 'One night the Messenger of Allah ﷺ was late for the '*Ishā*' prayer and then he came out into the mosque while the people were waiting for the prayer. He said, "There is no one among the people of the religions who remembers Allah Almighty at this hour except you." Then this *āyah* was revealed.' Ibn Wahb related the like of it.

Ibn 'Abbās said that: "*There is a community among the People of the Book who are upright. They recite Allah's Signs throughout the night, and they prostrate*" refers to those who believed with the Prophet ﷺ.

Ibn Isḥāq reported from Ibn 'Abbās that when 'Abdullāh ibn Salām, Tha'labah ibn Sa'yah, Usayd ibn Sa'yah, Usayd ibn 'Ubayd and others of the Jews became Muslim and affirmed and desired Islam and were firm in it, the rabbis of the Jews and the people of disbelief said, 'Only the worst of us believe in Muḥammad and follow him. If they had been among the best of us, they would not have left the religion of their fathers for another.' Then Allah revealed this.

Al-Afkhash said that it implies that some of the People of the Book have a good path. He recited:

Does someone with a community sin when he obeys?

It is said that there is some elision and it means: '*There is a community among the People of the Book who are upright* and another which is not upright.' It is like the words of Abū Dhu'ayb:

I disobeyed. My heart belongs to her. I obey its command
and do not know whether seeking her is right guidance [or error].

Al-Farrā' says that the noun '*community*' is in the nominative agreeing with the adjective '*same*' [which is in the nominative] and so it implies: 'A group among the People of the Book who are upright, reciting the signs of Allah are not the same as a group who disbelieve.' An-Naḥḥās says that this statement is incorrect for several reasons grammatically. One is that the word '*community*' is in the nominative because of the adjective '*same*' and so it does not refer to a noun which has no action on it. Because of this it is in the nominative by something which does not act on the verb and implies what is not needed. That is because the unbelieving [group] was already mentioned and so there is no need for that implication. Abū 'Ubaydah said, 'This is like their words, "The fleas ate me" and "your companions left."' An-Naḥḥās said, 'This is an error because they were already mentioned, and in the case of "The fleas ate me" [which is literally "they ate me, the fleas"] because they were already mentioned.'

They recite Allah's Signs throughout the night, and they prostrate.

The word *ānā' 'throughout'* means its hours. Its singular is *inan, anan* or *inyin*. The word '*prostrate*' here means doing the whole prayer. Al-Farrā' and az-Zajjāj said that it necessarily means that because there is no recitation in *rukū'* and *sujūd*. It is like Allah's words: *'they prostrate to Him,'* meaning that they do the prayer. We find in *al-Furqān*: *'When they are told to prostrate to the All-Merciful...'* (25:60) and elsewhere: *'Prostrate before Allah and worship Him.'* (53:62) It is also said that it just means normal prostration, but the reason for its revelation refutes that. What is meant is the *'Ishā'* prayer, as we mentioned from Ibn Mas'ūd. The idolaters went to sleep when it became dark, while the people of *tawḥīd* stood before Allah in the *'Ishā'* prayer reciting the Signs of Allah. Do you not see that when Allah mentions their standing, He is including their prostration? Ath-Thawrī said that it is prayer done between *Maghrib* and *'Ishā'*. It is also said that it refers to night prayers. It is related that a man of the Banū Shaybah who used to study the Divine Books said, 'We find among the words of the Lord: "Does a camel herder or shepherd reckon that when night covers him and he is helpless that he is like someone who stands and prostrates in prayer at the end of the night?"'

They believe in Allah and the Last Day, and enjoin the right and forbid the wrong, and compete in doing good. They are among the righteous.

'They believe' here means they affirm Allah and affirm what Muḥammad ﷺ says. It is said that the phrase *'enjoin the right'* has a general meaning and it is also said that it means to command that the Prophet ﷺ be followed and that the phrase *'forbid the wrong'* means to forbid the bad and to forbid opposing him. The words *'compete in doing good'* mean they do good actions and hasten to them without finding them burdensome since they know the value of their reward. It is said that it means that they hasten to act before they miss the time prescribed for that action. *'They are among the righteous,'* means they will be with the righteous, who are the Companions of Muḥammad ﷺ, in the Garden.

You will not be denied the reward for any good thing you do.

Al-A'mash, Ibn Waththāb, Ḥamzah, al-Kisā'ī, Ḥafṣ, and Khalaf read this as 'They will not ... they do,' reporting about the upright community. That is the recitation of Ibn 'Abbās and it is preferred by Abū 'Ubayd. The rest read it as 'You,' as direct address following from *'you are the best nation...'* That is preferred by Abū Ḥātim. Abū 'Amr reads it both ways. The *āyah* means: even if you deny the reward for any good you do, you will be thanked for it and rewarded for it.

إِنَّ الَّذِينَ كَفَرُوا لَن تُغْنِيَ عَنْهُمْ أَمْوَالُهُمْ وَلَا أَوْلَادُهُم مِّنَ اللَّهِ شَيْئًا
وَأُولَٰئِكَ أَصْحَابُ النَّارِ هُمْ فِيهَا خَالِدُونَ ﴿١١٦﴾

116 As for those who disbelieve, their wealth and children will not help them against Allah in any way. They are the Companions of the Fire, remaining in it timelessly, forever.

Muqātil said, 'After Allah mentions the believers of the People of the Book, He then mentions the unbelievers among them.' Al-Kalbī said, 'He made this an inceptive and He says, "Those who disbelieve will not be helped by a lot of wealth or a lot of children against the punishment of Allah."' He singles out children here because they are their closest relatives. The rest of this has already been mentioned.

مَثَلُ مَا يُنفِقُونَ فِي هَٰذِهِ الْحَيَاةِ الدُّنْيَا كَمَثَلِ رِيحٍ فِيهَا صِرٌّ أَصَابَتْ حَرْثَ
قَوْمٍ ظَلَمُوا أَنفُسَهُمْ فَأَهْلَكَتْهُ وَمَا ظَلَمَهُمُ اللَّهُ وَلَٰكِنْ أَنفُسَهُمْ يَظْلِمُونَ ﴿١١٧﴾

117 The metaphor of what they spend in their life in this world is that of a wind with an icy bite to it which strikes the crops of a people who have wronged themselves and destroys them. Allah did not wrong them; rather it was themselves they were wronging.

The *mā* (what) here can act like a verbal noun or it can mean 'which' and what it refers to is elided. It is like 'a wind that blows' which is a blowing wind. Ibn 'Abbās says that the word *ṣirr* means intense cold. It is said that its root is *ṣarīr*, which is a screeching sound, and so it is the sound of a strong wind. Az-Zajjāj says that it is the sound of the flames of the fire in that wind. This was mentioned in *al-Baqarah*. In a hadith it says that locusts which have been killed by *ṣirr* are forbidden. So the *āyah* means: the metaphor of the spending of the unbelievers, in its falsity, disappearance and lack of benefit, is like crops hit by a cold wind or by a fire which burns them up and destroys them. So their owners have no benefit at all from the crops after having had high hopes for their use and benefit.

Allah did not wrong them by that, but they wronged themselves by disbelief and disobedience and denying the right of Allah. It is said that they wronged themselves by cultivating outside the proper time of cultivation and in other than its proper place and so Allah punished them for putting the thing in other than its proper place, as al-Mahdawī stated.

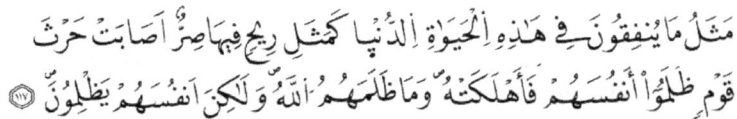

يَٰٓأَيُّهَا ٱلَّذِينَ ءَامَنُوا۟ لَا تَتَّخِذُوا۟ بِطَانَةً مِّن دُونِكُمْ لَا يَأْلُونَكُمْ خَبَالًا
وَدُّوا۟ مَا عَنِتُّمْ قَدْ بَدَتِ ٱلْبَغْضَآءُ مِنْ أَفْوَٰهِهِمْ وَمَا تُخْفِى صُدُورُهُمْ أَكْبَرُ
قَدْ بَيَّنَّا لَكُمُ ٱلْءَايَٰتِ إِن كُنتُمْ تَعْقِلُونَ ﴿١١٨﴾

118 You who believe, do not take any outside yourselves as intimates. They will do anything to harm you. They love what causes you distress. Hatred has appeared out of their mouths, but what their breasts hide is far worse. We have made the Signs clear to you if you use your intellect.

Allah is emphasising the blameworthy nature of relying on unbelievers. This is connected to His previous words: '*…if you obey a group of those given the Book.*' (3:100). The word *biṭānah* (intimates) is a verbal noun used for both singular and plural. The *biṭānah* of a man are his closest companions who have deep knowledge of his affairs. It is derived from *baṭn*, the opposite of outward. A poet said:

Those are my closest friends and inner circle.
They, rather than any relative, are my weak spot.

In this *āyah* Allah forbade the believers to take the unbelievers, Jews and people of sects as intimates, to consult them for their opinions and to rely on them in their affairs. It is said that you should not converse with anyone who is opposed to your school and *dīn*. A poet says:

Do not ask about a man. Ask about his close companion.
Every close companion follows the one he is close to.

We find in the *Sunan* of Abū Dāwūd that Abū Hurayrah reported that the Prophet ﷺ said, 'A man follows the religion of his close friend, so each of you should be very careful about whom he takes as a close friend.' It is related that Abū Mas'ūd said, 'Reckon people by their brethren.' Then Allah clarified the reason why connection is forbidden.

They will do anything to harm you.

This means to corrupt you, meaning that they will spare no effort to corrupt you. Even if they do not fight you openly, they will not stop striving to deceive and betray you, as will be explained.

Abū Umāmah said that this refers to the Khārijites. It is related that Abū Mūsā al-Ash'arī employed a *dhimmī* as a scribe and 'Umar wrote to him to reprimand him and recited this *āyah* to him. Abū Mūsā came to 'Umar with the accounts and presented then to 'Umar who liked them. A letter came to Abū Mūsā and he said, 'Where is your scribe so that he can read this letter to the people?' He replied, 'He does not enter the mosque.' He asked, 'Is he in *janābah*?' 'He is a Christian,' he answered. He rebuked him and said, 'Do not bring them near. Put them far away. Do not honour them. Allah has abased them. Do not trust them when Allah has said that they are treacherous.' 'Umar said, 'Do not employ the People of the Book. They think bribes are lawful. Seek help in your affairs with those who fear Allah.' 'Umar was told, 'There is a man among the Christians of Hira and no one writes better than he does. Should he not write for you?' He replied, 'I will not take staff from anyone other than the believers.' So it is not permitted to employ the *dhimmīs* as scribes nor put them in charge of other matters of buying and selling.

Circumstances have changed at this time as the People of the Book have been taken as scribes and trustees and entrusted with those roles by wealthy ignorant governors and amirs. Al-Bukhārī reported that Abū Sa'īd al-Khudrī transmitted that the Prophet ﷺ said, 'Allah did not send a Prophet nor appoint a caliph without him having two counsellors, one counsellor commanding the right and encouraging it, and one counsellor commanding the wrong and encouraging it. The one protected is the one that Allah protects.' Anas ibn Mālik reported that the Prophet ﷺ said, 'Do not seek light from the fire of the idolaters nor engrave an Arab on your signet-rings.' Al-Ḥasan ibn Abi-l-Ḥasan explained it as meaning, 'Do not consult the idolaters in any of your affairs and do not engrave Muḥammad on your rings.' Al-Ḥasan said, 'The confirmation of that is found in the Book of Allah: *"You who believe! do not take any outside yourselves as intimates."*'

The expression *'outside yourselves'* means from other than yourselves with regard to conduct and good position. It means that they will not fall short in anything designed to corrupt you. The verb *alā* means 'to fall short'. The phrase *'lā ālū juhdan'* means 'I did not omit any effort,' i.e. 'I did not fall short.' The verbal usage *'alawtu uluwwan'* means 'I fell short.' Imru'u-l-Qays said:

As long as a man still has a spark of life
to reach the end of matters and does not fall short (*āl*)

'Khabāl' or *khabl* is corruption. That can be in respect of actions, bodies and minds. *Khabl* is a wound which renders a limb unsound. *Khabl* is the handicapping

of limbs, as it refers to disorder. A man who is described as *khabil* or *mukhabbal* is dim-witted or mad. A person can become disordered (*khabala*) by love. Aws said:

Son of Lubaynā, you have no hand
but a hand whose strength is disordered (*makhbūlah*).

Al-Farrā' said:

Ibn Sa'd gave a glance and prepared for it.
Your companions and mount are disordered (*khabāl*).

The word '*khabāl*' is in the accusative on account of being the second object, as the verb 'falling short' is transitive, taking two objects. If you wish, it can be a verbal noun, or it can be genitive. The word *mā* in '*love what causes you*' acts as a verbal noun. They love what is hard for you. *'Anat* is hardship and it was already mentioned in *al-Baqarah.*

Hatred has appeared out of their mouths.

This means: enmity and denial of you have appeared from their mouths. Hatred is the opposite of love. *Baghḍā'* is a feminine verbal noun. Mouths are mentioned rather than tongues to indicate their bragging and prattle. This is greater than the concealed hatred that shows in their eyes. In this sense, the Prophet ﷺ forbade a man to speak openly about his brother's honour. The verb used in the hadith means to open the mouth. A donkey opens its mouth when it brays (*shahy*) as horses do when they neigh. It describes horses with their mouths open. This hadith is not understood to be evidence for it being permitted to attack someone's reputation by whispering. Scholars agree that it is forbidden as the revelation says: *'Do not backbite one another.'* (49:12) The Prophet ﷺ said, 'Your blood, your property and your honour is forbidden to you.' Mentioning '*shaḥw*' alludes to bragging and presumptuousness. Know that.

This *āyah* provides evidence that the testimony of an enemy against his enemy is not permitted. That is the position of the people of Madīnah and the people of the Hijaz. It is related from Abū Ḥanīfah that it is permitted. Ibn Baṭṭāl and Ibn Sha'bān said, 'Scholars agree that it is not permitted for someone to testify against his enemy, even if he is reputable. Enmity removes fairness, so how much more is that the case with the enmity of the unbeliever?'

But what their breasts hide is far worse.

This reports that their concealed enmity is worse than their open enmity.

'Abdullāh ibn Mas'ūd recited '*badā*' (appeared) in the masculine because *baghḍā'* and *baghḍ* mean the same.

هَٰٓأَنتُمۡ أُوْلَآءِ تُحِبُّونَهُمۡ وَلَا يُحِبُّونَكُمۡ وَتُؤۡمِنُونَ بِٱلۡكِتَٰبِ كُلِّهِۦ وَإِذَا لَقُوكُمۡ قَالُوٓاْ ءَامَنَّا وَإِذَا خَلَوۡاْ عَضُّواْ عَلَيۡكُمُ ٱلۡأَنَامِلَ مِنَ ٱلۡغَيۡظِۚ قُلۡ مُوتُواْ بِغَيۡظِكُمۡۗ إِنَّ ٱللَّهَ عَلِيمُۢ بِذَاتِ ٱلصُّدُورِ ١١٩

119 There you are, loving them when they do not love you, even though you believe in all the Books. When they meet you, they say, 'We believe.' But when they leave they bite their fingers out of rage against you. Say, 'Die in your rage.' Allah knows what your hearts contain.

There you are, loving them when they do not love you,

This refers to the hypocrites. The evidence for that is the words of the Almighty: *'When they meet you, they say, "We believe."'* Abu-l-'Āliyah and Muqātil stated that.

Love here means true friendship, in other words, 'You, Muslims, offer them true friendship but they do not offer you true friendship because of their hypocrisy.' It is said that it means: 'You desire Islam for them while they desire unbelief for you.' It is said that what is meant are the Jews. The majority say that.

Kitāb (Book) is generic. Ibn 'Abbās says that it means 'Books'. The Jews believe in some, as the Almighty says: *'When they are told, "Believe in what Allah has sent down," they say, "We believe in what was sent down to us.' And they reject anything beyond that."'* (2:91)

When they meet you, they say, 'We believe.'

They say that they believe in Muḥammad ﷺ and that he is the Messenger of Allah.

But when they leave they bite their fingers out of rage against you.

"But when they leave" and are among themselves, they bite the ends of their fingers in exasperated hatred against you and say to one another, 'Do you not see that these people are victorious and numerous?' Biting the fingers is due to the frustration of not being able to act on the rage they feel. It is as Abū Ṭālib said:

They bite their fingers in anger after you leave.

Someone else said:

May Allah make their rage last long! When they see me,
they bite the ends of their fingers out of rage.

The verb used is *'aḍḍa*. *'Uḍḍ* is the fodder of animals in the cities. It is like dregs and crushed date-stones. Form IV of the verb is used for feeding camels this kind of fodder and a plump camel is called *'uḍāḍī*. *'Iḍḍ* is a cunning man who has many schemes. Biting the fingers is the action of someone who is angry and cannot act on his anger or someone who has something happen to him that he cannot change. This biting (*'aḍḍ*) with the teeth is like biting the hand when someone has missed something or gnashing the teeth in regret. It is like other things that one does like counting pebbles and drawing lines in the sand when grieved. It is written with a *ḍād*. *'Aẓẓ* with a *ẓā'* refers to the hardness of time as in the poem:

The hardness of time, Ibn Marwan, does not leave any wealth
other than worn out and empty.

Anāmil (fingers) is the plural of *anmalah* or *anmulah*. When Abu-l-Jawzā' recited this *āyah*, he said that it referred to the Ibāḍīyyah. Ibn 'Aṭiyyah said, 'This description applies to many of the people of innovation among mankind until the Day of Rising.'

Say, 'Die in your rage.' Allah knows what your hearts contain.

If it is asked how did they not die since when Allah says to a thing, 'Be!' it is, there are two answers. One is made by aṭ-Ṭabarī and many commentators who say that it is a supplication against them, with the meaning: 'Say to them, "May Allah make your rage last until you die."' This would make it a directive to pray against them. The second is that Allah is telling them that they will not obtain what they hope for. Death will occur before that happens. According to this the meaning of supplication is removed and the meaning of harsh rebuke remains. This idea is found in the words of Musāfir ibn Abī 'Amr:

We grow in our desires
and gouge out the eye of the envier.

It is similar in implication to Allah's words: *'Anyone who thinks that Allah will not help him in this world and the Next should stretch a rope up to the ceiling and then hang himself.'* (22:15)

إِن تَمۡسَسۡكُمۡ حَسَنَةٞ تَسُؤۡهُمۡ وَإِن تُصِبۡكُمۡ سَيِّئَةٞ يَفۡرَحُواْ بِهَاۖ وَإِن تَصۡبِرُواْ
وَتَتَّقُواْ لَا يَضُرُّكُمۡ كَيۡدُهُمۡ شَيۡـًٔاۗ إِنَّ ٱللَّهَ بِمَا يَعۡمَلُونَ مُحِيطٞ ١٢٠

120 If something good happens to you, it galls them. If something bad strikes you, they rejoice at it. But if you are steadfast and godfearing, their scheming will not harm you in any way. Allah encompasses what they do.

If something good happens to you, it galls them.

As-Sulamī recited it with *yā'* (*yamsaskum* rather than *tamsaskum*) and the rest with *tā'*. The expression is general to all that is good and bad. What the commentators mention of fertility and drought, the cohesion of the believers and disunity and other things are examples, not disagreement.

The meaning of the *āyah* is: 'Anyone who has this description of intense enmity, rancour and joy at hardships befalling the believers, is not worthy to be your intimate, especially in the weighty matter of *jihād* which is the basis of this world and the Next.' How excellent are the words:

It is hoped that every enmity will be mended
except for the one who envies you out of envy.

But if you are steadfast and godfearing, their scheming will not harm you in any way.

'But if you are steadfast' in the face of their attempts to harm you and in remaining obedient to Allah and taking the believers as friends. The verb for 'harm' is *ḍāra, yaḍūru*. Allah's precondition for negating their harm is steadfastness and *taqwā*. This is meant to console the believers and strengthen their souls.

The Makkans and Madinans and Abū 'Amr recited *'yaḍirkum'* from *ḍāra* as we mentioned. Part of that is the expression, *'lā ḍayr'*, 'no causing of harm'. Al-Kisā'ī related that he heard *'ḍāra, yaḍūru'* and allowed *'yaḍurkum'* and claimed that the copy of the Qur'an of Ubayy ibn Ka'b had *'yaḍrurkum'*. The Kufan reading is *yaḍurrukum* from *ḍarra*, which also means to harm. It can also be in the nominative by an implied *fā'*. It means: 'it will not harm you'. [POEM] This is the position of al-Kisā'ī and al-Farrā'. Or it can be in the nominative with the intention of advancement. Sībuwayh composed:

If your brother is felled, you will be felled.

It means: it will not harm you if you are steadfast and godfearing.

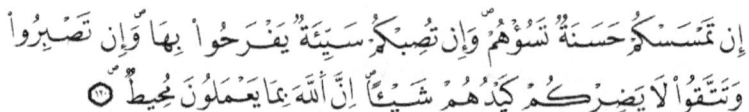

It can be in the jussive with a *ḍammah* on the *rā'* because of the meeting of two silent letters, following the *ḍammah*. The same is true of those who put a *fatḥah* on the *rā'* if the verb is in the jussive and the *fatḥah* is because of the meeting of two silent letters since the *fatḥah* is light. Abū Zayd related it from al-Mufaḍḍal from 'Āṣim. Al-Mahdawī related it. An-Naḥḥās related, 'Al-Mufaḍḍal aḍ-Ḍabbī related from 'Āṣim: "*yaḍurrikum*" with a *kasrah* on the *rā'* because of the meeting of two silent letters.'

وَإِذْ غَدَوْتَ مِنْ أَهْلِكَ تُبَوِّئُ الْمُؤْمِنِينَ مَقَاعِدَ لِلْقِتَالِ وَاللَّهُ سَمِيعٌ
عَلِيمٌ ﴿١٢١﴾

121 Remember when you left your family early in the day to install the believers in their battle stations. Allah is All-Hearing, All-Knowing.

The regent in 'when' is implied: 'Remember when you left early in the day.' It means, 'You went out in the morning.' *'Your family'* refers to 'your house with 'Ā'ishah'. This refers to the battle of Uḥud and the entire *āyah* was revealed about it. Mujāhid, al-Ḥasan, Muqātil and al-Kalbī, however, say that it is about the Battle of the Ditch, and it is also reported that al-Ḥasan said that it is the Battle of Badr that is being referred to.

Most, however, say that it is about Uḥud, as is indicated by the words in the following *āyah*: *'And remember when two of your clans were on the point of losing heart.'* This happened at Uḥud. The idolaters moved towards Madīnah with 3000 men to take their revenge for Badr. They camped at Uḥud on the side of a wadi on a canal facing Madīnah on Wednesday, 12 Shawwāl 3 AH at the beginning of the thirty-first month of the Hijrah. They remained there during Thursday while the Prophet ﷺ was in Madīnah. The Messenger of Allah ﷺ dreamt that the blade of his sword was dented and some cows of his were slaughtered and that he put his hand in a strong coat of mail. He interpreted it as meaning that a group of his Companions would be killed and that a man of his house would be struck down and that the coat of mail was Madīnah. This is found in Muslim. All of that is according to what is known about the battle of Uḥud.

The root of 'install' (*tabawwu'*) is to take positions, as when one moves into a house to live in it. Using the same verb, the Prophet ﷺ said, 'Let anyone who tells a lie about me take his seat in the Fire.' Here the verb means to place them in their military positions.

Al-Bayhaqī reports that Anas said that the Messenger of Allah ﷺ said, 'I dreamt that I was following a ram and the handle of my sword broke. I interpreted it to mean that I would kill the ram of the people and the breaking of the handle of the sword to be the killing of a man of my family.' Ḥamzah was killed and the Messenger of Allah ﷺ killed Ṭalḥah, the banner-bearer.

Mūsā ibn 'Uqbah mentioned that Ibn Shihāb reported, 'The banner-bearer of the Muhājirūn was one of the Companions of the Messenger of Allah ﷺ. He said, "I am 'Āṣim (the protector), Allah willing, of what is with me!" Ṭalḥah ibn 'Uthmān said to him, "Will you, 'Āṣim, come forth to individual combat?" "Yes," he replied. That man went forth and struck the head of Ṭalḥah until the sword went through his beard and killed him. So the banner-bearer was killed as in the dream of the Messenger of Allah ﷺ about the ram.'

إِذْ هَمَّت طَّآئِفَتَانِ مِنكُمْ أَن تَفْشَلَا وَٱللَّهُ وَلِيُّهُمَا ۗ وَعَلَى ٱللَّهِ فَلْيَتَوَكَّلِ
ٱلْمُؤْمِنُونَ ﴿١٢٢﴾

122 And remember when two of your clans were on the point of losing heart and Allah was their Protector. Let the believers put their trust in Allah.

The agent in 'when' is 'to install' or 'All-Hearing, All-Knowing.' The two clans are the Banū Salimah of Khazraj and the Banū Ḥārithah of Aws. They were the two flanks of the army in the Battle of Uḥud. *'Losing heart'* means to lose courage. We find in al-Bukhārī that Jābir reported that when this was revealed, he said, 'We are the two clans, the Banū Ḥārithah and Banū Salimah. We do not wish that it had not been revealed because Allah says: *"Allah was their Protector."*' It is said that they were the Banū al-Ḥārith, Banū al-Khazraj and Banū an-Nabīt. An-Nabīt was 'Amr ibn Mālik of Aws. *'Losing heart'* alludes to cowardice. That is its linguistic meaning.

After they went out and 'Abdullāh ibn Ubayy went back with the hypocrites who were with him, the two clans were on the point of losing heart, but Allah preserved their hearts and they did not turn back. That is known from the words of Allah: *'Allah was their Protector,'* in other words the Protector of their hearts from following up on this thought. It is said that they wanted not to go out and that was a small wrong action for them. It is said that it was a suggestion of the self, something that occurred to their minds, and so Allah acquainted His Prophet ﷺ with it and their insight was increased. They did not succumb to that weakness; Allah protected them from it; so they censured one another and went with the Prophet ﷺ.

The Messenger of Allah ﷺ proceeded until he was looking down on the idolaters. He set out from Madīnah with a thousand men. 'Abdullāh ibn Abī Salūl went back with three hundred men in anger since in his opinion it was better to remain and fight in Madīnah when the enemy came to them. His opinion coincided with that of the Messenger of Allah ﷺ but most of the Anṣār rejected it. The Messenger of Allah ﷺ went out with the Muslims and those of them whom Allah honoured with martyrdom were martyred. Mālik said, 'Four Muhājirūn were killed at Uḥud and seventy Anṣār.'

Maqā'id are positions, like *mawāqif*, and it is used for firm positions, especially that of archers. This is the the story of Uḥud in brief, and its details will be sufficiently dealt with.

Accompanying the idolaters were a hundred cavalry under the command of Khālid ibn al-Walīd while the Muslims did not have a single horse. In the battle the Messenger of Allah ﷺ was wounded on his face, his lower right incisor was broken with a stone and his helmet cut into his head. May He reward him on behalf of his community and the *dīn* for the staunchest steadfastness that any Prophet could have had. Those who did that to the Prophet ﷺ were 'Amr ibn Qamī'ah al-Laythī and 'Utbah ibn Abī Waqqāṣ. It is said that 'Abdullāh ibn Shihāb, the grandfather of the famous *faqīh*, Muḥammad ibn Muslim ibn Shihāb, was the one who inflicted the face injury on the Prophet ﷺ. Al-Wāqidī said, 'What is established with us is that the one who shot at the face of the Prophet ﷺ was Ibn Qamī'ah and the one who broke the incisor was 'Utbah ibn Abī Waqqāṣ.'

Al-Wāqidī said with his *isnād* that Nāfi' ibn Jubayr said, 'I heard a man of the Muhājirūn say, "I was present at Uḥud and saw arrows coming from every side and the Messenger of Allah ﷺ was in the midst of them and they were all diverted from him. I saw 'Abdullāh ibn Shihāb az-Zuhrī saying on that day, 'Direct me to Muḥammad! Direct me to Muḥammad! I will not survive if he survives!' The Messenger of Allah ﷺ was actually beside him without anyone else with him. Then he passed by him. Ṣafwān rebuked him and he replied, 'By Allah, I did not see him! I swear by Allah, he is protected from us! Four of us went out, having promised each other and made a pact that we would kill him, but we were unable to do that.'

Stones were thrown at the Messenger of Allah ﷺ until he fell into a ditch which had been dug by Abū 'Āmir ar-Rāhib to trap the Muslims. The Prophet ﷺ fell on his side and Ṭalḥah helped him to stand up again. Mālik ibn Sinān, the father of Abū Sa'īd al-Khudrī, sucked the blood from the wound of the Messenger of Allah

ﷺ and two rings of his helmet were stuck in his face. Abū 'Ubaydah ibn al-Jarrāḥ extracted them using his front teeth and his two front teeth fell out, so he had no front teeth.'"'

Ḥamzah was killed in this battle by Waḥshī, a slave of Jubayr ibn Muṭ'im. Jubayr had told him, 'If you kill Muḥammad, we will give you the reins of horses. If you kill 'Alī ibn Abī Ṭālib, we will give you a hundred camels. If you kill Ḥamzah, you are free.' Waḥshī said, 'As for Muḥammad, he is protected by Allah and no one will reach him. As for 'Alī, everyone he fights is killed. Ḥamzah is a brave man but perhaps I might get lucky and kill him.' Hind said when he was getting ready or passed by him, 'Heal me and heal yourself, Abū Dasamah!' Waḥshī hid behind a rock while Hamzah was attacking some of the idolaters. When he came back from his sortie and passed Waḥshī, he threw a javelin at him and it struck him and he fell down dead. Hind cut out Ḥamzah's liver and chewed it but could not swallow it and threw it away. She went up on a high rock and shouted some verses at the top of her voice. She said:

We have paid you back for the day of Badr!
  A war following a war is frenzied.

I could not bear the loss of 'Utbah
  nor my brother, his uncle and my first-born.

I have satisfaction and have fulfilled my vow.
  Waḥshī, you slaked the rancour in my breast.

I will thank Waḥshī for all my life,
  even until my bones have rotted in the grave!

Hind bint Uthāthah ibn 'Abbād ibn al-Muṭṭalib answered her:

You were disgraced at Badr and after Badr,
  daughter of a slanderer, great only in disbelief.

Allah brought against you in the dawn
  tall, radiant men from Hāshim,

Each slashing with a sharp sword:
  Ḥamzah my lion and 'Alī my falcon.

When Shaybah and your father desired treachery towards me,
We dyed their breasts with blood.

Your evil vow was the worst of vows.

'Abdullāh ibn Rawāḥah said while he was weeping for Ḥamzah:

My eye wept, and it was right to weep,
although weeping and lamentation is of no use,

for the lion of Allah on the morning that they said,
'Is that slain man Ḥamzah?'

All the Muslims were distressed about him there.
The Messenger was distressed by it.

O Abū Ya'lā, your pillars are smashed,
you, the glorious, pious, generous.

Allah's peace be upon you in the Gardens,
enjoying an everlasting bliss.

O Hāshim, the best of men, be steadfast.
All your deeds are good and fine.

The Messenger of Allah is noble and patient.
He speaks by Allah's command when he speaks.

Who will inform Lu'ayy for me?
After today fortunes will change.

Before today, they knew and tasted
Our fighting in which rancour was slaked.

You have forgotten our blows at the pool of Badr
when quick death came to you in the morning,

The mourning when Abū Jahl lay fallen,
the vultures wheeling over him.

'Utbah and his son fell together
as well as Shaybah, bitten by the polished sword.

We left Umayyah flat out
with a spear in his belly.

Ask the skulls of the Banū Rabī'ah.
There are notches in our swords from them.

So Hind, do not gloat about Ḥamzah,
Your might is abased.

Weep, Hind, and do not tire.
Shed tears as one bereaved for her child.

There is also an elegy for him by his sister, Ṣafiyyah which is mentioned in the *Sīrah*. May Allah be pleased with all of them.

Let the believers put their trust in Allah.

This contains clarification of the meaning of trust or reliance (*tawakkul*). Linguistically *tawakkul* means to display incapacity and rely on others, meaning literally to lean on someone else. Scholars disagree about the reality of *tawakkul*. Sahl ibn 'Abdullāh was asked about it and said, 'One group say that it is contentment with Allah's guarantee and having no expectation from created beings.' Others have said, 'It is abandoning means and relying on the Causer of means. If the means distracts someone from the Causer, it strips them of the name of trust.' Sahl also said, 'Whoever says that trust entails abandoning means has attacked the *Sunnah* of the Messenger of Allah ﷺ because Allah says: "*So make full use of any booty you have taken which is lawful and good.*" (8:69) Booty is earning. The Almighty also says: *"So strike their necks and strike all their finger joints!"* (8:12) This is action.' The Prophet ﷺ said, 'Allah loves the person with a profession.'

Someone else said, 'This is the position of the common *fuqahā'*: trust in Allah is trusting in Allah and believing that His decree will be carried out, and that it is necessary to follow the *Sunnah* of His Prophet ﷺ in striving with the means of obtaining food and drink, and defence against the enemy and preparing weapons and using what the usual *sunnah* of Allah demands. This is also the position of recognised Sufis, but in their view the term of '*tawakkul*' is not merited if someone puts their confidence in these means and their hearts turn to them. That is because the means do not in themselves bring benefit nor avert harm. Rather the cause and the result are the action of Allah alone. All is from Him and by His will. When someone relies on those means, the name 'trusting' is stripped from him.

Those who trust have two states. One is the state of the one who is firm in trust and does not turn to any of those means with his heart and he is only occupied with the ruling of the matter. The second is the state of the one who is not firm, and he is the one who turns at times to those means, sometimes without averting them from himself by scholarly reasoning, definitive evidence and experience. So he remains like that until Allah raises him by His generosity to the station of those with firm trust and joins him to the degrees of those with direct knowledge of Allah.

وَلَقَدْ نَصَرَكُمُ ٱللَّهُ بِبَدْرٍ وَأَنتُمْ أَذِلَّةٌ فَٱتَّقُوا۟ ٱللَّهَ لَعَلَّكُمْ
تَشْكُرُونَ ﴿١٢٣﴾ إِذْ تَقُولُ لِلْمُؤْمِنِينَ أَلَن يَكْفِيَكُمْ أَن يُمِدَّكُمْ رَبُّكُم بِثَلَٰثَةِ
ءَالَٰفٍ مِّنَ ٱلْمَلَٰٓئِكَةِ مُنزَلِينَ ﴿١٢٤﴾ بَلَىٰٓ إِن تَصْبِرُوا۟ وَتَتَّقُوا۟ وَيَأْتُوكُم مِّن فَوْرِهِمْ
هَٰذَا يُمْدِدْكُمْ رَبُّكُم بِخَمْسَةِ ءَالَٰفٍ مِّنَ ٱلْمَلَٰٓئِكَةِ مُسَوِّمِينَ ﴿١٢٥﴾

123 Allah helped you at Badr when you were weak so have *taqwā* of Allah, so that hopefully you will be thankful. 124 And when you said to the believers, 'Is it not enough for you that your Lord reinforced you with three thousand angels, sent down?' 125 Yes indeed! But if you are steadfast and are godfearing and they come upon you suddenly, your Lord will reinforce you with five thousand angels, clearly identified.

Allah helped you at Badr when you were weak

The battle of Badr took place on the Friday 17th Ramaḍān eighteen months after the Hijrah. Badr is the name of some wells there from which the place takes its name. Ash-Sha'bī said that the water belonged to a man of Juhaynah called Badr, but the first derivation is more frequently cited. Al-Wāqidī and others say that it is the name of the place and its origin is not transmitted. This will be further dealt with in *al-Anfāl*.

The weakness referred to is about the Muslims being few in number and that is because they numbered three hundred and thirteen or fourteen while their enemy were between nine hundred and a thousand strong. The word, *adhillah*, the plural of *dhalīl*, literally means 'abased', but the use of abasement here is metaphorical. In themselves they were nothing but mighty, but in relation to their enemy and to all the unbelievers on the earth it seemed that they were in a state of abasement and that they would be overcome.

Naṣr is help. Allah helped them at Badr and killed the leaders of the idolaters. On that day Islam was firmly established. It was the first battle which the Prophet ﷺ fought. We find in *Ṣaḥīḥ Muslim* that Buraydah said, 'The Messenger of Allah ﷺ went on seventeen expeditions and he fought in eight of them.' Abū Isḥāq said, 'I met Zayd ibn Arqam and asked him, "How many expeditions did the Messenger of Allah ﷺ go on?" "Nineteen," he answered. I asked, "How many times did you go with him?" "Seventeen," was the answer. I asked, "What was the first expedition he went on?" "Al-'Usayr or al-'Ushayr," he said.' All of this disagreement is found in histories and Prophetic biographies.

Muḥammad ibn Sa'd said in the *Ṭabaqāt*: 'The Messenger of Allah ﷺ went on twenty-seven expeditions (*ghazwah*) himself and sent out fifty-six expeditions (*sariyyah*). (One variant has forty-six.) Those the Messenger of Allah ﷺ personally fought in are: Badr, Uḥud, al-Muraysī', the Ditch, Qurayẓah, the Conquest of Makkah, Ḥunayn and Ṭā'if.' Ibn Sa'd stated: 'This is what there is consensus on. Some transmissions state that he fought against the Banu-n-Naḍīr, and at Wadī al-Qurā in the return from Khaybar and al-Ghābah.'

If this is confirmed, we say that Zayd and Buraydah each reported about what they knew or witnessed. Zayd said, 'The first expedition he ﷺ took part in was Dhāt al-'Usayrah.' This differs from what historians and biographers say. Muḥammad ibn Sa'd said that there were three expeditions before al-'Ushayrah, meaning that he ﷺ took part in them personally.

Ibn 'Abd al-Barr said in *Kitāb ad-Durar* on expeditions: 'The first expedition that the Messenger of Allah ﷺ himself made was the Waddān expedition in Ṣafar. He arrived in Madīnah on the 12th of Rabī' al-Awwal and remained there for the rest of the month and for the entire year until Ṣafar 2 AH. Then he went out in Ṣafar, appointing Sa'd ibn 'Ubādah over Madīnah, and reached Waddān. He made peace with the Banū Ḍamrah and then returned to Madīnah and there was no fighting. That is the expedition which is called al-Abwā'. Then he remained in Madīnah until Rabī' al-Ākhir of that year. Then he went out, appointing as-Sā'ib ibn 'Uthmān ibn Maẓ'ūn over Madīnah, until he reached Buwāṭ in the neighbourhood of Raḍwā. He returned to Madīnah without any fighting and remained there for the rest of Rabī' al-Ākhir and part of Jumāda-l-Ūlā. He then went out on an expedition and appointed Abū Salamah ibn 'Abd al-Asad over Madīnah and took the route to al-'Usayrah.'

Ibn Isḥāq mentioned that 'Ammār ibn Yāsir said, "Alī ibn Abī Ṭālib and I were comrades in the 'Usayrah expedition in the valley of Yanbu'. When the Messenger of Allah ﷺ halted there, we stayed there for a month and there he concluded a truce with the Banū Mudlij and their allies among the Banū Ḍamrah and then left them. 'Alī ibn Abī Ṭālib said to me, "Abu-l-Yaqẓān, do you want to go to those men and see what they are doing?" There was a group of the Banū Mudlij working on a well of theirs. We went and watched them for a while and then felt sleepy. So we went to a group of palm-trees in a cleared part of the ground and slept in the soft dust. By Allah, we were only awoken by the Messenger of Allah ﷺ nudging us with his foot. We sat up, covered in dust, and the Messenger of Allah ﷺ said to 'Alī, "What are you doing, Abū Turāb ('father of dust')?" We told him what we were doing. He said, "Shall I tell you of the two most wretched of men?" "Yes indeed, Messenger of Allah," we answered. He said, "Uḥaymir of Thamūd who slaughtered the She-camel, and the one who will strike you, 'Alī, here," and the Messenger of Allah ﷺ put his hand on his head, "until this is soaked with it," and he put his hand on his beard.' Abū 'Umar said, 'He stayed there for the rest of Jumāda-l-Ūlā and some nights of Jumāda-l-Ākhirah. He left the Banū Mudlij and returned without any fighting.'

After that, a few days later, the first expedition to Badr took place. There is no uncertainty about this on the part of historians and biographers. Zayd ibn Arqam reported about what he knew. Allah knows best. He said that the name was al-'Ushayr or al-'Usayr to which a *hā'* was added and so it becomes al-'Ushayrah. After that came the great expedition of Badr. Badr was the greatest of encounters in excellence for those who attended it. In it, according to the scholars, Allah helped His Prophet ﷺ and the believers with His angels, as is indicated by the literal words of the *āyah*. That did not happen at Uḥud. Those who state that it refers to the Battle of Uḥud make the words: *'Allah helped you at Badr ... you will be thankful'* an interpolation. This is the position of 'Āmir ash-Sha'bī but some people disagree with that. There are many reports which state that the angels were present at Badr and fought there.

Confirming that is what is stated by Abū Usayd Mālik ibn Rabī'ah who was present at Badr: 'If I were with you today at Badr and had my sight back, I would show you the ravine from which the angels emerged. I have no doubt about it whatsoever.' 'Aqīl related it from az-Zuhrī from Abū Ḥāzim Salamah ibn Dīnār.

Abū Ḥātim said, 'Only this one hadith is known from Abū Ḥāzim. It is said that Abū Usayd was the last of the people of Badr to die. Abū 'Umar mentioned him in *al-Isti'āb* and elsewhere.'

In *Ṣaḥīḥ Muslim* we find that 'Umar ibn al-Khaṭṭāb said, 'On the Day of Badr, the Messenger of Allah ﷺ looked at the idolaters who numbered one thousand while his Companions were only three hundred and thirteen in number. The Prophet ﷺ faced the *qiblah* and raised his hands and began to speak to his Lord, "O Allah, fulfil what You promised me! O Allah, bring what You promised me! O Allah, if You destroy this band of the people of Islam, You will not be worshipped on the earth!" He continued to speak to his Lord with his hands raised until the cloak fell from his shoulders. Abū Bakr came to him, picked up his cloak and put it back on his shoulders and then held him from behind and said, "Prophet of Allah, you have entreated your Lord enough. He will fulfil His promise to you." So Allah revealed: *"Remember when you called on your Lord for help and He responded to you: 'I will reinforce you with a thousand angels riding rank after rank.'"* (8:9) So Allah reinforced him with angels.'

Abū Zumayl related that Ibn 'Abbās said, 'While a man of the Muslims was chasing an idolater ahead of him, he heard the crack of a whip above him and the sound of a horseman saying, "Forward, Ḥayzūm!" He looked at the idolater and he fell down. He looked at him and his nose had been struck and his head cut by the whip. The Anṣārī told the Messenger of Allah ﷺ about that and he said, "You spoke the truth. That was from the help of the third heaven." On that day they killed seventy and captured seventy.'

More about this will come in *al-Anfāl*, Allah willing. The *Sunnah* and Qur'an support what the majority say about the help of the angels. Praise be to Allah. Khārijah ibn Ibrāhīm related that his father said, 'The Messenger of Allah ﷺ asked Jibrīl, "In the battle of Badr which angel said, 'Forward, Ḥayzūm'?" Jibrīl answered, "Muḥammad, I do not know all of the people of heaven!"'

'Alī told the people, 'While I was drawing water from the well of Badr, a strong wind came whose like I had never seen and then went. Then another strong wind came whose like I had never seen except for the wind before it. (I think he said, 'Then a strong wind came.') The first wind was Jibrīl who descended with a thousand angels to the Messenger of Allah ﷺ. The second wind was Mikā'īl who descended with a thousand angels to the right of the Messenger of Allah ﷺ. Abū Bakr was on his right. The third wind was Isrāfīl who descended with a thousand angels to the left of the Messenger of Allah ﷺ. I was on the left.'

Sahl ibn Ḥunayf said, 'In the Battle of Badr, one of us would point with his sword at the head of an idolater and his head would fall from his body before he reached him.' Ar-Rabī' ibn Anas said, 'In the Battle of Badr, the people recognized those slain by the angels by the blows on their necks and their fingertips, which were as if fire had burned them.' Al-Bayhaqī mentioned all of this. Some of them said that the angels fought and the sign of their striking the unbelievers was evident because every place they struck caught fire. Abū Jahl said to Ibn Mas'ūd, 'You have killed me? I have only been killed by someone so fast that I could not reach the hoof of his horse with my steed if I tried.' The benefit of the great number of angels was to give tranquillity to the hearts of the believers and Allah Almighty appointed those angels to fight until the Day of Rising. Every Muslim army that is steadfast and anticipating, the angels come to them and fight with them.

Ibn 'Abbās and Mujāhid said, 'The angels only fought in the Battle of Badr. They were present at other battles, but did not fight. They were reinforcements.' Some of them said, 'The reason why there was a large number of angels present was that those who were fighting that day made much supplication and glorification.' According to this view, the angels did not fight on that day but were present by the supplication to be firm. The first view is more frequently held.

Qatādah said, 'In the Battle of Badr, Allah reinforced them with a thousand and then three thousand and then it became five thousand.' That is borne out by His words: *'Remember when you called on your Lord for help and He responded to you: "I will reinforce you with a thousand angels riding rank after rank"* (8:9)', and *'Is it not enough that your Lord reinforced you with three thousand angels, sent down?'* (3:124), and *'Yes indeed! But if you are steadfast and godfearing and they come upon you suddenly, your Lord will reinforce you with five thousand angels, clearly identified.'* (3:125) On the Day of Badr the believers were steadfast and were godfearing and so Allah reinforced them with five thousand angels as He promised. This was all in the Battle of Badr. Al-Ḥasan said, 'Those five thousand will reinforce the believers until the Day of Rising.'

Ash-Sha'bī said, 'On the day of the Battle of Badr, the Prophet ﷺ and his Companions heard that Kurz ibn Jābir al-Muḥāribī wanted to reinforce the idolaters and that was hard for the Prophet ﷺ and the Muslims. Therefore, Allah revealed this *āyah*. Kurz heard about the defeat and did not reinforce them, but returned. So Allah also did not reinforce them with five thousand. They were reinforced with a thousand.' It is said that Allah promised the believers on the Day of Badr that if they were steadfast in obeying Him and feared and avoided what He prohibited, He would help them in all their wars. They were not steadfast and did not fear forbidden things except in the Battle of the Confederates and so He reinforced them when they laid siege to Qurayẓah.

It is said that this is about Uḥud: Allah promised them help if they were steadfast, but they were not steadfast and so He did not reinforce them with a single angel. If He had reinforced them, they would not have been defeated. 'Ikrimah and aḍ-Ḍaḥḥāk said that.

It is said that it is confirmed that Sa'd ibn Abī Waqqāṣ said, 'I saw two men to the right and left of the Messenger of Allah ﷺ in the Battle of Badr who were wearing white clothing and fighting fiercely. I never saw them before that nor after that.' It is said that perhaps this is particular to the Prophet ﷺ and he had two angels who fought with him, and that was not reinforcements for the Companions. Allah knows best.

The descent of the angels was one of the means of help which the Lord does not need. The creature needs it. The heart should be connected to Allah and trust in Him. He is the Helper with or without means: *'His command when He desires a thing is simply to say to it, "Be!" and it is.'* (36:82). But He reports about that so that creation will obey what they are commanded to follow in respect of those secondary means that have been followed in the past: *'You will not find any alteration in the pattern of Allah.'* (33:62) That does not detract from trust. It refutes the one who says, 'Secondary means are for the weak, not the strong.' The Prophet ﷺ and his Companions were strong and others were weak. This is clear.

The verb *madda* (reinforce) is the form used for evil and *amadda* for good. This was already mentioned in *al-Baqarah*. *'Sent down'* is recited by Abū Ḥaywah as *'munzalīna'*, meaning that they bring down help. Ibn 'Āmir recited *'munazzalīna'*, indicating its frequency.

The words end with *'Yes indeed!'* and then there is a new sentence. 'If you are steadfast' means against the enemy, and 'are godfearing' is added to it, meaning fear to disobey Him. The apodosis of the precondition is 'reinforce you'

But if you are steadfast and godfearing and they come upon you suddenly,

The meaning of *'min fawrihim'* is 'in a headlong manner,' according to 'Ikrimah, Qatādah, al-Ḥasan, ar-Rabī', as-Suddī and Ibn Zayd. It is said by Mujāhid and aḍ-Ḍahhāk that it means 'out of their anger'. They were angry about Badr on the Day of Uḥud. The root of *fawr* is to aim for something and take it seriously. *Fawr* means boiling, and so describes vehement anger. It is used to describe a boiling pot as in 10:40. A poet said:

Their pots boiled over us and we made them continue.

Your Lord will reinforce you with five thousand angels, clearly identified.

'Clearly identified' means they were marked with signs. Ibn 'Āmir, Ḥamzah, al-Kisā'ī read it in the active tense (*musawwimīn*), which would mean, 'they clearly identified themselves with signs'. Abū 'Amr, Ibn Kathīr and 'Āṣim prefer the passive, implying known by a sign and making their horses known. Aṭ-Ṭabarī and others preferred this reading. Most commentators said that it refers to their releasing their horses in the attack. Al-Mahdawī said that Allah released them against the unbelievers. Ibn Fūrak said that.

Based on the first reading, there is disagreement about the mark of the angels. 'Alī ibn Abī Ṭālib and Ibn 'Abbās and others said that they wore white turbans with tails. Al-Bayhaqī mentioned it from Ibn 'Abbās and al-Mahdawī related it from az-Zajjāj. The exception was Jibrīl who had a yellow turban like that of az-Zubayr ibn al-'Awwām. Ibn Isḥāq said that. Ar-Rabī' said that their sign was that they were on piebald horses. Al-Bayhaqī mentioned that Suhayl ibn 'Amr said, 'In the Battle of Badr, I saw white men on piebald horses between heaven and earth with distinguishing marks, killing and taking captives.' So *'clearly identified'* indicates the piebald horses, not the marks. Allah knows best.

Mujāhid said that their horses had short tails and manes, and their forelocks and tails were marked with wool. Ibn 'Abbās also said that at Badr the angels were marked by white wool in the forelocks and tails of their horses. 'Abbād ibn [Ḥamzah ibn] 'Abdullāh ibn az-Zubayr, Hishām ibn 'Urwah, and al-Kalbī said that the angels descended in the mien of az-Zubayr, wearing yellow turbans with the tails between their shoulders. That was stated by 'Abdullāh and 'Urwah, the sons of az-Zubayr. 'Abdullāh said, 'Az-Zubayr had a yellow turban.'

The *āyah* is evidence for adopting a sign and identification mark for tribes and squadrons, which the ruler appoints for them, so that each is distinct from the others in fighting, and for the excellence of piebald horses since the angels rode them. Perhaps they descended on them with horses like that of al-Miqdād, which was piebald. They had no other horses and they descended on these horses in honour of al-Miqdād in the same way that Jibrīl wore a yellow turban in honour of az-Zubayr. Allah knows best.

The *āyah* also is evidence for wearing wool, which was worn by the Prophets and righteous. Abū Dāwūd and Ibn Mājah related from Abū Burdah from his father: 'My father said to me, "I wish that you could have seen us with the Messenger of Allah ﷺ when we were hit by the rain; I think that we smelled like goats."' The Prophet ﷺ wore a Greek woollen *jubbah* with narrow sleeves. The imams related that. Yūnus also wore one. This will be discussed in *an-Naḥl*, Allah willing.

As for what Mujāhid mentioned about their horses having cropped tails and manes, it is unlikely. We find in the *Muṣannaf* of Abū Dāwūd that 'Uqbah ibn 'Abd as-Sulamī heard the Messenger of Allah ﷺ say, 'Do not cut short the forelocks, manes or tails of horses. Their tails keep the flies away, their manes keep them warm, and good is tied to their forelocks.' There must be some doubt about what Mujāhid said because according to that the horses of the angels were like that. Allah knows best.

The *āyah* also indicates the excellence of white and yellow as colours since the angels wore them. Ibn 'Abbās said, 'If someone wears yellow sandals, his needs are fulfilled.' The Prophet ﷺ said, 'Wear white garments. They are the best of your garments. Shroud your dead in them. Turbans are the crowns of the Arabs and their dress.' Rukānah, who is the one who wrestled with the Prophet ﷺ and the Prophet ﷺ threw him down, said, 'The difference between us and the idolaters are the turbans over our caps.' Abū Dāwūd transmitted it. Al-Bukhārī said that its *isnād* is unknown and it is not known who listened to whom.

وَمَا جَعَلَهُ ٱللَّهُ إِلَّا بُشْرَىٰ لَكُمْ وَلِتَطْمَئِنَّ قُلُوبُكُم بِهِۦ ۗ وَمَا ٱلنَّصْرُ إِلَّا مِنْ عِندِ
ٱللَّهِ ٱلْعَزِيزِ ٱلْحَكِيمِ ﴿١٢٦﴾ لِيَقْطَعَ طَرَفًا مِّنَ ٱلَّذِينَ كَفَرُوٓا۟ أَوْ يَكْبِتَهُمْ
فَيَنقَلِبُوا۟ خَآئِبِينَ ﴿١٢٧﴾

126 Allah only did this for it to be good news for you and so that your hearts might be set at rest by it (help comes from no one but Allah, the Almighty, the All-Wise) 127 and so that He might cut off a group of those who disbelieve or crush them and they might be turned back in defeat.

The word '*this*' refers to their being reinforced by the angels, the promise, or reinforcements. That is indicated by the previous words '*reinforce you*', the clear identification, the sending down or the number, which may have been as many as five thousand. The *lām* connected to '*set at rest*' is the *lām* of becoming, meaning 'so that your hearts might be put at rest by it, He made…' A similar usage is seen in 41:12. The phrase '*Help comes from no one but Allah,*' means for the believers. The unbelievers are not included in that because any victory they gain is full of disappointment and loss and has a bad outcome.

And so that He might cut off a group of those who disbelieve or crush them and they might be turned back in defeat.

Allah cuts them off by killing them. The thrust of the sentence is: 'Allah helped you at Badr *so that He might cut off…*' It is also said that the meaning is: 'Help is only from Allah *so that He might cut off…*' It could also be connected to the idea of help, meaning, 'He helped you *so that He might cut off…*' It is a reference to the idolaters who were killed at Badr, according to al-Ḥasan and others. As-Suddī said that it refers to the idolaters killed at Uḥud, who numbered eighteen.

The meaning of *'crush'* is to make them sad. Someone who is *'makbūt'* is sad. It is related that the Prophet ﷺ went to Abū Ṭalḥah and saw that his son was sad (*makbūt*). He asked, 'What is wrong with him?' He answered, 'His sparrow has died.' According to those who study language, the root of 'crush them' (*yakbitahum*) is *'yakbidahum'* to cause sorrow and exasperation in their livers (*akbād*), and the *dāl* has been replaced by a *tā'* as we see in *sabara* and *sabada* (shave). The verb *kabata* is used for diverting and humbling the enemy, and *kabada* is to afflict him in his liver. One refers to sorrow or enmity 'burning' one's liver. The Arabs call an enemy someone with 'a black liver' because when livers are burned by enmity, they become black. Al-A'shā said:

What you suffered from the arrival of a people
who are the enemy with blackened livers

The phrase *'turned back in defeat'* (*khāba, yakhību*) means with disappointed hopes. *Khā'ib* is someone whose hopes are cut off. *Khayyāb* is a steel which does not produce fire.

لَيْسَ لَكَ مِنَ ٱلْأَمْرِ شَيْءٌ أَوْ يَتُوبَ عَلَيْهِمْ أَوْ يُعَذِّبَهُمْ فَإِنَّهُمْ ظَـٰلِمُونَ ﴿١٢٨﴾
وَلِلَّهِ مَا فِى ٱلسَّمَـٰوَٰتِ وَمَا فِى ٱلْأَرْضِ يَغْفِرُ لِمَن يَشَآءُ وَيُعَذِّبُ مَن
يَشَآءُ وَٱللَّهُ غَفُورٌ رَّحِيمٌ ﴿١٢٩﴾

128 You have no part in the affair. Either He will turn towards them or He will punish them, for they are wrongdoers. 129 Everything in the heavens and everything in the earth belongs to Allah. He forgives whoever He wills and punishes whoever He wills. Allah is Ever-Forgiving, Most Merciful.

You have no part in the affair.

It is confirmed in *Ṣaḥīḥ Muslim* that the Prophet's incisor was broken at Uḥud and his head cut so that it bled. He said, 'How can a people prosper when they injure the head of their Prophet and break his tooth while he is calling them to Allah Almighty?' and Allah revealed this.

Aḍ-Ḍaḥḥāk said, 'The Prophet ﷺ wanted to invoke against the unbelievers and Allah sent down this. It is said that he asked for permission to call for their extermination, but when the *āyah* was revealed, he knew that some of them would become Muslim, and so many of them did, including Khālid ibn al-Walīd, 'Amr ibn al-'Āṣ, 'Ikrimah ibn Abī Jahl, and others.' At-Tirmidhī related that Ibn 'Umar said, 'The Prophet ﷺ made invocation against four people and Allah revealed: "*You have no part in the affair.*" Allah guided them to Islam.' He said that it is a sound *gharīb ḥasan* hadith.

It is said that the phrase *'either He will turn towards them'* is added to *'cut off a group'*. It means: 'so that He might kill a group of them or sadden them with defeat or turn to them or punish them.' *'Aw'* here can mean 'until'.

Our scholars said that the words of the Prophet ﷺ refer to finding it unlikely that those who did that to him would prosper. The words of Allah: *'You have no part in the affair'* bring close what he had thought unlikely and desiring their Islam. When he desired that, he said, 'O Allah, forgive my people. They do not know.' We find in *Ṣaḥīḥ Muslim* that Ibn Mas'ūd said, 'It is as if I could see the Messenger of Allah ﷺ recounting that the people of one of the Prophets struck and wounded him, and he said, as he wiped the blood from his face, "O Allah, forgive my people. They do not know." They said to him, "You should curse them!" He said, "I was not sent as a curser. I was sent as a caller and a mercy. O Allah, forgive my people! They do not know."'

Our scholars said that the one reported about in the hadith of Ibn Mas'ūd is the Prophet ﷺ. He is, in fact, relating about himself as proven by the fact that it is explicitly reported that when the teeth of the Prophet ﷺ were broken and his face injured in the Battle of Uḥud, that was very hard for his Companions to bear. They said, 'You should curse them!' He answered, 'I was not sent as a curser. I was sent as a caller and a mercy. O Allah, forgive my people! They do not know.' It was as if that had been revealed to him ﷺ before that happened to him at Uḥud. The Prophet ﷺ did not make that specific. When that occurred to him, then it was clear that it was about him as we mentioned.

It is also made clear by what 'Umar said to him: 'May my mother and father be your ransom, Messenger of Allah! Nūḥ invoked against his people. He said, *"My Lord, do not leave a single one of the unbelievers on earth!"* (71:26) If you were to invoke against us in the same way, we would be destroyed to the last one of us. Your back has been trodden on, your face bloodied and your teeth broken, but you refuse to speak other than good!' He answered ﷺ, 'Lord, forgive my people! They do not know.'

[One variant of the account has that] 'Allah was very angry with people who broke the teeth of their Prophet,' meaning with the actual person who did that. We have mentioned his name along with the disagreement about who it was. We said that the statement became specific because a group of those who were present at Uḥud later became good Muslims.

The Kufans claim that this *āyah* abrogates the *qunūt* which the Prophet ﷺ used to perform in the *rukū'* of the last *rak'ah* of *Ṣubḥ.* They use as evidence the hadith of Ibn 'Umar who heard the Prophet ﷺ say in the *Fajr* prayer after raising his head from *rukū'*, 'O Allah, our Lord and praise is yours in the last.' Then he said, 'O Allah, curse so-and-so and so-and-so.' Allah revealed: *'You have no part in the affair.'* Al-Bukhārī transmitted it. Muslim reported it from Abū Hurayrah in a more complete form. This is not abrogation. Allah is informing His Prophet ﷺ that the business is not up to him and that he only knows of the Unseen what Allah acquaints him with and that the entire affair belongs to Allah. He will turn to those He wishes and punish those He wishes. It implies: 'You have no part in the affair. Everything in the heavens and in the earth belongs to Allah, both you and them. He forgives whomever He wishes and turns to whomever He wishes.' There is no abrogation, and Allah knows best. His words explain that all matters are by the decision and decree of Allah. This also refutes the Qadariyyah and others in their views about Allah's decree.

Scholars disagree about the *qunūt* in *Fajr* and other prayers. The Kufans forbid it in *Fajr* and other prayers, and that is the position of al-Layth and Yaḥyā ibn Yaḥyā al-Laythī al-Andalūsī, the companion of Mālik. Ash-Sha'bī disliked it. It says in the *Muwaṭṭā'* about Ibn 'Umar, 'He did not do the *qunūt* in any prayer.' An-Nasā'ī related from Qutaybah from Khalaf that Abū Mālik al-Ashjā'ī reported that his father said, 'I prayed behind the Prophet ﷺ and he did not do the *qunūt.* I prayed behind Abū Bakr and he did not do the *qunūt.* I prayed behind 'Umar and he did not do the *qunūt.* I prayed behind 'Uthmān and he did not do the *qunūt.* I prayed behind 'Alī and he did not do the *qunūt.*' Then he said, 'My son, it is an innovation.'

It is said that the *qunūt* is always done in *Fajr* and other prayers when a disaster befalls the Muslims. Ash-Shāfi'ī and aṭ-Ṭabarī said that. It is said that it is recommended in *Fajr* and that is reported from ash-Shāfi'ī. Al-Ḥasan and Saḥnūn said that it is *sunnah.* That is demanded by the transmission of 'Alī ibn Ziyād from Mālik that the one who deliberately omits it must repeat it. Aṭ-Ṭabarī related the consensus that missing it out does not invalidate the prayer. Al-Ḥasan said that one does the *sujūd* of forgetfulness for it and that is one of the positions of ash-Shāfiʿī. Ad-Dāraquṭnī related from Saʿīd ibn ʿAbd al-ʿAzīz that the one who forgets the *qunūt* in *Ṣubḥ* should do the *sujūd* of forgetfulness.

Mālik preferred it to be done before *rukūʿ*, which is the position of Isḥāq. It is also related from Mālik that it can be done after *rukūʿ*. That is related from the four caliphs and it is also the position of ash-Shāfiʿī, Aḥmad, and Isḥāq. It is related from a group of Companions that there is a choice regarding that. Ad-Dāraquṭnī related with a sound *isnād* that Anas said, 'The Messenger of Allah ﷺ continued to do the *qunūt* in the morning prayer until he left this world.' Abū Dāwūd mentioned in *al-Marāsīl* that Khālid ibn Abī ʿImrān said, 'While the Prophet ﷺ was invoking against Muḍar, Jibrīl came to him and indicated to him that he should be silent and so he was. He said, "Muḥammad, Allah has not sent you as an abuser or curser. He sent you as a mercy. He did not send you as a punishment: *'You have no part in the affair. Either He will turn towards them or He will punish them, for they are wrongdoers.'*" Then he taught him this *qunūt*: 'O Allah! Truly we seek Your help and Your forgiveness and believe in You and praise You for all good. We thank You and are not ungrateful to You and submit ourselves to you and surrender and abandon all who reject You. O Allah You alone we worship. We pray and prostrate to You. We strive and struggle in Your Way. We hope for Your mercy and fear Your harsh punishment. Certainly Your punishment encircles the unbelievers.'

يَٰٓأَيُّهَا ٱلَّذِينَ ءَامَنُوا۟ لَا تَأْكُلُوا۟ ٱلرِّبَوٰٓا۟ أَضْعَٰفًا مُّضَٰعَفَةً ۖ وَٱتَّقُوا۟ ٱللَّهَ لَعَلَّكُمْ
تُفْلِحُونَ ﴿١٣٠﴾ وَٱتَّقُوا۟ ٱلنَّارَ ٱلَّتِىٓ أُعِدَّتْ لِلْكَٰفِرِينَ ﴿١٣١﴾ وَأَطِيعُوا۟
ٱللَّهَ وَٱلرَّسُولَ لَعَلَّكُمْ تُرْحَمُونَ ﴿١٣٢﴾

130 You who believe, do not feed on usury, multiplied and then remultiplied. Have *taqwā* of Allah so that hopefully you will be successful. 131 Have fear of the Fire which has been prepared for the unbelievers. 132 Obey Allah and the Messenger so that hopefully you will gain mercy.

You who believe, do not feed on usury, multiplied and then remultiplied.

This is a prohibition against consuming usury interpolated into the story of Uḥud. Ibn ʿAṭiyyah said, 'I do not recall anything transmitted about that.' Mujāhid said, 'They used to sell on credit and, when the term came, they would increase the price for a delay and so Allah revealed: *"You who believe, do not feed on usury multiplied and then remultiplied."'*

Usury is singled out among acts of disobedience because it is that against which Allah has declared war when He says: *'If you do not, know that it means war from Allah and His Messenger.'* (2:279). War allows killing, and so it is as if He were saying, 'If you do not fear usury, you will be defeated and killed.' So he commanded them to give up usury because they used to practise it, and Allah knows best.

'Multiplied' is in the accusative for the *ḥāl*, and *'remultiplied'* is recited as *'muḍa''afah'* as well as *'muḍā'afah'*. It indicates that they increased the usury time after time. The usury practised by the Arabs was that they increased the debt. The one owed the money would say, 'Will you settle or increase it?' as we mentioned in *al-Baqarah*. This went on year after year and the expression stresses the ugliness of what they were doing. That is why Allah mentions that it was being 'remultiplied'.

Have *taqwā* of Allah so that hopefully you will be successful.

Fear Him regarding any wealth gained from usury and do not consume it.

Have fear of the Fire which has been prepared for the unbelievers.

Then He alarms them by saying: *'Have fear of the Fire.'* Most commentators say that this is a threat directed at those who allow usury. Whoever allows usury disbelieves and is called an unbeliever. It is said that it means: fear the action which will strip faith from you and make the Fire mandatory for you, because usury is one of the wrong actions which make it inevitable that a person will be stripped of their faith and causes one to fear for them.

Another such action is lack of respect for one's parents. A tradition has come that a man called 'Alqamah who was disobedient to his parents was dying. He was told, 'Say: "There is no god but Allah,"' and he was unable to do that until his mother came and was pleased with him. Other things are cutting off relatives, usury, and treachery in respect of a trust. Abū Bakr al-Warrāq reported that Abū Ḥanīfah said, 'It is that which most removes faith from a person when he dies.' Abū Bakr said, 'We looked at wrong actions which remove faith and we did not find anything quicker in doing that than wronging people.'

This *āyah* indicates that the Fire is already created, which refutes the Jahmites who said that it is non-existent and not prepared.

Obey Allah and the Messenger so that hopefully you will gain mercy.

The instruction *'Obey Allah'* means you should obey Allah in respect the obligations of the *dīn* *'and the Messenger'* in respect of *sunnahs*. It is said that it specifies obedience to Allah in respect of forbidding usury and to the Messenger in respect of the prohibition which he conveyed. *'So that hopefully you will gain mercy'* means so that Allah will be merciful to you.

سَارِعُوٓاْ إِلَىٰ مَغْفِرَةٍ مِّن رَّبِّكُمْ وَجَنَّةٍ عَرْضُهَا ٱلسَّمَٰوَٰتُ وَٱلْأَرْضُ أُعِدَّتْ لِلْمُتَّقِينَ ١٣٣

133 Race each other to forgiveness from your Lord and a Garden as wide as the heavens and the earth, prepared for the godfearing:

Race each other to forgiveness from your Lord

Nāfi' and Ibn 'Āmir read it without *wāw* (and) before it, as in the copies of the Qur'an of the people of Madīnah and Syria. The rest of the seven have a *wāw* (and) before it. Abū 'Alī said that both are correct and well-known. If it is read with a *wāw*, it is adding a sentence to the sentence before it. If it is read without the *wāw*, it is because the second sentence is related to the first, but has no need of being joined to it by 'and'. *'Race each other'* is the verbal noun form of Form III.

There is some elision in the *āyah*, meaning: 'Race to that which will make forgiveness mandatory,' which is obedience. Anas ibn Mālik and Makḥūl said that it means racing to the *takbīr al-iḥrām*. 'Alī ibn Abī Ṭālib said that it means racing to the performance of the obligations. 'Uthmān ibn 'Affān said that means racing to sincerity. Al-Kalbī said that it means racing to repentance from usury. It is said it means racing to steadfastness in fighting. Other things are said as well. The *āyah* is general and means the same as the earlier *āyah*: *'Race each other to the good.'* (2:148)

a Garden as wide as the heavens and the earth.

The *muḍāf* is elided in this sentence. [POEM] Scholars disagree about its interpretation. Ibn 'Abbās said that the heavens and the earth are connected to one another as when a garment is opened up and it is clear that its parts are connected. That is the breadth of the Garden and only Allah knows how high it is. That is what the majority say and it is not denied. We find in a hadith reported by Abū Dharr from the Prophet ﷺ: 'The seven heavens and seven earths in comparison to the Footstool are only like some dirhams cast into a desert, and the Footstool in comparison to the Throne is only like a ring cast into a desert.' These things are much greater than the heavens and the earth, and the power of Allah is greater than all that.

Al-Kalbī said, 'There are four Gardens: the garden of 'Adn, the Garden of Refuge, the Garden of Firdaws, and the Garden of Bliss. The dimensions of each Garden is the same as the heavens and the earth if they were all joined together.' Ismā'īl as-Suddī said, 'If the heavens and the earth were broken into mustard seeds, each mustard seed would be a garden whose breadth was like that of the heaven and the earth.' We find in the *Ṣaḥīḥ*: 'The least of the people of the Garden in rank will be the one who wishes and wishes until wishes are no more. Allah Almighty says, "You will have that and ten like it."' Abū Sa'īd al-Khudrī related it, and Muslim and others transmitted it.

Ya'lā ibn Abī Murrah said, 'In Homs I met at-Tanūkhī, the emissary of Heraclius to the Messenger of Allah ﷺ. He was a very old man. He said, "I brought the letter of Heraclius to the Messenger of Allah ﷺ. He handed the letter to a man on his left. I asked, 'Who is your companion who is reading?' 'Mu'āwiyah,' they replied. The letter I was sent with said: 'You have written inviting me to a Garden whose breadth is like that of the heaven and the earth. Where is the Fire?' The Messenger of Allah ﷺ said, 'Glory be to Allah! Where is the night when the day comes?'"'

'Umar al-Fārūq used this argument against the Jews when they said to him, 'I think that you say, "A Garden whose breadth is like that of the heaven and the earth." So where is the Fire?' They told him, 'You have taken this from what is in the Torah.'

Breadth is used instead of height because height is usually greater than width. When height is mentioned, it does not indicate the extent of the breadth. Az-Zuhrī says, 'No one knows its height except Allah.' This is like Allah's words: '*They will be reclining on couches lined with rich brocade.*' (55:54) He described the lining as being the most excellent that is possible since it is known that the outside of something is always better than its lining. The Arabs say, 'a wide land' and 'a wide wilderness'. A poet says:

It is as the lands of Allah which, although they are wide,
are like the palm of the snatcher of a fearful fugitive.

People also say that this is simply a metaphorical usage in Arabic. Since the Garden has the greatest possible dimensions in respect of space and breadth, it is good to refer to it as 'the breadth of the heavens and the earth.' It like referring to a man by saying, 'This one is an ocean' and to a large animal by saying, 'This one is a mountain.' The *āyah* does not intend to define its breadth, but it means that it is the widest thing you could possibly imagine.

prepared for the godfearing.

Most scholars say that the Garden is already created since Allah uses the word, '*prepared*'. We also have the evidence provided by the hadiths about the Night Journey and other sound hadiths. The Mu'tazilites claim that neither the Garden nor the Fire is created now and that Allah will create them when He rolls up this world. He will start with the creation of the Garden and the Fire in whatever way He wishes because they are the Abode of Repayment in respect of both reward and punishment. They say that they will be created after the acknowledgment of responsibility at the moment of repayment and that, just as the responsibility and repayment are not combined in this world, they are not combined in the Next World either.

Ibn Fūrak said, 'What is in the Garden will increase on the Day of Rising.' Ibn 'Aṭiyyah said, 'This is a reference to what Mundhir ibn Sa'īd and others say about the Garden not being created yet.' Ibn 'Aṭiyyah also said, 'The words "What is in the Garden will increase on the Day of Rising" indicate that it already exists, but it needs addition for the increase to occur.'

Ibn 'Aṭiyyah spoke the truth. He said, 'In respect of the Footstool, the seven heavens and the seven earths are like a dirham thrown into a wilderness on earth. In respect of the Throne, the Footstool is like a ring cast into a wilderness. The Garden is now as it will be in the Next World. Its breadth is like the breadth of the heavens and the earth. According to what is related in *Ṣaḥīḥ Muslim*, the Throne is its ceiling. It is known that the ceiling contains what is under it and more. If all created things are like a ring in comparison to it, who is capable of estimating its dimensions? Only Allah, its Creator whose power has no end and the vastness of whose kingdom is without limit knows its height and breadth. Glory be to Him and exalted is He!'

ٱلَّذِينَ يُنفِقُونَ فِي ٱلسَّرَّآءِ وَٱلضَّرَّآءِ وَٱلْكَٰظِمِينَ ٱلْغَيْظَ وَٱلْعَافِينَ
عَنِ ٱلنَّاسِ ۗ وَٱللَّهُ يُحِبُّ ٱلْمُحْسِنِينَ ﴿١٣٤﴾

134 those who give in times of both ease and hardship, those who control their rage and pardon other people – Allah loves the good-doers –

those who give in times of both ease and hardship,

This is one of the qualities of the godfearing for whom the Garden is prepared. The literal meaning of the *āyah* is that it is praise for doing acts that are recommended. Ibn 'Abbās, al-Kalbī and Muqātil said that *sarrā'* is ease and *ḍarrā'* is difficulty. 'Ubayd ibn 'Umayr and aḍ-Ḍaḥḥāk said that they mean comfort and hardship. It is said that they mean health and illness. Ease and hardship can also refer to health and illness, or life and bequests after death. It is also said to refer to weddings and wedding feasts and to calamities and tragedies. It is said to mean spending which delights you, like spending on your children and relatives on the one hand, and giving to your enemies on the other. Or it can refer to hospitality and gifts on the one hand, and to what is spent on those who cause harm on the other. The *āyah* is universal.

those who control their rage.

Controlling rage is to retract it into yourself. It is said that it refers to someone who does not display his rage when he is able to inflict it on his enemy. The verb is also used in irrigation when the onward flow is blocked so that the water builds up. *Kiẓāmah* is something that blocks the flow of water. From it comes the word *kiẓām* which is a stopper for a bottle or waterskin. When the cud is stopped before it reaches an animal's mouth, the verb for that is *kaẓama*, as az-Zajjāj said. One describes a male camel and she-camel in that way. [POEM] It is said that that happens to the camel in a state of alarm when it refuses to move. The word *akẓūm* is used of a man filled with sorrow and grief. We find in the Revelation: *'His eyes turned white from sorrow, hidden within him* (kaẓīm). ' (12:84), *'His face darkens and he is furious (*kaẓīm)' (16:58) and *'when he called out in absolute despair* (makẓūm).' (68:48)

Ghayẓ (rage) is the source of anger and they often go together. The difference between them is that rage does not show on the limbs while anger shows through action. That is why anger is ascribed to Allah when it designates His actions against those with whom He is angry. Some people explain rage as being anger, but this is not good. Allah knows best.

pardon other people

Pardoning people is the most majestic form of good action when a person pardons another when he sees he is in the right. When someone deserves punishment and is spared, he has been pardoned. There is disagreement about the identity of the 'people' referred to here. Abu-l-'Āliyah, al-Kalbī and az-Zajjāj said that it means slaves. Ibn 'Aṭiyyah says that this is good as an example since they are servants and often commit wrong action and power over them is easy to have and they are easy to punish.

It is reported that one day, when he had guests, the slavegirl of Mihrān ibn Maymūn brought in a bowl of hot broth. She stumbled and the broth went over him. He wanted to beat her and the girl said, 'My master, implement the words of Allah: *"those who control their rage."* 'I have done it,' he answered. She said, 'And act by what follows it: *"pardon other people."*" He stated, 'I have pardoned you.' The slave-girl then said: *'Allah loves the good-doers.'* He said, 'I will act well by you. You are free for the sake of Allah.' Something similar is related from al-Aḥnaf ibn Qays.

Zayd ibn Aslam said that what is meant is pardoning their wrongdoing and evil. This is general and it is the literal meaning of the *āyah*. Muqātil ibn Ḥayyān said about this *āyah*, 'We heard that the Messenger of Allah ﷺ said about it, "There are only a few of those among my community; only someone protected by Allah. They were numerous in the nations of the past."' Allah praises those who forgive when they are angry when He says: *'When they are angry, they forgive'* (42:38). Here He praises those who control their rage. He says that He loves them for acting well in that respect.

There are many hadiths reported about controlling rage, pardoning people and controlling oneself when angry. It is one of the greatest acts of worship and *jihād* of the *nafs*. The Prophet ﷺ said, 'The strong man is not the one who throws people down in wrestling. The strong man is the one who has control of himself when he is angry.' And he said ﷺ, 'There is nothing which one can swallow better and with a greater reward than swallowing one's rage for the sake of Allah.' Anas reported that a man asked, 'Messenger of Allah, what is the strongest thing of all?' 'The anger of Allah,' he replied. He asked, 'And what will save a person from the anger of Allah?' 'Not getting angry,' he replied. Al-'Arjī said:

When you are angry, be dignified and control your rage.
Then you will see what you say and hear.

It is enough of an honour that you are patient for a time:
Allah will be pleased with you and you will be elevated.

'Urwah ibn az-Zubayr said about pardon:

People will not achieve glory, even if they are noble,
until they are humble even though they are mighty against people.

They are insulted and you see their colours shining.
It is not pardon due to abasement, but rather the pardon of honour.

Abū Dāwūd and at-Tirmidhī related from Mu'ādh ibn Anas al-Juhanī that the

Prophet ﷺ said, 'If anyone controls his rage when he is able to act on it, Allah will summon him in front of creatures and give him a choice to have whichever of the *houris* he wishes.' He said that it is a *ḥasan gharīb* hadith. Anas reported that the Prophet ﷺ said, 'On the Day of Rising, a caller will call out, "Whoever is due a wage from Allah should enter the Garden." It will be asked, "Who is due a wage from Allah?" The reply will come, "Those who pardoned others will stand and enter the Garden without any reckoning."'

Ibn al-Mubārak said, 'I was sitting with Manṣūr when he ordered a man to be killed. I said, "Amīr al-Mu'minīn! The Messenger of Allah ﷺ said, 'On the Day of Rising a caller will call out before Allah, "Whoever has a hold on Allah should come forward." None will come forward except the one who pardoned a wrong action.'" He ordered that he be let go.'

Allah loves the good-doers

This means that He will reward them for their doing good. Sarī as-Saqaṭī said, 'Doing good is to do good at the moment when it is possible. Not every moment has good-doing possible in it.' A poet said:

Hasten to do good when you are able to do so.
You will not be able to do so all the time.

Abu-l-'Abbās al-Jummānī said:

Not every moment and time
Provides scope for acts of charity.

When you are able, then make haste
out of fear of the time when it is not possible.

All of this was already discussed in *al-Baqarah*.

وَالَّذِينَ إِذَا فَعَلُوا فَاحِشَةً أَوْ ظَلَمُوا أَنفُسَهُمْ ذَكَرُوا اللَّهَ فَاسْتَغْفَرُوا
لِذُنُوبِهِمْ وَمَن يَغْفِرُ الذُّنُوبَ إِلَّا اللَّهُ وَلَمْ يُصِرُّوا عَلَىٰ مَا فَعَلُوا وَهُمْ
يَعْلَمُونَ ١٣٥

135 those who, when they act indecently or wrong themselves, remember Allah and ask forgiveness for their bad actions (and who can forgive bad actions except Allah?) and do not knowingly persist in what they were doing.

Those who, when they act indecently or wrong themselves,

In this *āyah* Allah speaks of a group who are lesser than the first group but connects them with them out His mercy and favour. They are those who repent. 'Aṭā' related that Ibn 'Abbās said, 'This *āyah* was revealed about Nabhān at-Tammār. His *kunyah* was Abū Muqbil. A beautiful woman came to him to sell him some dates. He pulled her to him and kissed her and then regretted doing that. He went to the Prophet ﷺ and mentioned it and this *āyah* was revealed.'

In the *Musnad* of Abū Dāwūd aṭ-Ṭayālisī, 'Alī ibn Abī Ṭālib and Abū Bakr reported that the Messenger of Allah ﷺ said, 'There is no one who commits a wrong action and prays two *rak'ah*s and then asks Allah for forgiveness without Allah forgiving him.' Then he recited this *āyah* and the *āyah*: *'Anyone who does evil or wrongs himself...'* (4:110) At-Tirmidhī transmitted it and said that it is a *ḥasan* hadith.

The *āyah* is general. It was sent down about a particular occasion but then applies to all who have done that or worse. It is said that the reason that this *āyah* was revealed was that a Thaqafī man went on an expedition and left an Anṣārī friend of his to look after his family. That man betrayed him by attempting to force himself on his wife. She defended herself and he only kissed her hand. He regretted doing that and went out wandering about the place in regret and repentance. The Thaqafī came and his wife told him what his friend had done. He went out after him and took him to Abū Bakr and 'Umar hoping that there would be some relief for him but they just rebuked him. He went to the Prophet ﷺ and told him what he had done and then this *āyah* was revealed. It is more fitting that it is general because of the hadith.

Ibn Mas'ūd reported that the Companions said, 'Messenger of Allah, the tribe of Israel is more honoured by Allah than we are. When one of them committed a wrong action, in the morning his punishment was written on the door of his house. (One variant has 'the expiation of his wrong action was written on the lintel of his house.'): "Cut off your nose. Cut off your ear," and so on.' Then Allah revealed this *āyah* as expansion, mercy and replacement for that which was done among the tribe of Israel. It is related that Iblīs wept when this *āyah* was revealed.

The word '*fāḥishah*' (indecency) is used for all types of disobedience but is often specific to fornication so that Jābir ibn 'Abdullāh and as-Suddī said that this *āyah* is about fornication. In the words *'or wrong themselves'*, it is said that 'or' here means 'and' what is meant are actions less than the major wrong actions.

remember Allah and ask forgiveness for their bad actions

'Remember Allah' here means accompanied by fear of His punishment and shame before Him. Aḍ-Daḥḥāk said, 'They remember the Great Day of Presentation

before Allah, and it is said that they realise in themselves that Allah will question them about what they did,' as is also stated by al-Kalbī and Muqātil. Muqātil also says that they remember Allah on the tongue when they commit wrong actions.

The phrase *'ask forgiveness for their bad actions,'* means that they seek forgiveness because of their wrong actions and this applies to every expression or supplication of this sort. We already mentioned at the beginning of this *sūrah* the 'master of asking forgiveness' and that its time is before dawn. Asking forgiveness is a tremendous matter and its reward huge, so that at-Tirmidhī reported that the Prophet ﷺ said, 'If anyone says, "I ask forgiveness of Allah, and there is no god but Him, the Living, the-Self-Sustaining and I turn to Him in repentance," he will be forgiven, even if he had fled from the heat of battle.' Abū Hurayrah said, 'I did not see anyone who asked for forgiveness more than the Messenger of Allah ﷺ.' Makḥūl said, 'I did not see anyone who asked for forgiveness more than Abū Hurayrah.' Makḥūl used also to often pray for forgiveness.

Our scholars said that the form of asking forgiveness which is desired is one that removes persistence in the wrong action and whose effect is confirmed in the heart, not just the expression on the tongue. As for someone who says, 'I ask Allah's forgiveness' with his tongue while persisting in the disobedience he is asking forgiveness for, he must ask forgiveness for doing that, and his minor wrong action is joined to the major ones. Al-Ḥasan al-Baṣrī said, 'Our asking forgiveness requires asking forgiveness.' This was in his time, so what is it like in our time when a person is seen to be bent on doing wrong and eager for it while the prayer beads are in his hand and he is claiming that he is asking for Allah's forgiveness for his wrong actions? That is nothing but mockery on his part. Allah says: *'Do not make a mockery of Allah's signs.'* (2:231)

Who can forgive bad actions except Allah?

This means that there is no one who forgives disobedience nor removes its punishment except Allah.

and do not knowingly persist in what they were doing.

'Do not persist' means that they should not remain fixed and resolved on continuing what they were doing. Mujāhid said, 'They do not continue in it.' Ma'bad ibn Ṣubayḥ said, 'I prayed behind 'Uthmān with 'Alī at my side. He turned to us and said, "I prayed without *wuḍū'*." Then he left and did *wuḍū'* and prayed.'

Persisting is to resolve on a matter with the heart and not refrain from it. The verb is used for tying up dirhams in a purse. Al-Ḥaṭī'ah said when describing horses:

Faces frowning, not curried, brave.
When they are asked to gallop with whips, they persist.

They are firm in running. Qatādah said that 'persisting' is being obdurate in disobeying Allah. A poet said:

He persists at night when his deeds are hidden.
Woe! Everyone with an obdurate heart is a cheat.

Sahl ibn 'Abdullāh said, 'The ignorant man is dead. The forgetful man is asleep. The rebellious man is drunk. The persistent man is destroyed. Persistence lies in procrastination. Procrastination is to say, "I will repent tomorrow." This is the claim of the *nafs*. How can it repent tomorrow when it has no control over it!' Someone else said, 'Persistence is to intend not to repent. When someone intends to repent, their persistence ceases.' Sahl's version is better. It is reported that the Prophet said ﷺ, 'There is no repentance when there is persistence [in the action].'

Our scholars say that what brings about repentance and not persisting is constant reflection on the Book of Allah, the Almighty, Ever-Forgiving, and what He has mentioned of the details of the Garden promised for the obedient and what He has described of the punishment of the Fire threatened for the disobedient. A person continues doing that until his fear and hope are strong and he calls on Allah with the awe and longing that are the fruits of hope and fear. He fears the punishment and hopes for the reward. It is Allah Who gives success in doing what is correct. It is said that what brings it about is a Divine awakening by which Allah alerts those for whom He desires happiness to the ugliness and harm of wrong actions since they are a deadly poison.

I say that this does not exactly accord with the expression, but does accord with the meaning. A person does not reflect on the promise and threat of Allah unless He alerts him to it. When, by success granted by Allah, someone looks at himself and finds himself filled with the wrong actions he has done and the evils he has committed, and regrets his excess and abandons it out of fear of Allah's punishment, then Allah affirms that he repents. If he does not do that, he persists in disobedience. Sahl ibn 'Abdullāh said, 'The sign of true repentance is that the wrong action distracts him from food and drink, as happened with the three who stayed behind [the Tabūk expedition].'

There are various things said about the word *'knowingly'*. It is said that it means that they remember their wrong actions and repent of them. An-Naḥḥās says that this is a good understanding. It is said that it means that they know that Allah will punish persistence in wrongdoing. 'Abdullāh ibn 'Ubayd ibn 'Umayr said that it means that they know that if they repent, Allah will turn to them. It is said that it means that they know that if they ask for forgiveness, Allah will forgive them. It is said that they know what is forbidden for them. That was stated by Ibn Isḥāq. Ibn 'Abbās, al-Ḥasan, Muqātil and al-Kalbī said that it means that they know that persistence is harmful and that it is better to leave it than to persist in it. Al-Ḥasan ibn al-Faḍl said that it means that they know that they have a Lord who forgives wrong actions.

This is taken from the hadith of Abū Hurayrah in which the Prophet ﷺ said, 'Someone committed a wrong action and said, "O Allah, forgive me my wrong action!" Allah, Blessed and Exalted, said, "My slave committed a wrong action and then acknowledged that he had a Lord who forgives wrong action and punishes wrong action." That person again committed a wrong action and said, "O Lord, forgive me my wrong action!" Allah, Blessed and Exalted, said, "My slave committed a wrong action and then acknowledged that he had a Lord who forgives wrong action and punishes wrong action." Then the same person again committed a wrong action and said, "O Lord, forgive me my wrong action!" Allah, Blessed and Exalted, said, "My slave committed a wrong action and then acknowledged that he had a Lord who forgives wrong action and punishes wrong action. I have forgiven My slave so let him do what he likes."' Muslim transmitted it.

This is evidence for the validity of repentance after breaking it by repeating the wrong action because the first repentance was obedience. Then it was broken and another new act of repentance is required. Returning to wrong action is uglier than doing it the first time because undoing repentance is ascribed to the second wrong action. Returning to repentance is better than doing it the first time because it entails clinging to the Gate of the Generous because none but Him can forgive wrong actions.

His words at the end of the hadith, 'Let him do what he likes,' is a command which actually means honour according to one view. It is like Allah's words: *'Enter it in peace.'* (15:46) The end of the words is a report about the state of the person who is told that he has been forgiven his earlier wrong actions and, Allah willing, is protected in his future affairs.

The *āyah* indicates the immense benefit of acknowledging one's wrong actions and asking for forgiveness for them. The Prophet ﷺ said, 'When someone acknowledges his wrong action and then repents to Allah, Allah turns to him.' It is transmitted in both *Ṣaḥīḥ* collections. Someone said:

A lad is entitled to pardon when he admits to
    the wrong actions he committed.

Someone else said:

Admit your wrong action and then ask to have it excused.
Denial of the wrong action means there are two wrong actions.

We find in another hadith in *Ṣaḥīḥ Muslim* that Abū Hurayrah reported that the Messenger of Allah ﷺ said, 'By the One in Whose hand my soul is, if you had not sinned, Allah would have removed you and brought other people who did commit wrong actions and asked for the forgiveness of Allah Almighty so that He could forgive them.' This is the benefit which comes from the names of Allah, the Ever-Forgiving (*al-Ghafūr*) and the One Who Turns to His slaves (*at-Tawwāb*), as we explained in *Kitāb al-Asnā*.

The wrong actions for which one can repent are either *kufr* or something else. The repentance of the unbeliever is to believe while regretting his past disbelief. Faith on its own does not constitute repentance. Repentance for anything other than *kufr* is either on account of a right due to Allah or a right due to others. In the case of the right of Allah, it is enough repentance to abandon not observing it, although in some cases the Sharī'ah is not satisfied with simple abandonment but requires the action to be made up, like the prayer and fasting, and in other cases expiation is necessary, such as for breaking oaths and *ẓihār*. Where the rights of other people are concerned, they must be fulfilled to those to whom they are owed. If they are not found, then one gives *ṣadaqah* on their behalf. If someone finds no way to come up with what he owes due to hardship, then it is hoped that Allah will pardon him. His bounty is freely given. How many He has provided surety against consequences and changed their evil deeds into good deeds. This will be explained later.

If someone does not remember his wrong action and recognise it, he does not have to repent for it specifically, but when he remembers a wrong action, he must repent of it. The interpretation of many people of what our Shaykh Abū Muḥammad 'Abd al-Mu'ṭī al-Iskandarānī mentioned from al-Muḥāsibī, namely that repentance for a category of actions is not valid, means that regret for them as a whole is not sufficient. A person has to repent of each transgression by his limb or heart specifically. People thought that that was his position but it is not what he meant and his words do not demand that understanding. The ruling is that when someone recognises the ruling of actions, and the disobedience he has done, then it is valid for him to repent of all of them that he acknowledges. If he does not recognise that the action was in disobedience to Allah, then he cannot repent of it, either as a whole or in particular. That is like when a man is involved in one of the categories of usury without knowing that it is usury. When he hears the words of Allah: *'You who believe, have taqwā of Allah and forgo any remaining usury if you are believers. If you do not, know that it means war from Allah and from His Messenger'* (2:2778-279), he finds the threat terrible but thinks that he is safe from usury. When he learns the reality of usury now and thinks about what he has done in the past and knows that he has been involved in a lot of usury in the past, then it is sound for him to repent of all of it now and he does not have to specify each instance of it.

That is true of all the wrong actions and evil deeds someone has done, such as slander, tale-bearing and other forbidden actions which they did not know were forbidden. When they understand the import of their past words, then they can repent of all of that and regret being remiss in what was due to Allah. When they ask the one they wronged to release them and he releases them overall and is content with forgoing his right, that is permitted because it comes under the legal principle of giving something which is unknown. This happens in spite of a people's greed and avarice in seeking their due, so how is it then with the Most Generous of the generous Who bounteously bestows acts in which Allah is obeyed and gives the means to do them and pardons disobedience, both small and great?

Our Shaykh said that this is what the imam means and it is that which his words indicate for the one who studies it. What someone thinks about regret only being valid for the actual action done or movement made or a specific silence would be attributing responsibility for something no one is actually capable of undertaking and that is not prescribed in the Sharī'ah, even if it is logically possible. The person would have to know exactly how many sips of wine he had taken, exactly how many movements he had made when fornicating, and exactly how many steps he had taken towards the *ḥarām*. No one is able to do that and therefore repent in an exactly specific way. More concerning the rulings and preconditions of repentance will be dealt with in *an-Nisā'* and elsewhere, Allah willing.

and do not knowingly persist in what they were doing.

This is clear evidence for what Qāḍī Abū Bakr ibn aṭ-Ṭayyib said, 'A person is punished for any disobedience he prepares for consciously and resolves on with his heart.' We find in revelation: *'Those who desire to profane it with wrongdoing, We will let them taste a painful punishment.'* (22:25). Allah says: *'In the morning it was like burnt land stripped bare.'* (68:30) The people referred to here were punished before their action because of their resolve as will be explained in the appropriate place. In a hadith in al-Bukhārī we find, 'When two Muslims clash with their swords, then both the killer and killed are in the Fire.' They asked, 'Messenger of Allah, we can understand this with regard to the killer, but what about the murdered man?' He said, 'He also was eager to kill his companion.' So threat is directed at the desire, which is the resolve and unsheathing of weapons.

Evidence of this is also found what at-Tirmidhī related in a sound *marfū'* report from Abū Kabshah al-Anmārī: 'This world consists of four types of people. There are those whom Allah provides with money and knowledge and they are fearful of their Lord in respect of it and maintain ties of kinship with it and acknowledge the right of Allah over it. Such a person is in the best position. There are those whom Allah provides with knowledge but does not provide with money. They have a sincere intention and say, "If I had money, I would have acted as so-and-so acted." Such a person is rewarded according to his intention, so the reward of both types is the same. There are those whom Allah provides with money but does not provide with knowledge, so they proceed haphazardly with their money without any knowledge. Such a person is not fearful of his Lord in respect of it nor does he maintain ties of kinship with it nor acknowledge the right of Allah over it. This person is in the worst position. Then there are those whom Allah does not provide with either money nor knowledge, so such a person says, "If I had money, I would have acted as so-and-so acted." He is repaid according to his intention, so the burden of sin of both of them is the same.'

This is the position of the Qāḍī and it is that of the generality of the early generations and people of knowledge among the *fuqahā'*, hadith scholars and *mutakallimūn*. One pays no attention to any disagreement about this on the part of those who say that a person is not taken to task for what he only intends to do and mentally prepares for.

There is no contrary evidence in the words of the Prophet ﷺ: 'If someone intends to commit an evil action and does not do it, it is not recorded for him. If he does it, one wrong action is recorded.' That is because 'if he does not do it' means that he does not resolve on doing it as indicated by what we mentioned. 'If he does it' means that he actually does it or resolves to do it. Success is by Allah.

أُوْلَٰٓئِكَ جَزَآؤُهُم مَّغْفِرَةٌ مِّن رَّبِّهِمْ وَجَنَّٰتٌ تَجْرِي مِن تَحْتِهَا ٱلْأَنْهَٰرُ
خَٰلِدِينَ فِيهَا وَنِعْمَ أَجْرُ ٱلْعَٰمِلِينَ ﴿١٣٦﴾

136 Their recompense is forgiveness from their Lord, and Gardens with rivers flowing under them, remaining in them timelessly, for ever. How excellent is the reward of those who act!

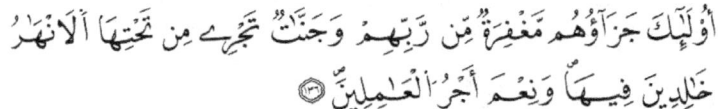

After forgiving wrong actions, Allah is generous towards those who are sincere in repentance and do not persist in wrong action. This can also be connected to the story of Uḥud and refer to those who fled, but then turned in repentance and did not persist. Allah will forgive them.

قَدْ خَلَتْ مِن قَبْلِكُمْ سُنَنٌ فَسِيرُوا۟ فِى ٱلْأَرْضِ فَٱنظُرُوا۟
كَيْفَ كَانَ عَٰقِبَةُ ٱلْمُكَذِّبِينَ ﴿١٣٧﴾

137 Whole societies have passed away before your time, so travel about the earth and see the final fate of the deniers.

This is solace from Allah for the believers. *Sunan* here is the plural of *sunnah*, which is the Straight Path. A person who is on a straight path does not incline to any lower desires. Al-Hudhalī said:

Do not be alarmed by a *sunnah* that you are travelling on.
The first to be pleased with a *sunnah* is the one who travels on it.

Sunnah also means a leader or imām who is followed, and one says, 'So-and-so is an excellent *sunnah*' when people imitate him in good. It is also used for a bad leader in the same way. Labīd said:

There is a group whose fathers are their *sunnah*.
Each group of people have a *sunnah* and their leader.

Sunnah also refers to a nation. *Sunnah*s are nations. The poem goes:

People have not seen any virtue like their virtue
and have not seen their like in past nations (*sunan*).

Az-Zajjāj says that what is meant are the people of *sunnah*s. There is elision. Ibn Zayd said it means 'likes'. 'Aṭā' said that it means laws. Mujāhid says that it refers to those nations like 'Ād and Thamūd who were destroyed before you.

The 'final fate' is the end of the business and refers to the Battle of Uḥud. Allah is saying, 'I give them a delay and a respite and draw them on until the book reaches its term,' meaning the victory of Allah and the believers, and the destruction of the enemy who are unbelievers.

هَٰذَا بَيَانٌ لِّلنَّاسِ وَهُدًى وَمَوْعِظَةٌ لِّلْمُتَّقِينَ ﴿١٣٨﴾

138 This is a clear explanation for all mankind, and guidance and admonition for those who are godfearing.

This means the Qur'an, as al-Ḥasan and others said. It is said that it indicates the previous *āyah*: *'Whole societies have passed away before your time'* and is a threat.

وَلَا تَهِنُوا وَلَا تَحْزَنُوا وَأَنتُمُ الْأَعْلَوْنَ إِن كُنتُم مُّؤْمِنِينَ ﴿١٣٩﴾

139 Do not give up and do not be downhearted. You shall be uppermost if you are believers.

Allah comforted and consoled them for the killing and wounding they suffered at Uḥud and encouraged them to fight their enemy and forbade them to be feeble and lose heart. The phrase *'Do not give up'* means 'Do not be weak and cowardly, Companions of Muḥammad, about fighting your enemies because of what befell you.' *'Do not be downhearted'* for your losses or the defeat. *'You shall be uppermost'* means: 'You will have the victory in the end if *"you believe"* in the truth of My promise.' It is said that 'if' (*in*) here means 'when'.

Ibn 'Abbās said, 'The Companions of the Messenger of Allah ﷺ were defeated at Uḥud and while they were in that condition, Khālid ibn al-Walīd came with his cavalry and wanted to look down on them from the mountain. The Prophet ﷺ said, "O Allah, do not let them be above us! O Allah, we have no strength except by You, O Allah, only this group worship you in the land," and Allah revealed this *āyah*. A group of Muslims archers went up the mountain and shot at the horses of the idolaters until they routed them.' That is what His words, *'You shall be the uppermost'* are referring to.

The *āyah* means that after Uḥud they will always overcome their enemies. Indeed after that no army went out during the time of the Messenger of Allah ﷺ without being victorious, and in every battle after the Messenger of Allah ﷺ, where even one of the Companions was present, they had victory. All these lands were conquered during the time of the Companions of the Messenger of Allah ﷺ. When they came to an end, no land was conquered as they had conquered them all in their time.

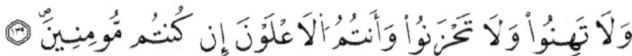

This *āyah* is conclusive evidence of the excellence of this community because they are addressed directly in the same way that Allah addressed His Prophets. Allah said to Mūsā: *'You will be uppermost.'* (20:68) He told this community: *'You*

shall be the uppermost.' This is derived from His Name, *al-A'lā* (Most High).

إِن يَمْسَسْكُمْ قَرْحٌ فَقَدْ مَسَّ ٱلْقَوْمَ قَرْحٌ مِّثْلُهُۥ ۚ وَتِلْكَ ٱلْأَيَّامُ نُدَاوِلُهَا بَيْنَ ٱلنَّاسِ وَلِيَعْلَمَ ٱللَّهُ ٱلَّذِينَ ءَامَنُوا۟ وَيَتَّخِذَ مِنكُمْ شُهَدَآءَ ۗ وَٱللَّهُ لَا يُحِبُّ ٱلظَّـٰلِمِينَ ﴿١٤٠﴾

140 If you have received a wound, they have already received a similar wound. We deal out such days to people turn by turn, so that Allah will know those who believe and can gather martyrs from among you – Allah does not love wrongdoers –

If you have received a wound, they have already received a similar wound.

'Wound' is read both as *qarḥ* and *qurḥ*. According to al-Kisā'ī and al-Akhfash, they are two dialectical forms. Al-Farrā', however, said that *qarḥ* means a wound and *qurḥ* means pain. It means: If you were wounded at Uḥud, they were wounded at Badr. Muḥammad ibn as-Samayfa' recited '*qaraḥ*'.

We deal out such days to people turn by turn,

This is said to be in war: sometimes to the believers so that Allah gives victory to His *dīn*, and sometimes to the unbelievers when the believers disobey, in order to test them and purify them of their wrong actions. When they do not disobey Allah, the party of Allah will be the victors. It is said that it refers to the alternation of joy and sorrow, health and illness, wealth and poverty. '*Dawlah*' is to come around again. A poet said:

One day is for us and one day is against us.
One day of delay and one day of victory.

so that Allah will know those who believe

This alternation is to set apart the believer from the hypocrite and distinguish between them as is clear in Allah's words: '*What assailed you on the day the two armies met was by Allah's permission, so that He would know the believers, and so that He would know the hypocrites.*' (3:166-167) It is said that it is in order to know the steadfastness of the believers for which they will be rewarded just as He informed them that they are responsible.

and can gather martyrs from among you.

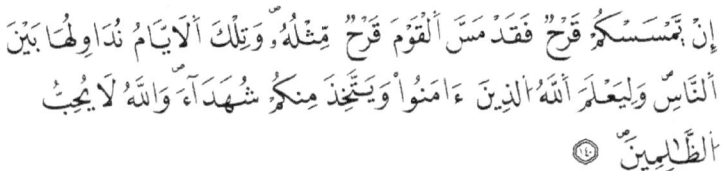

This means to honour you with martyrdom, with the implication that some people will be slain so that they can be witnesses against people by their actions. It is said, 'This is why he is called a martyr (*shahīd*).' It is also said to be because the Garden bears witness for him, and it is said that their spirits are present in the Abode of Peace because they are alive in the presence of their Lord while the souls of others have not yet reached the Garden. So *shahīd* in fact means *shāhid*, or present in the Garden. This is sound, as will come later.

The virtue of martyrdom is immense. Enough for you regarding that are the words of the Almighty: *'Allah buys from the believers their selves…'* (9:111) and *'O you who believe! shall I direct you to a transaction which will save you from a painful punishment? It is to believe in Allah and His Messenger and do jihad in the Way of Allah with your wealth and your selves … That is the Great Victory.'* (61:10-12)

We find in the *Ṣaḥīḥ* of al-Bustī from Abū Hurayrah that the Messenger of Allah ﷺ said, 'What the martyr experiences from being killed is no more than one of you experiences from a wound.' An-Nasā'ī related from Rāshid ibn Sa'd from one of the Companions of the Prophet ﷺ that a man said, 'Messenger of Allah, why is the martyr excused from what other believers are tested with in their graves?' He replied, 'The flash of the sword at his head is his test.'

We find in al-Bukhārī: 'Those Muslims killed in the Battle of Uḥud included Ḥamzah, al-Yamān, an-Naḍr ibn Anas and Muṣ'ab ibn 'Umayr.' 'Amr ibn 'Alī related from Mu'ādh ibn Hishām from his father that Qatādah said, 'We do not know of any tribe of the Arabs with more martyrs and mightier on the Day of Rising than the Anṣār.' Qatādah said, 'Anas ibn Mālik related to us that seventy were killed in the Battle of Uḥud, seventy at Bi'r Ma'ūnah and seventy in the Battle of Yamāmah.' He added, 'Bi'r Ma'ūnah was in the time of the Prophet ﷺ and the Battle of Yamāmah was in the time of Abū Bakr against Musaylimah the Liar.'

Anas said, "Alī ibn Abī Ṭālib was brought to the Prophet ﷺ with over sixty wounds from stabbings, blows or thrusts. The Prophet ﷺ began to pass his hand over him and they were healed by Allah's permission as if they had not been there.'

The words *'gather martyrs from among you'* indicate that Allah's Will is not the same as His Command, which is the position of the people of the *Sunnah*. Allah forbade the unbelievers to kill the believers – Ḥamzah and others – while He willed that they be killed. He forbade Ādam to eat from the tree while He willed that he would do so. He ordered Iblīs to prostrate but did not will that he do so and so Iblīs refused. That is indicated by His words: *'but Allah was averse to their setting out so He held them back.'* (9:46) He commanded all of them to do *jihād* but created laziness and the reasons that stop people from doing it.

It is reported that 'Alī ibn Abī Ṭālib said, 'Jibrīl came to the Prophet ﷺ at Badr and said to him, "Give your Companions a choice regarding the captives. They can either kill them or let them be ransomed, but if they do that the like number of them will be killed next year." They said, "The ransom and let us be killed."' At-Tirmidhī related it and said that it is a *ḥasan* hadith. Allah fulfilled His promise by the martyrdom of His friends after He had given them a choice and they chose being killed.

Allah does not love wrongdoers

This means the idolaters. Even if they receive injury from the believers, Allah does not love the unbelievers, but if He allows pain to be afflicted on the believers, it is a sign that He loves them.

وَلِيُمَحِّصَ ٱللَّهُ ٱلَّذِينَ ءَامَنُوا۟ وَيَمْحَقَ ٱلْكَٰفِرِينَ ﴿١٤١﴾

141 and so that Allah can purge those who believe and wipe out the unbelievers.

There are three things said about this. One is that the word *'purge'* means 'to test'. The second is that it means 'to purge' them of their wrong actions, which would apply some elision. Al-Farrā' said that. The third is that the meaning is 'to purify'. Al-Khalīl says the verb is used for a rope which is smoothed. Part of that usage is: 'O Allah, purge us of our wrong actions,' meaning to save us from being punished for them.

Abū Isḥāq az-Zajjāj said, 'I read out to Muḥammad ibn Zayd that al-Khalīl said that purging is delivering.' It means that He tests the believers to make them firm and purify them of their wrong actions. He will wipe out the unbelievers by destruction.

أَمْ حَسِبْتُمْ أَن تَدْخُلُوا۟ ٱلْجَنَّةَ وَلَمَّا يَعْلَمِ ٱللَّهُ ٱلَّذِينَ جَٰهَدُوا۟ مِنكُمْ وَيَعْلَمَ
ٱلصَّٰبِرِينَ ﴿١٤٢﴾

142 Or did you imagine that you were going to enter the Garden without Allah knowing those among you who had struggled and knowing the steadfast?

'Am' can mean 'indeed' or it is said that the *mīm* is extra. It means: 'Did you suppose, you who were defeated at Uḥud, that you would enter the Garden as

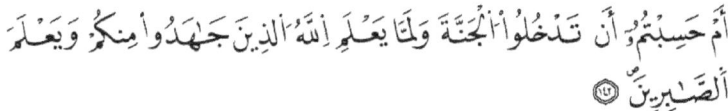

those who entered who were killed and endured the pain of wounds and killing without proceeding on their path and being steadfast as they were steadfast?' The words *'without Allah knowing those among you who had struggled,'* refer to knowledge of witnessing so that there is repayment. It means: without knowing those who did not struggle so that He knows that from you.

In the phrase '*knowing the steadfast*,' the verb has a *fatḥah* (*ya'lama*) because of an implied '*an*' according to al-Khalīl. Al-Ḥasan and Yaḥyā ibn Ya'mar recited '*ya'lami*' in the jussive case based on the context. It can also be recited as '*ya'lamu*' as a separate sentence, and this is the reading of 'Abd al-Wārith from Abū 'Amr. The *wāw* means 'so that'.

وَلَقَدْ كُنتُمْ تَمَنَّوْنَ ٱلْمَوْتَ مِن قَبْلِ أَن تَلْقَوْهُ فَقَدْ رَأَيْتُمُوهُ وَأَنتُمْ تَنظُرُونَ ١٤٣

143 You were longing for death before you met it. Now you have seen it with your own eyes.

'You were longing for death,' in other words martyrdom, before you met it. It is before killing or before meeting the causes of death. That is because many of those who had not been at Badr used to wish for a day of fighting. Then they were defeated at Uḥud. Some of them remained firm until they were killed, including Anas ibn an-Naḍr. When the Muslims withdrew, he said, 'O Allah, I am free of what those have done!' He joined the fight and exclaimed, 'It is the fragrance of the Garden that I sense!' He fought until he was martyred. Anas said, 'We only recognised him by his finger tips. He had about eighty wounds.' It is about him and those like him that Allah revealed: *'men who have been true to the contract they have made with Allah.'* (33:23)

The *āyah* censures those who were defeated, especially those who encouraged the Prophet ﷺ to leave Madīnah. So this refers to those Muslims who wished for martyrdom based on standing firm and being steadfast in jihad, not for the unbelievers to kill them, because such a wish would be disobedience and disbelief, which one cannot long for. So this question on the part of the Muslims is asking for Allah to grant them martyrdom as well as asking for steadfastness in jihad, even if it results in being killed.

'Now you have seen it with your own eyes.' Al-Akhfash said that this is repetition for the sake of stress. It is said that it means: 'while you are looking with no defect in your eyes' which is an expression used in Arabic for actually seeing something.

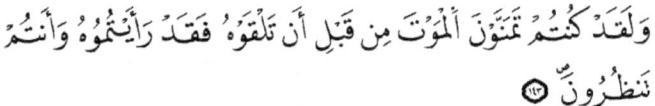

This conveys stress. Some of them said that it means: "You were looking at Muḥammad ﷺ. So why were you defeated?'

وَمَا مُحَمَّدٌ إِلَّا رَسُولٌ قَدْ خَلَتْ مِن قَبْلِهِ الرُّسُلُ أَفَإِيْن مَّاتَ أَوْ قُتِلَ انقَلَبْتُمْ عَلَىٰ أَعْقَابِكُمْ وَمَن يَنقَلِبْ عَلَىٰ عَقِبَيْهِ فَلَن يَضُرَّ اللَّهَ شَيْئًا وَسَيَجْزِي اللَّهُ الشَّاكِرِينَ ﴿١٤٤﴾

144 Muḥammad is only a Messenger and he has been preceded by other Messengers. If he were to die or be killed, would you turn on your heels? Those who turn on their heels do not harm Allah in any way. Allah will recompense the thankful.

This was revealed because of the defeat of the Muslims at Uḥud when Shayṭān shouted, 'Muḥammad has been killed!' 'Aṭiyyah al-'Awfī said, 'Some people said, "Muḥammad has been struck down, so surrender to them. They are your brothers." Others said, "If Muḥammad had been struck down, should you not continue as your Prophet did until you join him!" So Allah revealed this *āyah* about that along with the *āyah*s after it up to *āyah* 148.'

The *mā* in the sentence is negative. Ibn 'Abbās recited 'Messengers' without the definite article. Allah informs us in this *āyah* that the Messengers do not remain among their people forever and that He desires us to hold to what the Messengers brought, even if they die or are killed. He honoured and chose two names for His Prophet ﷺ which are derived from His Name. These names are Muḥammad and Aḥmad. This is used in Arabic for someone with many praiseworthy qualities. A poet said:

To the noble glorious praised (*muḥammad*) chief.

This was discussed in *al-Fātiḥah*. 'Abbās ibn Mirdās said:

O Seal of the Prophets, you are sent
with good! Every guidance to the Path is your guidance.

Allah built love for you for His creation
and named you Muḥammad.

This *āyah* is the end of the censure of those defeated and conveys that they will not be defeated, even if Muḥammad ﷺ is killed. Prophethood is not endangered by death. Allah knows best.

This *āyah* is the clearest evidence of the courage and boldness of Abū Bakr aṣ-Ṣiddīq. Courage and boldness are defined by the firmness of the heart in the face of affliction, and there could be no calamity greater than the death of the Prophet ﷺ as we explained in *al-Baqarah*, and at that time his courage and knowledge became clear. People, including 'Umar, said, 'The Messenger of Allah ﷺ is not dead!' 'Uthmān was mute and 'Alī hid and things were unsettled. Then the Ṣiddīq removed the confusion with this *āyah* when he came from his house in Ṣunḥ. The hadith is found in al-Bukhārī.

We find in the *Sunan* of Ibn Mājah that 'Ā'ishah said, 'When the Messenger of Allah ﷺ died while Abū Bakr was with his wife, the daughter of Khārijah, at al-'Awālī, people began to say, "The Prophet ﷺ has not died. It is just what happens when he is overcome by the revelation!" Abū Bakr came, uncovered his face, kissed him between the eyes and said twice, "You are too noble for Allah to make you die twice! By Allah, the Messenger of Allah ﷺ has died." 'Umar was in a corner of the mosque, saying, "By Allah, the Messenger of Allah ﷺ has not died and will not die until he cuts off the hands and feet of many of the hypocrites!" Abū Bakr rose and went up the minbar and said, "Whoever worships Allah, Allah is alive and will never die. Whoever worships Muḥammad, Muḥammad has died. *'Muḥammad is only a Messenger and he has been preceded by other Messengers. If he were to die or be killed, would you turn on your heels? Those who turn on their heels do not harm Allah in any way. Allah will recompense the thankful.'*" 'Umar said, "It was as if I had not read it until that day." He retracted what he had been saying.'

This is what Abū Naṣr 'Ubaydullāh al-Wā'ilī mentioned in *Kitāb al-Ibānah*. He said that Anas ibn Mālik heard 'Umar ibn al-Khaṭṭāb give allegiance to Abū Bakr in the mosque of the Messenger of Allah ﷺ. He sat on the minbar of the Messenger of Allah ﷺ to testify before Abū Bakr. He said, 'Yesterday I said something to you, and it is not as I said. By Allah, I did not find what I said in a Book revealed by Allah nor in anything given to me by the Messenger of Allah ﷺ, but I hoped that the Messenger of Allah ﷺ would live so that he could direct us – so that he would be the last of us to die – and Allah chose for His Messenger what is with Him instead of what is with us. This is the Book by which Allah guided His Messenger. Take it and you will be guided by what the Messenger of Allah ﷺ was guided by.'

Abū Naṣr al-Wā'ilī said, 'The statement that he made and then retracted was: "The Messenger of Allah ﷺ has not died and will not die until he cuts off the hands and feet of many of the hypocrites!" That was due to the immensity of what had happened and his fear of civil unrest and the appearance of hypocrites. When he saw the strength of the greater certainty of Abū Bakr aṣ-Ṣiddīq when he spoke the words of Allah: *"Every self will taste death"* (3:185), and: *"You will die and they too will die"* (39:30) and what he said, he came to his senses and was firm. He said, "It was as if I had never heard the *āyah* before Abū Bakr spoke." People went out and about in the streets of Madīnah repeating it as if it had only been revealed on that day. There is no dispute about the fact that he ﷺ died on a Monday, at the same time he entered Madīnah on his Hijrah, when it was well into morning, and was buried on Tuesday or Wednesday night.'

Ṣafiyyah bint 'Abd al-Muṭṭalib composed an elegy for the Messenger of Allah ﷺ:

O Messenger of Allah! You were our hope!
You were good to us and not harsh.

You were merciful, a guide and a teacher.
Today, everyone who weeps must weep for you.

By your life, I do not weep for the Prophet because of his loss,
but out of fear that bloodshed will come.

It is as if it comes on my heart when Muḥammad is mentioned
and the burning brands I fear after the Prophet.

May Allah, the Lord of Muḥammad,
bless a grave in Yathrib again.

May my mother, maternal aunt, uncle, fathers
and my life and property be the ransom of the Messenger of Allah!

You spoke the truth, and conveyed the Message truthfully.
You died a firm staff, bright and clear.

If the Lord of mankind had made our Prophet live
we would have been fortunate, but His command is carried out.

May the greeting of people be to you from Allah
and may He admit you in the Gardens of Eden in pleasure.

I see Ḥasan as his orphan and legacy,
a young man weeping and praying for his grandfather today.

Why was the burial of the Messenger of Allah ﷺ delayed when he had said to the people of a house who delayed burying their dead, 'Hurry to bury your corpse. Do not delay it'?

There are three points in the answer. The first is what we mentioned about the lack of agreement over his death. The second was because they did not know where to bury him. Some people said that it should be in al-Baqī' and others said in the mosque. Some people said that he should be kept until he could be carried to his ancestor Ibrāhīm, until the greatest scholar said, 'A Prophet is only buried where he dies."' Ibn Mājah, the *Muwaṭṭā'* and other sources mentioned it. The third is that they were preoccupied with the dispute which occurred between the Muhājirūn and the Anṣār about allegiance and waited until the business was settled, unity restored, and the situation was secure, and they gave their allegiance to Abū Bakr. Then they gave him a second allegiance on the following day in a group and with their assent. By him Allah delivered them from the catastrophe of the Riddah and the *dīn* was established. Praise be to Allah, the Lord of the worlds. Then they went back to the Prophet ﷺ and looked into burying him and washed and shrouded him. Allah knows best.

They disagree about whether the funeral prayer was performed for him or not. Some say that it was and some said that it was not but that each person stood to make supplication because he was too elevated to have someone pray over him. Ibn al-'Arabī said that this is weak because the Sunnah is that there is a prayer in the *janāzah* as there is a prayer over him in supplication when someone says, 'O Allah, bless Muḥammad until the Day of Rising,' and that benefits us.

It is said that the prayer was not said over him because there was no imām. This is weak because whoever establishes the obligatory prayer is their imām. It is also said that people prayed individually because each of them wanted his blessing individually and not subject to anyone else. Allah knows best whether that is sound.

Ibn Mājah transmitted with a *ḥasan isnād* which is sound from Ibn 'Abbās: 'When we finished preparing him on Tuesday, he was placed on the bed in his room and then the people came in and prayed over the Messenger of Allah ﷺ, and when the men had finished, the women came in. When the women were finished, the children came in. None of the people acted as imām over the Messenger of Allah ﷺ.' It is transmitted from Naṣr ibn 'Alī al-Jahḍamī from Wahb ibn Jarīr from his father from Muḥammad ibn Isḥāq. He said that Ḥusayn ibn 'Abdullāh related it from 'Ikrimah from Ibn 'Abbās.

Concerning the change of circumstance after the death of the Messenger of Allah ﷺ, Anas said, 'On the day when the Messenger of Allah ﷺ entered Madīnah, every part of it was illuminated. On the day he died, every part was cast into darkness. We had not shaken off the dust from our hands after burying the Messenger of Allah ﷺ until we doubted our own hearts.' Ibn Mājah transmitted it. Muḥammad ibn Bashshār related from 'Abd ar-Raḥmān ibn Mahdī from Sufyān from 'Abdullāh ibn Dīnār that Ibn 'Umar said, 'We used to be careful about our words and delighting with our wives in the time of the Messenger of Allah ﷺ fearing that the Qur'an would be revealed about us. When the Messenger of Allah ﷺ died, we spoke.'

Umm Salamah bint Abī Umayyah, the wife of the Messenger of Allah ﷺ, said, 'In the time of the Messenger of Allah ﷺ, when people stood to pray, their eyes would not leave the spot where their feet were. When the Messenger of Allah ﷺ died and Abū Bakr was in charge and people stood to pray, their eyes would not leave the place of their brow. When Abū Bakr died and 'Umar was in charge, when people stood to pray, their eyes would not leave the place of the *qiblah*. When 'Uthmān ibn 'Affān was in charge, the *fitnah* came and then people would look to the right or the left in the prayer.'

If he were to die or be killed, would you turn on your heels?

This is a metaphor for reverting to being unbelievers after faith, according to Qatādah and others. It is said to mean to return to being what they were before. It is said that this refers to actually and not metaphorically being routed. It is said that it means you would behave like apostates.

Those who turn on their heels do not harm Allah in any way.

They will harm themselves and expose themselves to punishment for opposition. Obedience does not help Allah and disobedience does not harm Him. He is free of need of any sort.

Allah will recompense the thankful.

Those who were steadfast, fought, and were martyred. This is a promise connected to a threat.

وَمَا كَانَ لِنَفْسٍ أَن تَمُوتَ إِلَّا بِإِذْنِ ٱللَّهِ كِتَٰبًا مُّؤَجَّلًا ۗ وَمَن
يُرِدْ ثَوَابَ ٱلدُّنْيَا نُؤْتِهِۦ مِنْهَا وَمَن يُرِدْ ثَوَابَ ٱلْءَاخِرَةِ نُؤْتِهِۦ مِنْهَا ۚ
وَسَنَجْزِى ٱلشَّٰكِرِينَ ﴿١٤٥﴾

145 No self can die except with Allah's permission, at a predetermined time. If anyone desires the reward of this world, We will give him some of it. If anyone desires the reward of the Next World, We will give him some of it. We will recompense the thankful.

No self can die except with Allah's permission, at a predetermined time.

This is encouragement to perform *jihād* and information that death is necessary and that every human being will die, slain or not slain, when the time written for him to die comes. *'Mu'ajjal'* means at a certain term. *'With Allah's permission'* means according to His decision and decree. *'Kitāb'* here means written by Allah. *'A predetermined time'* is the time in which Allah knows that the spirit of the person will leave his body. When someone is killed, we know that that is his time and it is not correct to say, 'If he had not been killed, he would have lived.' The evidence for this is found in the words of the Almighty: *'When their time comes, they cannot delay it a single hour or bring it forward'* (7:34), *'Allah's appointed time is certainly coming'* (29:5), and *'There is a prescribed limit to every term.'* (13:38) The Mu'tazilites claim that the term can be moved forward and back, and that if someone is murdered, he died before his time because the killer is responsible and must pay blood money. Here in this *āyah* the Almighty makes it clear that no self can die before its time. This will be further discussed in *al-A'rāf*, Allah willing. The evidence for this is found in the books of knowledge as will be explained in *Ṭaha* (20:52).

If anyone desires the reward of this world, We will give him some of it.

This means booty. This was revealed about those who left their post to get booty. It is said that it is general to all who desire this world rather than the Next World. It means: 'We will give him what is allotted for him of it.' We find in the Revelation: *'As for anyone who desires this fleeting existence, We hasten in it whatever We will.'* (17:18)

If anyone desires the reward of the Next World, We will give him some of it.

This means We will give him the reward of his actions, as Allah can multiply the reward for whomever He wishes. It is said that it refers to 'Abdullāh ibn Jubayr and those who remained at their posts until they were killed.

We will recompense the thankful.

We will give them the eternal reward for not fleeing. It is said that it means provision in this world, so that the thankful person does not imagine that he has been deprived of what was allotted him which the unbelievers obtained.

وَكَأَيِّن مِّن نَّبِيٓءٍ قُتِلَ مَعَهُۥ رِبِّيُّونَ كَثِيرٌ فَمَا وَهَنُواْ لِمَآ أَصَابَهُمْ فِي
سَبِيلِ اِ۬للَّهِ وَمَا ضَعُفُواْ وَمَا اَ۪سْتَكَانُواْ وَاللَّهُ يُحِبُّ اُ۬لصَّٰبِرِينَ ﴿١٤٦﴾ وَمَا
كَانَ قَوْلَهُمُۥٓ إِلَّآ أَن قَالُواْ رَبَّنَا اَ۪غْفِرْ لَنَا ذُنُوبَنَا وَإِسْرَافَنَا فِيٓ أَمْرِنَا
وَثَبِّتْ أَقْدَامَنَا وَانصُرْنَا عَلَى اَ۬لْقَوْمِ اِ۬لْكَٰفِرِينَ ﴿١٤٧﴾

146 Many a Prophet has been killed, when there were many thousands with him! They did not give up in the face of what assailed them in the Way of Allah, nor did they weaken, nor did they yield. Allah loves the steadfast. 147 All they said was, 'Our Lord, forgive us our wrong actions and any excesses we went to in what we did and make our feet firm and help us against these unbelieving people.'

Many a Prophet has been killed.

Az-Zuhrī said, 'Shayṭān shouted at Uḥud, "Muḥammad has been killed!" and a group of the Muslims were routed.' Ka'b ibn Mālik said, 'I was the first to recognise the Prophet ﷺ. I saw his eyes shining under the helmet. I called out in my loudest voice, "This is the Messenger of Allah!" He indicated for me to be silent, and then Allah revealed: *"Many a Prophet has been killed when there were many thousands with him!..."*'

'Ka-ayyin' means 'how many?' Al-Khalīl and Sībuwayh said that it is *'ayy'* with the *kāf* of resemblance added to it and so it is indeclinable with it and means: 'how many?' In the copy of the Qur'an it has a *nūn* because it is a word that has been moved from its basic meaning and its expression has changed because the meaning has changed and then it has been used frequently and there is elision in it.

There are four dialectical forms of the word. Ibn Kathīr recited *'kā'in'*, like *'kā'in'*, as an active participle, its root being *kay'* where the *yā'* has been changed into an *alif* as happens with *yay'as* and thus some say *yā'as* with *ya's*. [POEMS] Ibn

Muḥayṣin recited '*ka'in*' with a *hamzah* and the *alif* shortened, like *ka'in*, which is from *kā'in* and the *alif* has been elided. He also has '*ka'yin*' like *ka'yin* and it is a reversal of *kay'* and it has been lightened. The rest have '*ka-ayyin*' like *ka'ayyin*. It is the root. [POEMS] A fifth version is '*kay'in*' like *kay'in*. It is as if lightened from *kayyi'* and reversed. [MORE DISCUSSION] An-Naḥḥās said that Abū 'Amr stopped at '*ka'ayy*' without a *nūn* because it is *tanwīn*. Sawrah ibn al-Mubārak related that from al-Kisā'ī. The rest stop with a *nūn* following the script of the Qur'an.

The *āyah* is meant to encourage the believers and is a command to follow those before them who followed the Prophets. It means: many Prophets were killed while there were devout people with them, or many Prophets were killed and their communities did not apostasise. Two things are said here. The first was said by al-Ḥasan and Sa'īd ibn Jubayr. Al-Ḥasan said, 'No Prophet has ever been killed in battle,' while Ibn Jubayr said, 'We have not heard of any Prophet being killed in battle.' The second is transmitted from Qatādah and 'Ikrimah and then one is permitted to stop after 'killed'. This is according to the reading of Nāfi', Ibn Kathīr, Abū 'Amr, and Ya'qūb (which is *qutila*, killed.) It is the reading of Ibn 'Abbās, and Abū Ḥātim preferred it.

There are two aspects to it. One is that 'killed' refers to the Prophet ﷺ alone and the words end at 'killed' and there is some elision in the words, meaning that there were many with him, and it is as you would say, 'In spite of the huge army with him, the general was killed.' 'I went out and there were goods with me.' The second is that killing affected the Prophet ﷺ and the many with him, and the words mean, 'some of those with him were killed.' The Arabs say, 'We killed Banū Tamīm and Banū Sulaym,' when some of them were killed. So 'they did not give up' refers to those with him. I think that this is more appropriate to the context in which the *āyah* was revealed. The Prophet ﷺ was not killed while some of his Companions were killed.

The Kufans and Ibn 'Āmir read *qātala* (How many a Prophet has fought). That is the reading of Ibn Mas'ūd and Abū 'Ubayd preferred it. Allah's praise of those who fight includes those who are killed, but praise of those who were killed does not include those who fought. So 'fought' is more universal.

'Many thousands is read as *ribbiyyūna, rubbiyyūna* and *rabbiyyūna*. Most read it as *ribbiyyūna*. 'Alī read it as *rubbiyyūna* and Ibn 'Abbās as *rabbiyyūna*. *Ribbiyyūna* refers to many groups, according to Mujāhid, Qatādah, aḍ-Ḍaḥḥāk and 'Ikrimah. The singular is *ribbiyy* or *rubbiyy*. 'Abdullāh ibn Mas'ūd says that it means many thousands. Ibn Zayd said that it means followers. The first

is better known linguistically. *Ribbah* and *rubbah* is a bag in which arrows are collected. *Rabāb* is a confederation of tribes. Abān ibn Tha'lab said that *ribbiyy* means ten thousand. Al-Ḥasan said that they are steadfast scholars. Ibn 'Abbās, Qatādah, ar-Rabī' and as-Suddī said that it is a large group. Ḥassān said:

When a company withdraw from the truth,
we attack them in a large company (*ribbiyy*).

Az-Zajjāj said that the two readings with *ḍammah* refers to large groups. It is said that it is ten thousand. It is related from Ibn 'Abbās that *rabbiyyūna* with *fatḥah* is derived from *rabb* (Lord). Al-Khalīl said that it is a singular for those who are steadfast with the Prophets. They are the *rabbāniyūn* who are attributed to devotion, worship and recognition of Allah's lordship. Allah knows best.

They did not give up in the face of what assailed them in the Way of Allah.

The verb '*give up*' means to weaken. It was already mentioned. *Wahn* is the shattering of resolve by fear. Al-Ḥasan and Abu-s-Sammāl recited '*wahunū*' instead of '*wahanū*'. Abū Zayd said that they are two dialectical usages. The verb is *wahana*, and *awhana*, Form IV, is to weaken. *Wāhinah* is the shortest rib and *wahan* camels are bulky. *Wahn* is also a time in the middle of the night. It means they did not become weak when their Prophet was killed or their comrades were slain. It means: 'the rest of them did not become weak.' The *muḍāf* is elided.

nor did they weaken, nor did they yield.

'They did not weaken' in the face of the enemy and *'they did not yield,'* because of what they suffered in *jihād*. *Istikānah* is humility and abasement. Its root is *istakanū* on the measure of Form VIII and the *fatḥah* of the *kāf* is filled and an *alif* results from it. For those who make it come from *kawn* it is Form X. The first is more in keeping with the meaning of the *āyah*. It has been recited as '*famā wahnū wamā ḍa'fū*'. Al-Kisā'ī related '*ḍa'afū*'.

Then Allah reports that after some of them were killed or their Prophet was killed, they were steadfast and did not flee and remained steady in the face of death. They asked for forgiveness so that their death would be accompanied by repentance for their wrong actions if they were given martyrdom. They asked for firmness so that they would not be routed and for help against the enemy. Feet are singled out for firmness because they are what one stands on. He is saying, 'Did you do and say the like of that, Companions of Muḥammad?' He answered their supplication and granted them help, victory and booty in this world and forgiveness in the Next World when they go there. That is how Allah treats His sincere servants who are true in repentance, support His *dīn* and are firm in meeting His enemy by His true promise and true words.

Allah loves the steadfast.

He means here those who are steadfast in *jihād*.

All they said was, 'Our Lord, forgive us our wrong actions and any excesses

Some recite *'mā kāna qawluhum'* in the nominative, making *'qawl'* the noun of *kāna*. So it means: 'All that they say is'. For those who read it in the accusative, *qawl* is the predicate of *kāna* whose meaning is 'all they said'.

'Wrong actions' are minor wrong actions and *'excesses'* are major wrong actions. Excess (*isrāf*) describes being excessive in something and exceeding the limits. We find in *Ṣaḥīḥ Muslim* that Abū Mūsā al-Ash'arī reported that the Prophet ﷺ used to make this supplication: 'O Allah, forgive my error, ignorance and excess in my business and what you know better than I do.' So a person must use the supplications found in the Book of Allah and sound *Sunnah* and leave others based on their own choice. Allah has chosen for His Prophet and His friends and instructed them how they should make supplication.

فَـَٔاتَىٰهُمُ ٱللَّهُ ثَوَابَ ٱلدُّنْيَا وَحُسْنَ ثَوَابِ ٱلْـَٔاخِرَةِ وَٱللَّهُ يُحِبُّ ٱلْمُحْسِنِينَ ١٤٨

148 So Allah gave them the reward of this world and the best reward of the Next World. Allah loves good-doers.

The reward of this world is help and victory over one's enemies. *'The best reward of the Next World'* is the Garden. Al-Jaḥdarī recited *'fa-athābahum'* from *thawāb* (reward).

يَـٰٓأَيُّهَا ٱلَّذِينَ ءَامَنُوٓا۟ إِن تُطِيعُوا۟ ٱلَّذِينَ كَفَرُوا۟ يَرُدُّوكُمْ
عَلَىٰٓ أَعْقَـٰبِكُمْ فَتَنقَلِبُوا۟ خَـٰسِرِينَ ١٤٩ بَلِ ٱللَّهُ مَوْلَىٰكُمْ وَهُوَ
خَيْرُ ٱلنَّـٰصِرِينَ ١٥٠

149 You who believe! if you obey those who disbelieve, they will turn you round on your heels and you will be transformed into losers. 150 No, Allah is your Protector. And He is the best of helpers.

When Allah commanded people to follow in the footsteps of the helpers of the earlier Prophets, He also warned them against obeying the unbelievers, meaning the Arab idolaters, Abū Sufyān and his people. It is said that it means the Jews and Christians. 'Alī said that it is in reference to what the hypocrites said to the believers when they suffered that defeat: 'Return to your father's religion.'

'They will turn you round on your heels,' making you revert to disbelief. Then you will return defeated. Allah is the One who will help and preserve you if you obey Him. It is recited as *'bali-llāha'* in the accusative, implying 'Rather, obey Allah, your Master.'

سَنُلْقِى فِى قُلُوبِ ٱلَّذِينَ كَفَرُواْ ٱلرُّعْبَ بِمَآ أَشْرَكُواْ بِٱللَّهِ مَا لَمْ يُنَزِّلْ بِهِۦ سُلْطَٰنًا وَمَأْوَىٰهُمُ ٱلنَّارُ وَبِئْسَ مَثْوَى ٱلظَّٰلِمِينَ ۝

151 We will cast terror into the hearts of those who disbelieve because they have associated others with Allah for which He has not sent down any authority. Their shelter will be the Fire. How evil is the abode of the wrongdoers!

This echoes Allah's words: *'He cast terror into their hearts.'* (59:2) 'Terror' is recited with two syllables as *ru'ub* (rather than *'ru'b'*) by Ibn 'Āmir and al-Kisā'ī. These are two dialectical forms. *Ru'b* means fear, a verbal noun from *ra'aba*. Someone terrified is described as *mar'ūb*. It is possible that *ru'b* is a verbal noun and *ru'ub* a simple noun. The root of *ru'b* (terror) comes from filling, and the verb is used for the filling of a watering-trough or of a torrent filling a valley. It means: 'We will fill the hearts of the idolaters with fear and alarm.' As-Sakhtiyānī recited it with *yā'*, *'sa-yulqī'* ('He will cast') while the rest use the Divine *nūn* ('We will cast').

As-Suddī and others said, 'When Abū Sufyān and the idolaters left for Makkah after Uḥud, they went part of the way and then regretted doing that. They said, "What we have done is bad! We should have killed them until none of them was left except the odd runaway. Let us go back and wipe them out!" When they resolved on that, Allah cast terror into their hearts so that they did not do it.' 'Casting' is used for the actual throwing down of physical objects as in 7:150 where it refers to the Tablets, in 26:44 where it refers to ropes and staffs, and in 36:45 where it is used for a staff. It is used metaphorically in this *āyah* as it is in 20:39 in reference to love.

because they have associated others with Allah for which He has not sent down any authority

This is the reason Allah cast terror into their hearts. *Shirk* is to make someone else a partner. The phrase *'for which He has not sent down any authority'* is further explanation. *'Sulṭān'* is supporting proof, clarification and excuse. This is why the ruler is called a 'sultan' because he is the proof of Allah on the earth. It is also said that *sulṭān* is derived from *salīṭ*, the oil used in a lamp, which is from sesame seed. Imru'u-l-Qays said:

He tipped the sesame oil (*salīṭ*) with the twisted wicks.

So the sultan gives light by giving victory to the truth and curbing the false. *Salīṭ* is also used for a sharp edge and so it refers to force (*salāṭah*). The root of *sulṭān* is strength because by it he overcomes and the *nūn* is additional to the root. *Salīṭah* is used for a sharp-tongued woman and for a man with an eloquent tongue. He means that Allah has given no authority for the worship of idols in any religion and it is not logical to permit that. Then He says where their final resting place will be: the Fire, and then blames them. *Mathwā* is the place in which one resides, derived from the verb *thawā*. *Ma'wā* is any sort of shelter to which one resorts either in the night or the day.

وَلَقَدْ صَدَقَكُمُ ٱللَّهُ وَعْدَهُۥٓ إِذْ تَحُسُّونَهُم بِإِذْنِهِۦ ۖ حَتَّىٰٓ إِذَا
فَشِلْتُمْ وَتَنَٰزَعْتُمْ فِى ٱلْأَمْرِ وَعَصَيْتُم مِّنۢ بَعْدِ مَآ
أَرَىٰكُم مَّا تُحِبُّونَ ۚ مِنكُم مَّن يُرِيدُ ٱلدُّنْيَا وَمِنكُم
مَّن يُرِيدُ ٱلْـَٔاخِرَةَ ۚ ثُمَّ صَرَفَكُمْ عَنْهُمْ لِيَبْتَلِيَكُمْ ۖ
وَلَقَدْ عَفَا عَنكُمْ ۗ وَٱللَّهُ ذُو فَضْلٍ عَلَى ٱلْمُؤْمِنِينَ ﴿١٥٢﴾

152 Allah fulfilled His promise to you when you were slaughtering them by His permission. But then you faltered, disputing the command, and disobeyed after He showed you what you love. Among you are those who want this world and among you are those who want the Next World. Then He turned you from them in order to test you – but He has pardoned you. Allah shows favour to the believers.

Muḥammad ibn Ka'b al-Quraẓī said, 'When the Messenger of Allah ﷺ

returned to Madina from Uḥud after they had suffered, they said to one another, "How did this happen to us when Allah has promised us victory?" Then this was revealed. That is because they killed the banner-bearer of the idolaters and the seven after him who held the banner. Victory was going to the Muslims but, when they were distracted by booty, some of the archers left their positions for booty and that led to the rout.'

Al-Bukhārī reports that al-Barā' ibn 'Āzib said, 'In the Battle of Uḥud when we met the idolaters, the Messenger of Allah ﷺ positioned the archers and put 'Abdullāh ibn Jubayr in charge of them, saying: "Do not leave your position. Even if you see that we have defeated them, do not leave. If you see that they have defeated us, do not help us against them." When we met them, the Muslims defeated them so that we saw the women running for the mountain, their garments raised and anklets showing. The [archers] began to say, "Booty! Booty!" 'Abdullāh said, "The Prophet ﷺ made you promise that you would not leave." They left, became confused, and seventy were struck down. Abū Sufyān ibn Ḥarb looked down and asked, "Is Muḥammad among the people?" He said, "Do not answer him." Then he asked, "Is the son of Abū Quḥāfah among the people?" He said, "Do not answer him." Then he said, "Is the son of al-Khaṭṭāb among the people?" Then he said, "Those have been killed. If they had been alive, they would have answered." 'Umar could not restrain himself and said, "By Allah, you have lied, enemy of Allah! All of those you numbered are among the living! That which will vex you remains!" Abū Sufyān said twice, "Hubal be high!" The Prophet ﷺ said, "Answer him!" They said, "What shall we say?" He said, "Say: 'Allah is Higher and More Majestic.'" Abū Sufyān said, "We have al-'Uzzā and you have no 'Uzzā." The Prophet ﷺ said, "Answer him!" They asked, "What shall we say?" He said, "Say: 'Allah is our Protector and you have no Protector.'" Abū Sufyān said, "A day which is in return for the day of Badr. Victory in war goes in turns. You will find some of the people mutilated. I did not order it, but it does not disturb me."'

It is related from Sa'd ibn Abī Waqqāṣ in al-Bukhārī and Muslim: 'I saw the Messenger of Allah ﷺ on the Day of Uḥud and two men were with him fighting for him as fiercely as possible.' One transmission from Sa'd has: 'They were wearing white clothes. I never saw them before or after.' He meant that they were Jibrīl and Mikā'īl. Another variant has: 'They were fighting for the Messenger of Allah ﷺ as fiercely as possible. I never saw them before or after.' Mujāhid, however, says that the angels did not fight with them that day and that the only day they fought with them was Badr. Al-Bayhaqī says that Mujāhid means that they left when the people disobeyed the Messenger and were not steadfast in what they had been commanded to do.

'Urwah ibn az-Zubayr said, 'If they were steadfast and godfearing, Allah Almighty promised that He would reinforce them with five thousand angels, clearly identified, and He did that. When they disobeyed the command of the Messenger and abandoned their positions and the archers, out of desire for this world, failed to follow the instruction that the Messenger of Allah ﷺ had given them about not leaving their positions, the reinforcement of the angels was taken from them. Allah revealed: *"Allah fulfilled His promise to you when you were slaughtering them by His permission."* So Allah was true to His promise and showed them victory. When they disobeyed, He punished them with affliction.'

'Umayr ibn Isḥāq said, 'In the Battle of Uḥud, they left the Messenger of Allah ﷺ exposed while Sa'd was shooting from in front of him with a lad handing him arrows. Whenever one arrow was gone, he brought him another. He said "Shoot, Abū Isḥāq!" When they finished, they looked to see where the young man was and did not see or recognise him.'

Muḥammad ibn Ka'b said, 'When the banner-bearer of the idolaters was killed and their banner fell, 'Amrah bint 'Alqamah al-Ḥārithah raised it up. Ḥassān said about that:

Had it not been for the Ḥārithī woman,
They would have been sold in the markets like chattels.

'*Taḥussūnahum*' means to kill and eradicate them. A poet said:

We slaughtered (*ḥasasnāhum*) them with swords
and their remnants were scattered and separated.

Jarīr said:

The swords slaughter (*taḥussuhum*) them utterly
and their remnants took flight and scattered.

Abū 'Ubayd said that *ḥass* is eradication by killing. Locusts are described as '*maḥsūs*' when they are killed by cold. Cold is a killer which burns off (*maḥassah*) plants. A year that is *ḥasūs* has a drought that consumes everything. Ru'bah said:

We suffered a severe (*ḥasūs*) year
that consumed and left everything dry after it was green.

Its root is *ḥiss* which is perceiving something by touch (*ḥāssah*). *Ḥassa* is to remove his senses by killing.

'With His permission' means with His knowledge, or according to His decree and command.

But then you faltered, disputing the command,

You lost courage and weakened. The verb is *fashila, yafshalu,* and verbal noun *fashil* and *fashl.* The apodosis of *'ḥattā'* is elided. This sort of form is permissible and is, in fact, seen elsewhere in the Qur'an as in 6:25. Al-Farrā' said that the apodosis is 'disputing' and the *wāw* is redundant as we see elsewhere. [OMISSION] Some people said that the *wāw* before 'disobeyed' is redundant, meaning 'then you faltered and disputed, disobeying.' On this basis, there is a change in the word order here; it means 'when you disputed and disobeyed, then you faltered.'

Abū 'Alī said that the apodosis can be *'He turned you from them* and 'then' is redundant. It implies: 'until when you faltered, disputed and disobeyed, He turned you from them.' [ILLUSTRATIVE POEM] Al-Akhfash permitted it to be redundant as in the case in 9:118.

It is said that *'ḥattā'* means *'ilā'* (to) and then it has no apodosis, i.e. 'Allah fulfilled His promise to you until you faltered,' meaning that the promise was contingent on remaining firm. *'Disputing'*, or disagreeing, refers to the archers arguing with one another when some wanted to go after booty and others said that they would remain firm following the command of the Prophet ﷺ.

and disobeyed after He showed you what you love.

They disobeyed the command of the Messenger ﷺ to remain firm. The words *'after He showed you what you love'* refer to the victory which was going to the Muslims at the beginning of Uḥud when the banner-bearer of the idolaters fell. When he fell, the Prophet ﷺ and his Companions spread out in separate squadrons and began to slaughter the enemy. The enemy cavalry charged three times but the barrage of arrows drove them back. When the fifty archers saw that victory had gone to their brothers, some of them said, 'Why are we standing here when Allah has defeated the enemy?' So they left their positions that they had promised the Messenger of Allah ﷺ they would not leave. They disputed, faltered and disobeyed the Messenger and then the cavalry attacked and killed them. The words of the *āyah* express rebuke for them. The manner of the rebuke is that they saw the beginning of a victory, but they must know that complete victory lies in standing firm, not in being routed.

Among you are those who want this world and among you are those who want the Next World.

Then He explains the cause of the dispute: '*this world*' here means booty. Ibn Mas'ūd said, 'None of us was aware that any of the Companions of the Prophet ﷺ desired this world and its goods until the Day of Uḥud.' Those who wanted the Next World were those who stayed firm in their position and did not dispute the command of their Prophet ﷺ with their commander, 'Abdullāh ibn Jubayr. Khālid ibn al-Walīd and 'Ikrimah ibn Abī Jahl, who were still idolaters then, attacked him and killed those who had remained with him. May Allah have mercy on them.

The blame lies with those who retreated, not with those who stood firm. Those who stood firm won the reward. This is because it is said that when general punishment descends on a people in which the righteous and children are destroyed, the punishment does not actually happen to them. It was the means to their gaining their reward. Allah knows best.

Then He turned you from them in order to test you

This means: 'after He had let you overpower them, He turned you from them in flight.' That indicates that both disobedience and disagreement are created by Allah. The Mu'tazilites say that it means: 'then you turned,' and it is connected to the terror of the Muslims which Allah removed from the hearts of the unbelievers to test them. Al-Qushayrī points out that this would not help because removing terror from the hearts of the unbelievers so that they would disdain the Muslims is ugly and not permitted, and would make the *āyah* meaningless. It is said that '*He turned you from them*" means that 'He did not oblige you to pursue them.'

He has pardoned you. Allah shows favour to the believers.

He did not eradicate you after your disobedience and opposition. It is said that this is addressed to everyone, and it is said that it is only addressed to the archers who disobeyed, which an-Naḥḥās prefers. Most commentators say that it is like Allah's words: '*Then He pardoned you.*' (2:52) Allah shows favour by pardon and forgiveness.

Ibn 'Abbās said, 'The Prophet ﷺ was not helped in any place as he was helped at Uḥud.' He ['Ubaydullāh, the transmitter] said, 'We do not acknowledge that.' Ibn 'Abbās said, 'The Book of Allah stands between me and those who deny that. Allah Almighty says about the Battle of Uḥud: "*Allah fulfilled His promise to you when you were slaughtering them by His permission. But then you faltered, disputing the command, and disobeyed after He showed you what you love. Among you are those who want this world and among you are those who want the Next World. Then He turned you from them in order to test you – but He has pardoned you. Allah shows favour to the believers.*" (3:152) He means the archers. The Prophet ﷺ had put them in a position and told them, "Guard our backs. If you see us being killed, do not help us. If you see us taking booty, do not join us."

'When it looked as if the Messenger of Allah ﷺ had won and they had exposed the camp of the idolaters, the archers all turned away and went to loot the camp, joining the ranks of the Companions of the Prophet ﷺ and becoming mixed up with them (and he intertwined the fingers of his hands). After the archers deserted their position, the enemy cavalry attacked the Companions of the Prophet ﷺ from that position. They fought one another in a confused melée and many Muslims were slain.

'At the beginning of the day, the Messenger of Allah ﷺ and his Companions were in the ascendancy to the point that seven or nine standard-bearers of the idolaters were struck down. The Muslims charged towards the mountain but did not reach the place that people call "the Cave" which is under the hollowed-out rock. Then Shayṭān shouted out: "Muḥammad has been killed!" People were in no doubt at that moment that it was it true and we continued to think the Messenger of Allah ﷺ had been killed until he appeared to us between two men of Sa'd. We recognised him by the way he walked. We were so happy that it was as if what had happened to us had not happened. He came towards us, saying, "Allah will be very angry with a people who have bloodied the face of their Prophet!"'

Ka'b ibn Mālik said, 'I was the first Muslim to recognise the Messenger of Allah ﷺ. I recognised him by his eyes shining from under his helmet. I called out in my loudest voice, "Company of Muslims! This is the Messenger of Allah ﷺ coming!" He indicated that I should be quiet.'

إِذْ تُصْعِدُونَ وَلَا تَلْوُۥنَ عَلَىٰٓ أَحَدٍ وَالرَّسُولُ يَدْعُوكُمْ فِي
أُخْرِيكُمْ فَأَثَٰبَكُمْ غَمًّا بِغَمٍّ لِّكَيْلَا تَحْزَنُواْ عَلَىٰ مَا فَاتَكُمْ
وَلَا مَآ أَصَٰبَكُمْ وَاللَّهُ خَبِيرٌۢ بِمَا تَعْمَلُونَ ﴿١٥٣﴾

153 Remember when you were scrambling up the slope, refusing to turn back for anyone, and the Messenger was calling to you from the rear. Allah rewarded you with one distress in return for another so you would not feel grief for what escaped you or what assailed you. Allah is aware of what you do.

Remember when you were scrambling up the slope, refusing to turn back for anyone,

'When' can be connected to *'He pardoned you.'* Most recite *'scrambling up'* as *'tuṣ'idūna'*. Abū Rajā' al-'Uṭāridī, Abū 'Abd ar-Raḥmān as-Sulamī, al-Ḥasan and Qatādah recite *'taṣ'adūna'*, meaning climbing the mountain. Ibn Muḥayṣin and Shibl recited both verbs with *yā'* in the third person. Al-Ḥasan recited *'talūna'* with one *wāw*. Abū Bakr ibn 'Ayyāsh related from 'Āṣim *'tulūna'* with a *ḍammah* on the *tā'* which is an aberrant dialect. An-Naḥḥās said that.

Abū Ḥātim said that *aṣ'ada* is to travel forward and *ṣa'ida* is to ascend a mountain or something else. *Iṣ'ād* is travelling on level land, the bottom of valleys, and ravines. *Ṣu'ūd* is an elevation on a mountain, plateau, steps and stairs. It is possible that they were on an elevated place on the mountain after climbing up from the valley and so both readings convey the meaning.

Qatādah and ar-Rabī' said, 'They climbed up the valley in the Battle of Uḥud. Ibn 'Abbās said that they climbed at Uḥud while they were fleeing. Both of the readings are correct as those who retreated on that day climbed and were made to climb. Allah knows best.

Al-Qutabī and al-Mubarrad said that Form IV is used when the distance is far and so it as if the distance is far on the ground just as it is in climbing. A poet said:

O those who ask where she went (*aṣ'adat*),
she has a promised rendezvous in the valley of Yathrib.

Al-Farrā' said that *iṣ'ād* is to begin a journey and *inḥidār* is to return from it. One can say, 'We "climbed"' from Baghdad to Makkah and to Khorasan and similar places when you set out for them and began the journey, and *inḥadara* is to return. Abū 'Ubaydah said:

You wept for the departure (*iṣ'ād*).
Today you have been sent and the camel driver shouts.

Al-Mufaḍḍal said that *ṣa'ida, aṣ'ada* and *ṣa''ada* mean the same. *'Refusing to turn back'* means to ascend and continue without looking at one another in the flight. Someone simply going up can turn his head or his animal.

'For anyone' refers to Muḥammad ﷺ according to al-Kalbī. *'Ukhrā'* means 'behind them' Al-Bukhārī says that it is the feminine of *'ākhir'*. 'Amr ibn Khālid related from Zuhayr that Abū Isḥāq heard al-Barā' ibn 'Āzib say, 'On the day of the Battle of Uḥud, the Prophet ﷺ put 'Abdullāh ibn Jubayr in charge of the men on foot. Then they were routed and the Messenger of Allah ﷺ was calling to them from behind them. The Prophet ﷺ was left with only twelve men.' Ibn 'Abbās and

others said that he called out, 'Servants of Allah! Return!' while they were fleeing. He was calling to change what was objectionable. It is impossible that he would see something objectionable, in this case the rout, and not forbid it. According to this, the rout was an act that amounted to disobeying Allah, but this is not the case as will be explained, Allah willing.

Allah rewarded you with one distress in return for another.

Ghamm (grief) linguistically comes from 'to cover', as when the day becomes dark or the crescent moon is covered so that it cannot be seen. So one says that something grieves (*ghamma*) a person.

Mujāhid, Qatādah and others said that the first grief was killing and wounding, and the second was the alarm at the killing of the Prophet ﷺ when shayṭān shouted that out. It is said that the first grief was on account of the victory and booty that eluded them, and the second was on account of the killing and defeat they suffered. It is said that the first was the defeat and the second was Abū Sufyān and Khālid looking down on them, which grieved the Muslims since they thought that they would attack and kill them. This made them forget what had afflicted them. That is when the Prophet ﷺ said, 'O Allah, do not let them be over us.'

The *bā'* in '*bi-ghamm*' has the meaning of '*'alā*'. It means that they grieved the Prophet ﷺ by opposing him and Allah repaid them for that by their distress over what afflicted some of them. Al-Ḥasan said that the first grief was Uḥud in return for what happened to the idolaters at Badr. 'Distress' is called a reward as the repayment for a wrong action is called a wrong action. It is said that Allah gave them success in spite of their wrong action and so they were distracted by that from what afflicted them.

So you would not feel grief for what escaped you or what assailed you.

This is connected to *'He pardoned you'* or to *'Allah rewarded you.'* It means: 'This is sorrow after sorrow so that you would not grieve over the booty you missed or your defeat.' The first view is better. It can also mean: 'so that you would not be sad about what missed you and your punishment for disobeying the Messenger of Allah ﷺ.' The same usage is found in 7:12 and 58:29. It is said that it means a succession of sorrows so that after this you will not be distracted by booty. His words: *'Allah is aware of what you do'* is a threat.

ثُمَّ أَنزَلَ عَلَيْكُم مِّن بَعْدِ الْغَمِّ أَمَنَةً نُّعَاسًا يَغْشَىٰ طَائِفَةً مِّنكُمْ ۖ وَطَائِفَةٌ
قَدْ أَهَمَّتْهُمْ أَنفُسُهُمْ يَظُنُّونَ بِاللَّهِ غَيْرَ الْحَقِّ ظَنَّ الْجَاهِلِيَّةِ ۖ يَقُولُونَ
هَل لَّنَا مِنَ الْأَمْرِ مِن شَيْءٍ ۗ قُلْ إِنَّ الْأَمْرَ كُلَّهُ لِلَّهِ ۗ يُخْفُونَ فِي أَنفُسِهِم مَّا لَا
يُبْدُونَ لَكَ ۖ يَقُولُونَ لَوْ كَانَ لَنَا مِنَ الْأَمْرِ شَيْءٌ مَّا قُتِلْنَا هَاهُنَا ۗ قُل لَّوْ كُنتُمْ
فِي بُيُوتِكُمْ لَبَرَزَ الَّذِينَ كُتِبَ عَلَيْهِمُ الْقَتْلُ إِلَىٰ مَضَاجِعِهِمْ ۖ وَلِيَبْتَلِيَ اللَّهُ مَا
فِي صُدُورِكُمْ وَلِيُمَحِّصَ مَا فِي قُلُوبِكُمْ ۗ وَاللَّهُ عَلِيمٌ بِذَاتِ الصُّدُورِ ﴿١٥٤﴾

154 Then He sent down to you, after the distress, security, restful sleep overtaking a group of you, whereas another group became prey to anxious thoughts, thinking other than the truth about Allah – thoughts belonging to the Time of Ignorance – saying, 'Do we have any say in the affair at all?' Say, 'The affair belongs entirely to Allah.' They are concealing things inside themselves which they do not disclose to you, saying, 'If we had only had a say in the affair, none of us would have been killed here in this place.' Say, 'Even if you had been inside your homes, those people for whom being killed was decreed would have gone out to their place of death.' So that Allah might test what is in your breasts and purge what is in your hearts. Allah knows the contents of your hearts.

Then He sent down to you, after the distress, security

It is said that *amn* and *amānah* mean the same. It is also said that *amānah* is security when there is cause for fear and *amn* is when there is no cause for fear. It is in the accusative by the effect of 'sent down' and 'sleep' is an appositive for it. It is also said that it is in the accusative as the object as if He were saying, 'He sent down sleep on you for security.' Ibn Muḥayṣin recited '*amnah*'. After the sorrows the believers experienced at Uḥud, Allah granted them sleep and most of them fell asleep. Those who feel secure sleep and fearful people do not sleep. In al-Bukhārī, Anas reported that Abū Ṭalḥah said, 'We were overcome with slumber when we were in the lines on the Day of Uḥud.' He said, 'My sword would fall from my hand and I would pick it up, and it would fall from my hand I would pick it up again.'

'Overtaking' is read both as *taghshā* and *yaghshā*. *Yaghshā* refers to sleep and *taghshā* to security.

Another group became prey to anxious thoughts, thinking other than the truth about Allah – thoughts belonging to the Time of Ignorance

Ṭā'ifah (group) can be applied to both one person and to a group. Here it refers to the hypocrites: Mu'attab ibn Qushayr and his companions. They went out hoping for booty and fearing the believers. They did not sleep and regretted taking part in the expedition and said all sorts of things.

'*Qad ahammathum anfusuhum*' means that it impelled them to worry. *Hamm* is anything someone is concerned about. The verb *ahamma* is used for something being of concern to someone. Something that is *muhimm* is significant. '*Ahamma*' is used when something causes you disquiet and *hamma* is to concern you. The *wāw* before 'group' makes it adverbial and so means 'when they became prey'. They thought that the business of Muḥammad ﷺ was false and that he would not win. The phrase '*thoughts belonging to the Time of Ignorance*' has an omission: 'thinking the thoughts of the people of the Time of Ignorance.'

'Do we have any say in the affair at all?'

This is a question which indicates denial, and implies 'We did not have any say in the business about going out. We were forced to go out.' This is indicated by what Allah reports that they said. Az-Zubayr said, 'On that day sleep was released on us and while sleep was overcoming me, I heard Mu'attab ibn Qushayr say, "*If we had only had a say in the affair, none of us would have been killed here in this place.*"' It is said that it means that he says, 'We do not have any of the victory which Muḥammad promised us.' Allah knows best.

Say, 'The affair belongs entirely to Allah.'

Abū 'Amr and Ya'qūb recited '*kulluhu*' in the nominative for the inceptive whose predicate is 'to Allah' while the rest have '*kullahu*' in the accusative, as you say, 'The business is all Allah's' for stress. This is stress on its universality and total encompassment. This encompassing meaning is only stress. It is also said that it is an adjective modifying 'affair'. Al-Akhfash said that it is an appositive, meaning 'Success is in Allah's hand. He gives success to whomever He wishes and disappoints whomever He wishes.' Juwaybir said from aḍ-Ḍaḥḥāk from Ibn 'Abbās that the words '*thoughts belonging to the Time of Ignorance*' allude to denial of the Decree and that is what they were saying, and so Allah replied with this *āyah*, stating that the Decree, both good and evil, belongs to Allah.

They are concealing things inside themselves which they do not disclose to you, saying, 'If we had only had a say in the affair, none of us would have been killed.'

What they are concealing is *shirk*, disbelief and denial. They did not show this to you. They said, 'Our tribes would not have been killed.' It is said that the hypocrites said, 'If we had known, we would not have gone out to fight the people of Makkah and our leaders would not have been killed.' Allah then refutes them:

Say: 'Even if you had been inside your homes, those people for whom being killed was decreed would have gone out to their place of death.'

The time when people will die is written on the Preserved Tablet. '*Maḍāji*'' means the places where they will be struck down. It is also said that 'killing' here means 'fighting', because fighting leads to death. Abū Ḥaywah recited '*burriza*' meaning 'made to go out'. It is said: 'If you had failed to go out, hypocrites, you would have been brought out to another place in which you would have fallen so that Allah might test what is in your breasts and show it to the believers.'

So that Allah might test what is in your breasts and purge what is in your hearts.

The *wāw* in the beginning is interpolated as in 6:75. The verb is elided with the *lām* which indicates 'in order to be'. This implies: 'He obliged fighting for you and did not give you victory at Uḥud in order to test what is in your breasts and to purge your evil deeds when you return and are sincere.' It is said that 'test' is to put through a trial in order to test. It is said that it is so that you will witness what is invisible of His knowledge. It is said that there is some elision and it implies: 'so that He might test the friends of Allah.'

Allah knows the contents of your hearts.

He knows the good and evil they contain. It is said that the contents of the hearts are the hearts themselves.

إِنَّ الَّذِينَ تَوَلَّوْا مِنكُمْ يَوْمَ الْتَقَى الْجَمْعَانِ إِنَّمَا اسْتَزَلَّهُمُ الشَّيْطَانُ
بِبَعْضِ مَا كَسَبُوا وَلَقَدْ عَفَا اللَّهُ عَنْهُمْ إِنَّ اللَّهَ غَفُورٌ حَلِيمٌ ﴿١٥٥﴾

155 Those of you who turned their backs on the day the two armies clashed – it was Shayṭān who made them slip for what they had done. But Allah has pardoned them. Allah is Ever-Forgiving, All-Forbearing.

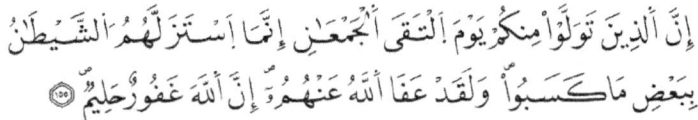

This refers to those who turned their backs on the idolaters at Uḥud, as 'Umar and others said. As-Suddī said that it means those who fled to Madīnah when defeated rather than those who went up the mountain. It is also said to refer to certain people who remained behind the Prophet ﷺ for three days when they were defeated and then left.

The meaning of *'made them slip'* means to induce them to slip by reminding them of their previous errors. They disliked staying firm because they might be killed. That is what is meant by the words *'for what they had done'*. It is said that it means to move them to slip. It is Form X from *zallah*, which is an error. It is said that the verbs *zalla* and *azalla* mean the same. Then it is said that they disliked fighting before sincere repentance. This is the first position. The second is that their repentance is for their disobeying the Prophet ﷺ by abandoning their position for booty.

Al-Ḥasan said that the words *'what they had done'* refer to their acceptance of the whispering of Iblīs. Al-Kalbī said, 'Shayṭān made their actions seem good to them.' It is also said that their retreat was not disobedience because, when they heard that the Prophet ﷺ had been killed, they wanted to fortify Madīnah and cut off what the enemy wanted to do to them. It is possible that they did not hear the call of the Prophet ﷺ because of their terror. It is also possible to say that the numbers of the enemy were more than twice their number because they were 700 and the enemy were 3000 so in theory retreat in such circumstances was permissible, but to retreat from the Prophet ﷺ was an error which is not permitted. Perhaps they imagined that the Prophet ﷺ had retreated to the mountain. The best view is the first one.

In general, if the affair is taken to be a definite wrong action, Allah pardoned it. If it is taken to be a permissible retreat, then the *āyah* is about those who retreated a great distance, more than the permitted amount. Abu-l-Layth Naṣr ibn Muḥammad ibn Ibrāhīm as-Samarqandī mentioned from al-Khalīl ibn Aḥmad from as-Sarrāj from Qutaybah from Abū Bakr ibn Ghaylān from Jarīr that 'Uthmān and 'Abd ar-Raḥmān ibn 'Awf had words, and 'Abd ar-Raḥmān ibn 'Awf said to him, 'Do you abuse me when I was present at Badr and you were not. I gave allegiance under the Tree and you did not, and you were one of those who turned in retreat on the day of the Meeting (meaning Uḥud)?' 'Uthmān responded to him: 'As for what you said about being present at Badr while I was not, I was not absent from anything where the Messenger of Allah ﷺ was present except when the daughter of the Messenger of Allah ﷺ was ill and I was tending to her. The Messenger of Allah ﷺ gave me one of the shares of the Muslims. As for the Pledge of the Tree, the Messenger of Allah ﷺ had sent me as an envoy to

Makkah and the Messenger of Allah ﷺ put his right hand on his left and said, "This is for 'Uthmān." The right hand and left hand of the Messenger of Allah ﷺ are better for me than my own right hand and left hand. As for the day of the Meeting, Allah has said, *"Allah has pardoned them,"* so I am among those Allah has pardoned.' 'Uthmān defeated 'Abd ar-Raḥmān in that argument.

This idea is also validated by Ibn 'Umar as we find in *Ṣaḥīḥ Bukhārī*. 'Abdān reported from Abū Ḥamzah that 'Uthmān ibn Mawhab said, 'A man came and made the *ḥajj* to the House. He saw some people sitting there and asked, "Who are those people?" They answered, "They are Quraysh." He inquired, "Who is that old man among them?" They replied, "'Abdullah ibn 'Umar." He said, "If I ask you about something, will you answer me?" He continued, "I entreat you by the sanctity of this House, do you know that 'Uthmān fled on the Day of Uḥud?" He answered, "Yes." He said, "Do you know that he was absent from Badr and not present at it?" He replied, "Yes." He said, "Do you know that he was absent from the Pledge of Riḍwān and not present at it?" He answered, "Yes." The man said, "Allah is greater!" Ibn 'Umar said, "Let me now explain to you what you asked me about. As for his fleeing at Uḥud, I testify that Allah pardoned him. As for being absent from Badr, he was married to the daughter of the Messenger of Allah ﷺ who was ill and the Messenger of Allah ﷺ said to him, 'You will have the reward and share of a man who was present at Badr.' As for his being absent from the Pledge of Riḍwān, if there had been anyone dearer than 'Uthmān in the valley of Makkah, he would have sent him in his place. The Messenger of Allah ﷺ sent 'Uthmān and the Pledge of Riḍwān took place after 'Uthmān had gone to Makkah. Therefore the Messenger of Allah ﷺ said of his right hand, 'This is the hand of 'Uthmān,' and struck it against his other hand and said, 'This is for 'Uthmān.'" Ibn 'Umar said to him, "Take this with you now."'

This *āyah* is like Allah's turning to Ādam and the words of the Prophet ﷺ, 'Ādam overcame Mūsā in a argument.' That was when Mūsā criticised Ādam for being the cause, when he ate from the tree, of him and his descendants leaving the Garden. Ādam replied, 'Do you blame me for something which Allah decreed for me forty years before I was created? And then He turned to me. Whoever He turns to incurs no wrong action and whoever has no wrong action is not subject to blame.' That is the case with those whom Allah pardons. This is a report from Allah and His report is true. Others who commit wrong action and repent hope for His mercy and fear His punishment. They fear that their repentance might not be accepted. Even if it is accepted, their fear dominates them since they do not definitively know that.

يَٰٓأَيُّهَا ٱلَّذِينَ ءَامَنُواْ لَا تَكُونُواْ كَٱلَّذِينَ كَفَرُواْ وَقَالُواْ لِإِخْوَٰنِهِمْ إِذَا ضَرَبُواْ
فِى ٱلْأَرْضِ أَوْ كَانُواْ غُزًّى لَّوْ كَانُواْ عِندَنَا مَا مَاتُواْ وَمَا قُتِلُواْ لِيَجْعَلَ ٱللَّهُ
ذَٰلِكَ حَسْرَةً فِى قُلُوبِهِمْ وَٱللَّهُ يُحْىِۦ وَيُمِيتُ وَٱللَّهُ بِمَا تَعْمَلُونَ
بَصِيرٌ ١٥٦

156 You who believe! do not be like those who disbelieve and say of their brothers, when they are going on journeys or military expeditions, 'If they had only been with us, they would not have died or been killed,' so that Allah can make that anguish for them in their hearts. It is Allah Who gives life and causes to die. Allah sees what you do.

The words *'do not be like those who disbelieve'* refer to the hypocrites. *'Their brothers'* are their brothers in hypocrisy or in lineage. They said this about the expedition which the Prophet ﷺ sent to Bi'r Ma'ūnah. The Muslims were forbidden to say what the hypocrites said. The words *'when they are going'* refer to what was already mentioned because the words have the meaning of a precondition since 'those' was indefinite and not determined and so '*idha*' is in the position of '*idh*' as the past tense in the apodosis takes the place of the future.

The verb *'going'* means travelling for trade or something else in the course of which they die. *Ghuzzā* (expeditions) is the plural of *ghāzi*. It is a broken plural and does not change whatever case it is in. The plural is like *rāki', rukka', ṣā'im, ṣuwwam, nā'im, nuwwam, shāhid, shuhhad*, and *ghā'ib, ghuyyub*. The plural can be *ghuzāh* like *quḍāh*, and *ghuzzā* with *maddah*, like *ḍurrāb* and *ṣuwwām*. It is said that *ghaziyy* is the plural of *ghuzāh*. It is related that az-Zuhrī recited *'ghuzzā'*. A woman whose husband is on an expedition is called *mughziyah*. A donkey which is late in reproducing is a *mughziyah*. The verb *aghzat* describes a she-camel which is hard to impregnate. *Ghazw* is aspiring for a thing and *maghzā* is the goal. That which has to do with an expedition is *'ghazawī'*.

so that Allah can make that anguish for them in their hearts

This refers to their thoughts and words. The *lām* is connected to His words, *'they said'*. This makes their statement that if they had not gone out, they would not have been killed, a cause of regret for them. *Ḥasrah* is regret. It is concern for what was missed and could not be obtained. A poet said:

O my anguish that I have not obtained my goal with her.
I did not enjoy proximity or nearness.

It is said that it is connected to something elided and means: 'Do not be like them so that Allah makes that statement a regret because those words display their hypocrisy. It is also said that it means: 'Do not believe them nor pay any attention to that,' and that caused anguish in their hearts. It is said that their anguish and disgrace will be on the Day of Rising because of the honour and blessing the believers will enjoy.

It is Allah Who gives life and causes to die.

He decrees those who go out to fight and remain alive and those who stay behind and die among their families.

Allah sees what you do.

It is recited as both *ta'malūna* (what you do) and *ya'malūna* (what they do). Then He reports that being killed in the Way of Allah and death in it is better than the entire world.

وَلَئِن قُتِلْتُمْ فِي سَبِيلِ ٱللَّهِ أَوْ مُتُّمْ لَمَغْفِرَةٌ مِّنَ ٱللَّهِ وَرَحْمَةٌ خَيْرٌ مِّمَّا
يَجْمَعُونَ ﴿١٥٧﴾ وَلَئِن مُّتُّمْ أَوْ قُتِلْتُمْ لَإِلَى ٱللَّهِ تُحْشَرُونَ ﴿١٥٨﴾

157 If you are killed in the Way of Allah or if you die, forgiveness and mercy from Allah are better than anything you can acquire. 158 If you die or you are killed, it is to Allah that you will be gathered.

The apodosis here is elided and there is no need for it because of the apodosis of the oath in forgiveness. It is more fitting for there to be no need for it with the apodosis of the oath because it has the beginning of the words and means 'He will forgive you.'

The word '*die*' is read as *mittum* with the people of the Hijaz, as in *nimtum*, from the verb *māta yamātu*, like *kiftu yakhāfu*. Lower Muḍar say *muttum*, like *ṣumtum*, from *māta yamūtu*, *kāna yakūnu*, and *qāla yaqūlu*. This is the position of the Kufans and it is good.

The phrase '*it is to Allah that you will be gathered*' is a warning. By saying this, Allah warns them: 'Do not flee from the battle and from what you have been commanded to do. Rather flee from His punishment which is painful. You will return to Him and no one but He has the power to harm or benefit you.' Allah knows best.

فَبِمَا رَحْمَةٍ مِّنَ ٱللَّهِ لِنتَ لَهُمْ ۖ وَلَوْ كُنتَ فَظًّا غَلِيظَ ٱلْقَلْبِ لَٱنفَضُّوا۟ مِنْ
حَوْلِكَ ۖ فَٱعْفُ عَنْهُمْ وَٱسْتَغْفِرْ لَهُمْ وَشَاوِرْهُمْ فِى ٱلْأَمْرِ ۖ فَإِذَا عَزَمْتَ
فَتَوَكَّلْ عَلَى ٱللَّهِ ۚ إِنَّ ٱللَّهَ يُحِبُّ ٱلْمُتَوَكِّلِينَ ﴿١٥٩﴾

159 It is a mercy from Allah that you were gentle with them. If you had been rough or hard of heart, they would have scattered from around you. So pardon them and ask forgiveness for them, and consult with them about the matter. Then when you have reached a firm decision, put your trust in Allah. Allah loves those who put their trust in Him.

It is a mercy from Allah that you were gentle with them.

The use of '*mā*' in '*it is a mercy*' is connective and used for stress as is the case elsewhere in the Qur'an (4:155, 38:11). It is not redundant in general although Sībawayh applies the idea of redundancy to it since its governing function is removed.

The meaning of the *āyah* is that when the Prophet ﷺ was kind to those who had retreated at Uḥud and did not rebuke them, Allah made it clear that it was by Allah's success that he did that.

It is also said that '*mā*' is interrogative, meaning, 'By what mercy from Allah were you gentle to them?' and expresses wonder. This is unlikely. If that were the case, *mā* would be written without the *alif.* The verb for being gentle is *lāna yalīnu.*

If you had been rough or hard of heart, they would have scattered from around you.

The word '*rough*' (*faẓẓ*) implies coarseness and roughness, from the verb *faẓẓa.* The plural is *afẓāẓ*. The Prophet ﷺ was not rough or harsh nor did he shout in markets. The expression '*hard of heart*' refers to scowling, lack of indulgence, and lack of compassion and mercy. Al-Mufaḍḍal said about a reminder:

He is not rough (*faẓẓ*) with the lowly.
They aim for his gifts, but he is easy.

He is rough (*faẓẓ*) with his enemies who are cautious of him,
as his attack is death, and its recipient is cut.

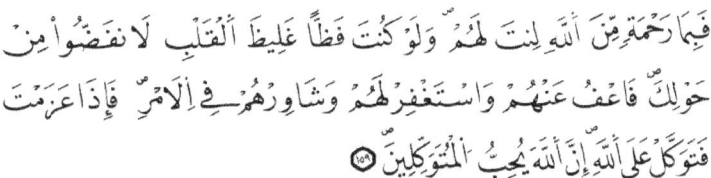

Another said:

I will die of deprivation in my house
While others die of surfeit.

This world is generous to the ignorant
and harsh and rough (*faẓẓ*) to those of intelligence.

Hardness of the heart is expressed through the frowning of the face, lack of reaction to the desires of others, and lack of compassion and mercy. A poet said:

He weeps for us, but we do not weep for anyone.
Our livers are harder than those of camels.

The verb *'scattered'* means split up. You separate (Form I) people and they are split up. The root of the word *faḍḍ* means to break and snap. An illustration of that is the words of Abu-n-Najm describing camels:

Early to water, not bare.
The pebbles scatter from them on the high plateau.

The root of *faḍḍ* has a *kasrah*. That can be seen from the expression: '*lā yafḍuḍu-llāhu fāk*' (May Allah not break your teeth).

The meaning is: 'O Muḥammad, were it not for your kindness, their shame and awe of being near to you would have prevented them from coming back to you after they had retreated and abandoned you.'

So pardon them and ask forgiveness for them and consult with them about the matter.

Scholars say that Allah commanded His Prophet ﷺ to do these things in a specific order. First He commanded him to pardon them for what was due to him in particular. Once he had done this, He commanded him to ask forgiveness for what they owed to Allah. Then when they were in this degree they were worthy of being consulted about matters.

Linguists say that consultation (*istishārah*) is derived from a verb which means 'to train an animal to run and other things.' *Mishwār* is a place where animals are made to run. *Mashūr* and *mushtār* are those who gather honey from its hives. 'Adī ibn Zayd said:

The Shaykh gave him permission to listen
and for hadiths like white honey (*mushār*).

Ibn 'Aṭiyyah said, '*Shūrā* (consultation) is one of the principles of the Sharī'ah and a firmly established ruling. Anyone who does not consult the people of knowledge and *dīn* should be dismissed. There is no disagreement concerning that. Allah praises the believers when He says: *"They manage their affairs by mutual consultation."* (42:38) A bedouin said, "I have never been cheated, allowing my people to be cheated." "How is that?" he was asked. He replied, "I do not do anything until I consult them."' Ibn Khuwayzimandād said, 'It is mandatory for rulers to consult scholars about things they do not know and matters of the *dīn* which are unclear to them, as it is also mandatory for army leaders in matters connected to warfare, for important people in matters connected to public welfare, and for notable scholars, ministers and governors in matters connected to the best interests of the land and its government.' It used to be said, 'The one who consults never regrets it,' as it also said, 'The one who prides himself on his own opinion is misguided.'

Consult with them about the matter.

This indicates the permissibility of *ijtihād* in deciding matters and taking other people's opinions into account when that is allowed by revelation. Allah permitted His Messenger ﷺ to do that. The people of interpretation disagree about the meaning of Allah commanding His Prophet ﷺ to consult his Companions. One group say that it was simply about military tactics, to encourage them, and raise their standing and draw them to their *dīn*. Allah has no need of anyone's opinion concerning His revelation. This is related from Qatādah, ar-Rabī', Ibn Isḥāq and ash-Shāfi'ī. Ash-Shāfi'ī said that it is on the same line as the words, 'Consult the virgin' which is meant to set her heart at ease, but it is not that it is actually mandatory.

Muqātil, Qatādah and ar-Rabī' said that when the Arab leaders were not consulted, it was upsetting for them, and so Allah commanded His Prophet ﷺ to consult them about the matter out of kindness to them, to assuage their rancour and to elevate them. When he consulted them, they recognised the honour he showed them.

Others say that this is about things concerning which there is no revelation. Al-Ḥasan al-Baṣrī and aḍ-Ḍaḥḥāk said, 'Allah did not command his Prophet ﷺ to consult out of any need for their opinion, but to instruct them in the virtue of consultation and so that his community would follow it after him.' The reading if Ibn 'Abbās has '*fī ba'ḍi-l-amr*' (some of the matter). Excellent are the words of a poet:

Consult your friend regarding what is hidden and abstruse.
Accept the advice of a gracious counselor.

Allah instructed His Prophet to do that
when He said, "Consult with them" and "trust".

It is reported in the *Muṣannaf* of Abū Dāwūd from Abū Hurayrah that the Messenger of Allah ﷺ said, 'The one consulted is trusted.'

Scholars say that if someone is consulted about legal rulings, he should have knowledge of the *dīn*. That is rarely found in other than someone of intelligence. Al-Ḥasan said, 'The *dīn* of a person is not complete as long as his intellect is not complete.' When someone like this is consulted and strives in righteousness and makes an effort and there is an error in what he indicates, then he is not blameworthy. Al-Khaṭṭābī and others said that.

The description of the one consulted in matters of this world should be that he is intelligent, experienced and friendly to the one who consults him. He said:

Consult your truthful friend about any unclear, hidden matter.

Another said:

If the door to a matter is difficult of access for you,
then consult someone intelligent and do not disobey him.

Shūrā is a blessing. The Prophet ﷺ said, 'The one who consults does not regret and the one who does *istikhārah* is not disappointed.' Sahl ibn Sa'd as-Sā'idī reported that the Messenger of Allah ﷺ said, 'No one is ever made wretched by consultation nor made happy by being satisfied with his own opinion.' One of them said, 'Consult someone who is experienced in matters. He will give you his opinion based on what usually happens to him, and you take it free of charge.' 'Umar ibn al-Khaṭṭāb made the appointment of a *khalīfah*, which is the greatest of matters, a matter of counsel.

Al-Bukhārī said, 'The rulers after the Prophet ﷺ used to consult the trustworthy people of knowledge in allowable matters in order to adopt the easiest of them.' Sufyān ath-Thawrī said, 'Let the people you consult be people of *taqwā* and trust and those who fear Allah Almighty.' Al-Ḥasan said, 'By Allah, a people do not consult one another without being guided to the best of what is with them.' It is reported from 'Alī that the Messenger of Allah ﷺ said, 'There are no people who have a council and someone named Aḥmad or Muḥammad attends it and they admit him to it, but that it is good for them.'

Shūrā is based on differences of opinion and the person who consults is looking into those differences and trying to ascertain which is the closest possible position to the Book and the *Sunnah*. When Allah guides him to whatever He wishes, then he should resolve firmly on it and carry it out, trusting in it, since this is the aim of *ijtihād*. This is what Allah commanded the Prophet ﷺ to do in this *āyah*.

Then when you have reached a firm decision, put your trust in Allah.

Qatādah said, 'Allah Almighty commanded His Prophet ﷺ that, when he reached a firm decision, he should act on it and trust in Allah, not in the advice he had been given. Resolving on a firm decision is the correct thing to do. Following opinion rather than firm resolve is only based on the decision of those who strive among the bold Arabs. It is as is said:

> "When he aspires, he has resolve firmly before him
> and sets aside any mention of outcomes.
>
> He only consults himself in his opinion
> and is only content with handle of the sword as companion."'

An-Naqqāsh said, 'Resolve is the intention to carry something out. *Ḥazm* (determination) is putting a *ḥā'* in place of the *'ayn* (*'azm*) in resolve. Ibn 'Aṭiyyah said, 'This is an error. *'Azm* is the intention to carry out something. Allah says: *"Consult with them about the matter. Then when you have reached a firm decision..."*.' Consultation and that which has the same meaning amounts to resolve. The Arabs say, 'I will be firm if I resolve.'

Ja'far aṣ-Ṣādiq and Jābir ibn Zayd recited '*'azamtu*', 'When I have decided,' attributing the resolve to Allah Himself by His guidance and granting success as when He said: *'You did not throw when you threw. It was Allah who threw.'* (8:17) Thus the words mean: 'When I have resolved for you, given you success and guided you, then put your trust in Allah.' The rest recite '*'azaymta*', meaning 'when you have decided.'

Al-Muhallab said, 'The Prophet ﷺ accepted this and said, "It is not proper for a Prophet who has donned armour on behalf of His community to take it off until Allah decides." It means that when he has made a decision, he should not turn away from it because that would be contrary to the trust in Allah which Allah stipulated should accompany resolve. He put on his armour when it was suggested by those whom Allah would honour with martyrdom to go forth with him. They were the righteous believers who had missed Badr. They said, "Messenger of Allah, lead us out against our enemies!"

'The Prophet ﷺ had indicated that they should stay and that was also the view of 'Abdullāh ibn Ubayy. He said, "Messenger of Allah, stay and do not lead the people out to them. If they stay, they will stay in a bad situation. If they come against us in Madīnah, we will fight them in the courtyards and alleyways and the women and children will throw stones at them from the walls. By Allah, we have never fought an enemy in this city without defeating them and we have never gone out to an enemy without their defeating us." Others rejected this view and kept urging the people and calling for battle. The Prophet ﷺ prayed *Jumu'ah* and went into his house afterwards and donned his armour. Then those people regretted that and said, "We forced the Messenger of Allah." When he came out to them in his armour, they said, "Messenger of Allah, stay if you wish. We do not want to force you." Then the Prophet ﷺ said, "It is not proper for a Prophet who has donned armour on behalf of His community to take it off until he fights."'

Allah loves those who put their trust in Him.

Tawakkul is reliance on Allah while displaying lack of power. The noun is *tuklān*. One says, '*ittakaltu 'alayhi*' (I relied on him). Its root is '*iwtakaltu*' and the *wāw* has been changed to a *yā'* because of the *kasrah* before it. Then the *tā'* has replaced it and assimilated into the *tā'* of Form VIII. One also uses Form II and says, '*wakkaltu bi*.' The noun is *wikālah* or *wakālah*.

Scholars disagree about *tawakkul*. A group of Sufis say that the only ones entitled to it are those whose hearts are not mixed with fear of other than Allah, not of wild animals or anything else, and until they give up seeking for provision since Allah has guaranteed it.

The position of most *fuqahā'* was already mentioned (3:122). It is sound as we made clear. Mūsā and Hārūn experienced fear since Allah said to them: '*Have no fear*,' (20:67-68) and Ibrāhīm is mentioned as fearing the angels when they came to him. (11:70) If Ibrāhīm the Friend and Mūsā the One-spoken-to, can show fear, that is enough evidence for us, and it is more likely that others will be fearful. This idea will be further explained.

إِن يَنصُرْكُمُ ٱللَّهُ فَلَا غَالِبَ لَكُمْ ۖ وَإِن يَخْذُلْكُمْ فَمَن ذَا ٱلَّذِى يَنصُرُكُم مِّنۢ
بَعْدِهِۦ ۗ وَعَلَى ٱللَّهِ فَلْيَتَوَكَّلِ ٱلْمُؤْمِنُونَ ﴿١٦٠﴾

160 If Allah helps you, no one can vanquish you. If He forsakes you, who can help you after that? So the believers should put their trust in Allah.

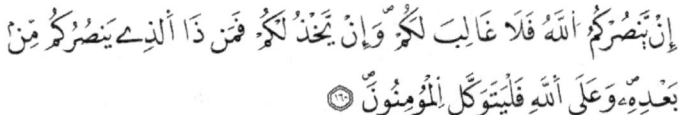

If you rely on Him and trust in Him, He will help you and defend you against your enemies and you will not be overcome. If He were to forsake you, then no one could help you. The one forsaken is the one who is not helped as He says: '*If He forsakes you…*' Forsaking (*khidhlān*) is absence of help and someone who is *makhdhūl* is abandoned and of no concern. A gazelle which abandons (*khadhalat*) its fellow females and stands over its calf in the field is called *khadhūl*. Ṭarafah said:

Isolated (*khadhūl*), grazing in a dense grove,
Eating the edges of the fruit of the arak, adorned.

He also said:

She looked at you with the eye of a girl.
She has left (*khadhalat*) her fellow does for her calf.

It is said that there is some reversal because she is *makhdhūlah* when she is forsaken. *Takhādhala* describes legs when they become weak. [Al-A'shā] said:

The leg is weak (*khadhūl*) without being lame. A leg that is *khadhulah* is one that continues to be weak. Allah knows best.

وَمَا كَانَ لِنَبِيٓءٍ اَنْ يُّغَلَّ وَمَنْ يَّغْلُلْ يَاتِ بِمَا غَلَّ يَوْمَ اَلْقِيَٰمَةِ ثُمَّ تُوَفّ۪يٰ
كُلُّ نَفْسٍ مَّا كَسَبَتْ وَهُمْ لَا يُظْلَمُونَ ﴿١٦١﴾

161 No Prophet would ever be guilty of misappropriation. Those who misappropriate will arrive on the Day of Rising with what they have misappropriated. Then every self will be paid in full for what it earned. They will not be wronged.

When the archers left their positions at Uḥud out of fear that the other Muslims would seize all the booty and not leave anything for them, Allah made it clear that the Prophet ﷺ would not be unjust in the distribution and they did not have the right to loot.

Aḍ-Ḍaḥḥāk said, 'The reason is that on one of his expeditions the Messenger of Allah ﷺ sent out scouts and they took booty before they came to him. He divided the spoils among the people, but not the scouts and Allah revealed in criticism: *"No Prophet would ever be guilty of misappropriation,"* by allotting to some and not others.' Something similar is related from Ibn 'Abbās, 'Ikrimah, Ibn Jubayr and others. They said that it was revealed because a piece of red velvet was missing from the booty at Badr. One of those with the Prophet ﷺ said, 'Perhaps the Prophet ﷺ took it,' and this was revealed. Abū Dāwūd and at-Tirmidhī transmitted it. He said that it is a *gharīb ḥasan* hadith. Ibn 'Aṭiyyah said, 'It is said that this was spoken by the believers, who saw no harm in that. It is said that it was the hypocrites. It is also related that it was a sword which was missing.' This is based on reading: '*yaghulla*'.

Abū Ṣakhr related from Muḥammad ibn Ka'b: '"*No Prophet would ever be guilty of misappropriation*" means that no Prophet would conceal something of the Book of Allah.' It is said that the *lām* is one that indicates a transfer. It is also recited as *yughalla*. Ibn as-Sikkīt said, 'We have only heard *ghalla* used about booty. And it is recited as "*yaghulla*" and "*yughalla*". The first means to act falsely and the second is that acting thus is falsely attributed to him. The verb means to take something secretly.'

Ibn 'Arafah said that misappropriation is called *ghulūl* because the hands are prevented (*maghlūlah*) from doing that. Abū 'Ubayd said that *ghulūl* is only used in reference to booty. He said that he did not think that it is used for treachery or malice. It is, however, clear that *aghalla* is part of treachery, *ghalla yaghillu* is part of malice, and *ghalla yaghullu* is part of misappropriation of booty. The verb is also used of a camel that cannot quench its thirst. It is also used for being treacherous as in the poem by an-Namir:

May Allah repay Ḥamzah ibn Nawfal from us
with the repayment of a traitor (*mughill*) false to his trust.

We find in a hadith, 'There should be no treachery (*ighlāl*) and no theft.' It is said, 'No bribery.' Shurayḥ said, 'There is no liability for a borrower unless he is treacherous (*mughill*).' The Prophet ﷺ said, 'There are three to whom the heart of a believer is not treacherous...' If the word is read with a *fatḥah*, then it is about rancour.

The verb *ghalla* can be either transitive or intransitive. '*Ghalla-l-mafāwiz*' means 'he entered the midst of the deserts.' The verb is used for water running between trees. Linguistically, it is to take something from the booty while concealing it from one's companions. The verb *taghalghala* is used for water running in between the trees. *Ghalal* is the water flowing at the roots of trees because it is concealed by the trees. It is as is said:

The torrents played with it and its water disappeared
amid the trees, stopping at the roots of the castor-oil plant.

Ghilālah is an undergarment. *Ghāll* is depressed land with trees in it. Places where the trees called Salam and Ṭalḥ grow are called *ghāll*. It is also the name of a plant. The plural is *ghullān*.

Some people say that '*yughalla*' means that a *ghāll* exists. According to this interpretation, the reading is based on the meaning of '*yaghulla*'. According to most scholars, the meaning of '*yughalla*' is that no one should accuse him of misappropriation in the booty.

The *āyah* forbids people to misappropriate booty and threatens those who do that. That should not be done to anyone, and it is worse still when applied to the Prophet ﷺ. He is singled out for mention because treachery towards him is a greater sin because wrong actions in his presence are magnified since it is mandatory to respect him. The rulers follow the command of the Prophet ﷺ and so they have their portion of respect. It is said that it means that no Prophet has ever misappropriated and so what is meant by the sentence is not a prohibition, but a report.

Those who misappropriate will arrive on the Day of Rising with what they have misappropriated.

He will bear it on his back and shoulder, being punished by carrying it and its weight, terrified by its voice and displaying his treachery before witnesses. This is the disgrace which Allah will inflict on the misappropriator similar to what He will do to the traitor who will have a banner set up behind him stating the extent of his treachery. Allah assigned punishments according to what human beings know and understand. Do you not see what a poet said?

Do you name me? Woe to you! Have you heard
of the banner of treachery regarding her raised in the gathering?

The Arabs used to raise banners because of treachery and similarly a criminal would be paraded with his crime.

In *Ṣaḥīḥ Muslim*, Abū Hurayrah said, 'The Messenger of Allah ﷺ stood among us one day and mentioned *ghulūl* and how terrible it was and then said, "I should not like to see any of you come on the Day of Resurrection, carrying round his neck a camel that will be grunting. Such a man will say, 'Messenger of Allah, help me!' I will say, 'I can do nothing for you. I conveyed the Message to you.' I should not like to see any of you come on the Day of Resurrection, carrying round his neck a horse that will be neighing. Such a man will say, 'Messenger of Allah, help me!' I will say, 'I can do nothing for you. I conveyed the Message to you.' I should not like to see any of you come on the Day of Resurrection, carrying round his neck a sheep that will be bleating. Such a man will say, 'Messenger of Allah, help me!' I will say, 'I can do nothing for you. I conveyed the Message to you.' I should not like to see any of you come on the Day of Resurrection, carrying round his neck a soul that will be shouting. Such a man will say, 'Messenger of Allah, help me!' I will say, 'I can do nothing for you. I conveyed the Message to you.' I should not like to see any of you come on the Day of Resurrection, carrying round his neck rags that will be fluttering. Such a man will say, 'Messenger of Allah, help me!' I will say, 'I can do nothing for you. I conveyed the Message to you.' I should not like to see any of you come on the Day of Resurrection, carrying round his neck gold and silver. Such a man will say, 'Messenger of Allah, help me!' I will say, 'I can do nothing for you. I conveyed the Message to you.'"'

Abū Dāwūd related that Samurah ibn Jundub said, 'When the Messenger of Allah ﷺ gained some booty, he commanded Bilāl to make an announcement among the people and they would bring their booty, and then he would take the fifth and divide it. A day after the announcement a man brought a halter of hair and said, "Messenger of Allah, this is part of what we got in the booty." He asked, "Did you hear Bilāl call out three times?" "Yes," he replied. He asked, "What kept you from bringing it?" He made some excuse and the Prophet ﷺ said, "No, you will bring it on the Day of Rising. I will not accept it from you."'

Some scholars say that it means that the person will be given the burden of that on the Day of Rising. It is as Allah says in another *āyah*: *'They will bear their burdens on their backs. How evil is what they bear!'* (8:30) It is said that the report conveys the great seriousness of the matter. It means that on the Day of Rising a person will come and Allah will make his situation known, just as it would be known if he were carrying a grunting camel or a neighing horse on his back. This is making it metaphorical and not actual. When, however, words can be actual or metaphorical, the actual is the basis, as we read in the books of fundamental principles. The Prophet ﷺ was informing about the reality. [As the proverb goes,] 'There is no perfume after 'Arūs,' [meaning that there is no glossing after the fact.]

It is said that if someone misappropriates something in this world, its form will appear to him on the Day of Rising in the Fire, and he will be told to go down and get it. When he goes down to it, it will continue to drop until it reaches the bottom of Hell. It will continue like that for as long as Allah wishes. It is said the words *'arrive with what he has misappropriated'* means that that treachery and misappropriation will testify against him on the Day of Rising.

Scholars say that *ghulūl* is one of the great wrong actions on the strength of this *āyah* and the hadith already mentioned by Abū Hurayrah about a person carrying it on their neck. The Prophet ﷺ also said about Mid'am, 'No! By the One who has my self in his hand! The cloak which he took from the spoils on the Day of Khaybar before they were distributed will blaze with fire on him.' When the people heard that, a man brought a sandal-strap – or two sandal-straps – to the Messenger of Allah ﷺ. The Messenger of Allah ﷺ said, 'A sandal-strap – or two sandal-straps – of fire!' That is transmitted in the *Muwaṭṭā'*. The fact that the Prophet ﷺ said, 'By the One Who has my self in His hand' and did not pray over the one who committed *ghulūl* is evidence of its gravity. It is one of the rights of people for which there must be retaliation in good and bad actions. Then the person is left to Allah's will. His words, 'A sandal-strap – or two sandal-straps – of fire' is like his words ﷺ, 'Bring the needle and thread.' This indicates that it is not lawful to take anything, great or small, from the booty before it is distributed.

The only exceptions that are agreed upon is food eaten, firewood and game caught in enemy territory. Az-Zuhrī reported that food can only be taken in enemy territory with the permission of the leader. This is baseless since traditions contradict it. Al-Ḥasan said, 'When the Companions of the Messenger of Allah ﷺ conquered a city or fortress, they ate from the pottage, flour, ghee and honey.' Ibrāhīm said that they may eat and fodder animals in enemy territory before the fifth is taken. 'Aṭā' also said that people on an expedition can eat ghee, honey and food they take and the rest must be handed over to the leader. This is the position of the majority of scholars.

This hadith is evidence for the fact that the baggage of the misappropriator is not burned because the Messenger of Allah ﷺ did not burn the baggage of the man who had taken the cloak nor that of the other man over whom he did not pray. If he had burned it, that would have been transmitted as an obligation. As for the hadith related from 'Umar ibn al-Khaṭṭāb saying that the Prophet ﷺ said, 'If you find a man who has misappropriated, burn his baggage and beat him,' which is reported by Abū Dāwūd and at-Tirmidhī from Ṣāliḥ ibn Muḥammad ibn Zā'idah, it is weak and not used as evidence. At-Tirmidhī said, 'I asked Muḥammad (meaning al-Bukhārī) about this hadith and he said, 'This is related by Ṣāliḥ ibn Muḥammad who is Abū Wāqid al-Laythī. His hadiths are *munkar*.'

Abū Dāwūd also related that he said, 'We went on an expedition with al-Walīd ibn Hishām and were accompanied by Sālim ibn 'Abdullāh ibn 'Umar and 'Umar ibn 'Abd al-'Azīz. A man took some goods from the booty and Ibn Hishām commanded that his baggage be burned. He was paraded about and not given a share of the booty.' Abū Dāwūd said, 'This is the sounder of the two hadiths.'

It is related from 'Amr ibn Shu'ayb from his father from his grandfather that the Messenger of Allah ﷺ, Abū Bakr and 'Umar burned the baggage of misappropriators and beat them. Abū Dāwūd said, "Alī ibn Baḥr added in it from al-Walīd (whom I have not heard of), "they denied him his share."" Abū 'Umar said, 'Some of those who related this hadith said, "His head is cut off and his baggage is burned."' This hadith goes back to Ṣāliḥ ibn Muḥammad who is not considered to be authoritative. It is confirmed that the Prophet ﷺ said, 'A Muslim's blood is only lawful for one of three reasons.' So, on this basis, there can be no execution for stealing from the booty.

Ibn Jurayj related from Abu-z-Zubayr from Jābir that the Prophet ﷺ said, 'There is no hand amputation in the case of someone who is treacherous, someone who loots or someone who snatches.' This contradicts the hadith of Ṣāliḥ ibn Muḥammad and has a stronger *isnād*. A misappropriator is treacherous both linguistically and in the Sharī'ah. If amputation is forbidden, then it is even more appropriate that execution would be as well. Aṭ-Ṭaḥāwī said, 'If this hadith of Ṣāliḥ is sound, then it may have been at a time when there were punishments for crimes of property, as with the person who refused to pay *zakāt* indicated by the words: 'I will take it along with half of his property, one of the firm commands of Allah Almighty.' It is as Abū Hurayrah said about a lost camel that was concealed: 'Its indemnity is owed and its like along with it.' It is as 'Abdullāh ibn 'Amr ibn al-'Āṣ said about hanging dates: 'Its indemnity is twice the amount and some lashes as a deterring punishment.' All of this is abrogated. Allah knows best.

If a man commits this crime and the object is found, it is taken from him and he is disciplined and punished. Mālik, ash-Shāfi'ī, Abū Ḥanīfah and their people, and al-Layth say that his baggage is not burned. Ash-Shāfi'ī, al-Layth and Dāwūd say that if he knows of the prohibition, he is punished. Al-Awzā'ī said that all his baggage is burned except for his weapons, the clothes he is wearing and his saddle, but his mount is not taken from him and what he stole is not burned. This is the position of Aḥmad and Isḥāq. Al-Ḥasan said that but excluded animals or a copy of the Qur'an.

Ibn Khuwayzimandād said that it is reported that Abū Bakr and 'Umar burned the baggage of people who misappropriated and beat them. Ibn 'Abd al-Barr said that those who said that the saddle and baggage of misappropriators are burned include Makḥūl and Sa'īd ibn 'Abd al-'Azīz. Their evidence is the hadith reported, but in our view a hadith does not oblige violation of vested rights nor carrying out a judgment when there are stronger traditions than it. What Mālik and his followers believed regarding this question is sounder in respect of investigation and sound tradition. Allah knows best.

Mālik's school does not differ about physical punishment. As for property, it is said that what when a *dhimmī* sells wine to a Muslim, the wine he sold to a Muslim is poured out and the price taken from the *dhimmī* as a punishment so that he does not sell wine to other Muslims. Thus financial penalties are permitted. 'Umar poured out milk diluted with water.

Scholars agree that misappropriators must return all they took to the one in charge of the division before people separate if they can do that. If they do it, that is their repentance and requital of their wrong action. They disagree about what they do if the army has separated and they cannot reach the leader. A group of the people of knowledge say that they must give a fifth to the ruler and the rest as *ṣadaqah*. This is the position of az-Zuhrī, Mālik, al-Awzā'ī, al-Layth and ath-Thawrī. It is also related from 'Ubādah ibn aṣ-Ṣāmit, Mu'āwiyah and al-Ḥasan al-Baṣrī and is similar to the position of Ibn Mas'ūd and Ibn 'Abbās because they thought that they should give it away as *ṣadaqah,* and that is also the school of Aḥmad ibn Ḥanbal. Ash-Shāfi'ī says that they cannot give away someone else's property as *ṣadaqah*.'

Abū 'Umar said, 'I consider this to be the case when the owners or the heirs no longer exist. If none of them exist, then ash-Shāfi'ī does not dislike *ṣadaqah* in that case, Allah willing. They agree that a found object can be given as *ṣadaqah* after it has been announced and not claimed. If the owner arrives after that, then he has a choice between a reward or liability. The same principle applies to misappropriated property. Success is by Allah.

The fact that there is liability for misappropriation indicates that those who take booty share equally in the booty and it is not lawful for anyone to be preferred in part of it over someone else. There is agreement that if someone steals some of it, he should be disciplined, as we already stated.

If someone has sexual intercourse with a slavegirl or steals a share, scholars disagree about carrying out the *ḥadd* punishment on him. One group think that there should be no amputation in this case.

Gifts to governors are equivalent to misappropriation. The disgrace of that in the Next World will be the same as that of the misappropriator. In the *Sunan*, Abū Dāwūd, and Muslim in the *Ṣaḥīḥ,* report from Abū Ḥumayd as-Sā'idī that: 'The Prophet ﷺ appointed a man called Ibn al-Lutbiyyah from Azd to collect the *zakāt.* When he arrived back, he said, "This is for you and this was given as a gift to me." The Prophet ﷺ stood on the minbar, praised and glorified Allah and then said, "I appointed one of your men to be in charge of an activity for which Allah has made me responsible, and then he came and said, 'This is for you and this was given as a gift to me.' Why did he not sit in the house of his father or mother until his gift came to him if he is speaking the truth? By Allah, none of you will take anything without right but that he will meet Allah Almighty carrying it on the Day of Rising, a camel which is grumbling, or a cow which is mooing, or a sheep which is bleating." Then he raised his hands until the whites of his armpits could be seen, and said, "O Allah! Have I conveyed it?" three times.' Abū Dāwūd reported from Buraydah that the Prophet ﷺ said, 'If we appoint someone to a post and we pay him a wage, anything he takes after that is *ghulūl*.'

It is also related that Abū Mas'ūd al-Anṣārī said, 'The Messenger of Allah ﷺ sent me as a collector and said, "Go, Abū Mas'ūd, and I should not like to see you come on the Day of Rising with one of the *zakāt* camels grumbling on your back, saying, 'You have misappropriated me.'" When I did not go, he said, "I will not force you."'

These hadiths specify what Abū Dāwūd related from al-Mustawrid ibn Shaddād who said, 'I heard the Messenger of Allah ﷺ say, "Whoever is an agent for us should acquire a wife. If he does not have a servant, he should acquire a servant. If he does not have a house, he should acquire a house."' Abū Bakr said, 'I was told that the Prophet ﷺ said, "Whoever takes other than that is a thieving misappropriator."'

Another aspect of *ghulūl* is keeping back books from their people, and other things are included as well. Az-Zuhrī said, 'Beware of *ghulūl* in books.' He was asked what that was and replied, 'Keeping them from their people.' It is said that it can mean to conceal from people something of revelation out of desire, fear or flattery. That is when people disliked something in the Qur'an that criticised their religion and abused their gods. They asked for it to be concealed. Muḥammad ibn Bashshār said that. What we began with is the position of the majority.

أَفَمَنِ ٱتَّبَعَ رِضْوَٰنَ ٱللَّهِ كَمَنۢ بَآءَ بِسَخَطٍ مِّنَ ٱللَّهِ وَمَأْوَىٰهُ جَهَنَّمُ وَبِئْسَ
ٱلْمَصِيرُ ﴿١٦٢﴾ هُمْ دَرَجَٰتٌ عِندَ ٱللَّهِ وَٱللَّهُ بَصِيرٌۢ بِمَا يَعْمَلُونَ ﴿١٦٣﴾

162 Is someone who pursues the pleasure of Allah the same as someone who incurs displeasure from Allah and whose refuge is Hell? What an evil destination! 163 They have different ranks with Allah. Allah sees what they do.

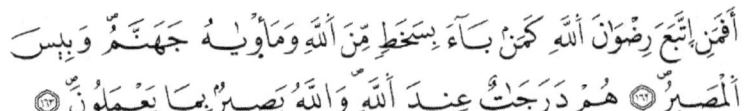

The one who follows the pleasure of Allah is the one who abandons *ghulūl* and is steadfast in *jihād*. The one who incurs His displeasure is the one who espouses disbelief, *ghulūl*, or not following the Prophet ﷺ in battle. Such a person will go to the Fire if he does not repent or Allah does not pardon him. It is an evil place to return to. 'Pleasure' is read as both *riḍwān* and *ruḍwān*, like *'udwān* and *'idwān*.

They have different ranks with Allah.

The one who gains Allah's pleasure is not like the one who incurs His displeasure. It is said that their ranks vary with Allah. Whoever gains His pleasure will have honour and immense reward and the one who incurs His displeasure will have abasement and painful punishment. It means that they will have different ranks, or be arranged in different ranks, or will be in different ranks, or will possess different ranks.

The People of the Fire also have different ranks, as in the words, 'I found him in the depths of the Fire and brought him out to the shallows.' A believer is not the same as an unbeliever in rank, and then the believers differ from one another, some having higher ranks than others, as is the case with the unbelievers. *Darajah* is a rank. *Darj* is to go through rank after rank. The stations in the Fire are referred to as '*darakāt*' as Allah says: *'The hypocrites are in the lowest level of the Fire.'* (4:145) Those who do not misappropriate will have ranks (*darajāt*) in the Garden, and those who do so will have levels (*darakāt*) in the Fire. Abū 'Ubaydah said that Hell has levels (*adrāk*), each of which is a *darak* or *dark*. That refers to descending levels while *darajāt* refers to ascending ones.

لَقَدْ مَنَّ ٱللَّهُ عَلَى ٱلْمُؤْمِنِينَ إِذْ بَعَثَ فِيهِمْ رَسُولًا مِّنْ أَنفُسِهِمْ يَتْلُوا۟
عَلَيْهِمْ ءَايَٰتِهِۦ وَيُزَكِّيهِمْ وَيُعَلِّمُهُمُ ٱلْكِتَٰبَ وَٱلْحِكْمَةَ وَإِن كَانُوا۟ مِن قَبْلُ
لَفِى ضَلَٰلٍ مُّبِينٍ ١٦٤

164 Allah showed great kindness to the believers when He sent a Messenger to them from among themselves to recite His Signs to them and purify them and teach them the Book and Wisdom, even though before that they were clearly misguided.

Allah made it clear that He has given them a great favour by sending Muḥammad ﷺ to them. Several things are said about the meaning of the kindness (*minnah*) referred to here. One is that *'from among themselves,'* means he is a human being like them. Since he showed definitive evidence and is a human being like them, they knew that that was from Allah. It is said that it is because he is one of them and so they are honoured by him ﷺ and that is the favour. It is said that he is one of them so that they know his condition and nothing of his path is hidden from them. Since his place was among them, it would be more fitting for them to fight for him and not retreat from him. There is an irregular reading which has '*min anfasihim*', meaning 'from the noblest of them' because he is from the Banū Hāshim and the Banū Hāshim are the best of Quraysh, and Quraysh are the best of the Arabs, and the Arabs are better than anyone else.

It is said that although 'believers' is general, its meaning here is particular to the Arabs because there is no Arab tribe which he is not descended from and they have lineage related to him, except for the Banū Taghlib who were Christians until Allah purified them of that. This interpretation is further elaborated by Allah's words: *'It is He who raised up among the unlettered people a Messenger from them.'* (62:2)

Abū Muḥammad 'Abd al-Ghanī mentioned from Abū Aḥmad al-Baṣrī from Qāḍī Abū Bakr Aḥmad ibn 'Alī ibn Sa'd al-Marwazī from Yaḥyā ibn Ma'īn from Hishām ibn Yūsuf from 'Abdullāh ibn Sulaymān an-Nawfalī from az-Zuhrī from 'Urwah that 'Ā'ishah said, 'Allah showed great kindness to the believers when He sent a Messenger to them from among themselves.' She said, 'This is particular to the Arabs.' Others have said that Allah means all believers here and '*from among themselves*' means that he is one of them and a human being like them, but he was singled out for the Revelation. This is the meaning of Allah's words: *'A Messenger has come to you from among yourselves.'* (9:128) The believers are singled out because they benefit from it. The favour to them is therefore greater.

'Yatlū' is in the accusative to describe the Messenger. It means that he recites. *Tilāwah* is recitation. *'Before that'* means that before Muḥammad ﷺ they were in clear misguidance. It is said that '*in*' means *mā* and the *lām* in the predicate means '*illā*'. It is like the phrase *'even though before this you were astray'* (2:198), meaning that previously they were only among those who were misguided. This is the school of the Kufans. The meaning of this *āyah* was already discussed in *al-Baqarah*.

أَوَلَمَّا أَصَٰبَتۡكُم مُّصِيبَةٞ قَدۡ أَصَبۡتُم مِّثۡلَيۡهَا قُلۡتُمۡ أَنَّىٰ هَٰذَاۖ قُلۡ هُوَ مِنۡ
عِندِ أَنفُسِكُمۡۗ إِنَّ ٱللَّهَ عَلَىٰ كُلِّ شَيۡءٖ قَدِيرٞ ١٦٥

165 Why is it that when a calamity happens to you, when you have already inflicted twice as much, you say, 'How could this possibly happen?' Say, 'It has come from your own selves.' Allah has power over all things.

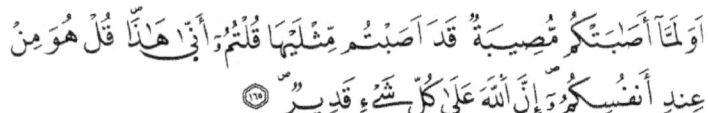

The *alif* at the beginning denotes a question and the *wāw* adds it to what comes before it. The *'calamity'* referred to is their defeat at Uḥud and the words *'you already inflicted twice as much'* refer to Badr. There they killed seventy and took seventy captive. A captive is like someone killed because he can be killed by his captor. You defeated them at Badr and at the beginning of Uḥud and killed about twenty of them then. You killed them in two battles and they afflicted you at Uḥud.

You say, 'How could this possibly happen?'

'How could we suffer this defeat and killing when we are fighting in the Way of Allah and are Muslims, and the Prophet and revelation are among us, and they are idolaters?'

Say, 'It has come from your own selves.'

This refers to the disobedience of the archers. There are no people who obey their Prophet in war without being victorious because when they obey, they are the Party of Allah, and the Party of Allah are necessarily the victors.

Qatādah and ar-Rabīʿ ibn Anas said, 'Allah means their asking the Prophet ﷺ to go out when he wanted to remain in Madīnah and the interpretation of the dream of armour being a fortress.'

ʿAlī ibn Abī Ṭālib ﵁ said, 'It is their choosing ransom at Badr instead of killing.' They were told, 'If you let the captives be ransomed, an equal number of you will be killed.' The Prophet ﷺ said about the captives at Badr, 'You can kill them if you wish or, if you wish, let them be ransomed and enjoy the ransom, and then a like number of you will be martyred.' The last of the seventy was Thābit ibn Qays who was in the Battle of Yamāmah. According to the first two views, *'from your own selves'* refers to your wrong actions. According to the last view, it is your choice.

وَمَآ أَصَٰبَكُمۡ يَوۡمَ ٱلۡتَقَى ٱلۡجَمۡعَانِ فَبِإِذۡنِ ٱللَّهِ وَلِيَعۡلَمَ ٱلۡمُؤۡمِنِينَ ﴿١٦٦﴾ وَلِيَعۡلَمَ ٱلَّذِينَ
نَافَقُواْۚ وَقِيلَ لَهُمۡ تَعَالَوۡاْ قَٰتِلُواْ فِي سَبِيلِ ٱللَّهِ أَوِ ٱدۡفَعُواْۖ قَالُواْ لَوۡ نَعۡلَمُ
قِتَالٗا لَّٱتَّبَعۡنَٰكُمۡۗ هُمۡ لِلۡكُفۡرِ يَوۡمَئِذٍ أَقۡرَبُ مِنۡهُمۡ لِلۡإِيمَٰنِۚ يَقُولُونَ
بِأَفۡوَٰهِهِم مَّا لَيۡسَ فِي قُلُوبِهِمۡۚ وَٱللَّهُ أَعۡلَمُ بِمَا يَكۡتُمُونَ ﴿١٦٧﴾

166 What assailed you on the day the two armies met was by Allah's permission, so that He would know the believers, 167 and so that He would know the hypocrites. They were told, 'Come and fight in the Way of Allah or at least help defend us.' They said, 'If we knew that there would be a fight, we would certainly follow you.' They were closer to unbelief that day than to belief, saying with their mouths what was not in their hearts. And Allah knows best what they are hiding.

What assailed you on the day the two armies met was by Allah's permission, so that He would know the believers

The '*day*' here is Uḥud, and it refers to the killing, wounding and defeat that took place there. *'By Allah's permission'* means 'with His knowledge' or 'by His decision and decree'. Al-Qaffāl said, 'By leaving you and them, not that He willed that.' This is the Mu'tazilite interpretation. The *fā'* is added because *mā* means 'which' here. That which assailed them when the two armies met was by Allah's permission, and so it is like a precondition as Sībawayh said.

so that He would know the believers and so that He would know the hypocrites.

'Knowing' the believers and the hypocrites means to distinguish between them or to reveal them. It is said that it means to show the faith of the believers by their firmness in fighting and to show the disbelief of hypocrites by showing their abuse so that they will know that.

They were told, 'Come and fight in the Way of Allah or at least help defend us.'

'They were told': the hypocrites here mean 'Abdullāh ibn Ubayy and his people who ceased to help the Prophet ﷺ. They numbered 300. 'Abdullāh ibn 'Amr ibn Ḥarām al-Anṣārī went after them and said to them, 'Fear Allah and do not abandon your Prophet! Fight in the Way of Allah or defend!' Ibn Ubayy said to him, 'I do not think that there will be fighting. If we knew that there would be fighting, we would be with you.' When 'Abdullāh despaired of them, he said, 'Go,

enemies of Allah. Allah and His Messenger have no need of you!' He went with the Prophet ﷺ and was martyred.

People disagree about the meaning of *'defend'* here. As-Suddī, Ibn Jurayj and others said, 'Make our numbers seem larger even if you do not fight with us.' That is defence against the enemy and deterrence. Making numbers seem larger deters the enemy.

Anas ibn Mālik said, 'At the battle of al-Qādisiyyah, I saw 'Abdullāh ibn Umm Maktūm wearing armour whose ends were dragging. He had a black banner in his hand. He was asked, "Did not Allah excuse you [from fighting]?" [He was blind.] He said, "Indeed, but I want to increase the numbers of the believers with myself."' It is related that he said, 'So how is my increasing the numbers in the Cause of Allah!' Abū 'Awn al-Anṣārī said, 'The meaning of "defend" is "to take up position *(rābitū)*".' This is close to the first meaning as a *murābiṭ* must be a defender because if it had not been for the stationing of the *murābitūn* at the borders, the enemy would have entered.

Some commentators believe that the words of 'Abdullāh ibn 'Amr, 'Defend' were a summons to fight because he called them to fight in the Way of Allah and so that the word of Allah be uppermost. When he saw that they were not following that, he turned his face from them to shame them and show his disdain. Do you not see that Quzmān said, 'By Allah, I only fought for the honour of my people!' And do you not see that one of the Anṣār said on the day of the battle of Uḥud when he saw that Quraysh had released their animals in the fields of the canal, 'Are we going to let them graze in the fields of the Banū Qaylah without us fighting?" That means: 'You are not fighting for the Cause of Allah. You are just fighting for yourselves and your territory.'

They were closer to unbelief that day than to belief.

Their state was evident and the veils covering them ripped apart and their hypocrisy disclosed to those who thought they were Muslims. So they were closer to disbelief in their outward state, even though they were actually unbelievers anyway.

The words *'saying with their mouths what was not in their hearts'* means that they were making a show of faith but concealing disbelief. The word *'mouths'* stresses that.

ٱلَّذِينَ قَالُوا۟ لِإِخْوَٰنِهِمْ وَقَعَدُوا۟ لَوْ أَطَاعُونَا مَا قُتِلُوا۟ ۗ قُلْ فَٱدْرَءُوا۟
عَنْ أَنفُسِكُمُ ٱلْمَوْتَ إِن كُنتُمْ صَٰدِقِينَ ﴿١٦٨﴾

168 They are those who said of their brothers, when they themselves had stayed behind, 'If they had only obeyed us, they would not have been killed.' Say, 'Then ward off death from yourselves if you are telling the truth.'

They are those who said of their brothers, when they themselves had stayed behind,

'They are those who said of their brothers,' means 'on behalf of their brothers'. They were the martyrs of Khazraj who had been killed. They were their brothers in lineage and proximity, but not in the *dīn*. They said of these martyrs, 'If they had stayed in Madīnah, they would not have been killed.' It is said that 'Abdullāh ibn Ubayy and his fellow hypocrites said about them: 'If those who were killed had obeyed us, they would not have been killed.' So *'obeyed us'* means by not going out against Quraysh. *'They stayed behind'* means 'They said this and sat by themselves, not going out on *jihād*.' Allah then answered them.

Say, 'Then ward off death from yourselves if you are telling the truth.'

This means: 'Say to them, Muḥammad: "If you are speaking the truth, then avert death from yourselves."' The word *dar'* means defence. This makes it clear that there is no defence against the Decree. A person who is killed can only be killed at the end of his life-span. What Allah knows and reports will be must happen. It is said that on that day seventy hypocrites died. Abu-l-Layth as-Samarqandī said, 'I heard one of the commentators in Samarqand say, "On the day this *āyah* was revealed, seventy hypocrites died."'

وَلَا تَحْسَبَنَّ ٱلَّذِينَ قُتِلُوا۟ فِى سَبِيلِ ٱللَّهِ أَمْوَٰتًۢا ۚ بَلْ أَحْيَآءٌ عِندَ رَبِّهِمْ
يُرْزَقُونَ ﴿١٦٩﴾ فَرِحِينَ بِمَآ ءَاتَىٰهُمُ ٱللَّهُ مِن فَضْلِهِۦ وَيَسْتَبْشِرُونَ بِٱلَّذِينَ
لَمْ يَلْحَقُوا۟ بِهِم مِّنْ خَلْفِهِمْ أَلَّا خَوْفٌ عَلَيْهِمْ وَلَا هُمْ يَحْزَنُونَ ﴿١٧٠﴾

169 Do not suppose that those killed in the Way of Allah are dead. No indeed! They are alive and well provided for in the very presence of their Lord, 170 delighting in the favour Allah has bestowed on them, rejoicing over those they left behind who have not yet joined them, feeling no fear and knowing no sorrow,

When Allah made it clear that what happened at Uḥud was a test to distinguish the hypocrites from the truthful, He made it clear that the one who did not flee and was killed enjoyed honour and life with Him. The *āyah* is about the martyrs of Uḥud. It is also said that it is about martyrs of Bi'r Ma'ūnah or that it is general to all martyrs.

We find in the *Muṣannaf* of Abū Dāwūd, that Ibn 'Abbās reported that the Messenger of Allah ﷺ said, 'When your brothers were struck down at Uḥud, Allah placed their spirits in the mouths of green birds which go to the rivers of the Garden, eating from their fruits and returning to gold lamps hanging in the shadow of the Throne. When they found their delightful food and drink and resting-places, they said, "Who will convey to our brothers from us that we are alive and well provided for in the Garden so that they do not turn from doing *jihād* and do not flinch in battle?" Allah said, "I will convey it for you." and then Allah revealed, *"Do not suppose…"*'

Baqī ibn Mukhallad related that Jābir said, 'The Messenger of Allah ﷺ met me and said, "Jābir, why do I see you downcast and worried?" I replied, "Messenger of Allah, my father was martyred and left dependents and he had debts." He said, "Shall I give you the good news about what your father has received from Allah?" "Yes, indeed," I replied. He said, "Allah has given life to your father and spoken to him directly – and He speaks to no one except from behind a veil – and said to him, 'My slave, wish and I will give to you.' He said, 'Lord, return me to the world so that I can be killed for You a second time.' So the Lord said, 'It has already been decided by Me that people do not return to it.' He said, 'Lord, then convey to those after me.' So Allah revealed, *'Do not suppose…'*"' It is transmitted by Ibn Mājah in the *Sunan* and at-Tirmidhī in his *Jāmi'* and he said that it is a *ḥasan gharīb* hadith.

Wakī' related from Sālim ibn al-Afṭas that Sa'īd ibn Jubayr said, 'When Ḥamzah ibn 'Abd al-Muṭṭalib and Muṣ'ab ibn 'Umayr were struck down and saw the good they had been given, they said, "Would that our brothers knew the good with which we have been provided so that it would increase their desire for *jihād*!" Allah Almighty said, "I will convey it to them from you," and He revealed this.'

Abu-ḍ-Ḍuḥā said, 'This *āyah* was revealed about the people of Uḥud in particular.' The first hadith indicates that this view is sound. Some of them said that it was revealed about the martyrs of Badr. They were fourteen men: eight of the Anṣār and six of the Muhājirūn. It is also said that it was revealed about the martyrs of the Bi'r Ma'ūnah whose story is well known. Muḥammad ibn Isḥāq and others mentioned it. Others said that when the relatives of the martyrs obtained blessings and happiness, they were filled with regret and said, 'We are in blessing and happiness while our fathers, sons and brothers are in the grave.' So Allah revealed this *āyah* to console them and tell them about the state of those who had been killed.

Generally speaking, even though it is possible for revelation to have a specific cause, Allah reports in it that martyrs are alive in the Garden and provided for, and it is not impossible that, while they have died and their bodies are in the earth, their spirits are still alive, like those of all the believers. They are given provision in the Garden at the moment of their death and so it is as if their life in this world was continuing.

Scholars disagree about this. The majority take the position we mentioned and say that their life is real. Some say that their spirits are returned to them in their graves and they enjoy bliss, in the same way that the unbelievers are revived in their graves and are punished.

Mujāhid said, 'They are provided with the fruits of the Garden,' in other words they experience its scent while not actually being in it. Other people say that the *ayah* is metaphorical and it means that Allah has judged that they will be blessed in the Garden and so it is praise for them. That is like when you say, 'So-and-so is not dead,' meaning that his renown lives on. It is said:

The death of someone godfearing is life without annihilation.
Some people die among people and yet they remain alive.

It means that they continue to be remembered with excellent praise.

Others say that their spirits are in the mouths of green birds and they are provided for in the Garden, eating and enjoying bliss. This is the sound position because the sound transmission about it is that it is actual and the hadith of Ibn 'Abbās removes any dispute. The same is true of the hadith of Ibn Mas'ūd that Muslim transmitted. We have further explained the states of the dead and the Next World in *Kitāb at-Tadhkirah*. Praise be to Allah.

There we mentioned how the martyrs are and the fact that they have different states. As for the interpretation of the martyrs being 'alive' meaning that they will be brought back to life here, this is unlikely and is refuted by the Qur'an and *Sunnah*. Allah's word *'alive'* indicates their everlasting life and only those who are alive are provided for. It is said that every year the reward of an expedition is written for them and they share in the reward of every *jihād* after them until the Day of Rising because they made *jihād* a *sunnah*. It is like Allah's words: *'So We decreed for the tribe of Israel that if someone kills another person...'* (5:32) That will be dealt with in that *sūrah*, Allah willing.

It is said that their spirits bow and prostrate under the Throne until the Day of Rising just as the souls of living believers who spend the night in *wuḍū'* also do. It is said that it is said because a martyr does not decay in the grave and the earth does not consume him. We mentioned this idea in *at-Tadhkirah.* The earth does not consume Prophets, martyrs, scholars, *mu'adhdhins* whose wage is with Allah and those who know the Qur'an.

Since a martyr is adjudged to be alive, there is no prayer said over him, as is the ruling of someone physically alive. Scholars disagree about washing martyrs and praying over them. Mālik, ash-Shāfi'ī Abū Ḥanīfah and ath-Thawrī believe that all martyrs should be washed and prayed over, except for those killed in actual battle against the enemy, based on the hadith of Jābir in which the Prophet ﷺ said, 'Bury them in their blood,' i.e. at Uḥud they were not washed. Al-Bukhārī related it.

Abū Dāwūd related that Ibn 'Abbās said, 'The Messenger of Allah ﷺ commanded that those killed at Uḥud should have their weapons and armour removed from them and be buried in their blood and clothing.' That is the position of Aḥmad, Isḥāq, al-Awzā'ī, Dāwūd, a group of the *fuqahā'* and People of Hadith of the cities and Ibn 'Ulayyah. Sa'īd ibn al-Musayyab and al-Ḥasan said that they should be washed. One of them said that the martyrs of Uḥud were not washed because they were so many and the situation distracted them from doing that.

Abū 'Umar says that no one takes the position of Sa'īd and al-Ḥasan among the *fuqahā'* except for 'Ubaydullāh ibn al-Ḥasan al-'Anbārī. What they mentioned about them being distracted from doing it is not a valid reason because each of them had relatives who could wash them and see to them. The reason – and Allah knows best – is, as in the hadith: 'It will be like the scent of musk on the Day of Rising.' So it is clear that the reason is not as some of them said about them being distracted from doing it and there is no place for analogy and investigation in this matter. It is simply a question of following the tradition about those killed at Uḥud not being washed.

One of the later scholars who took the position of al-Ḥasan argued, using the words of the Prophet ﷺ about the martyrs of Uḥud, 'I will be a witness for these people on the Day of Rising.' He said that this indicates that they are special and others do not share with them in that. Abū 'Umar said that this is aberrant and the position that they are not washed is more appropriate since that was confirmed from the Prophet ﷺ about those killed at Uḥud and others. Abū Dāwud related that Jābir said, 'A man was hit by an arrow in his chest or his throat and died. He was buried in his clothes as he was. He said, "We are with the Messenger of Allah ﷺ."'

As for praying over them, scholars also disagree about that. Mālik, al-Layth, ash-Shāfi'ī, Aḥmad and Dāwūd believe that the prayer should not be performed over them, based on the hadith of Jābir which states that two of the dead of Uḥud were buried in the same cloth. It was asked, 'Which of them knew the most Qur'an?' One of them was indicated and he was put first in the grave. Then he ﷺ said, 'I will be a witness for these people on the Day of Rising.' He commanded that they should be buried in their blood and not washed or prayed over. The *fuqahā'* of Kufa, Basra and Syria say that the prayer is said over them and they use as evidence *mursal* hadiths about the Prophet ﷺ performing the prayer over Ḥamzah. Scholars agree, however, that if someone is removed alive from the battlefield and does not die in the battle, but dies later, the prayer is performed over him, as 'Umar did.

They disagree about someone killed unjustly, like those killed by Khārijites, highwaymen and the like. Abū Ḥanīfah and ath-Thawrī said that anyone killed unjustly is not washed, but the prayer is said over him and over every martyr, and that is the position of most Iraqis, and they cite hadiths in support of this. They related by various paths that Zayd ibn Ṣūḥān, who was killed in the Battle of the Camel, said, 'Do not remove my garment nor wash away my blood.'

It is confirmed that 'Ammār ibn Yāsir said something similar. 'Ammār was killed at the Battle of Ṣiffīn and 'Alī did not wash him. Ash-Shāfi'ī has two positions: one is that they are washed like all the dead except those who are actually killed in battle. This is the position of Mālik. Mālik said that those killed by the unbelievers who die in battle are not washed. The one killed by unbelievers outside of battle is washed and prayed over, and this is the position of Aḥmad ibn Ḥanbal. The other position of ash-Shāfi'ī is that those killed by rebels are not washed. The position of Mālik is sounder. Washing the dead is confirmed by consensus and transmitted from Kufa. So it is mandatory to wash every dead person except for those excluded by consensus or a firm *sunnah*. Success is by Allah.

If the enemy surprises people in their camp and some of them are killed, is the ruling about them the same as someone killed in battle or the normal ruling of someone who has died? This question arose for us in Cordoba when the enemy attacked by surprise on the third morning of Ramadan 627 AH. Some were killed and some were captured. My father was among those who were killed. I asked our Shaykh, Abu Ja'far Aḥmad, known as Abū Ḥujjah, about this. He said, 'Wash him and pray over him. Your father was not killed in battle in the ranks.' Then I asked our Shaykh Rabī' ibn 'Abd ar-Raḥmān ibn Aḥmad ibn Rabi' ibn Ubayy and he said that his ruling is that of someone killed in battle. Then I asked the Qāḍī Abu-l-Ḥasan 'Alī ibn Qiṭrāl, while a group of *fuqahā'* were around him. They said, 'Wash him, shroud him and pray over him.' I did that. After that I found the question in *at-Tabaṣṣur* by Abu-l-Ḥasan al-Lakhmī and others. If I had found that before, I would not have washed him and I would have buried him in his blood in his clothes.

This *āyah* indicates the immense reward for being killed in the Way of Allah and martyrdom in respect of it so that it expiates wrong actions, as the Prophet ﷺ stated: 'Being killed in the way of Allah expiates everything except debt. That is what Jibrīl told me.' Our scholars say that the mention of debts alludes also to other rights for which one is responsible, like usurpation, taking property wrongfully, murder and deliberate injury and other matters which entail responsibility. None of that is forgiven by *jihād*, and there is requital in respect of all of that in the form of good actions and bad actions, as reported in the sound *Sunnah*.

'Abdullāh ibn Unays reported that he heard the Messenger of Allah ﷺ say, 'Allah will gather the slaves – or people (Hammām is unsure of the word used) – naked, uncircumcised, bare.' He was asked what that was and he answered, 'They will have nothing with them. A voice will call to them which will be heard by all, far and near: "I am the King. I am the Judge. None of the people of the Garden should enter the Garden while one of the people of the Fire is seeking requital of an injustice from him, and none of the people of the Fire should enter the Fire while one of the people of the Garden is seeking requital of an injustice from him, even a slap."' They asked, 'How will we be able to do that when we will come barefoot, naked and uncircumcised?' He replied, 'It will be with good actions and wrong actions.' Al-Ḥārith ibn Usāmah transmitted it.

It is also reported in Muslim from Abū Hurayrah that the Messenger of Allah ﷺ said, 'Do you know who is the true bankrupt?' They replied, 'The bankrupt is the person who has neither money nor goods.' He said, 'The bankrupt person of my community is the one who performs the prayer, fasts and pays *zakāt*, but insults this person, slanders that one, consumes the property of this person, sheds the blood of that one, and strikes this one. Some will be given some of his good deeds and others will be given some of his good deeds. If his good deeds are exhausted before he has given everyone their due, some of their wrong actions will be taken and cast on him and then he will be cast into the Fire.' He ﷺ also said, 'By the One who has my self in His hand, if a man is killed in the Way of Allah and then is brought to life and killed again and then brought to life and killed again, and owes a debt, he will not enter the Garden until his debt is settled.' Abū Hurayrah reported that the Prophet ﷺ said, 'The soul of the believer is suspended as long as he owes a debt.' Aḥmad ibn Zuhayr said, 'Yaḥyā ibn Ma'īn was asked about this hadith and said that it is sound.

If it is said, 'This indicates that some martyrs will not enter the Garden when they are killed and their spirits are not in the mouths of birds as was mentioned and they are not in their graves, so where then are they?' We reply that it is reported that the Prophet ﷺ said, 'The spirits of martyrs are at a river at the door of the Garden called Bāriq. Their provision is brought out to them from the Garden morning and evening.' Perhaps it is them, and Allah knows best. This is like what Imām Abū Muḥammad ibn 'Aṭiyyah said. He said, 'Those have different degrees and states, but all of them are provided for.'

Imām Abū 'Abdullāh Muḥammad ibn Yazīd ibn Mājah al-Qazwīnī has in his *Sunan* from Sulaym ibn 'Āmir who heard Abū Umāmah say that he heard the Messenger of Allah ﷺ say, 'A martyr at sea is like two martyrs on land and someone who suffers from seasickness is like someone stained in his own blood on land. The time between one wave and the next is like being cut off from this world in obeying Allah. Allah Almighty has appointed the Angel of Death to take all souls except for those of martyrs at sea: Allah Almighty Himself sees to taking their souls. The martyr on land is forgiven all wrong actions except for debts while the martyr at sea is forgiven all wrong actions and debts as well.'

The debt which holds a person back from the Garden, and Allah knows best, is when he left enough to settle the debt but did not mention it in his will, or which he could have paid but did not, or which he incurred in extravagance and stupidity and died before repaying. As for someone who incurred the debt out of his obligation to support his dependents or because of hardship, and died without leaving enough to pay it, Allah will not hold him back from the Garden, Allah willing, because it is the duty of the ruler to pay his debt for him, either from the *zakāt*, from the share of the debtors, or from the booty. The Prophet ﷺ said, 'If anyone leaves a debt or loss, it is up to Allah and His Messenger. Whoever leaves property, it is for his heirs.' We have further explained this in a chapter in *Kitāb at-Tadhkirah*. Praise be to Allah.

well provided for in the presence of their Lord, delighting in the favour Allah has bestowed on them,

There is an elision here which implies, 'in the honour of their Lord'. The word *''inda'* necessarily indicates proximity. Here it denotes honour. The verb *'provided for'* has its normal meaning. Some people say that the life referred to is that of being remembered and they are given beautiful praise. The first view is that it is actual and real.

It is said that when the spirits rove in that state, they perceive the scents, fragrance, blessing and delight of the Garden appropriate for spirits, but which act as provision and stimulation for them. As for physical pleasures, when those spirits are returned to their bodies, they will enjoy the full bliss prepared for them. This is a sound statement and it is a sort of metaphor. It agrees with what we have reported. Allah grants success.

The verb *'delighting'* is a *ḥāl* 'circumstantial expression' of what is implied in 'well-provided for'. It is also possible that *'delighting'* is an adjective stemming from the earlier word *'alive'*. *'Delight'* is joy and the *'favour'* is the bliss mentioned in this *āyah*. Ibn as-Samayfa' recited *'fāriḥīna'* with an *alif*. They are two dialectical forms, like *farih* and *fārih*, *ḥadhir* and *ḥādhir*, *ṭami'* and *ṭāmi'*, and *bakhil* and *bākhil*. An-Naḥḥās said that it is permitted to be in the nominative outside of the Qur'an as an adjective of *'alive'*.

rejoicing over those they left behind who have not yet joined them.

Those who have not joined them in favour, even though they have favour. The word *'rejoicing'* comes from *basharah* (skin) because when a man is happy, the effect of joy shows in his face. As-Suddī said, 'Martyrs will be given a book which mentions those of their brothers they have preceded and they will be delighted as people in this world rejoice when someone who has been away returns.'

Qatādah, Ibn Jurayj, ar-Rabī' and others said that they rejoice by saying, 'Our brothers we left in this world are fighting in the Way of Allah with their Lord. They will be martyred and obtain an honour like ours.' So they delight in that.

It is said that the indication of the good news for those who have not yet joined them refers to all the believers, but when they see the reward of Allah there is certainty that the *dīn* of Islam is the Truth for which Allah has rewarded them and so they rejoice in the favour that Allah has given them. They rejoice for the believers because *'they will feel no fear and know no sorrow'*. Az-Zajjāj and Ibn Fūrak believed this.

يَسْتَبْشِرُونَ بِنِعْمَةٍ مِّنَ ٱللَّهِ وَفَضْلٍ وَأَنَّ ٱللَّهَ لَا يُضِيعُ أَجْرَ ٱلْمُؤْمِنِينَ ﴿١٧١﴾

171 rejoicing in blessings and favour from Allah and that Allah does not let the wage of the believers go to waste.

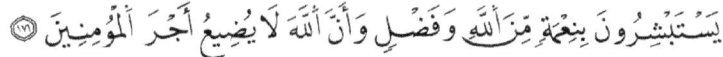

They are rejoicing in obtaining the Garden from Allah or in forgiveness from Allah. *'Favour'* is extra clarification since favour is a part of blessing and indicates its great expanse and that it is not like the blessings of this world. It is said that favour comes after blessing by way of stress. At-Tirmidhī reports from al-Miqdām ibn Ma'dīkarib that the Messenger of Allah ﷺ said, 'The martyr has six distinguishing features with Allah. [Some variants have seven.] Allah forgives him immediately, he sees his seat in the Garden, he is protected from the punishment of the grave, he is safe from the greatest fear, a ruby crown of gravity will be placed on his head which is better than this world and everything in it, he will be married to seventy-two houris, and he will intercede for seventy of his relatives.' This is a sound *ḥasan gharīb* hadith. This is the explanation of blessing and favour, and there are many traditions about that.

Mujāhid said, 'Swords are the keys to the Garden.' It is related that the Messenger of Allah ﷺ said, 'Allah Almighty honoured the martyrs with five marks of honour with which He did not honour any of the Prophets nor me. One of them is that all Prophets have their souls taken by the Angel of Death who is the one who will take my soul. Allah is the One who takes the souls of the martyrs by His power however He wishes and the Angel of Death has no power over their souls. The second is that all the Prophets are washed after death and I will be washed after death. The martyrs are not washed and they have no need for the water of this world. The third is that all the Prophets are shrouded and I will be shrouded. The martyrs are not shrouded, but buried in their clothes. The fourth is that when the Prophets die, they are called dead and when I die, I will be called dead. The martyrs are not called dead. The fifth is that the Prophets are given their intercession on the Day of Rising and my intercession will be on the Day of Rising. The martyrs intercede every day for those they intercede for.'

Al-Kisā'ī recited '*inna-llāha*' and the rest have it as '*anna*'. If someone recites it as '*anna*', it means 'rejoicing in blessing from Allah and rejoicing in the fact that Allah will not let the wage of the believers go to waste.' If it is recited with '*inna*', then it is for the inceptive. Its proof is in the reading of Ibn Mas'ūd: '*Allahu*'.

ٱلَّذِينَ ٱسْتَجَابُوا۟ لِلَّهِ وَٱلرَّسُولِ مِنۢ بَعْدِ مَآ أَصَابَهُمُ ٱلْقَرْحُ ۚ لِلَّذِينَ أَحْسَنُوا۟
مِنْهُمْ وَٱتَّقَوْا۟ أَجْرٌ عَظِيمٌ ﴿١٧٢﴾

172 Those who did good and were godfearing, among those who responded to Allah and the Messenger after the wound had been inflicted, will have an immense reward:

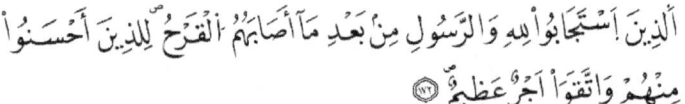

'*Those*' is in the nominative for the inceptive whose predicate is '*after the wound had been inflicted*'. It can also be in the position of the genitive as an appositive for '*believers*' or for '*who have not yet joined them*'. '*Istajābū*' means 'respond', and the *sīn* and *tā'* are redundant. [VERSE]

In the two *Ṣaḥīḥ* Collections, 'Urwah ibn az-Zubayr said, "Ā'ishah said to me, "Your father is one of those who responded to Allah and the Messenger after they had been wounded." 'Ā'ishah said, "Nephew, your fathers (meaning az-Zubayr and Abū Bakr) are among those who responded to Allah and the Messenger after they were wounded." She continued, "When the idolaters left Uḥud and the Prophet ﷺ and his Companions had suffered the injuries they suffered, they feared that they would return, so he ﷺ said, 'Who will volunteer to go to those so that they know that we have strength?' Abū Bakr and az-Zubayr went out with seventy men after the people. They heard them and departed by the favour of Allah.'"

'Ā'ishah indicated what happened in the expedition of Ḥamrā' al-Asad which is about eight miles from Madīnah. That was on the Sunday, the second day after Uḥud. The Messenger of Allah ﷺ called on the people to pursue the idolaters. He said, 'Only those who were with us yesterday will go with us.' So two hundred of the believers went with him. We find in al-Bukhārī: 'He asked, "Who will go after them?" He selected seventy men from them. Abū Bakr and az-Zubayr were among them. They reached Ḥamrā' al-Asad, meaning to frighten the enemy. Some of them were seriously wounded and could not walk or ride, and were carried. All of that was to obey the command of the Messenger of Allah ﷺ and out of desire for *jihād*.'

It is said that the *āyah* was revealed about two men of the Banū 'Abd al-Ashhal who were seriously wounded, one leaning on the other. They went out with the Prophet ﷺ. When they reached Ḥamrā' al-Asad, Nu'aym ibn Mas'ūd met them and told them that Abū Sufyan ibn Ḥarb and the Quraysh with him had gathered under their banner to return to Madīnah and eradicate its people. They said what Allah tells us: '*Allah is enough for us and the Best of Guardians.*' When Quraysh gathered like that, Ma'bad al-Khuzā'ī went to them. Khuzā'ah were allies of the Prophet ﷺ. When he saw the state of the Companions of the Prophet ﷺ and saw the resolve of Quraysh to return and eradicate the people of Madina, he was alarmed by that and his faithfulness to the Prophet ﷺ and His Companions led him to alarm Quraysh, so he said to them, 'I have left Muḥammad and his Companions at Ḥamrā' al-Asad in a large army. He has gathered those who stayed behind and they are coming against you. Save yourselves! Save yourselves! I forbid you to do that! By Allah, what I saw of them led me to compose some verses of poetry!' 'What are they?' he was asked. He said:

My horse almost fell at the rumble
when the earth streamed with swarms of steeds.

Galloping with noble lions astride them,
not feeble in the fight, firm in the saddle, fully armed.

I continued to run, thinking the ground itself was moving,
when they brought a leader who is never deserted.

I said, 'Woe to Ibn Ḥarb in your encounter
when the land is surging with horses!'

I warn the people of the Ḥaram clearly,
speaking to every wise and sensible man among them,

Of the army of Aḥmad, not some contemptible troop,
and my warning should not be described as hearsay.

That made Abū Sufyan and those with him turn back. Allah cast fear into their hearts and they returned to Makkah swiftly in fear, and the Prophet ﷺ returned victorious to Madīnah with his Companions as Allah says: *'So they returned with blessings and bounty from Allah and no evil touched them.'* That means that there was no fighting or terror.

Jābir ibn 'Abdullāh asked for permission from the Prophet ﷺ to go out with him and he gave him permission. Allah had told them of the immense reward that this group would have, and the Messenger of Allah ﷺ said, 'It refers to this expedition.' This is the commentary of the majority on this *āyah*.

Mujāhid and 'Ikrimah have an aberrant view and say that this *āyah* is connected to the two after it and it is about the Prophet ﷺ going out to Lesser Badr. He went out for the appointment he made with Abū Sufyan at Uḥud when he said, 'Our meeting is Badr next year.' The Prophet ﷺ said, 'Say: "Yes."' So the Prophet ﷺ set out for Badr where there was a great market and gave his Companions some dirhams. He approached Badr and Nu'aym ibn Mas'ūd al-Ashjā'ī came to him and told him that Quraysh had gathered and were coming to fight them. The Muslims were alarmed at that, but they said: *'Allah is enough for us and the best of Guardians.'* They were determined and went to Badr and did not find anyone except the market. They bought some condiments and traded with their dirhams and returned safely and with a profit, as Allah says: *'They returned with blessings and bounty from Allah.'* (3:174) This means the profit from their trade. Allah knows best.

ٱلَّذِينَ قَالَ لَهُمُ ٱلنَّاسُ إِنَّ ٱلنَّاسَ قَدْ جَمَعُوا۟ لَكُمْ فَٱخْشَوْهُمْ
فَزَادَهُمْ إِيمَٰنًا وَقَالُوا۟ حَسْبُنَا ٱللَّهُ وَنِعْمَ ٱلْوَكِيلُ ﴿١٧٣﴾

173 those to whom people said, 'The people have gathered against you, so fear them.' But that merely increased their belief and they said, 'Allah is enough for us and the Best of Guardians.'

There is disagreement about who is meant by *'those to whom people said'*. Mujāhid, Muqātil, 'Ikrimah and al-Kalbī said that this refers to Nu'aym ibn Mas'ūd al-Ashjā'ī. The expression is general but its meaning is particular. A similar usage in seen in *'Do they in fact envy other people'* (4:54) when Muḥammad ﷺ is meant. As-Suddī said that it was a bedouin who was given a wage for doing that.

Ibn Isḥāq and a group said that *'people'* here refers to a troop of the 'Abd al-Qays who passed by Abū Sufyān who sent them to the Muslims to impede them. It is said that the *'people'* referred to are the hypocrites. As-Suddī said, 'When the Prophet ﷺ and his Companions prepared to go out to Lesser Badr for the appointment with Abū Sufyān, the hypocrites came to them and said, 'We are your friends. We forbade you to go out to them and you disobeyed us and they fought you and won. If you go to them, none of you will return.' They replied, *'Allah is enough for us and the Best of Guardians.'*

Abū Ma'shar said, 'Some of Hudhayl came to Madīnah from Tihāmah and the Companions asked them about Abū Sufyān and they said. "They have gathered many troops against you, so fear them and be on guard against them. You have no power to resist them."' According to these statements, the word *'people'* means troops. Allah knows best.

But that merely increased their belief

The words of the people increased their belief, meaning their confirmation and certainty in their *dīn*, helping them in strength, boldness, and readiness. So according to this, the increase of belief lies in actions. People disagree about increase and decrease in belief. Scholars disagree about the increase and decrease in actions, taking different positions. One creedal position regarding this is that belief itself is one thing and affirmation (*taṣdīq*) is another thing. Together they form a single whole which does not increase once it is obtained, and of which nothing remains when it vanishes. So there is only increase and decrease in things connected to it rather than belief itself.

Another group of scholars believe that belief increases and decreases according to the actions which issue from it. This applies especially to many of the scholars who apply the term 'belief' to acts of obedience, going by the words of the Prophet ﷺ: 'Belief has over seventy branches. The best of which is the words: "There is no god but Allah," and the least of which is removing an obstruction from the road.' At-Tirmidhī transmitted it. Muslim added, 'Modesty is a branch of belief.' We find in the hadith of 'Alī, 'Belief appears like a white spot in the heart. Whenever belief increases, the spot increases.' Al-Aṣma'ī said that the word for 'spot', '*lumẓah*', is like a speck which is white. For instance a horse is '*almaẓ*' when it has some whiteness on its lower lip. Hadith scholars have '*lamẓah*', but in Arabic it is *lumẓah.*

This is evidence against those who deny that belief increases and decreases. Do you not see that he said, 'Whenever belief increases, the spot increases until the entire heart is white'? It is the same with hypocrisy. It appears as a black spot in the heart. Whenever hypocrisy increases, the heart blackens until it becomes entirely black.

Some of them said that faith is non-essential, not being fixed for two moments at a time, and it comes to the Prophets and righteous in an uninterrupted sequence. It increases by the frequency of its arrival in the heart of the believer and the constancy of its presence there. It decreases by consecutive periods of negligence in the heart of the believer. Abu-l-Ma'ālī indicated this. This understanding is found in the hadith of intercession, transmitted by Abū Sa'īd al-Khudrī in Muslim: 'The believers say, "Our Lord, they used to fast with us and pray and make *ḥajj*" They will be told, "Go and bring out those you know. It is forbidden for the Fire to touch their faces." They will bring out many people, some of whom are in the Fire up to the middle of their thighs and some who are in it up to their knees. Then they will say, "Our Lord, not one of those You commanded us to bring out remains in it." He will say, "Return and take out of it anyone in whose heart you find good equal to the weight of one dinar." They will bring out many people and then they will say, "Our Lord, we have not left in it anyone You commanded us to bring out." Then He will say, "Return and take out of it anyone in whose heart you find good equal to the weight of half a dinar." They will bring out many people and then they will say, "Our Lord, we have not left in it anyone You commanded us to bring out." Then He will say, "Return and take out of it anyone in whose heart you find even an atom's weight of good."'

It is said that what is meant in the hadith are actions of the heart, such as intention, sincerity, fear, counsel and the like. That is called 'belief' since they are located in belief or indicate it. This is the linguistic usage in Arabic. They call something by the name of the thing that it is near it or is a result of it. The evidence for this interpretation is what the Shāfi'īs say in reference to the time after all those with an atom's weight of good are removed from the Fire, when [as it says in the hadith] they said, 'We have not left any good in it at all,' even though Allah will later remove from it a lot of people who simply said, 'There is no god but Allah.' They are believers, and if they had not been believers, He would not have removed them from it.

If the first thing on which a likeness is based does not exist, then it cannot be subject to increase or decrease. That [increase/decrease] is determined in respect of movement. When Allah created a single knowledge and then created a similar knowledge or knowledges of known things along with it, then the first knowledge is increased. If Allah makes those similar knowledges cease to exist, then knowledge decreases, meaning that increase is removed. That is also the case when He creates a movement and creates concomitant movements.

Some scholars believe that the increase and decrease of belief is by way of proofs and so as a person increases in proofs they are said to increase in belief. That is why, according to one position, the Prophets are superior to others. They know about belief from many more angles than most people do. This position, however, does not follow what the *āyah* implies since it is not conceivable that there be an increase in belief through proofs in this instance.

Some people believe that belief increased through the revelation of obligations and reports in the period of the Prophet ﷺ and in learning of them after having been ignorant of them. This does constitute a kind of increase of belief and would make increase metaphorical. From this point of view, decrease is inconceivable, and this is in respect of knowledge. Allah knows best.

Allah is enough for us and the Best of Guardians.

'Enough' (*ḥasb*) is derived from *aḥsāb* which is sufficiency. A poet says:

She killed our house with curds and ghee.
    It is enough for you in being sated and quenched.

Al-Bukhārī reported from Ibn 'Abbās that this is also what Ibrāhīm said when he was thrown into the fire and Muḥammad ﷺ said it when people told him, 'The people have gathered against you.' Allah knows best.

فَانقَلَبُوا۟ بِنِعْمَةٍ مِّنَ ٱللَّهِ وَفَضْلٍ لَّمْ يَمْسَسْهُمْ سُوٓءٌ وَٱتَّبَعُوا۟ رِضْوَٰنَ ٱللَّهِ ۗ وَٱللَّهُ
ذُو فَضْلٍ عَظِيمٍ ﴿١٧٤﴾

174 So they returned with blessings and bounty from Allah and no evil touched them. They pursued the pleasure of Allah. Allah's favour is indeed immense.

Our scholars say that when they entrusted their affairs to Allah and relied with their hearts on Him, He repaid them with four things: blessing, favour, averting evil and following His pleasure, and so He was pleased with them and they with Him.

إِنَّمَا ذَٰلِكُمُ ٱلشَّيْطَٰنُ يُخَوِّفُ أَوْلِيَآءَهُۥ فَلَا تَخَافُوهُمْ وَخَافُونِ إِن كُنتُم
مُّؤْمِنِينَ ﴿١٧٥﴾

175 It was only Shayṭān frightening you through his friends. But do not fear them – fear Me if you are believers.

Ibn 'Abbās and others said, 'The meaning is "by means of his friends", in other words he frightens the believers by means of the unbelievers.' The genitive particle is omitted and the verb connected to the noun which is why it is in the accusative, as we also see in 18:2. He alarmed the believers by means of the unbelievers. As-Suddī and al-Ḥasan said, 'He frightened them through the hypocrites to make them not fight the idolaters.' As for the friends of Allah, they are not frightened when he tries to alarm them.

It is said that what is meant is that a human shayṭān, either Nu'aym ibn Mas'ūd or someone else, alarmed them with the number of the unbelievers. *'But do not fear them,'* means do not fear the unbelievers mentioned earlier, or it refers to the friends if you say that it means that Shayṭān makes his friends alarm you.

Allah says *'fear Me'* in respect of doing what He commands if you believe in His promise. The word 'fear' (*khawf*) in Arabic means dread. *Khāwafahu fa-khāfahu* is to vie to see which of then would have a greater fear of the other. *Khawfā'* is a waterless desert and a camel which is *khawfa'* is one with mange. *Khāfah* is like a leather bag used for collecting honey.

Sahl ibn 'Abdullāh said, 'Some of the truly sincere gathered to Ibrāhīm the Friend and asked, "What is fear?" He replied, "Not feeling safe until you reach the place of safety."' Sahl also said, 'Whenever ar-Rabī' ibn Khaytham passed by

Bukayr, he used to faint. 'Alī ibn Abī Ṭālib was told about that and said, "When that happens to him, inform me." That happened and they told him and he went to his hand inside his shirt and found his heart beating rapidly. He said, "I testify that this is the most fearful of the people of your time."'

The one who fears Allah fears that He will punish him, either in this world or the Next. That is why it is said that the fearful person is not the one who weeps and wipes his eyes; the fearful person is rather the one who abandons that for which he fears he will be punished. Allah has made it obligatory on His slaves to fear Him. He says: *'Fear Me if you are believers.'* He praises the believers for having fear: *'They fear their Lord above them.'* (16:50) The people of subtle indications say many things about fear which connect with what we have mentioned. Abū 'Alī ad-Daqqāq said, 'I visited Abū Bakr ibn Fūrak when he was ill. When he saw me, he wept and I said to him, "May Allah restore you and heal you." He said to him, "Do you think that I am afraid of death? I am afraid of what comes after death."'

We find in the *Sunan* of Ibn Mājah that Abū Dharr reported that the Messenger of Allah ﷺ said, 'I see what you do not see and I hear what you do not hear. Heaven moans and it has the right to moan. There is no place in it the width of four fingers without an angel placing his brow on it, prostrating to Allah Almighty. By Allah, if you knew what I know, you would laugh little and weep much and you would not enjoy women on your beds and you would go out to the streets seeking the help of Allah Almighty. I wish that I were a felled tree.' At-Tirmidhī transmitted it and said that it is a *ḥasan gharīb* hadith. It is related by another path that 'I wish that I were a felled tree' were Abu Dharr's words. Allah knows best.

وَلَا يَحْزُنكَ ٱلَّذِينَ يُسَٰرِعُونَ فِى ٱلْكُفْرِ إِنَّهُمْ لَن يَضُرُّوا۟ ٱللَّهَ شَيْـًٔا يُرِيدُ ٱللَّهُ
أَلَّا يَجْعَلَ لَهُمْ حَظًّا فِى ٱلْءَاخِرَةِ وَلَهُمْ عَذَابٌ عَظِيمٌ ﴿١٧٦﴾

176 Do not let those who rush headlong into unbelief sadden you. They do not harm Allah in any way. Allah desires to assign no portion to them in the Next World. They will have a terrible punishment.

Do not let those who rush headlong into unbelief sadden you.

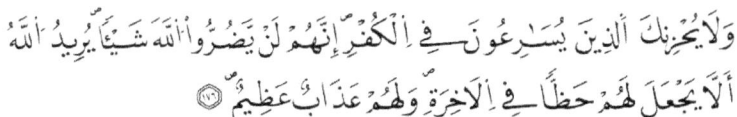

These are people who became Muslim and then apostatised out of fear of the idolaters. The Prophet ﷺ was saddened about them and Allah revealed this. Al-Kalbī said that it means the hypocrites and Jewish leaders who concealed the description of Prophet ﷺ in their Books and so this was revealed. It is said that it refers to the People of the Book when they did not believe. That was hard on the Messenger of Allah ﷺ because the people looked to them and said that they were the People of the Book and that if he what he said had been true, they would have followed him. So this was revealed.

Nāfi' reads this as *'yuḥzinuka'* (Form IV, to make sad) as he does throughout the Qur'an except in *al-Anbiyā'* (21:103) where he has *'yaḥzunuka'*. Abū Ja'far has the opposite. Ibn Muḥayṣin recited in all *'yuḥzinuka'* while the rest read it *'yaḥzunika'*. They are two dialects: *ḥazana, yaḥzunu*, and *aḥzana*, which is a rare dialectical form, but, according to an-Naḥḥās, the first is the more eloquent of the two. A poet said about *aḥzana*:

My companions have gone, and the houses sadden me.

Most recite 'rush' as *'yusāri'ūna'* and Ṭalḥah recited *'yusri'ūna'*.

Aḍ-Ḍaḥḥāk said that they are the unbelievers of Quraysh and others say that they are the hypocrites. It is said that it is those mentioned before, and it is said that it is all unbelievers and their rushing into disbelief to work against Muḥammad ﷺ.

Al-Qushayrī said, 'Sorrow over the disbelief of the unbeliever is a type of obedience, but the Prophet ﷺ had excessive sorrow over the disbelief of his people and was forbidden that: *'So do not let yourself waste away out of regret for them."* (35:8) and *'Perhaps you may destroy yourself with grief, chasing after them, if they do not believe in these words.'* (18:6)

They do not harm Allah in any way.

They will not diminish the kingdom of Allah and His power in any way by their disbelief. It is related by Abū Dharr that the Prophet ﷺ said in what He related from what Allah the Blessed and Almighty said: 'O My slaves! I have forbidden injustice to Myself and I have made it unlawful between you, so do not wrong one another. O My slaves! All of you are misguided except those that I guide, so seek My guidance and I will guide you. O My slaves! All of you are hungry except those that I feed so ask me for food and I will feed you. O My slaves! All of you are naked except those that I clothe so ask me for clothing and I will clothe you. O My slaves! You make mistakes by night and by day and I forgive all wrong actions so ask for My forgiveness and I will forgive you. O My slaves! You will never attain to My harm so as to be able to harm Me and you will never attain to My benefit so as to be able benefit Me. O My slaves! If the first and last of you, all the jinn and all the men among you, possessed the heart of the most godfearing man among you, that would not increase My kingdom in any way. O My slaves! If the first and last of you, all the jinn and all the men among you, possessed the heart of the most evil man among you, that would not decrease My kingdom in any way. O My slaves! If the first and last of you, all the jinn and all the men among you, were to stand in a single place and ask of Me, I could give to every man what he asks without that decreasing what I have any more than a needle when it enters the sea. O My slaves! It is your actions for which I call you to account and then repay you in full. So anyone who finds good should praise Allah and anyone who finds something else should blame none but himself.' It is transmitted by Muslim in the *Ṣaḥīḥ*, at-Tirmidhī and others. It is an immense hadith. It is said that the meaning is: 'You will not harm the friends of Allah when they relinquish their help since Allah is their Helper.'

Allah desires to assign no portion to them in the Next World.

Ḥaẓẓ (*portion*) is a share and fortune. You say that someone is more fortunate (*aḥaẓẓ*) than another and he is *maḥẓūẓ* or fortunate. The plural of *ḥaẓẓ* is *aḥāẓẓ*. Abū Zayd said that a man who is described as *ḥaẓīẓ* is fortunate since he has a portion of provision. The verb *ḥaẓẓa* is to be fortunate in something. Sometimes the plural is *aḥuẓẓ*. Allah means that He will not assign them a portion in the Garden. This is a text which illustrates that good and evil are subject to Allah's will.

إِنَّ الَّذِينَ اشْتَرَوُا الْكُفْرَ بِالْإِيمَانِ لَن يَضُرُّوا اللَّهَ شَيْئًا وَلَهُمْ عَذَابٌ أَلِيمٌ ١٧٧

177 Those who sell belief for unbelief do not harm Allah in any way.

Those who sell belief for disbelief were already mentioned in *al-Baqarah*. *'They do not harm Allah in any way'* is repetition for stress. It is said that part of bad management is to exchange belief for disbelief and sell the one for the other. '*Shay*'' is in the accusative in both places since it is in the position of a verbal noun. It is as if Allah were saying: they will not harm Allah either a little or a lot. It can also be in the accusative by the elision of an implied *bā'*, as if He were saying: it will not harm Allah at all.

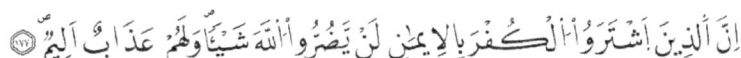

وَلَا يَحْسَبَنَّ ٱلَّذِينَ كَفَرُوٓا۟ أَنَّمَا نُمْلِى لَهُمْ خَيْرٌ لِّأَنفُسِهِمْ ۚ إِنَّمَا نُمْلِى لَهُمْ
لِيَزْدَادُوٓا۟ إِثْمًا ۚ وَلَهُمْ عَذَابٌ مُّهِينٌ ﴿١٧٨﴾

178 Those who disbelieve should not imagine that the extra time We grant to them is good for them. We only allow them more time so they will increase in evildoing. They will have a humiliating punishment.

This refers to His granting them a long life and luxury. It means: 'Those who alarm the Muslims should not imagine that Allah does not have the power to destroy them. They are given a long life so that they can disobey Allah, not because it is good for them.' It is said to mean: 'The extra time We have given them in the form of the victory at Uḥud is not good for them. That is just in order to increase their punishment.'

It is related that Ibn Mas'ūd said, 'There is no one, either good or bad, but that death is not better for him. If he is good, Allah says: "*What is with Allah is better for those who are truly good*" (3:198), and if he is bad, Allah says: "*We only allow them more time so they will increase in evildoing.*"'

Ibn 'Āmir and 'Āṣim read 'imagine' as '*yaḥsibanna*' whereas Ḥamzah reads it as '*taḥsabanna*' and the rest read it as '*yaḥsabanna*'. If it is read with *yā'*, '*those*' is the subject and it means, 'the unbelievers should not imagine,' and 'the extra time We grant to them' takes the place of two objects and '*mā'* means 'which' and the pronoun is elided. '*Better'* is the predicate of '*anna'*, and it is also possible to assume that *mā'* and the verb are verbal nouns and implies: 'those who disbelieve should not imagine that Our granting them a deferral is good for them'.

If it is read with a *tā'*, then the subject is the second person, who is Muḥammad ﷺ, and '*those*' is in the accusative based on the first object of '*imagine*' and what follows it is an appositive for '*those*' and takes the place of two objects as it would do if it were an appositive. It is not proper for '*an'* and what follows it to be a second object of '*imagine*' because the second object in this area is the first in meaning because '*ḥasiba'* and its sisters are added to the inchoative and the predicate, meaning 'you should not imagine that the extra time We grant them is good.' This is the view of az-Zajjāj.

Abū 'Alī said, 'If this is sound, then "*good*" would be in the accusative because "*anna*" would become an appositive for "those who disbelieve", and so it would be as if Allah were saying, "Do not imagine that the deferral of those who disbelieve is good for them." So His word "*good*" is the second object of "*imagine*". It is not permitted to recite it with *tā'* unless it is "*inna*" with a *kasrah* and "*good'* is in the accusative. That is not related from Ḥamzah. The reading from Ḥamzah has a *tā'* and so this reading is not sound.'

Al-Farrā' and al-Kisā'ī said, 'The reading of Ḥamzah is permitted for repetition. It implies: "Do not imagine that those who disbelieve, do not imagine that the deferral We grant them is good." So "*anna*" takes the place of two objects by the second "imagine". It acts as a second object of the first "*imagine*".' Al-Qushayrī said, 'This is close to what az-Zajjāj mentioned about the claim of the appositive, and the reading is sound and Abū 'Alī aimed to be harsh to az-Zajjāj.' An-Naḥḥās said, 'Abū Ḥātim claimed the recitation by Ḥamzah here and in 3:180 is poor Arabic. This is not permitted and a group corroborate him in that.'

Yahyā ibn Waththāb recited '*innamā*' and '*inna*', both with a *kasrah.* Abū Ja'far said, 'Yaḥyā's reading is good.' Abū Ḥātim said, 'I heard al-Akhfash mentioned that the *kasrah* of "*inna*" is used by the Qadariyyah as an argument and they make it entail a change in word order: "Those who disbelieve should not imagine that We give them more time so that they can increase in evildoing. Giving them a deferral is good for them."' He said, 'I saw in a copy of the Qur'an in the General Mosque in which a mode (*ḥarf*) had been added which said: "*innāmā numlī lahum [li-yazdādū] imānan.*" Ya'qūb al-Qāri' looked at it and the incorrect usage was clear and he scratched it out.'

This *āyah* is a text invalidating the position of the Qadariyyah because it reports that Allah extends their lives so that their unbelief will increase by their committing acts of disobedience to Allah and this occurs sequentially in the heart as is clear in respect of its opposite which is belief. Ibn 'Abbās said, 'There is no one who is pious or impious but that death is better for him.' Then he recited: *'We only allow them more time so that they will increase in evildoing'* and he recited: *'What is with Allah is better for those who are truly good.'* (3:198) Razīn transmitted it.

مَّا كَانَ ٱللَّهُ لِيَذَرَ ٱلْمُؤْمِنِينَ عَلَىٰ مَآ أَنتُمْ عَلَيْهِ حَتَّىٰ يَمِيزَ ٱلْخَبِيثَ مِنَ ٱلطَّيِّبِ ۗ
وَمَا كَانَ ٱللَّهُ لِيُطْلِعَكُمْ عَلَى ٱلْغَيْبِ وَلَٰكِنَّ ٱللَّهَ يَجْتَبِى مِن رُّسُلِهِۦ مَن
يَشَآءُ ۖ فَـَٔامِنُوا۟ بِٱللَّهِ وَرُسُلِهِۦ ۚ وَإِن تُؤْمِنُوا۟ وَتَتَّقُوا۟ فَلَكُمْ أَجْرٌ
عَظِيمٌ ﴿١٧٩﴾

179 Allah will only leave the believers in the position you now are in so that He can sift out the rotten from the good. Allah has not given you access to the Unseen. But Allah chooses those of His Messengers whom He wills. So believe in Allah and His Messengers. If you believe and are godfearing you will have an immense reward.

Allah will only leave the believers in the position you now are in so that He can sift out the rotten from the good. Allah has not given you access to the Unseen.

Abu-l-'Āliyah said, 'The believers asked to be given a sign by which a believer could be distinguished from a hypocrite and so Allah revealed: *"Allah will only leave the believers in the position you now are in ..."*' There is disagreement about who is addressed by this *āyah*. Ibn 'Abbās, aḍ-Ḍaḥḥāk, Muqātil, al-Kalbī and most commentators say that it is addressed to the unbelievers and hypocrites, implying, 'Allah would not leave the believers in the position you are in of disbelief, hypocrisy and enmity to the Prophet ﷺ.'

Al-Kalbī said, 'Some Quraysh from the people of Makkah said to the Prophet ﷺ, "You claim that one of our men is in the Fire. If he leaves our *dīn* and follows yours, you say that he is one of the people of the Garden. So tell us who this one is. Tell us which of us will come to you and who will not come." So Allah revealed: *"Allah will only leave the believers in the position you now are in"* of disbelief and hypocrisy *"so that He can sift out the rotten from the good."*'

It is said that it is addressed to the idolaters and that what is meant by the 'believers' are those still to be born who will believe, meaning that Allah would not leave children who will believe in the *shirk* you espouse until He has distinguished between you and them. If this is true, then *'Allah has not given'* is a new sentence. That is the position of Ibn 'Abbās and most commentators.

It is said that it is addressed to the believers, i.e. 'Allah would not leave you, O believers, in the position you are in where the believer is muddled with the hypocrites until he sifts you out through trial and responsibility so that you will recognise the rotten hypocrite from the good believer.' The two groups were sifted at Uḥud. This is the position of most of the people of meanings.

This is addressed to the believers, meaning, 'Allah would not single out the hypocrites for you so that you recognise them, but He helps you in that through responsibility and trial.' That was made clear at Uḥud. The hypocrites stayed behind and displayed malice. 'You did not know this Unseen reality before this happened. Now Allah has acquainted Muḥammad ﷺ with that.'

It is said that the words *'give you access'* mean Allah would not inform you of what will happen with them, and so this would be connected to what was before and is not a new sentence. That is because when the unbelievers said, 'Why has nothing been revealed to us?' Allah said: *'Allah has not given you access to the Unseen,'* in other words to the one whom [they think] deserves Prophethood so that revelation would be by their choice.

Allah chooses whomever He wishes to receive access to His Unseen. The verb for 'giving access' is *ṭala'a* and *iṭṭala'a* which is transitive. The verb used for 'sifting out' is recited as *'yumayyizu'* from Form II. It is also recited like that in *al-Anfāl* and it is the reading of Ḥamzah. The rest have *yamīzu* from Form I of *māza, yamīzu*. One says, *'miztu'* to separate one part of a thing from another, with the verbal noun *mayz*, and Form II with the verbal noun *tamyīz*. Abū Mu'ādh said, '"*Miztu'ash-shay*" means "I divided it into two." When it is into several parts, then you say, "*mayyaztuhā tamyīzan*". Similarly when you make one into two, you say, "*faraqtu baynahumā*". An example of that is the parting (*faraq*) of the hair. When you split something into several things, you say, "*farraqtuhu tafrīqan*."' An aspect of it is sifting (*imtāza*) people from one another. We also see its use in the *āyah*: *'It all but bursts with rage'* (67:8): *'yakādu yatamayyaza,'* meaning almost bursts apart. We also see in a report: 'If someone removes (*māza*) something harmful from the road, it is *ṣadaqah* for him.'

So believe in Allah and His Messengers.

It is said that when the unbelievers asked the Messenger of Allah ﷺ to make it clear to them who were believers, Allah revealed this. It means: 'Do not be occupied with what does not concern you. Be occupied with what concerns you, which is belief.' *'Believe'* means to affirm the truth, not to seek for the Unseen. *'The immense reward'* is the Garden.

It is reported that an astrologer was with al-Ḥajjāj ibn Yusūf and al-Ḥajjāj took some pebbles in his hand and, knowing how many they were, asked the astrologer, 'How many pebbles are in my hand?' He guessed and was right. Al-Ḥajjāj ignored him and took some pebbles which he had not counted and asked the astrologer, 'How many are in my hand?' He guessed and was wrong. Then he guessed again and was wrong. He said, 'Governor, I think that you do not know how many are in your hand.' 'No, I don't' he replied and then asked, 'So what is the difference between this and that?' He said, 'You counted the first one and so it was not an unseen matter. I guessed and was right. The number this time was unknown, and so it was unseen matter and only Allah Almighty knows the Unseen.' This will be further discussed in *al-An'ām*.

وَلَا يَحْسَبَنَّ ٱلَّذِينَ يَبْخَلُونَ بِمَآ ءَاتَىٰهُمُ ٱللَّهُ مِن فَضْلِهِۦ هُوَ خَيْرًا لَّهُم بَلْ هُوَ
شَرٌّ لَّهُمْ سَيُطَوَّقُونَ مَا بَخِلُوا۟ بِهِۦ يَوْمَ ٱلْقِيَٰمَةِ وَلِلَّهِ مِيرَٰثُ ٱلسَّمَٰوَٰتِ وَٱلْأَرْضِ
وَٱللَّهُ بِمَا تَعْمَلُونَ خَبِيرٌ ١٨٠

180 Those who are tight-fisted with the bounty Allah has given them should not suppose that that is better for them. No indeed, it is worse for them! What they were tight-fisted with will be hung around their necks on the Day of Rising. Allah is the inheritor of the heavens and the earth and Allah is aware of what you do.

Those who are tight-fisted with the bounty Allah has given them should not suppose that that is better for them.

'*Those*' is in the nominative and the first object is elided. Al-Khalīl, Sībawayh and al-Farrā' said that it means: 'They think miserliness is better for them,' meaning: 'The tight-fisted should not suppose that miserliness is better for them.' There is elision because 'miserliness' is indicated. This is common usage in Arabic. [POEM] As for the reading of Ḥamzah, it is very unlikely according to an-Naḥḥās. It is also possible that it means 'Do not suppose the miserliness of the tight-fisted is better for them.' Az-Zajjāj said, 'It is like "*Ask the town*" (12:82).' The pronoun '*huwa*' in '*it is better for them*' is separating according to the Basrans but is a disconnected pronoun according to the Kufans. An-Naḥḥās said that in Arabic it can be an inceptive and predicate.

It is worse for them. What they were tight-fisted with will be hung around their necks on the Day of Rising.

Miserliness is worse for them. The *sīn* of the future tense in '*will be hung*' is a threat. Al-Mubarrad said that. This *āyah* was revealed about miserliness in respect of wealth and spending in the Way of Allah and not paying the obligatory *zakāt*. This is like Allah's words: '*They do not spend it in the way of Allah.*' (9:34) A group of interpreters, including Ibn Mas'ūd, Ibn 'Abbās, Abū Wā'il, Abū Mālik, as-Suddī and ash-Sha'bī, said, 'The meaning of *"what they were tight-fisted with will be hung around their necks"* is that which is reported in hadith from Abū Hurayrah in which the Prophet ﷺ said, "If someone is given wealth by Allah and does not pay the *zakāt* due on it, on the Day of Rising it will take on the likeness of [a poisonous snake] with two spots which will coil about his neck under his ears on the Day of Rising, saying, 'I am your wealth. I am your treasure.'" Then he recited this *āyah.*' An-Nasā'ī transmitted it.

Ibn Mājah transmitted from Ibn Mas'ūd that the Messenger of Allah ﷺ said, 'If someone does not pay the *zakāt* due on his wealth, on the Day of Rising it will take on the likeness of [a poisonous snake] with two spots which will coil about his neck.' He said, 'Then the Prophet ﷺ recited an *āyah* confirming this in the Book of Allah Almighty: "*Those who are tight-fisted with the bounty Allah has given them should not suppose that that is better for them.*"' It is reported from the Prophet ﷺ: 'There is no one who has a relative who comes to him and asks him for some of the surplus wealth he has and then he is miserly towards him, but that on the Day of Rising a serpent of fire will be brought to him, smacking its lips, and wrapped around his neck.'

Ibn 'Abbās said, 'This *āyah* was revealed about the People of the Book and their miserliness in clarifying what they knew about Muḥammad ﷺ.' Mujāhid and a group of the people of knowledge said that. According to this interpretation, the words '*hung about their necks*' indicate the punishment for their miserliness. It comes from *ṭāqah* (ability) as the Almighty says: *'For those who are able to fast'* (2:184), but this is not part of ability. Ibrāhīm an-Nakha'ī said that on the Day of Rising Allah will give them a collar of fire. This coincides with the first interpretation which is the view of as-Suddī. It is said that their actions will cling to them as a collar clings to the neck. The ring of a dove is used metaphorically to denote this adhesion. Allah Almighty says: *'We have hastened the destiny of every man around his neck.'* (17:13) An example illustrating this is found in the words of 'Abdullāh ibn Jaḥsh to Abū Sufyān:

Convey to Abū Sufyan that he will come to regret the outcome of a matter.
You sold the house of your cousin to settle the debt you owed.

Your ally by Allah, the Lord of people, swears a strong oath:
Take it! Take it! Your treachery will cling to you like the ring of a dove!

This follows the second interpretation. Linguistically, *bukhl* (miserliness) is that person withholds a right he owes to another. The one who withholds what he is not obliged to give is not a miser because he is not censured for that. The people of the Hijaz say: *yabkhulūna*, *bakhulū* while the rest of the Arabs say: *yabkhalūna*, *bakhilū*. An-Naḥḥās related that.

An example of the result of miserliness is what is related of the Prophet ﷺ saying to the Anṣār, 'Who is your master?' They answered, 'Al-Jadd ibn Qays in spite of his miserliness.' He said, 'What illness could be worse than miserliness?' 'How is that, Messenger of Allah?' they asked. He said ﷺ, 'A people lived by the coast and, because of their miserliness, disliked guests staying there. They said, "Let our men be far from the women so that the men can use the distance of the women as an excuse for not receiving guests and the women can use the distance of the men as an excuse." They did that for a long time and so the men became involved with one another and the women with one another.' Al-Māwardī mentioned it in *Kitāb adab ad-dunyā wa'd-dīn*. Allah knows best.

There is disagreement about whether miserliness (*bukhl*) and avarice (*shaḥḥ*) are the same thing. It is said that miserliness is refusing to give what you have and avarice is desiring to obtain what you do not have. Avarice is miserliness coupled with greed. That is sound based on what Muslim transmits from Jābir ibn 'Abdullāh that the Messenger of Allah ﷺ said, 'Beware of injustice. Injustice will be darkness on the Day of Rising. Beware of avarice. Avarice destroyed those before you and prompted them to shed each other's blood and make lawful what was unlawful.' This refutes the idea of miserliness being refusing to give what is obligatory and avarice being refusing to give what is recommended, because if avarice had been refusing to give what is recommended, it would not have merited such a severe threat and strong censure about being the destruction of this world and the Next. This is supported by what an-Nasā'ī reported from Abū Hurayrah who reported that the Prophet ﷺ said, 'Dust in the Way of Allah will never be joined with the smoke of Hellfire in the nostrils of a Muslim man. Avarice and belief are never joined together in the heart of a Muslim man.' This indicates that avarice is more strongly censured than miserliness although there is something reported which indicates that they are the same: the words of the Prophet ﷺ who was asked, 'Is the believer miserly?' 'No,' he replied. Al-Māwardī related in *Kitāb adab ad-dunyā wa'd-dīn* that the Prophet ﷺ asked the Anṣār, 'Who is your master?' They answered, 'Al-Jadd ibn Qays in spite of his miserliness.'

Allah is the inheritor of the heavens and the earth.

Allah tells us about His going on and the eternal nature of His Kingdom and that He is after time as He was before time, free of any need of the universe. He will inherit the earth after the annihilation of His creation and departure of their kingdoms when there is no one left to claim their wealth. This is a reference to customary practice in human inheritance and this is not what actually happens because the heir is the one who inherits what he did not own before whereas Allah is, in any case, the Owner of the heavens and the earth and what is between them, the heavens and what is in them, and the earth and what is in it. Property and wealth are in reality merely loaned to their owners in this world and, when they die, return to their original Owner. It is also like the *āyah*: *'It is We who will inherit the earth and all those on it.'* (19:40) In both *āyahs* Allah Almighty commanded His servants to spend and not to be miserly before they die and leave that to be inherited by Allah Almighty. They only benefit from what they spend.

لَّقَدْ سَمِعَ ٱللَّهُ قَوْلَ ٱلَّذِينَ قَالُوٓا۟ إِنَّ ٱللَّهَ فَقِيرٌ وَنَحْنُ أَغْنِيَآءُ ۘ سَنَكْتُبُ مَا قَالُوا۟ وَقَتْلَهُمُ
ٱلْأَنۢبِيَآءَ بِغَيْرِ حَقٍّ وَنَقُولُ ذُوقُوا۟ عَذَابَ ٱلْحَرِيقِ ﴿١٨١﴾ ذَٰلِكَ بِمَا قَدَّمَتْ
أَيْدِيكُمْ وَأَنَّ ٱللَّهَ لَيْسَ بِظَلَّٰمٍ لِّلْعَبِيدِ ﴿١٨٢﴾

181 Allah has heard the words of those who say, 'Allah is poor and we are rich.' We will write down what they said and their killing of the Prophets without any right to do so and We will say, 'Taste the punishment of the Burning.' 182 That is on account of what you did. Allah does not wrong His slaves.

Allah has heard the words of those who say, 'Allah is poor and we are rich.'

Allah mentions here the ugly words of the unbelievers, especially the Jews. Commentators say that when Allah revealed: *'Is there anyone who will make Allah a generous loan?'* (2:245), some of the Jews, including Ḥuyayy ibn Akhṭab according to al-Ḥasan, and Finḥāṣ ibn 'Āzūrā' according to 'Ikrimah and others, said, 'Allah is poor and we are rich since He borrows from us.' They said this to confuse those who were weak, not because they believed it, because they were People of the Book. But in saying this they asserted disbelief because they wanted to cause doubt in the weak among them and among the believers and to deny the Prophet ﷺ. 'He is poor according to what Muḥammad ﷺ says, since He borrows from us.'

We will write down what they said

This means 'We will repay them for it.' It is said, 'We will record it in the records of their deeds,' in other words command the Guardian Angels to confirm what they said on the Day of Rising when they read what is in these books so that it will be evidence against them. It is like Allah's words: *'We are writing it down.'* (21:94) It is said that what is meant by writing is remembering, meaning 'We will remember what they said and repay them.' The *mā* in *'mā qālū'* is in the accusative by the action of 'write'. Al-A'mash and Ḥamzah recite *'sa-yuktabu'* ('what they said will be written down') and so *mā* is a passive subject. Ḥamzah thought that based on the reading of Ibn Mas'ūd: *'yuqālu'* (it will be said).

their killing of the Prophets without any right to do so.

We will also record their killing of the Prophets, in other words their approval of their being killed. What is being referred to is their ancestors killing of the Prophets, but they were pleased with that and so it was also ascribed to them. A man commended the killing of 'Uthmān in the presence of ash-Sha'bī and ash-Sha'bī told him, 'You have shared in his murder.' He made approval tantamount to actual killing.

This is a very serious matter since approval of disobedience is also disobedience. Abū Dāwūd reported from al-'Urs ibn 'Umayra al-Kindī that the Prophet ﷺ said, 'When you do something wrong on the earth, those who witness but dislike it – or object to it – are like the one who is absent from it. Those who are absent from it but approve of it are like those who are present.' This is a text. The meaning of the expression *'without any right'* was discussed in *al-Baqarah.*

We will say, 'Taste the punishment of the Burning.'

This will be said to them in Hellfire, or at their deaths, or at the Reckoning. The words are spoken by Allah or by the angels. The reading of Ibn Mas'ūd is *'yuqālu'*. *'Burning'* is a name for the blazing of the Fire. The 'Fire' includes that which is actually blazing and that which is not.

That is on account of what you did. (lit. 'what your hands sent ahead)

That punishment is for your prior wrong actions. The use of the word *'hands'* here indicates their personally undertaking the action since it ascribes it directly to the person doing it. An action can be ascribed to a person when he orders it to be done as in 28:4. The root of *'aydīkum'* is *'aydyukum'* and the *ḍammah* is elided because it is heavy. Allah knows best.

ٱلَّذِينَ قَالُوٓا۟ إِنَّ ٱللَّهَ عَهِدَ إِلَيْنَآ أَلَّا نُومِنَ لِرَسُولٍ حَتَّىٰ يَاتِيَنَا بِقُرْبَانٍ
تَاكُلُهُ ٱلنَّارُ قُلْ قَدْ جَآءَكُمْ رُسُلٌ مِّن قَبْلِي بِٱلْبَيِّنَٰتِ وَبِٱلَّذِي قُلْتُمْ
فَلِمَ قَتَلْتُمُوهُمْ إِن كُنتُمْ صَٰدِقِينَ ﴿١٨٣﴾ فَإِن كَذَّبُوكَ فَقَدْ كُذِّبَ رُسُلٌ
مِّن قَبْلِكَ جَآءُو بِٱلْبَيِّنَٰتِ وَٱلزُّبُرِ وَٱلْكِتَٰبِ ٱلْمُنِيرِ ﴿١٨٤﴾

183 Those who say, 'Allah has made a contract with us that we should not believe in any Messenger until he brings us a sacrifice consumed by fire.' Say, 'Messengers came to you before me with the Clear Signs and with what you say. So why did you kill them if you are telling the truth?' 184 If they deny you, Messengers before you were also denied, who brought the Clear Signs and written texts and the illuminating Book.

Those who say, 'Allah has made a contract with us that we should not believe in any Messenger until he brings us a sacrifice consumed by fire.'

'Those' is in the genitive as an appositive for *'those who say'* in the previous *āyah* or as an adjective of 'slaves' or the predicate of an inceptive meaning: 'they are those who say'.

Al-Kalbī and others said that it was revealed about Ka'b ibn al-Ashraf, Mālik ibn aṣ-Ṣayf, Wahb ibn Yahūdhā, Finḥāṣ ibn 'Āzūrā' and a group who came to the Prophet ﷺ and said to him, 'So you claim that Allah has sent you to us when He revealed to us a Book in which He made a contract with us that we should not believe in any Messenger until he brings us a sacrifice consumed by fire. If you bring that, then we will believe you.' Then Allah revealed this. It is said that this is in the Torah, but the Word was complete when both the Messiah and Muḥammad came to them. When they came to them, then they should believe in them without such a sacrifice.

It is said that the matter of that kind of sacrifice was established until it was abrogated by 'Īsā. Among them, a Prophet used to sacrifice and pray. A roaring smokeless white fire would descend and consume the sacrifice. This is what the Jews claimed, while concealing its abrogation. In holding to this, they were harassing the Prophet ﷺ. The miracles of the Prophet ﷺ were a definitive proof to invalidate their claim. It was the same with the miracles of 'Īsā. If his truthfulness is mandatory, then it is mandatory to affirm him. Then Allah established the proof against them.

Say, 'Messengers came to you before me with the Clear Signs and with what you say. So why did you kill them if you are telling the truth?'

This is addressed to Muḥammad and *'to you'* refers to the Jews. The *'Clear Signs'* the Prophets brought them were the sacrifices, but in spite of that they killed many of them, such as Zakariyyā, Yaḥyā, Shu'ayb, and the rest of the Prophets who were killed and not believed in. That, of course, refers to what their ancestors did.

This is the *āyah* which ash-Sha'bī recited and used as evidence against the one who commended the murder of 'Uthmān as we stated. Allah calls these Jews 'killers' because they approved of what their ancestors had done, even though there was about seven hundred years between them. *'Qurbān'* (sacrifice) is a practice by which one draws near to Allah, such as *ṣadaqah* and other righteous actions. It has the form *fu'lān* from the basis of *qurbah*. It can be a noun like *sulṭān* and *burhān* (proof), or a verbal noun like *'udwān* (aggression) and *khusrān* (loss). 'Īsā ibn 'Umar used to recite *'qurubān'*, following the *ḍammah* on the *qāf* as the plural of *ẓulmah* is *ẓulumāt* and that of *ḥujrah* is *ḥujurāt*.

If they deny you, Messengers before you were also denied, who brought the Clear Signs and written texts and the illuminating Book.

'Clear Signs' are proofs. *'Zubur'* are written texts. *Mazbūrah* means 'written'. *'Zubur'* is the plural of *zabūr* which is a book. The root of *zabara* means 'to write'. Every *zabūr* is a book. Imru'u-l-Qays said:

Whose are the remnants I see which grieve me,
like the writing of a book (*zabūr*) on Yamānī bark?

'I recognize my *tazbirah*', refers to handwriting. It is also said that it is derived from *zabr*, meaning to chide. The verb *zabara* can also mean to encircle a well with stones.

Ibn 'Āmir recited *'bi-z-zuburi wa bi-l-kitāb'* with two extra *bā*'s in both words. It is like that in the Syrian copies of the Qur'an.

'The Illuminating Book' is a book that is clear in itself and also makes things clear, from the verb *anāra, yunīru*. Form II and Form X are used as well as Form IV to mean the same. Each of them is intransitive and transitive. Allah combines *zubur* and *kitāb* which mean the same. We have already mentioned the root meaning of *kitāb*.

كُلُّ نَفْسٍ ذَآئِقَةُ ٱلْمَوْتِ وَإِنَّمَا تُوَفَّوْنَ أُجُورَكُمْ يَوْمَ ٱلْقِيَٰمَةِ فَمَن زُحْزِحَ عَنِ ٱلنَّارِ
وَأُدْخِلَ ٱلْجَنَّةَ فَقَدْ فَازَ وَمَا ٱلْحَيَوٰةُ ٱلدُّنْيَآ إِلَّا مَتَٰعُ ٱلْغُرُورِ ١٨٥

185 Every self will taste death. You will be paid your wages in full on the Day of Rising. Anyone who is distanced from the Fire and admitted to the Garden has triumphed. The life of this world is just the enjoyment of delusion.

Allah told us about the misers and their disbelief when they said, 'Allah is poor and we are rich,' and then commanded the believers to be steadfast in the face of their injury. In the next *āyah* He tells them: *'You will be tested,'* and thus makes it clear that this world will end and not continue. The duration of this world is brief and the Day of Rising is the Day of Repayment.

Every self will taste death.

Everyone will taste death because it is unavoidable for the living as Umayyah ibn Abī'ṣ-Ṣalt said:

Whoever does not die in the bloom of life dies decrepit.
Death is a cup from which everyone must drink.

Another said:

Death is a door which everyone must enter.
Would that I knew which Abode lies beyond the door!

The general reading is *'dhā'iqatu-l-mawti'* with *iḍāfah* while al-Aʿmash and Ibn Abī Isḥāq read *'dhā'iqatun al-mawta'* with *tanwīn* and '*mawt*' in the accusative. They said that that is because it has not been tasted yet. That is because there are two types of active participle. One indicates the past and the other the future. If it is the first, then it is only in *iḍāfah* with what follows it, as when you say, 'This one hit Zayd yesterday and killed Bakr yesterday' because it acts as an inert noun, which is knowledge like 'The slave of Zayd' and 'the companion of Bakr.' [POEM] If it is the second, then it is permitted to have the genitive, accusative and *tanwīn* because it acts like a present verb. If the verb is not transitive, it is not transitive, like '*qā'iumun Zaydun*'. If it is transitive, you make it transitive and it takes the accusative like '*Zaydun ḥārib ʿAmran.*' It is also permitted to elide the *tanwīn* and the *iḍāfah* is lighter. [POEM] We also see the same usage in 39:38.

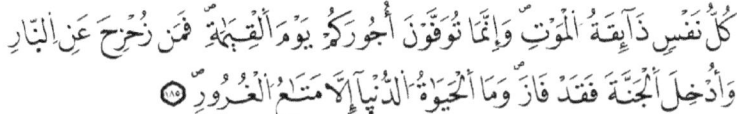

Know that death has causes and signs. One of the signs of the death of the believers is the sweat of the brow. An-Nasā'ī reported that Buraydah heard the Messenger of Allah ﷺ say, 'The believer dies with sweat on his brow.' We explained it in *at-Tadhkirah*.

When he is dying, he is told to say the *shahādah* since the Prophet ﷺ said, 'Instruct your dying to say, "There is no god but Allah"' so that it is his last words and his life is sealed with the *shahādah*. It should not be repeated to him so that he does not become irritated.

It is recommended to recite *Sūrat Yāsīn* based on the words of the Prophet ﷺ, 'Recite *Yāsīn* over your dying.' Abū Dāwūd transmitted it. Al-Ajurrī mentioned in the *Book of Advice* from Umm ad-Dardā' that the Prophet ﷺ said, 'There is no dying person who has *Sūrat Yāsīn* recited to him without death being easy for him.' In death the eyes follow the spirit, as is reported in *Ṣaḥīḥ Muslim*. Acts of worship and responsibility are removed. Rulings are then addressed to the living, some of which are not properly esteemed. His righteous brothers are informed about his death. Some people dislike that and say that it is tantamount to a death announcement which is disliked. The first view is sounder and we have elucidated it elsewhere. Another thing that is done is preparation of the dead person by washing and burial of them before any putrefaction occurs. The Prophet ﷺ said to some people who delayed burying their dead, 'Hurry to bury your dead' and he said ﷺ, 'Hurry to perform the funeral prayer.'

It is *sunnah* for the Muslims to wash all their dead except for martyrs. It is said that it is mandatory to wash them as well as Qāḍī 'Abd al-Wahhāb said. The first is the position of the Book. There are scholars who hold both views. The reason for the disagreement is what the Prophet ﷺ said to Umm 'Aṭiyyah about washing his daughter Zaynab, as in *Muslim*, or Umm Kulthūm as in Abū Dāwūd: 'Wash her three or five or more if you think that is necessary.' That is the basis of scholars for washing the dead. It is said that what is meant is the command to wash and it is said that what is meant is clarification of the ruling about washing and that it is mandatory. It is said that what is meant is instructing how that washing should be done and there is nothing in it which indicates that it is mandatory. They said that this is indicated by his words ﷺ, 'if you think'. This would imply that the literal meaning is not a mandatory command because it is left to their view. They are told, 'This is highly unlikely because the words "if you think" refer to a command, not to understanding. There is merely choice concerning the number of times.'

There is no disagreement that washing the dead is prescribed and acting on it is the Sharī'ah. It is not abandoned. It is done like the *ghusl* for *janābah*. The dead person is not washed more than seven times by consensus as Abū 'Umar related.

If something emerges from the corpse after the seventh time, only the place of emergence is washed. The ruling is the same as that of someone in *janābah* when he breaks *wuḍū'* after his *ghusl*.

The dead person is shrouded after they are washed. Shrouding is mandatory according to the generality of the Muslims. If they have money, the cost of the shroud is taken from the main part of their wealth according to most scholars, except for Ṭāwus who says that it is taken from the remaining third of their wealth, large or small. If the deceased was someone who had to be supported in his life – by a master, if it is a slave, or by a father, husband or son in other cases – there is agreement that, in the case of a slave, the master must pay, but there is disagreement about the husband, father and son. If there is no one, then it is up to the Muslim Treasury or the community of Muslims as a whole to provide what is needed.

The specific individual obligation is that the private parts must be covered. If more is available, but not enough to cover the entire body, then the head and face are covered as well to honour the face and cover the good features which will change. The basis for this is the story of Muṣ'ab ibn 'Umayr. He left a mantle after the Battle of Uḥud. When his head was covered, his feet showed, and when his feet were covered, his head showed. The Messenger of Allah ﷺ said, 'Put it over his head and cover his feet with idhkhir-herb.' Muslim transmitted it.

Most scholars recommend an odd number of cloths in shrouding, but all of them agree that there is no definitive number. White is recommended. The Messenger of Allah ﷺ said, 'Wear white. It is the best of your garments. Shroud your dead in it.' Abū Dāwud transmitted it. The Prophet ﷺ was shrouded in three white Saḥūlī cotton cloths. It is permitted to use other than white for shrouds unless it is silk.

The stinginess of heirs regarding shrouding is settled for them by stipulating the same sort of clothing used for *Jumu'ah* and for 'Īds. The Prophet ﷺ said, 'When one of you shrouds his brother, he should shroud him well.' Muslim transmitted it. That is unless the dead person has left instructions to use something inferior to that. If he leaves instructions for something more extravagant, it is said that such excess is void, and it is also said that it is paid for from the third he is allowed to use for legacies. The first view is sounder since Allah says: *'Do not be extravagant.'* (6:141) Abū Bakr said, 'It is for pus.'

When the washing and shrouding is finished, the deceased is placed on their bier and the men carry him. The ruling is to carry the bier quickly since the Prophet ﷺ said, 'Go briskly with the bier. If the dead is righteous, it is good that you are bringing him to. If he is other than that, it is evil that you are removing from your shoulders.' It is not as the ignorant do today by walking slowly and stopping time after time, and reciting the Qur'an with melodies and other things which are not lawful to do as the Egyptians do with their dead.

An-Nasā'ī related from Muḥammad ibn 'Abd al-A'lā from Khālid from 'Uyaynah ibn 'Abd ar-Raḥman that his father, 'Abd ar-Raḥman, said, 'I saw the funeral of 'Abd ar-Raḥman ibn Samurah. Ziyād was walking in front of the bier. Some men from family and clients of 'Abd ar-Raḥman began to get in front of the bier and walk backwards, saying, "Slowly! Slowly! May Allah bless you!" They went at a snail's pace until we were on part of the Mirbad road where we met Abū Bakrah on a mule. When he saw what they were doing, he attacked them with his mule and brought his whip down on them. He said, "Stop it! By the One who honoured the face of Abu-l-Qāsim ﷺ, when we were with the Messenger of Allah ﷺ, we went very quickly with it!" The people were glad.' Abū Mājidah related that Ibn Mas'ūd said, 'We asked our Prophet ﷺ about how to walk with the bier and he said, "Less than trotting. If it is good, he is hastened to it. If it is other than that, then may the people of the Fire be far away!"'

Abū 'Umar said, 'The majority of scholars agree that what is meant by going quickly is faster than sedately. They preferred going quickly to going slowly. It is disliked to go so quickly as to impose difficulty on any weak people who are following.' Ibrāhīm an-Nakha'ī said, 'Go slightly slowly but do not creep slowly like the Jews and Christians.' Some people interpreted the 'going quickly' mentioned in the hadith of Abū Hurayah as hastening the burial, not the manner of walking. That is of no import because of what we have mentioned. Success is by Allah.

The prayer over the deceased is a general obligation like *jihād*. This is the common position of the schools of the scholars, Mālik and others, since the Prophet ﷺ said about the Negus, 'Stand and do the prayer for him.' Aṣbagh, however, said that it is *sunnah* and related that from Mālik. This will be further discussed in *at-Tawbah*.

It is mandatory to bury the deceased in the earth and cover them since the Almighty says: *'Then Allah sent a crow which scratched at the earth to show him how to conceal his brother's corpse.'* (5:31) The ruling concerning digging the grave, what is recommended in it and how to place the dead in it will be mentioned in another place. The ruling concerning building a mosque over graves will be mentioned in *al-Kahf*.

These are rulings about the dead and what is obliged for the living. 'A'ishah said that the Messenger of Allah ﷺ said, 'Do not curse the dead. They have gone ahead to what they sent forward.' Muslim transmitted it. We find in the *Sunan* of an-Nasā'ī: 'Someone who had died was spoken ill of in the presence of the Prophet ﷺ and he said, "Only speak well of the dead."'

You will be paid your wages in full on the Day of Rising.

The wage of the believer is the reward and the wage of the unbeliever is punishment. Blessing and trial in this world are not counted as a reward and payment because they are subject to annihilation.

Anyone who is distanced from the Fire and admitted to the Garden has triumphed.

He has *'triumphed'* because he has obtained what he hoped for and was saved from what he feared. Al-A'mash related from Zayd ibn Wahb from 'Abd ar-Raḥmān ibn 'Abd Rabb al-Ka'bah from 'Abdullāh ibn 'Amr that the Prophet ﷺ said, 'Anyone who desires to be far from the Fire and to enter the Garden should have death come to him while he is testifying that there is no god but Allah and Muhammad is the Messenger of Allah, and he should give people what he must give them.' Abū Hurayrah related that the Messenger of Allah ﷺ said, 'A whip-sized space in the Garden is better than this world and everything in it. Recite if you wish: *"Anyone who is distanced from the Fire and admitted to the Garden has triumphed."'*

The life of this world is just the enjoyment of delusion.

This means that it deludes and deceives the believer so that he thinks it will last for a long time while in fact it is quickly passing. Enjoyment refers to articles that are enjoyed and used, such as an axe, pot and bowl. Then it is removed and does not last. That is what most commentators say. Al-Ḥasan said, 'It is like the green of plants and the games of girls which have no result.' Qatādah said, 'It is abandoned enjoyment which is about to vanish. So a person must take what he can from this enjoyment by obeying Allah.' A poet spoke excellent words about this:

It is the abode of harm and annoyance,
the abode of passing away and the abode of vicissitudes.

Even if you were to obtain it lock, stock and barrel,
you would still die without getting what you desire of it.

Ghurūr is delusion while *gharār* is shayṭān who deludes people by making them hope and giving them false promises. Ibn 'Arafah said, 'Delusion is things you see that have an outward appearance that you love while their inward is disliked or unknown.' Shayṭān is the Deluder because he moves people to what their lower selves love while what is behind it is harmful for them. Illustrating this is a sale that is *'gharār'* (entailing risk). Outwardly it is is uncertain and what is inside it is unknown.

لَتُبْلَوُنَّ فِي أَمْوَالِكُمْ وَأَنفُسِكُمْ وَلَتَسْمَعُنَّ مِنَ الَّذِينَ أُوتُوا الْكِتَابَ مِن
قَبْلِكُمْ وَمِنَ الَّذِينَ أَشْرَكُوا أَذًى كَثِيرًا وَإِن تَصْبِرُوا وَتَتَّقُوا فَإِنَّ ذَٰلِكَ مِنْ
عَزْمِ الْأُمُورِ ﴿١٨٦﴾

186 You will be tested in your wealth and in yourselves and you will hear many abusive words from those given the Book before you and from those who are idolaters. But if you are steadfast and godfearing, that is the most resolute course to take.

This is addressed to the Prophet ﷺ and His Community. It means: 'You will be tested and tried in your wealth by hardships and loss, through spending in the Cause of Allah and all the obligations of the Sharī'ah.' Testing in selves is through death, illness and loss of loved ones. He mentions wealth first because there are many afflictions in it.

In connection with the verb *'you may hear'*, if it is asked why the *wāw* is kept in *'la-tublawūnna'* (tested) when it is elided in *'wala-tasma'unna'*, the answer is that the *wāw* in *'la-tublawūnna'* has a *fatḥah* before it and so it takes a vowel because of two silent letters meeting, and the *ḍammah* is singled out because it is the *wāw* of the plural and it is not permitted to elide it because nothing before it indicates it. It is elided in *'wala-tasma'unna'* because what is before it indicates it. It is not permitted for the *wāw* to have a *hamzah* in *'la-tublawūnna'* because its vowel is accidental [not permanent].' An-Naḥḥās and others said that. One says for the masculine singular *'la-tublayanna'*, for the dual *'la-tublayānna'* and for the plural *'la-tublawunna'*.

The reason for this *āyah* being revealed was that Abū Bakr heard a Jew say, 'Allah is poor and we are rich' to refute the Qur'an and make light of it when Allah revealed: *'Is there anyone who will make Allah a generous loan?'* (2:245) He slapped him and the Jew complained about him to the Prophet ﷺ and this was revealed. 'Ikrimah said that the speaker was Finḥāṣ.

Az-Zuhrī said that it was revealed because of Ka'b ibn al-Ashraf, a poet, who used to satirise the Prophet ﷺ and His Companions; the Qurayshī unbelievers had incited him to do so. He abused the Muslim women to the point that eventually the

Messenger of Allah ﷺ sent Muḥammad ibn Maslamah and his comrades to kill him. This is known in the *Sīrah* and sound reports. Other things are said as well.

When the Prophet ﷺ came to Madīnah, there were Jews and idolaters there, and he and his Companions endured much verbal abuse. The *Ṣaḥīḥ* collections report that once, when the Prophet ﷺ was on a donkey, he passed by Ibn Ubayy and called him to Allah. He retorted, 'If what you say is true, do not annoy us with it in our gatherings! Return to your mount and just speak to whoever comes to you.' Ibn Ubayy covered his nose so that the dust raised by the donkey would not touch him. Ibn Rawāḥah exclaimed, 'Indeed, Messenger of Allah! Bring it to us in our gatherings. We like that!' The idolaters around Ibn Ubayy and the Muslims abused one another. The Prophet ﷺ kept on calming them down until they were quiet. Then he went to Sa'd ibn 'Ubādah to visit him since he was ill and said, 'Did you hear what so-and-so said?' Sa'd said, 'Pardon him and overlook it. By the One who sent down the Book on you, Allah has brought us the truth which He sent down on you at the very time that the people of this little town had agreed to crown him and bind his head with a (royal) turban. When Allah stopped that happening by the truth which Allah gave you, he was vexed on that account. That is why he did what you saw.' The Messenger of Allah ﷺ pardoned him and then this was revealed.

It is said that this was before fighting was revealed and Allah recommended His slaves have steadfastness and *taqwā* and reported that that is the most resolute course to take. This is found in al-Bukhārī. *'The most resolute course to take'* is the strongest and firmest.

It more evident that it is not abrogated. Argument should always be conducted in the best way and courtesy is always recommended. The Prophet ﷺ used to make peace with the Jews, flatter them and overlook the hypocrites. This is clear.

وَإِذْ أَخَذَ ٱللَّهُ مِيثَٰقَ ٱلَّذِينَ أُوتُوا۟ ٱلْكِتَٰبَ لَتُبَيِّنُنَّهُۥ لِلنَّاسِ وَلَا تَكْتُمُونَهُۥ
فَنَبَذُوهُ وَرَآءَ ظُهُورِهِمْ وَٱشْتَرَوْا۟ بِهِۦ ثَمَنًا قَلِيلًا فَبِئْسَ مَا يَشْتَرُونَ ١٨٧

187 Allah made a covenant with those given the Book: 'You must make it clear to people and not conceal it.' But they toss it in disdain behind their backs and sell it for a paltry price. What an evil sale they make!

Allah made a covenant with those given the Book.

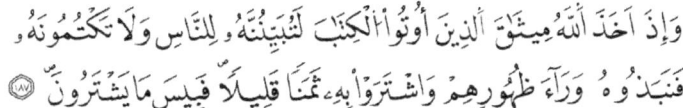

This is connected to the previous mention of the Jews. They were commanded to believe in Muḥammad ﷺ and to make his business clear, but they concealed it. So the *āyah* rebukes them. Then this is also a general report to them and others.

Al-Ḥasan and Qatādah said, 'This is about everyone who is given knowledge of the Book. Whoever knows something should teach it. Beware of concealing knowledge. That is destruction.' Muḥammad ibn Ka'b said, 'It is not lawful for a scholar to remain silent with his knowledge nor for someone ignorant to remain silent about his ignorance. Allah says: *"Allah made a covenant with those given the Book"* and *"Ask the People of the Reminder if you do not know."* (16:42)'

Abū Hurayrah said, 'If Allah had not criticised the People of the Book for not doing so, I would not have transmitted anything to you.' Then he recited this *āyah*. Al-Ḥasan ibn 'Umārah said, 'I went to az-Zuhrī after he had stopped transmitting hadith and I found him at his door. I said, "Will you transmit to me?" He replied, "Do you not know that I have stopped transmitting hadith?" I said, "You will relate to me or I will relate to you." He said, "Relate to me." I said, "Al-Ḥakam ibn 'Uyaynah related to me from Yaḥyā ibn al-Jazzār that he heard 'Alī ibn Abī Ṭālib say, 'Allah did not impose on the ignorant to learn until he imposed on scholars to teach.'" Then he related forty hadiths to me.'

You must make it clear to people and not conceal it.

It is said that the masculine pronoun 'it' can refer to Muḥammad ﷺ (meaning 'You must make 'him' clear'), and it is said that it refers to the Book. This would include clarifying the actions of the Prophet ﷺ because he is mentioned in the Book. *'Not conceal it'* is grammatically adverbial. Abū 'Amr, 'Āṣim in the variant of Abū Bakr and the people of Makkah have *'li-tubayyinunnahu'* in the second person while the rest have it with *yā'* (*li-yubayyinunnahu*) because they are not present. ('It must be made clear.')

Ibn 'Abbās recited *'mithāqa'n-nabiyyina'* (a covenant with the Prophets), and so His words, *'toss it'* refer to the people to whom the Prophets made things clear. The reading of Ibn Mas'ūd is *'la-tubayyinūnahu'* without the heavy *nūn*.

But they toss it in disdain behind their backs and sell it for a paltry price.

The word *nabdh* means casting aside as in: *'something to cast disdainfully behind your backs'* (11:92), and it was explained in *al-Baqarah*. The expression *'behind their backs'* stresses the tossing aside, as we see in *'cast disdainfully behind your backs.'* (11:92).

لَا تَحْسَبَنَّ ٱلَّذِينَ يَفْرَحُونَ بِمَآ أَتَوا۟ وَّيُحِبُّونَ أَن يُحْمَدُوا۟ بِمَا لَمْ يَفْعَلُوا۟ فَلَا تَحْسَبَنَّهُم
بِمَفَازَةٍ مِّنَ ٱلْعَذَابِ ۖ وَلَهُمْ عَذَابٌ أَلِيمٌ ﴿١٨٨﴾

188 Those who exult in what they have done and love to be praised for what they have not done should not suppose that they have escaped the punishment. They will have a painful punishment.

That is because they stayed behind the expeditions and brought the Prophet ﷺ their excuses. It is confirmed in the *Ṣaḥīḥ* collections from Abū Sa'īd al-Khudrī that when the Messenger of Allah ﷺ went on an expedition, some of the hypocrites stayed behind and exulted in doing that. When the Prophet ﷺ returned, they offered their excuses and oaths and wanted to be praised for what they had done, and this was revealed.

Also in the two *Ṣaḥīḥ* collections, Marwān said to his doorman, 'Go to Rāfi' ibn 'Abbās and tell him, "If every man of us who exults in what he had done and loves to be praised for what he has not done is going to be punished, then we will all be punished." Ibn 'Abbās said, "What do you have to do with this *āyah*! This *āyah* was revealed about the People of the Book." Then he recited: *"Allah made a covenant with those given the Book. You must make it clear to people and not conceal it"* and *"Those who exult in what they have done and love to be praised for what they have not done."* Ibn 'Abbās said, "The Prophet ﷺ asked them about something and they concealed it from him and told him something else. They left and reported what they had told him about what he asked them and wanted to be praised for that and exulted at their concealment of what he had asked them about."'

Muḥammad ibn Ka'b al-Quraẓī said, 'It was revealed about some scholars of the tribe of Israel who concealed the truth and gave to kings knowledge which supported their falsehoods. *"They sold it for a small price,"* in other words, for what the kings of this world gave them. So Allah said to His Prophet ﷺ: *"Those who exult in what they have done ..."* and told him that they would have painful punishment for their corrupting the *dīn* for the slaves of Allah.'

Aḍ-Ḍaḥḥāk said, 'The Jews used to say to the kings, "We find in our Book that Allah will send a Prophet at the end of time to seal Prophethood." Then when Allah sent him and the kings asked them, "Is this the one you find in their Book?", the Jews, desiring the wealth of the kings, replied, "It is not him." So the kings gave them treasures. Then Allah told them: *"Those who exult in what they have done..."* by way of lying to the kings to take the goods of this world *"...should not suppose...*'" The first hadith is contrary to the second one. It is possible that there were two reasons for its revelation since they occurred at the same time and it answers both. Allah knows best.

they love to be praised for what they have not done

They seek praise. Marwān's words, 'If every man of us who exults in what he has done...' indicate that the generality has a specific form and 'those' is part of it. This is definite in the case of those who understand that from the Qur'an and Sunnah.

If the *āyah* is about the People of the Book and not about the hypocrites who stayed behind, it is because they said, 'We are following the *dīn* of Ibrāhīm' but they were not following his *dīn*, and they used to say, 'We are the people of prayer, fasting and Scripture,' desiring to be praised for that.

Nāfi', Ibn 'Āmir, Ibn Kathīr and Abū 'Amr read it as 'They should not suppose' (*yaḥsabanna* or *yaḥsibanna*), meaning 'those who exult should not suppose that they have escaped the punishment.' It is said that the first object is elided, which is 'themselves' and the second is '*escaped*'. The Kufans read it with *tā'* meaning, 'You should not suppose (*taḥsabanna*), O Muḥammad, that those who exult have escaped the punishment.' The second 'suppose' is for stress. Its first object is '*hum*' and the second is elided. The *fā'* at the beginning is a conjunction or redundant in replacing the second object by the first.

Aḍ-Ḍaḥḥāk and 'Īsā ibn 'Umar recite it with a *tā'* and a *ḍammah* on the *bā'*: '*taḥsabunnahum*'. So it is addressed to Muḥammad ﷺ and his Companions. Mujāhid, Ibn Kathīr, Abū 'Amr and Yaḥyā ibn Ya'mur recite it with a *yā'* and a *ḍammah* on the *bā'*, reporting about those who exult, i.e. 'those who exult should not suppose'. '*Escape*' is the second object and '*suppose*' is for stress. It is said that 'those' is the subject of '*suppose*' and its two objects are elided... (more grammatical discussion).

Most of the seven readers and others recite '*ataw*' with a short *alif*, indicating the lying and concealment they have done.' Marwān ibn al-Ḥakam, al-A'mash and Ibrāhīm an-Nakha'ī recite '*ātaw*' with *maddah* which means 'give'. Sa'īd ibn Jubayr recited 'ūtū' without naming the subject, i.e. 'they are given'.

Mafāzah (escape) is deliverance. It is form *maf'alah* from the verb *fāza*, *yafūzu* to be saved. It means that they will not be saved (*fā'izūn*). A place of fear is called *mafāzah* for luck. Al-Aṣmā'ī said that. It is said that it is because of it is a place where the desert is crossed (*tafwīz*) where destruction is likely. The Arabs use '*fawwaza*' for a man when he dies. Tha'lab said, 'I related to Ibn al-A'rābī what al-Aṣmā'ī had said and he said, "He erred. Abu-l-Makārim said that it is called *mafāzah* because the one who crosses it wins (*fāza*)."' Al-Aṣma'ī said that someone who has been stung is called 'healthy' for luck. Ibn al-A'rābī said that it is because he will recover when he is afflicted. It is said that one should not suppose that they are in a place far from the punishment because success is a long way away from what is disliked. Allah knows best.

وَلِلَّهِ مُلْكُ السَّمَٰوَٰتِ وَالْأَرْضِ وَاللَّهُ عَلَىٰ كُلِّ شَيْءٍ قَدِيرٌ ﴿١٨٩﴾

189 The kingdom of the heavens and earth belongs to Allah. Allah has power over all things.

This is an argument against those who say, 'Allah is poor and we are rich' and refutes them. It is said that it means: 'Do not suppose that those who exult will be saved from the punishment. Everything belongs to Allah and is subject to His power.' So it is added to the first statement. It means that they will not be saved from His punishment. He will seize them whenever He wishes. The expression '*Allah has power over all things*' was explained in *al-Baqarah*.

إِنَّ فِي خَلْقِ السَّمَاوَاتِ وَالْأَرْضِ وَاخْتِلَافِ اللَّيْلِ وَالنَّهَارِ لَآيَاتٍ لِأُولِي الْأَلْبَابِ ﴿١٩٠﴾
الَّذِينَ يَذْكُرُونَ اللَّهَ قِيَامًا وَقُعُودًا وَعَلَىٰ جُنُوبِهِمْ وَيَتَفَكَّرُونَ فِي خَلْقِ السَّمَاوَاتِ
وَالْأَرْضِ رَبَّنَا مَا خَلَقْتَ هَٰذَا بَاطِلًا سُبْحَانَكَ فَقِنَا عَذَابَ النَّارِ ﴿١٩١﴾ رَبَّنَا إِنَّكَ مَنْ
تُدْخِلِ النَّارَ فَقَدْ أَخْزَيْتَهُ ۖ وَمَا لِلظَّالِمِينَ مِنْ أَنْصَارٍ ﴿١٩٢﴾ رَبَّنَا إِنَّنَا سَمِعْنَا مُنَادِيًا
يُنَادِي لِلْإِيمَانِ أَنْ آمِنُوا بِرَبِّكُمْ فَآمَنَّا ۚ رَبَّنَا فَاغْفِرْ لَنَا ذُنُوبَنَا وَكَفِّرْ
عَنَّا سَيِّئَاتِنَا وَتَوَفَّنَا مَعَ الْأَبْرَارِ ﴿١٩٣﴾ رَبَّنَا وَآتِنَا مَا وَعَدْتَنَا عَلَىٰ رُسُلِكَ وَلَا تُخْزِنَا يَوْمَ
الْقِيَامَةِ ۗ إِنَّكَ لَا تُخْلِفُ الْمِيعَادَ ﴿١٩٤﴾ فَاسْتَجَابَ لَهُمْ رَبُّهُمْ أَنِّي لَا أُضِيعُ عَمَلَ عَامِلٍ
مِنْكُمْ مِنْ ذَكَرٍ أَوْ أُنْثَىٰ ۖ بَعْضُكُمْ مِنْ بَعْضٍ ۖ فَالَّذِينَ هَاجَرُوا وَأُخْرِجُوا مِنْ دِيَارِهِمْ وَأُوذُوا فِي
سَبِيلِي وَقَاتَلُوا وَقُتِلُوا لَأُكَفِّرَنَّ عَنْهُمْ سَيِّئَاتِهِمْ وَلَأُدْخِلَنَّهُمْ جَنَّاتٍ تَجْرِي مِنْ تَحْتِهَا
الْأَنْهَارُ ثَوَابًا مِنْ عِنْدِ اللَّهِ ۗ وَاللَّهُ عِنْدَهُ حُسْنُ الثَّوَابِ ﴿١٩٥﴾ لَا يَغُرَّنَّكَ تَقَلُّبُ الَّذِينَ
كَفَرُوا فِي الْبِلَادِ ﴿١٩٦﴾ مَتَاعٌ قَلِيلٌ ثُمَّ مَأْوَاهُمْ جَهَنَّمُ ۚ وَبِئْسَ الْمِهَادُ ﴿١٩٧﴾ لَٰكِنِ
الَّذِينَ اتَّقَوْا رَبَّهُمْ لَهُمْ جَنَّاتٌ تَجْرِي مِنْ تَحْتِهَا الْأَنْهَارُ خَالِدِينَ
فِيهَا نُزُلًا مِنْ عِنْدِ اللَّهِ ۗ وَمَا عِنْدَ اللَّهِ خَيْرٌ لِلْأَبْرَارِ ﴿١٩٨﴾ وَإِنَّ مِنْ
أَهْلِ الْكِتَابِ لَمَنْ يُؤْمِنُ بِاللَّهِ وَمَا أُنْزِلَ إِلَيْكُمْ وَمَا أُنْزِلَ إِلَيْهِمْ
خَاشِعِينَ لِلَّهِ لَا يَشْتَرُونَ بِآيَاتِ اللَّهِ ثَمَنًا قَلِيلًا ۗ أُولَٰئِكَ لَهُمْ
أَجْرُهُمْ عِنْدَ رَبِّهِمْ ۗ إِنَّ اللَّهَ سَرِيعُ الْحِسَابِ ﴿١٩٩﴾ يَا أَيُّهَا الَّذِينَ
آمَنُوا اصْبِرُوا وَصَابِرُوا وَرَابِطُوا وَاتَّقُوا اللَّهَ لَعَلَّكُمْ تُفْلِحُونَ ﴿٢٠٠﴾

190 In the creation of the heavens and the earth, and the alternation of night and day, there are Signs for people with intelligence: 191 those who remember Allah, standing, sitting and lying on their sides, and reflect on the creation of the heavens and the earth: 'Our Lord, You have not created this for nothing. Glory be to You! So safeguard us from the punishment of the Fire. 192 Our Lord, those You cast into the Fire, You have indeed disgraced. The wrongdoers will have no helpers. 193 Our Lord, we heard a caller calling us to belief: 'Believe in your Lord!', and we believed. Our Lord, forgive us our wrong actions, erase our bad actions from us and take us back to You with those who are truly good. 194 Our Lord, give us what You promised us through Your Messengers,

and do not disgrace us on the Day of Rising. You do not break Your promise.' 195 Their Lord responds to them: 'I will not let the deeds of any doer among you go to waste, male or female – you are both the same in that respect. Those who made hijrah and were driven from their homes and suffered harm in My Way and fought and were killed, I will erase their bad actions from them and admit them into Gardens with rivers flowing under them, as a reward from Allah. The best of all rewards is with Allah.' 196 Do not be deceived by the fact that those who disbelieve move freely about the earth. 197 A brief enjoyment; then their shelter will be Hell. What an evil resting-place! 198 But those who have *taqwā* of their Lord will have Gardens with rivers flowing under them, remaining in them timelessly, for ever: hospitality from Allah. What is with Allah is better for those who are truly good. 199 Among the people of the Book there are some who believe in Allah and in what has been sent down to you and what was sent down to them, and who are humble before Allah. They do not sell Allah's Signs for a paltry price. Such people will have their reward with their Lord. And Allah is swift at reckoning. 200 You who believe, be steadfast; be supreme in steadfastness; be firm on the battlefield; and have taqwa of Allah; so that hopefully you will be successful.

In the creation of the heavens and the earth

This was already discussed in *al-Baqarah*. Allah concludes this *sūrah* with the command to look and deduce from His signs since they only come from the Living, Self-Subsistent, All-Powerful, Pure, Peace, who is free from the needs of created existence, so that their faith is based on certainty, not blind imitation.

Signs for people with intelligence

This means those who use their intellects to reflect on evidence. It is related that 'Ā'ishah said, 'When this *āyah* was revealed to the Prophet ﷺ, he rose and prayed. Then Bilāl came to give the *adhān* for the prayer and he recited it weeping. He said, "Messenger of Allah, why do you weep when Allah has forgiven you your past and any future errors?" He answered, "Bilāl, am I not a grateful slave?" Then Allah revealed this and he ﷺ said, "Woe to those who recite it without reflecting on it!"'

Scholars say that it is recommended for someone who wakes up from sleep to wipe his face and recite these ten *āyahs* in imitation of the Prophet ﷺ. That is confirmed in the *Ṣaḥīḥ* collections and elsewhere. Then he should pray what is prescribed for him and combine reflection and action, and the best action will be made clear in this *āyah*. It is related from Abū Hurayrah that the Messenger of Allah ﷺ used to recite these ten *āyahs* every night. Abū Naṣr al-Wā'ilī as-Sijistānī transmitted it in *Kitāb al-Inābah* from Sulaymān ibn Mūsā from Muẓāhir ibn Aslam al-Makhzūmī from al-Maqburī from Abū Hurayrah. It was already mentioned at the beginning of the *sūrah* that 'Uthmān said, 'If someone recites the end of *Āl 'Imrān* in the night, prayer during the whole night will be recorded for him.'

Those who remember Allah, standing, sitting and lying on their sides.

Allah mentioned the three postures which human beings necessarily adopt in most of their affairs and so it is as if it covers all their time. 'Ā'ishah said, 'The Messenger of Allah ﷺ used to remember Allah at all times.' Muslim transmitted it. That would include when he was in the lavatory and other places.

Scholars disagree about this. 'Abdullāh ibn 'Amr, Ibn Sīrīn and an-Nakha'ī allow it, and Ibn 'Abbās, 'Aṭā' and ash-Sha'bī dislike it. The first position is sounder because of the general nature of the text of the *āyah* and hadith. An-Nakha'ī said, 'There is nothing wrong in remembering Allah in the lavatory. It is taken up,' meaning recorded by by the angels and written in their books. The evidence for that is Allah's words: *'He does not utter a single word, without a watcher by him, pen in hand'* (50:18) and: *'Standing over you are guardians, noble, recording.'* (82:10) That is because Allah commanded His slaves to remember Him in every state without exception. He says: *'Remember Allah much'* (33:41), *'Remember Me – I will remember you'* (2:152) and *'We will not let the wage of good-doers go to waste.'* (18:30) So it is universal. The person who remembers Allah Almighty in all his states is rewarded, Allah willing.

Abū Nu'aym mentioned from Abū Bakr ibn Mālik from 'Abdullāh ibn Aḥmad ibn Ḥanbal from his father from Wakī' from Sufyān from 'Aṭā' ibn Abī Marwān from his father that Ka'b al-Aḥbar said, 'Mūsā ﷺ said, "O Lord, are You near so that I can speak intimately with You, or far, so that I must call out to You?" He said, "Mūsā, I sit with the one who remembers me." He said, "O Lord, what if we are in a situation in which we consider You too majestic and great to be remembered there?" "And what is what?" He asked. He said, "In a state of major impurity (*janābah*) or in the lavatory." He said, "Mūsā, remember Me in every situation."'

The dislike of that is either because of thinking that remembering Allah is too great to be done in places where He should not be remembered, as it is disliked to recite the Qur'an in the bath-house, or because it forces the noble scribes to remain in a place of filth and impurity to record what was said. Allah knows best.

'Standing, sitting' is in the accusative for the *ḥāl* and *'on their sides'* is also in the accusative for the *ḥāl* and means lying down, as in Allah's words: *'he calls on Us, lying on his side or sitting down or standing up.'* (10:12) This means that he calls on Him lying on his side.

A group of commentators, al-Ḥasan and others, think that the words from *'those who remember Allah'* are about the prayer, meaning that people must not fail to do it and should perform it in whatever state is possible. If someone has an excuse, then he can pray sitting down or lying down. According to Ibn Mas'ūd, that is reflected in this *āyah* as will be made clear.

If the *āyah* is about the prayer, the *fiqh* is that a person prays it standing. If he cannot do that, then sitting, and if he cannot manage that, then lying down. This is as it is confirmed from 'Imrān ibn Ḥuṣayn that Abu-l-Bawāsīr asked the Prophet ﷺ about the prayer. He said, 'Pray standing. If you cannot, then sitting. If you cannot, then lying down.' The imāms transmitted it. The Prophet ﷺ prayed *nāfilah* prayers sitting down a year before he died as we find in *Ṣaḥīḥ Muslim*. An-Nasā'ī related that 'Ā'ishah said, 'I saw the Messenger of Allah ﷺ praying cross-legged.' Abū 'Abd ar-Raḥmān said, 'I do not know of anyone who relates this hadith other than Abū Dāwud al-Ḥafarī, who is trustworthy. I can only think that this hadith is an error.' Allah knows best.

Scholars disagree about how a person who is ill should pray and how they should sit. Ibn 'Abd al-Ḥakam related from Mālik that they sit cross-legged in the standing portions. Al-Buwayṭī mentioned that from ash-Shāfi'ī. When they want to prostrate, they do as much as they are able to. That is also the position of ath-Thawrī, al-Layth, Aḥmad, Isḥāq, Abū Yūsuf and Muḥammad. In the transmission of al-Muzanī, ash-Shāfi'i said that they should sit in the prayer as they normally would in the *tashahhud*. This is related from Mālik and his people. The first is the well-known position and it is the apparent view of the *Mudawwanah*. Abū Ḥanīfah and Zafar said that they sit as he would for *tashahhud* and that is how they do *rukū'* and prostration as well.

If they cannot sit, then they can choose whether to pray on their side or their back. This is the position in the *Mudawwanah*. Ibn Ḥabīb related from Ibn al-Qāsim that they should pray on their backs. If they cannot do that, then on their right side, and finally on their left side. The book of Ibn al-Mawwāz has the opposite: they should pray on their right side. If they cannot do that, then on their left side. And if they cannot do that, then on their backs. Saḥnūn said that they should pray on their right side, in the same way as people are placed in their grave, then on their back, then on their left side. Mālik and Abū Ḥanīfah said, 'When someone prays lying down, their feet should be towards *qiblah*.' Ash-Shāfi'ī and ath-Thawrī said that they pray on their side with their face towards *qiblah*.

If someone regains their strength after illness during the prayer, Ibn al-Qāsim said that they should stand for the rest of the prayer and build on what they have done. That is the position of ash-Shāfi'ī, Zafar and aṭ-Ṭabarī. Abū Ḥanīfah and his two companions said that if someone prays one *rak'ah* lying down and then recovers, they should start the prayer again. If they were sitting and bow and prostrate and then recover, they build on what they have done according to Abū Ḥanīfah, but not according to Muḥammad. Abū Ḥanīfah and his people said that if someone starts the prayer standing and reaches a point where they can only indicate the movements, they build on what they have done. That is related from Abū Yūsuf. Mālik said about a sick person who cannot bow or prostrate, but is able to stand and sit, that they pray standing and indicate bowing, and when they want to prostrate, they should sit and indicate prostration. That is the position of Abū Yūsuf and analogous to the position of ash-Shāfi'ī. Abū Ḥanīfah and his people said that they should pray sitting.

As for the prayer of a healthy person not standing, it is related from the hadith of 'Imrān ibn Ḥuṣayn that the prayer of a healthy person lying down is worth half that of one sitting down. Abū 'Umar said that the majority of the people of knowledge do not permit *nāfilah* prayers lying down when someone is able to sit or stand. It is a hadith which is only related by Ḥusayn the Teacher, who is Ḥusayn ibn Dhakwān, from 'Abdullāh ibn Buraydah from 'Imrān ibn Ḥuṣayn. There is disagreement about its *isnād* as well as its text from Ḥusayn which means that one should hesitate about it. If it is sound, I do not know its true import. If one of the people of knowledge permits the performance of *nāfilah* prayers while lying down for someone able to sit or stand, then that is the meaning of this addition in the report. It is an argument for those who believe that to be the case. If they agree that it is disliked to perform *nāfilah* prayers while lying down in the case of someone able to sit or stand, then this hadith of Ḥusayn is either an error or abrogated.

It is said that what is meant by the *āyah* is that those who deduce evidence from the creation of the heaven and the earth say that that which changes must have a Changer, and that Changer must have the power to achieve it in perfection. He can send Messengers. If He sends a Messenger whose truthfulness is indicated by a single miracle, then no one has an excuse. Those people remember Allah in every state. Allah knows best.

reflect on the creation of the heavens and the earth.

We have explained the meaning of 'remember', which is either with the tongue or in prayer. Then Allah adds another form of worship to it: reflection on the power of Allah and His creation and the lessons to be gained from that so as to increase insight.

Every thing contains a sign of Him
which indicates that He is One

It is said that '*reflect*' is added to the *ḥāl*. It is also said that it is separate. The first view is more likely.

Reflection is that the heart returns to something. One says *tafakkara*, and a man who is *fikkīr* reflects often. The Prophet ﷺ passed by some people who were reflecting on Allah and said, 'Reflect on creation. Do not reflect on the Creator. You will not be able to value Him properly.' Reflection, consideration and expanding the mind is with respect to creatures, as Allah says here. It is related that Sufyān ath-Thawrī prayed two *rak'ah*s at the Maqām and then raised his head towards heaven. When he saw the stars, he fainted. He used to urinate blood on account of the depth of his sorrow and reflection.

Abū Hurayrah reported that the Messenger of Allah ﷺ said, 'Once, while a man was lying on his bed, he lifted his head, looked at the stars and the sky and said, "I testify that you have a Lord and a Creator. O Allah, forgive me." Allah looked at him and forgave him.' He ﷺ said, 'There is no act of worship like reflection.' It is related that the Prophet ﷺ said, 'An hour of reflection is better than a year of worship.' Ibn al-Qāsim reported that Mālik said, 'Umm 'd-Dardā' was asked, "What did Abu-d-Dardā' mostly do?" She said, "He mostly reflected."' He was asked, 'Do you think that reflection is best of actions?' 'Yes,' he replied, 'It is certainty.' Ibn al-Musayyab was asked about prayers between *Ẓuhr* and *'Aṣr* and he said, 'This is not worship. Worship is scrupulousness about what Allah has forbidden and reflecting on the command of Allah.' Al-Ḥasan said, 'Reflecting for an hour is better than praying all night.' Ibn 'Abbās and Abu-d-Dardā' said that. Al-Ḥasan said, 'Reflection is the mirror of the believer in which he sees his good actions and bad actions reflected.'

Part of that on which one should reflect are the terrors of the Next World, the Gathering, the Garden and its bliss, and the Fire and its punishment. It is related that Abū Sulaymān ad-Dārānī took a mug of water to do *wuḍū'* for the night prayer. He had a guest. The guest saw him put a finger in the handle of the mug and then he stopped, reflecting, until dawn. He said to him, 'What is this, Abū Sulaymān?' He said, 'When I put my finger in the mug's handle, I thought about the words of Allah Almighty: *"When they have shackles and chains around their necks and are dragged along the ground"* (40:71), and I reflected on my state and how I would meet the shackles when they are placed on my neck on the Day of Rising. I continued doing that until morning.' Ibn 'Aṭiyyah observed, 'This is extreme fear, and the best of matters is the middle one. The scholars of this community do not commend this course. Studying knowledge of the Book of Allah and the meanings of the *Sunna* of the Messenger of Allah ﷺ for someone who understands and hopes to benefit is better than this.'

Ibn al-'Arabī said, 'Scholars disagree about which of the two actions is better: reflection or the prayer. The Sufis believe that reflection is better. It results in gnosis, which is the best of stations. The *fuqahā'* believe that the prayer is better since its encouragement is reported in hadiths.' We find in the two *Ṣaḥīḥ* collections that Ibn 'Abbās spent the night with his aunt, Maymūnah. He said, 'The Messenger of Allah ﷺ got up and wiped the sleep from his face. Then he recited the final ten *āyah*s of *Sūrat Āl 'Imrān*. He went to a waterskin which was hanging and did *wuḍū'* quickly and then prayed thirteen *rak'ah*s.' Look at how he combined the two: he reflected on creatures and then turned to the prayer. This is the *sunnah* on which he relied. As for the method of those Sufis who say you should reflect day and night, month after month without break, that is far from what is correct, inappropriate and not following the *sunnah.*

Ibn 'Aṭiyyah said, 'My father, may Allah be pleased with him, reported to me that one of the scholars of the east said, "I used to spend the night in Al-Aqdām Mosque in Egypt. I prayed *'Ishā'* and saw a man lying down wrapped up in a garment in his cloak until morning. We prayed that night and stayed awake. When the *iqāmah* for the *Ṣubḥ* prayer was given, he got up and faced the *qiblah* and prayed with the people. I thought that he was terribly impudent to pray without doing *wuḍū'*. When the prayer was over, he went out and I followed him to admonish him. When I was close to him, I heard him recite:

"An enwrapped body is absent present,
a heart which is aware, a silent invoker.

Constricted in the unseen worlds, expanded –
that is the state of the gnostic invoker.

I spent the night as the brother of thought,
    and so for the whole of the night he is awake asleep."

Then I knew that he was one of those who worship by reflection and I left him.'

Our Lord, You have not created this for nothing. Glory be to You!

They say, 'You did not create this in vain or as a jest. You created this as evidence of Your wisdom and power.' The *bāṭil* is that which vanishes and departs. Labīd said:

Everything except Allah is false.

The word '*for nothing*' is in the accusative because it is the adjective of an elided verbal noun, meaning 'a vain creation'. It is said that it is in the accusative based on the removal of the genitive, meaning 'You did not create it for what is in vain. It is said that it is based on a second object and 'created' means 'make.'

As for the expression '*Glory be to You!*' Mūsā ibn Ṭalḥa reports that the Messenger of Allah ﷺ was asked about the meaning of 'Glory be to Allah.' He said, 'It means: to free Allah from every kind of evil.' This was already explained adequately in *al-Baqarah*.

So safeguard us from the punishment of the Fire.

'Protect us from its punishment.' This has already been discussed.

Our Lord, those You cast into the Fire, You have indeed disgraced.

It is said that they are disgraced and sent far away. Al-Mufaḍḍal said that it means that they are destroyed, and he recited:

Allah disgraces those who worship the cross
and bear the habits of monks.

It is said to imply distance and hatred. The verb means to put far away and hate. Ibn as-Sakīt said that *khizy* is when someone falls into trial. The people of threat hold to this *āyah* and say, 'Anyone who enters the Fire cannot be a believer because Allah would not disgrace the believers (cf. 66:8).' This is refuted since there are proofs that someone who commits a major wrong action is still a believer as we will mention.

What is meant here then is those who will be in the Fire forever, as Anas ibn Mālik said. Sa'īd ibn al-Musayyab said that the *āyah* deals with those who will never leave the Fire and that is why He says: *'The wrongdoers will have no helpers.'* These are the unbelievers.

The people of meanings said that disgrace can mean shame, and one says *khaziya, yakhzā, khazāyah* for being ashamed, and the shamed is *khazyān*. Dhu-r-Rummah said:

Shame reached him in his excursion
from ropes, disordered by anger.

So the believers will be ashamed about entering the Fire with the people of other religions until they are brought out from it. Disgrace for the unbelievers is their destruction in it without death. The believers will die and leave it, as is confirmed in the sound *sunnah* reported from Abū Sa'īd al-Khudrī in Muslim.

Our Lord, we heard a caller calling us to belief: 'Believe in your Lord!', and we believed.

That is Muḥammad ﷺ. Ibn Mas'ūd, Ibn 'Abbās and most commentators said that. Qatādah and Muḥammad ibn Ka'b al-Quraẓī said, 'It is the Qur'an.' Not all of them heard the Messenger of Allah ﷺ. The evidence for this is the fact that Allah reports that the believing jinn said: '*We have heard a most amazing Recitation. It leads to right guidance.'* (72:1-2) The first group answered that if someone hears the Qur'an, it is as if he has met the Prophet ﷺ. This is a sound concept. *'An'* in *'Believe in'* is in the accusative by the elided genitive participle, i.e. '*bi-anna āminū*'. There is a change in the normal order and it means: 'We heard a caller to belief calling.' Abū 'Ubaydah said that. The *lām* in the *āyah* means *'ilā'* (to) as is found frequently in other *āyah*s like 99:5 and 7:43. It is also said that it means 'for the sake of', meaning 'so that we believe'.

Our Lord, forgive us our wrong actions and erase our bad actions from us.

The repetition is for stress in the supplication, as both expressions have the same meaning of covering. In the words *'Take us back to You with those who are truly good'* the '*truly good'* are the Prophets. The root of *barr* has to do with amplitude, and the one who is 'truly good' (*barr*) is the one who goes to great lengths in obeying Allah and receives ample mercy from Allah.

Our Lord, give us what You promised us through Your Messengers.

This means on the tongues of Your Messengers, like *'ask the town'* (12:82). Al-A'mash and az-Zuhī recited *'ruslika'* with lightening. It is said that it is a reference to the Prophets and angels asking for forgiveness for the believers and the angels asking forgiveness for those on the earth. There is also Nūḥ's supplication for the believers, that of Ibrāhīm, and the Prophet ﷺ praying for forgiveness for his community.

and do not disgrace us on the Day of Rising.

This means 'Do not punish or destroy us or disgrace us. Do not abase us, distance us from You or hate us on the Day of Rising.'

You do not break Your promise.

There are three aspects to the meaning of Allah not breaking His promise. The first is that Allah has promised the Garden to those who believe and they asked to be among those who were promised that without disgrace and punishment. The second is that they asked this as an act of worship and humility. Supplication is the core of worship. This is like Allah's words: *'Say: "Lord, judge us with truth!"'* (21:112) when He only ever judges with the truth. The third is that they asked to be given their promised victory against their enemy immediately because it directly refers to the Companions of the Prophet ﷺ and they asked for that in order to exalt the *dīn*. Allah knows best.

Anas ibn Mālik reported that the Messenger of Allah ﷺ said, 'When Allah promises someone a reward for an action, He makes him accomplish it as mercy from Him. If he promises punishment for an action, then the person has a choice regarding it.' The Arabs censure failing to keep a promise but praise failing to follow through on a threat. One of them said:

My nephew does not fear my attack as long as I live
    and so does not hide out of fear of the threatener.

When I threaten or promise, I do not follow through on my threat
    but I fulfil my promise.

Their Lord responds to them:

He answers them. Al-Ḥasan said, 'They continue to say, "Our Lord, Our Lord," until He answers them.' Ja'far aṣ-Ṣādiq said, 'If someone says five times, "Our Lord," Allah will save him from what he fears and give him what he wants.' He was asked, 'How is that?' He replied, 'Recite if you wish, *"those who remember Allah"* to *"You do not break Your promise."* (3:191-194)'

Their Lord responds to them: 'I will not let the deeds of any doer among you go to waste, male or female –

'Īsā ibn 'Umar recited *'innī'* instead of *'annī'*. Al-Ḥakīm Abū 'Abdullāh related that Umm Salamah said, 'Messenger of Allah, why do I not hear Allah mention women in the *hijrah* at all?' Then Allah revealed: *'Their Lord responds to them "I will not let the deeds of any doer among you go to waste, male or female."'* At-Tirmidhī transmitted it.

'Min' in the sentence is for stress because it is preceded by a negative particle. The Kufans, however, say that it is explanatory and cannot be elided because it is included for the meaning which is not sound without it. It can be elided when it is stress for denial.

you are both the same in that respect.

This is an inceptive and predicate. It means: your *dīn* is the same. It is said that you (meaning male and female) are both the same with respect to reward, judgments, help and the like. Aḍ-Ḍaḥḥāk said, 'Your men are like your women in respect of obedience, and your women are like your men in respect of obedience.' This is similar to the phrase: *'The men and women of the believers are friends of one another.'* (9:71) When it is said, 'So-and-so is from me (*minnī*),' it means: 'He has my position and my character.'

Those who made hijrah and were driven from their homes and suffered harm in My Way and fought and were killed.

'Those who made hijrah' are those who left their homes and came to Madīnah *'and were driven from their homes'* in obedience to Allah Almighty. *'They fought'* My enemies and *'were killed'* in My Way (*qātalū wa qutilū*). Ibn Kathīr and Ibn 'Āmir have *'qātalū wa qattalū'* which is for stress. Al-A'mash recited *'qutilū wa qātalū,'* meaning 'fight My enemies and are killed in My path.'

It is said that the word *'qad'* is elided in the words, meaning 'They were killed and they fought (*qad qātilū*). [POEM ON USAGE] It is said: those of them who remained fought. The Arabs say, 'We fought the Banū Tamīm and some of them were killed.' Imru'u-l-Qays said:

If you kill us, we will kill you.

'Umar ibn 'Abd al-'Azīz recited *'qatalū wa qutilū'* without *alif.*

I will erase their bad actions from them

I will veil them from them in the Next World and will not rebuke them on account of them nor punish them for them because the reward is affirmed for those people. According to the Basrans, '*thawāb*' is a verbal noun of stress because the words '*I will admit them into Gardens with rivers flowing under them*' mean, 'I will give them a reward.' Al-Kisā'ī said that it is accusative for the disjunctive. Al-Farrā' said that it is explanatory. They will be given an excellent recompense. [GRAMMATICAL EXEGESIS]

Do not be deceived by the fact that those who disbelieve move freely about the earth.

It is said that this is addressed to the Prophet ﷺ while the Community is meant. It is said that it is addressed to all. That is because the Muslims said, 'The unbelievers trade, have wealth and are able to travel about in the land while we are dying from hunger,' and so it was revealed: 'Do not be deceived by the apparent safety of the unbelievers in their moving about in their journeys.'

A brief enjoyment; then their shelter will be Hell.

The words '*A brief enjoyment*' mean that they will only move about freely for a brief time and the benefit of that is only a very temporary one. Ya'qūb recited '*yaghurranka*'. [POEM] It is similar to: '*Do not let their free movement about the earth deceive you.*' (40:4) It is called 'brief' because it is passing. Everything which is passing, even if it is a lot, is actually little. We find in the *Ṣaḥīḥ* of at-Tirmidhī that al-Mustawrid reported that the Prophet ﷺ said, 'This world in comparison with the Next World is like putting your finger in the sea and seeing what comes back on it.''

What an evil resting-place!

The '*resting-place*' is evil for them because of their unbelief. It is what Allah has prepared for them in the Fire. Some find evidence in this *āyah* and ones like it: '*Those who disbelieve should not imagine that the extra time We grant to them is good for them.*' (3:178). '*I will give them more time. My strategy is sure.*' (7:183) '*Do they imagine that, in the wealth and children We extend to them…*' (23:55) and '*We will lead them, step by step, into destruction from where they do not know.*' (7:182), and say that these *āyah*s are evidence that the unbelievers are not in fact blessed in this world because the reality of blessing is free from the taint of both immediate and later harm. The blessing of the unbelievers is mixed with pain and punishment. So it is like someone who is given honey mixed with poison. Even if he enjoys eating it, it is not called a blessing because it will kill him. A group of scholars believe this. It is the position of Abu-l-Ḥasan al-Ash'arī.

A group of them, including Qāḍī Abū Bakr, the Sword of the Sunnah and Tongue of the *Ummah*, believe that Allah actually does bless them in this world. They say, 'The root of blessing (*ni'mah*) is *na'mah*, which is a comfortable life,' and we find this linguistically used in the Qur'an: *'What comfort and ease (na'mah) they delighted in!'* (44:27) One says that the flour is fine (*nā'im*) when it is very finely milled. This is sound and there is further evidence for it in that Allah obliges the unbelievers to be grateful as is it obliged on all of those subject to responsibility. He says: *'Remember the blessings of Allah'* (7:74) and *'thank Allah.'* (2:182) Thankfulness is only for blessing. He says: *'And do good as Allah has been good to you'* (28:77), and this was addressed to Qārūn. He says: *'Allah makes a likeness of a city which was safe and at peace'* (16:112). So Allah reports that He blessed them with worldly blessings and they were ungrateful for them. He says: *'They acknowledge Allah's blessing and then deny it'* (16:83) and *'Mankind! remember Allah's blessing upon you.'* (35:3) This is universal and includes the unbelievers and others.

When poisoned food is offered to someone, that is a kindness to him in that situation, since they are not made to swallow pure poison, but it is mixed with something sweet. So it is not unlikely for it to be said, 'He has blessed him.' If this is the case, then there are two types of blessings: a beneficial blessing and an averting blessing. A beneficial blessing is any kind of pleasure someone is given. An averting blessing is one that averts from them any type of disaster. According to this view, Allah does give blessings to the unbelievers. They do not disagree that Allah does not give them the blessing of the *dīn*. Praise be to Allah.

But those who have *taqwā* of their Lord will have gardens with rivers flowing under them

This concludes the negation of the unbelievers and their benefit of moving freely about the land. It is, however, the godfearing who will have the greatest and everlasting benefit. The word *'But'* is in the position of the nominative by the inceptive. Yazīd ibn al-Qa'qā' recited *'lakinna'*.

hospitality from Allah.

Nuzul is like *thawāb* according to the Basrans. Al-Kisā'ī said that it is a verbal noun, and al-Farrā' said that it is explanatory. Al-Ḥasan and an-Nakha'ī recited *'nuzl'*, finding two *ḍammah*s heavy. The rest have it as *nuzul*. The meaning of *nuzul* is hospitality prepared for a guest. *Nazīl* is a guest. A poet says:

The guest of a people has the greatest right
    and the right of Allah in respect of the guest's right.

The plural is *anzāl*. The portion of a guest (*nazīl*) is brought together. *Nuzl* is a lot of food served to the guest as is *nazal*.

Perhaps the specific meaning of hospitality here, and Allah knows best, is what appears in *Ṣaḥīḥ Muslim* from Thawbān, the client of the Messenger of Allah ﷺ, in the story about a rabbi who asked the Prophet ﷺ, 'Where will people be on the day the earth is changed to other than the earth and heavens?' He replied ﷺ, 'They will be in the darkness before the bridge.' He asked, 'Who will be the first person to cross?' He replied ﷺ, 'The poor Muhājirūn.' The Jew asked, 'What will be their hospitality they enter the Garden?' He answered ﷺ, 'The lobe of the liver of the whale.' He asked, 'And what will be their food after it?' He replied ﷺ, 'The oxen of the Garden will be slaughtered for them and they will eat from the best of them.' He asked, 'What will be their drink?' He replied ﷺ, 'It will be from a spring there called Salsabīl.'

Linguists say that *tuḥfah* (hospitality) in the hadith are fruits that one presents (*atḥafa*) and *ṭuḥaf* is the best of something. This corresponds to what we mentioned about hospitality. Allah knows best. 'The lobe of the liver' is a piece like a finger. Al-Harawī said that *'hospitality from Allah'* means a reward. It is said that it means provision.

The expression *'What is with Allah is better for those who are truly good,'* means that it it is better than what the unbelievers have in this world. Allah knows best.

Among the people of the Book there are some who believe in Allah and in what has been sent down to you and what was sent down to them,

Jābir ibn 'Abdullāh, Anas, Ibn 'Abbās, Qatādah and al-Ḥasan said that this was revealed about the Negus. That was because when he died, Jibrīl announced his death to the Messenger of Allah ﷺ and the Prophet ﷺ told his Companions, 'Stand and pray for your brother the Negus.' They remarked to one another, 'He commands us to pray for one of the Abyssinian barbarians!' Then Allah revealed this.

Aḍ-Ḍaḥḥāk said that the words *'what has been sent down to you'* refer to the Qur'an and the words *'and what was sent down to them'* refer to the Torah and Gospel. We find in the Revelation: *'They will be given their reward twice over.'* (28:54) We find in *Ṣaḥīh Muslim*, 'Three will be given their reward twice over.' A man of the People of the Book is mentioned who believes in his own Prophet and then meets the Prophet ﷺ and believes in him, follows him and affirms him. He will have two rewards. This was already mentioned in *al-Baqarah*. Mujāhid, Ibn Jurayj and Ibn Zayd said that it was revealed about all the believers of the People of the Book. It is general and the Negus is one of them. His name was Aṣḥamah which means gift.

and who are humble before Allah.

This means humble and abased. It is in the accusative for the *ḥāl* modifying what is implied in 'believe', and it is said that it is modifying the pronoun in '*to them*' or '*to you*'. The *āyah* contains clarification.

You who believe, be steadfast.

Allah ends the *sūrah* with the directives that this tenth *āyah* contains which include victory over the enemy in this world and success in obtaining the bliss of the Next World. So He encourages steadfastness in obedience and against one's appetites. *Ṣabr* means constraint, and was already discussed in *al-Baqarah*.

Be supreme in steadfastness.

This is *ṣābara*, and it is said that it means steadfastness against the enemy, as Zayd ibn Aslam stated. Al-Ḥasan said that it is being steadfast in the five prayers. It is said that it is being constant in opposing the appetites of the *nafs*. 'Aṭā' and al-Quraẓī said, 'Wait patiently for what you are promised,' in other words do not despair, but wait for relief. The Prophet ﷺ said, 'Waiting for relief with patience is worship.' Abū 'Umar preferred this. The first is the position of the majority. 'Antarah said:

> I have not seen any living person as steadfast we are,
> Nor any who struggled against the like of those we struggled against.

He means that they were steadfast against the enemy in war as we were steadfast, and displayed neither cowardice nor treachery.

Struggling (*mukāfajah*) is face-to-face combat. That is why they disagree about the meaning of '*rābiṭū*' in '*be firm on the battlefield*.' Most of the Community say that it means: 'line up horses against the enemy,' implying link them up as your enemies do, and that is seen in the words of the Almighty: '*with all the firepower and cavalry you can muster.*' (8:60)

In the *Muwaṭṭā'* Zayd ibn Aslam reports: "Ubayda ibn al-Jarrāḥ wrote to 'Umar ibn al-Khaṭṭāb mentioning to him the great array of Byzantine troops and the anxiety they were causing him. 'Umar wrote to him, "Whatever hardship befalls a believing slave, Allah will make an opening for him after it, and a hardship will not overcome two eases. Allah says in His Book: '*You who believe, be steadfast; be supreme in steadfastness; be firm on the battlefield; and have taqwa of Allah; so that hopefully you will be successful.*'""

Abū Salamah ibn 'Abd ar-Raḥmān said, 'This *āyah* is about waiting for the prayer after the prayer. There was no expedition in the time of the Messenger of Allah ﷻ in which horses were tied up.' Abū 'Abdullāh al-Ḥakam related it in his *Ṣaḥīḥ*. Abū Salamah used as evidence the words of Prophet ﷺ: 'Shall I direct you to something by which Allah will wipe out wrong actions and raise up degrees? Doing *wuḍū'* thoroughly, even in times of difficulty, taking many steps to the mosque and waiting for the prayer after praying the previous one. That is *ribāṭ*,' three times. Mālik related it.

Ibn 'Aṭiyyah said, 'The sound position is that *ribāṭ* is perseverance in the Way of Allah.' Its root meaning is the tying up of horses. Then anyone who devoted himself to defending one of the frontiers of Islam was called a *murābiṭ*, whether he was mounted or on foot. It is derived from *rabṭ* (tying up). The Prophet ﷺ said, 'That is your *ribāṭ*.' It resembles *ribāṭ* in the Way of Allah. This sort of usage is common as in the hadith: 'The strong person is not the one who throws people down. The strong person is the one who controls himself when he is angry.'

The first, which is the linguistic meaning, is not contestable. Al-Khalīl ibn Aḥmad, one of the imāms of linguistics, says, '*Ribāṭ* is clinging to the frontiers and being constant in the prayer.' Therefore, waiting for the prayer is a true linguistic meaning of *ribāṭ*, as the Prophet ﷺ said. Moreover, there is what ash-Shaybānī observed about it. Water can be described as '*mutarābiṭ*,' meaning remaining in one place and not leaving it. Ibn Fāris related it. That is demanded by the transitive nature of *ribāṭ* linguistically. *Murābiṭah* in Arabic denotes a contract regarding something, so that it does not peter out, and so it refers to something in which one is steadfast. So the heart is bound by good intention and the body by obedience. One of the most important aspects of this is lining up horses in the Way of Allah, as in the text of the Qur'an, '*with cavalry*' (8:60), but it also includes binding the self to performing the prayers as the Prophet ﷺ said, as related by Abu Hurayrah, Jābir and 'Alī.

According to the *fuqahā'*, a *murābiṭ* in the Way of Allah is someone who goes to one of the frontiers to bind himself there for a time. Muḥammad ibn al-Mawwāz says that. As for those who live at the frontiers who prosper and earn there, they are not *murābiṭūn* even if they are defenders. Ibn 'Aṭiyyah said that.

Ibn Khuwayzimandād said, 'There are two situations with respect to *ribāṭ*. One is that someone is secure and defended at the frontier. In that case it is permitted to live there with one's wife and children. If it is not safe, a man is permitted to stay there himself, if he is one of the people of fighting, but may not move his wife and children there to expose them to the enemy, since they might be captured and enslaved.' Allah knows best.

Many hadiths have come about the excellence of *ribāṭ*. They include what al-

Bukhārī reported from Sahl ibn Sa'd as-Sā'idī in which the Messenger of Allah ﷺ said, 'Manning the frontier (*ribāṭ*) for one day in the way of Allah is better than this world and everything in it.' In *Ṣaḥīḥ Muslim*, Salmān reported that he heard the Messenger of Allah ﷺ say, 'Fighting on the front line (*ribāṭ*) for a day and a night is better than fasting and praying at night for a month. If a man dies doing it, the actions which he used normally to do go on accruing for him and his provision is bestowed on him and he will be safe from the trials of the grave.' Abū Dāwūd reports from Faḍālah ibn 'Ubayd that the Messenger of Allah ﷺ said, 'The actions of every dead person are sealed except for the *murābiṭ* in the Way of Allah. His actions will go on increasing until the Day of Rising and he will be safe from the trials of the grave.'

These hadiths provide evidence that *ribāṭ* is the best of actions whose reward continues after death, as in the hadith reported from al-'Alā' ibn 'Abd ar-Raḥmān from his father from Abū Hurayrah in which the Prophet ﷺ said: 'When a man dies, his actions are cut off except for three: an on-going *ṣadaqah,* knowledge which brought benefit and a virtuous son who makes supplication for him.' This is a sound hadith in the transmission of Muslim. On-going *ṣadaqah*, beneficial knowledge, and a righteous son who makes supplication for his parents end when the *ṣadaqah* runs out, the knowledge is lost or the son dies, but the reward of *ribāṭ* goes on being multiplied until the Day of Rising because the only meaning of growth is multiplication. It does not depend on a cause so that it would cease when that cause disappears. Instead, it is a favour from Allah that will continue until the Day of Rising.

This is due to the fact that no actions of piety are possible except when there is security from the enemy and the territory of the *dīn* and hallmarks of Islam are protected. For this reason *ribāṭ* continues to enjoy a reward which comes from all other righteous actions that are performed. Ibn Mājah transmitted with a sound *isnād* from Abū Hurayrah that the Messenger of Allah ﷺ said, 'If someone dies as a *murābiṭ* in the Cause of Allah, he will be given the reward for the righteous actions he did, given his provision, and receive security from the Tempter and Allah will resurrect him on the Day of Rising safe from alarm.' This hadith has a second qualification, which is death while a *murābiṭ.* Allah knows best.

It is related that 'Uthmān ibn 'Affān heard the Messenger of Allah ﷺ say, 'Fighting on the frontier (*ribāṭ*) in the way of Allah is better than a thousand years of fasting and prayer at night.' Ubayy ibn Ka'b reported that the Messenger of Allah ﷺ said, '*Ribāṭ* for a day in the Way of Allah during Ramaḍān in the exposed areas of the Muslims, in anticipation of the reward, has a greater reward with

Allah and repayment from Him than the worship of fasting and night prayers for a thousand years. If Allah returns him safe to his family, no evil deed will be written against him for a thousand years, his good actions are written for him, and the reward of *ribāṭ* will continue for him until the Day of Rising.' This hadith indicates that *ribāṭ* in the month of Ramaḍān will bring him an abiding reward, even if he does not die while engaged in it. Allah knows best. Anas ibn Mālik said that he heard the Messenger of Allah ﷺ say, 'A night spent on guard in the Way of Allah is better than a man praying and fasting in his family for a thousand years. The year is three hundred and sixty days, and every day is like a thousand years.'

It is reported that waiting for the prayer after the prayer is *ribāṭ*. So the one who waits for the prayer also has that excellence, Allah willing. Al-Ḥāfiẓ Abū Nu'aym related from Sulaymān ibn Aḥmad from 'Alī ibn 'Abd al-'Azīz from Ḥajjāj ibn al-Minhāl, and from Abū Bakr ibn Mālik from 'Abdullāh ibn Aḥmad ibn Ḥanbal from his father from al-Ḥusayn ibn Mūsā from Ḥammād ibn Salamah from Thābit al-Bunānī from Abū Ayyūb al-Azdī from Nawf al-Bikālī that 'Abdullāh ibn 'Amr said, 'The Prophet ﷺ prayed *maghrib* one day and we prayed with him. Some people left and some stayed behind. The Messenger of Allah ﷺ came before the people had called the *'Ishā'* prayer. He came to the people who were there, raised his fingers indicating twenty-seven, and pointed to the sky. His garment exposed his knees while he was saying, "Good news, company of Muslims! Your Lord has opened one of the gates of heaven to boast of you to the angels, saying, 'Look at My slaves who have finished one obligation and are waiting for another.'"' Ḥammād ibn Salamah related from 'Alī ibn Zayd from Muṭarrif ibn 'Abdullāh from both Nawf and 'Abdullāh, the sons of 'Amr, from Nawf from the Torah, and 'Abdullāh ibn 'Amr related it from the Prophet ﷺ.

Have *taqwā* of Allah.

Allah never commands *jihād* without emphasising the need for *taqwā*.

so that hopefully you will be successful.

So that you will have the success you hope for. Here *'la'alla'* means 'so that'. Success is going-on. All of this was discussed fully in *al-Baqarah*. Praise be to Allah.

4. Sūrat an-Nisā' – Women

This is a Madinan *sūrah* except for one *āyah* which was revealed in Makkah in the year of the Conquest about 'Uthmān ibn Ṭalḥah al-Ḥajabī: *'Allah commands you to return to their owners the things you hold on trust.'* (4:58). An-Naqqāsh said that it was said that it was revealed during the Prophet's *hijrah* from Makkah to Madīnah. Some people say that since Allah says, 'O mankind' it means that it was revealed in Makkah. 'Alqamah and others said that, and so it seems that the beginning is Makkan and what is revealed after the Hijrah is Madinan. An-Naḥḥās said that it is all Makkan.

The first position is sounder because we find in *Ṣaḥīḥ Bukhārī* that 'Ā'ishah said, *'Sūrat an-Nisā'* was only revealed while I was with the Messenger of Allah ﷺ,' meaning married to him. There is no disagreement that Prophet ﷺ married 'Ā'ishah in Madīnah. Whoever examines its rulings will realise that there is no doubt that it is Madinan. As for the expression 'O mankind' making it Makkan, this is not sound. *Al-Baqarah* is Madinan, but 'O mankind' occurs twice in it. Allah knows best.

يَٰٓأَيُّهَا ٱلنَّاسُ ٱتَّقُوا۟ رَبَّكُمُ ٱلَّذِى خَلَقَكُم مِّن نَّفْسٍ وَٰحِدَةٍ وَخَلَقَ مِنْهَا
زَوْجَهَا وَبَثَّ مِنْهُمَا رِجَالًا كَثِيرًا وَنِسَآءً ۚ وَٱتَّقُوا۟ ٱللَّهَ ٱلَّذِى تَسَآءَلُونَ بِهِۦ
وَٱلْأَرْحَامَ ۚ إِنَّ ٱللَّهَ كَانَ عَلَيْكُمْ رَقِيبًا ﴿١﴾

1 O mankind, have *taqwā* of your Lord who created you from a single self and created its mate from it and then disseminated many men and women from the two of them. Have *taqwā* of Allah in whose name you make demands on one another and also in respect of your families. Allah watches over you continually.

O mankind, have *taqwā* of your Lord who created you

We already discussed the derivation of the terms 'mankind', '*taqwā*', 'Lord', 'creation', 'mate' and 'dissemination' in *al-Baqarah*. The *āyah* calls attention to the Creator.

The adjective *'single' (wāḥidah)* is in the feminine, because the word *nafs* is feminine, even if it denotes the masculine. Linguistically, one could use the masculine since Ādam is meant, as Mujāhid and Qatādah said, and that is found in the reading of Ibn Abī 'Ablah which has *'wāḥid'*. The verb *'baththa'* (disseminate) means to separate and spread out over the earth, as we see in *'spread-out rugs'* (88:16). *'The two of them'* are Ādam and Ḥawwā'. Mujāhid said that Ḥawwā' was created from the rib of Ādam, as in the hadith, 'Woman was created from a crooked rib' as we mentioned in *al-Baqarah.*

and then disseminated many men and women from the two of them.

Their descendants are of two categories. This means that the hermaphrodite is not a separate category, but has an actuality that refers to both categories. Such a person is a human being and must be connected to one sex or another as was already mentioned in *al-Baqarah.*

Have *taqwā* of Allah in whose name you make demands on one another and also in respect of your families

The repetition of '*have taqwa*' is for stress and notification to the selves of those who are commanded. The word *'whose'* is in the accusative as an adjective and '*families*' is added. The sentence means: 'Fear Allah lest you disobey Him and fear cutting off kin.'

The people of Madīnah read this as *'tassā'alūna'*, assimilating the *tā'* into the *sīn* while the Kufans read it *'tasā'alūna'* because the meaning is known. Ibrāhīm an-Nakha'ī, Qatādah, al-A'mash and Ḥamzah read *'al-arḥāmi'* in the genitive. Grammarians have discussed this. The leaders of the Basrans said that it is ungrammatical and it is not lawful to recite it like that. The Kufans said that it is ugly and do not add anything to this without mentioning the reason for it. An-Naḥḥās said, 'as far as I know.' Sībawayh said, 'It is not added to something implied in the genitive because it is in the position of *tanwīn* which is not added to it.'

One group say that it is added to something indicated. They used to make demands in that way. A man would say, 'I ask you by Allah and kinship.' That is how it is explained by al-Ḥasan, an-Nakha'ī and Mujāhid. It is a sound position with respect to the matter as will be explained.

Some people, including az-Zajjāj, said that it is weak. They said, 'It is ugly to add the substantive noun to the pronoun in the genitive unless what is in the genitive is in the substantive form, as in Allah's words: '*We caused the earth to swallow both him and his house.'* (28:81) It is ugly to say, 'I passed by him and Zayd(*in*).' Az-Zajjāj said that al-Māzinī said that it is because the coupled word and its antecedent are equal partners and either of them can take the place of the other.' As it is not permitted to say, 'I passed by Zayd and you (*ka*),' it is not permitted to say, 'I passed by you (*bika*) and Zayd.' Sībawayh said that he considers it ugly and only permitted in poetry. [POEMS]

In *Kitāb at-tadhkirah al-mahdiyyah*, al-Fārisī says that Abu-l-'Abbās al-Mubbarad said, 'If you pray behind an imam who recites "*mā antum bi-musrikhiyy*" (14:22) and this as "*tasā'alūna bihi wa-l-arḥāmi*", take your sandals and leave.'

Az-Zajjāj said, 'In addition to being weak and ugly in Arabic, the reading of Ḥamzah is an serious error in respect of the principles of the *dīn* because the Prophet ﷺ said, "Do not swear by your fathers." If it is not permitted to swear by other than Allah, how can it be permitted to swear by kinship? I also saw that Ismā'īl ibn Isḥāq believed that swearing by other than Allah is something terrible and that one should only swear by Allah.'

An-Naḥḥās said, 'Some of them say that "*al-arḥāmi*" as an oath is an error both in grammar and meaning because the hadith from the Prophet ﷺ indicates that it should be in the accusative (*al-arḥāma*), and it is related that Jarīr said, "We were with the Prophet ﷺ when some people of Muḍar came who were naked and barefoot. I saw the expression on the face of the Messenger of Allah ﷺ change because of what he saw of their dire poverty. Then he prayed *Ẓuhr* and addressed the people and quoted this *āyah*." Then he said, "One man gave a dinar in *ṣadaqah*, another a dirham and yet another a *ṣā'* of dates."' So the reason that it is in the accusative is because it is encouraging maintaining ties of kinship. It is also sound that the Prophet ﷺ said, 'Whoever swears should swear by Allah or be silent.' This refutes the one who says: 'I ask you by Allah and my kin.' Abū Isḥāq said that it means 'by which you demand your rights.' There is also no sense to the genitive here. This is what I know about the position of language scholars who forbid reciting it as '*al-arḥāmi*' in the genitive. Ibn 'Aṭiyyah preferred that.

Imām Abū Naṣr 'Abd ar-Raḥīm ibn 'Abd al-Karīm al-Qushayrī rejected that, saying, 'Such words are rejected by the imams of the *dīn* because the readings of the imams of recitation are confirmed from the Prophet ﷺ by multiple transmissions which are known. Whoever rejects that, rejects the Prophet ﷺ and finds the recitation ugly. This is a position which one should be aware of and wary about. One should not follow the imams of language and grammar in it. Arabic is learned from the Prophet ﷺ and no one doubts his eloquence.'

As for what is mentioned about the hadith, it is debatable because the Prophet

ﷺ said to Abu-l-'Usharā', "By your father, stabbing it in the thigh is sufficient." It is prohibited to swear an oath by other than Allah. This is entreating someone by the right of kinship, and it is not forbidden.'

Al-Qushayrī said, 'It is said that this is an adjuration by kinship, meaning "Have *taqwā* of Allah and the right of kinship." It is like when you say, "Do that, by your father's right." Revelation has, "By the star," 'By the Mount," "By the fig" and so forth. This is unnatural.' In fact, this is not unnatural, because it is not unlikely that *'al-arḥām'* is like this. Swearing by that is as Allah swears by that which He has created and which indicates His oneness and power for stress. Allah knows best. Allah can swear by whatever He wishes, forbid whatever He wishes and allow whatever He wishes. So this can be an oath, as the Arabs swear by kinship. It is sound that the *bā'* is meant and elided as we see in poems [POEMS]

'Abdullāh ibn Yazīd recited *'al-arḥāmu'* in the nominative as the inceptive and the predicate is implied. It implies: 'And relatives are family with whom ties are maintained.' It is also possible that it is instigation because the Arabs put that in the nominative. [POEM] It is also said that it is in the accusative added to 'bihi' because its position is accusative. [POEM] They used to say, 'I ask you by Allah and by kinship.' What is most apparent is that it is in the accusative by an implied verb as we already mentioned.

The religion agrees that it is mandatory to maintain ties of kinship and that it is forbidden to cut them off. It is confirmed that when Asmā' asked the Prophet ﷺ, 'Shall I give to my mother?' he replied, 'Yes, give to your mother,' and he commanded her to maintain her tie of kinship although her mother was an unbeliever. So it includes within the favour even giving to an unbeliever. This is such that Abū Ḥanīfah and his people said that relatives inherit from one another if there are no paternal kin (*'aṣabah*) or prescribed shares.

One should buy and free relatives who are slaves. That is supported by what Abū Dāwud related that the Prophet ﷺ said: 'If someone comes into possession of a *maḥram* relative, then he is free.' That is the position of most of the people of knowledge, and is related from 'Umar ibn al-Khaṭṭāb and 'Abdullāh ibn Mas'ūd and it is not known that any of the Companions objected to it. It is the position of al-Ḥasan al-Baṣrī, Jābir ibn Zayd, 'Aṭā', ash-Sha'bī and az-Zuhrī. That is the view taken by ath-Thawrī, Aḥmad and Isḥāq. Our scholars have three positions. One is that it is specific to fathers and grandfathers. The second that it applies to both sides, meaning siblings, and the third is like what Abū Ḥanīfah says about it applying to any relatives. Ash-Shāfi'ī said that someone is only obliged to free children and parents, but not siblings or any other relatives.

The sound position is the first one based on the hadith which we mentioned and which was transmitted by at-Tirmidhī and an-Nasā'ī. The best of its paths is that which is in an-Nasā'ī which he related from Ḍamrah from Sufyān from 'Abdullāh ibn Dīnār from Ibn 'Umar that the Messenger of Allah ﷺ said, 'If someone comes into possession of a *maḥram* relative, he must free him.' This is a firm hadith transmitted from one reputable transmitter to another and there is no criticism of it by any of the imams for any reason which would demand that it be abandoned, other than the fact that an-Nasā'ī said at the end of it that it is a *munkar* hadith. Others said that he alone has Ḍamrah and this is the meaning of *munkar* and *shādhdh* in the terminology of hadith scholars. Ḍamrah is reputable and trustworthy. When someone trustworthy is the only one with a hadith, that does not impair it. Allah knows best. They disagree about whether this applies to milk relatives. Most say that it does not and the hadith does not demand that. Qāḍī Sharīk said that he must emancipate them.

The literalists and some *mutakallimūn* believe that a son is not forced to free his father if he owns him. Their argument is based on the hadith in which the Prophet ﷺ said, 'A child cannot repay his parent unless he finds him a slave and buys him and sets him free.' They said that if it is valid to buy him, ownership is confirmed and an owner has free disposal of his property.

This is ignorance of the goals (*maqāṣid*) of the Sharī'ah on their part. Allah Almighty says: *'you should show kindness to your parents.'* (17:23) So He connects worship of Him to kindness to parents in respect of obligation. It is not part of kindness for a son to allow his parent to remain his property and to be subject to his authority. Therefore he is obliged to free him either because of his ownership and acting by the hadith, or for the sake of being kind to him, acting by the *āyah*. According to the majority, the hadith applies when the son has the means to free his father by buying him and the Sharī'ah applies emancipation to him as coming from him.

The disagreement of scholars is about who is set free when he or she is owned. The reason for the first position is what we mentioned from the Book and the Sunnah. The reason for the second view is the connection of close kinship to the father which is mentioned in the hadith, not the closeness of a man to his son so that it is applied to the father. A brother is close to him in that respect because of the connection by paternity. He says, 'I am your father's son.' The reason for third view is connected to the hadith of Ḍamrah. Allah knows best.

Al-arḥām: raḥm is the name for all relatives without difference between *maḥram* or non-*maḥram*. Abū Ḥanīfah thinks that the *maḥram* relationship prevents taking a gift back, while it is permitted to take it back in the case of cousins even if severance exists when there is kinship. That is why inheritance, guardianship and other rulings are connected to it. The quality of being *maḥram* is additional to the text of the Book, and is not relied on. They also think that it is abrogated, especially when it indicates the cause of severance. It is allowed in respect of cousins. Allah knows best.

Allah watches over you continually.

He is Watcher, meaning Guardian, according to Ibn 'Abbās and Mujāhid. Ibn Zayd says a Knower. It is said that *Raqīb* means Guardian, and it is one of the attributes of Allah Almighty. *Ar-Raqīb* is the One who guards and watches. The verb is *raqaba*. *Marqab* is a high place which overlooks the area where the Watcher is. *Raqīb* is also the third share of the seven parts, and it is said that it is a type of snake. So it is a word with different meanings, and Allah knows best.

وَءَاتُوا۟ ٱلْيَتَـٰمَىٰٓ أَمْوَٰلَهُمْ ۖ وَلَا تَتَبَدَّلُوا۟ ٱلْخَبِيثَ بِٱلطَّيِّبِ ۖ وَلَا تَأْكُلُوٓا۟
أَمْوَٰلَهُمْ إِلَىٰٓ أَمْوَٰلِكُمْ ۚ إِنَّهُۥ كَانَ حُوبًا كَبِيرًا ۝٢

2 Give orphans their property, and do not substitute bad things for good. Do not assimilate their property into your own. Doing that is a serious crime.

Give orphans their property,

'Orphans' means those who *were* orphans. It is like Allah's words: *'The magicians threw themselves down in prostration'* (7:120) when there was no longer any magic in them when they prostrated. Similarly, although an adult is not actually considered 'an orphan', the Prophet ﷺ was nevertheless called 'the orphan of Abū Ṭālib' based on what had previously been the case. The verb *'ātū'* means 'give' and *'ītā''* is giving. *'Atw'* is a gift. Abū Zayd said that a bribe is a gift (*itāwah*). The word 'orphan' only applies to someone who has not yet reached maturity as mentioned in *al-Baqarah*.

This *āyah* is addressed to guardians and executors. According to Muqātil and al-Kalbī it was revealed about a man of Ghaṭafān who had a lot of property belonging to a nephew who was an orphan. When the orphan came of age, he asked for his property and the uncle refused to hand it over, and this was revealed. The uncle said, 'We seek refuge with Allah from serious crime!' and he returned the property. The Prophet ﷺ said, 'Whoever is protected from the avarice of his *nafs* and returns it, will alight in his house,' referring to the Garden. When the lad took the money, he spent it in the Way of Allah, and the Prophet ﷺ said, 'The wage is confirmed and the burden remains.' He was asked, 'How is that, the Messenger of Allah?' He said, 'The wage is established for the lad and the sin remains for his father,' because he was an idolater.

There are two aspects to giving orphans their property. One is that their guardian gives them their food and clothing as long he is in that position, since that is not possible for someone who does not have full control, such as a child or an adult fool. The second is to give them money when they are capable. That is when they are tested and sensible. So the term 'orphan' is metaphorical since it no longer applies to someone like that. It means the one who was an orphan. It is continuing to keep the name as in the words: *'The magicians fell down in prostration'* (26:46), which means those who had been magicians, and just as the Prophet ﷺ was called 'the orphan of Abū Ṭālib'. When a guardian realises that his charges are properly responsible, it is forbidden for him to withhold their money. Abū Ḥanīfah said, 'When someone is twenty-five, they are given their money in any case.'

Allah did not mention in this *āyah* about being aware of sensibleness (*rushd*). He mentioned it later: *'Keep a close check on orphans until they reach a marriageable age, then if you perceive that they have sound judgment, hand over their property to them.'* (4:6) Abū Bakr ar-Rāzī al-Ḥanafī says in *Aḥkām al-Qur'an*: 'Since good judgment is not made a condition in one place, while it is in another, it should not be applied to both situations. So when someone is twenty-five and is a fool, and good sense is not discerned in him, his money must still be given to him. If he is younger than that, then it is not mandatory, based on the two *āyahs*.' Abū Ḥanīfah said, 'It is possible that someone can be a grandfather before they reach sound judgment. If they can be a grandfather, how is it sound to give them money on account of being an orphan and in the name of an orphan? Is that not extremely unlikely?'

Ibn 'Arabī refuted this as being baseless, especially on the basis that he sees that such payments cannot be confirmed by analogy. They must be derived from texts and no texts exist regarding this matter. What the scholars say about being debarred will be discussed later, Allah willing.

Do not substitute bad things for good.

So do not exchange a fat sheep of the orphan's property for a thin one, nor a good dirham for an adulterated one. In the Jāhiliyyah, due to lack of *dīn*, people did not refrain from consuming the property of orphans. They would take what was good from the property of orphans and replace it with bad property of their own and say, 'A name for a name and capital for capital.' Allah forbade that. This is the position of Sa'īd ibn al-Musayyab, az-Zuhrī, as-Suddī, and aḍ-Ḍaḥḥāk. It is the literal meaning of the *āyah*.

It is said that the meaning is: 'Do not consume the property of orphans which is unlawful for you and therefore bad, claiming that it is good and your own property.' Mujāhid, Abū Ṣāliḥ and Bādhān said, 'Do not hasten to consume any bad things in their property and claim it is good and lawful provision.'

Ibn Zayd that in the Jāhiliyyah they did not allow women and children to inherit. The eldest would take the legacy. 'Aṭā' said, 'Do not take profit from an orphan in your care when he is young and naïve.' These two positions are outside the apparent meaning of the *āyah*. The verb *tabaddala* is to exchange one thing for another in its place. The grammatical term appositive (*badal*) comes from this verb.

Do not assimilate their property into your own.

Mujāhid said, 'This *āyah* forbids mixing property when spending. The Arabs used to mix their expenses with those of orphans and then were forbidden to do that. Then it was abrogated by the *āyah* in *al-Baqarah*: *'If you mix your property with theirs, they are your brothers.'* (2:220) Ibn Fūrak said that al-Ḥasan said, 'People interpret this *āyah* as being a prohibition against mixing property, and so they avoided it and then the *āyah* in *al-Baqarah* made things easier for them.'

A group of later scholars said that '*ilā*' means 'with'. It is like His words, '*be helpers of (ilā) Allah*'. (61:14). [POEM] Others say that it has its normal meaning of 'to' which conveys ascription, implying, 'Do not add their property to yours in consumption.' So they were forbidden to think of the property of orphans as being like their own property over whose use and consumption they had full control.

Doing that is a serious crime.

The word '*that*' refers to assimilating property. Consuming the property of orphans is great wrong action, according to Ibn 'Abbās, al-Ḥasan and others. '*Crime*' (*ḥūb*) is derived from the verb *hāba*, meaning to commit a wrong action. The root of the verb comes from chiding a camel. A sin is called *ḥūb* because a person is chided about it and encouraged to refrain from it. One says in supplication, 'O Allah, forgive my sin (*ḥūb*)!'

Ḥūbah is also a need as we see in the supplication, 'I present my need (*ḥūbah*) to You!' *Ḥūb* is alienation, as we see from the words of the Prophet ﷺ, 'Umm

Ya'qūb's divorce is on account of alienation.' There are a couple of dialectal forms: *ḥūb*, which is the common reading and the dialect of Hijaz; *ḥawb*, as decided by al-Ḥasan which al-Akhfash says is the dialect of Tamīm and Muqātil says is the dialect of Abyssinia. *Ḥūb* is a verbal noun as is *ḥiyābah*. Ubayy ibn Ka'b recited '*ḥāb*' as a verbal noun. *Ḥaw'ab* is a wide place and also means water. One says, '*Alḥaqa-llāhu bihi-l-ḥawbah*' (May Allah bring poverty on him). *Ḥībah* is a state. The origin of the *yā'* is *wāw*. Form V of the verb, *taḥawwaba*, means to worship and remove *ḥūb* from oneself. The verb also means expressing sorrow and crying out loudly, as when chiding. *Taḥawwaba* is also to cry out from pain. Ṭufayl said:

Taste as we tasted a morning burned
by rage in our livers and grief (*taḥawwab*).'

وَإِنْ خِفْتُمْ أَلَّا تُقْسِطُوا فِي الْيَتَامَىٰ فَانكِحُوا مَا طَابَ لَكُم
مِّنَ النِّسَاءِ مَثْنَىٰ وَثُلَاثَ وَرُبَاعَ فَإِنْ خِفْتُمْ أَلَّا تَعْدِلُوا فَوَاحِدَةً
أَوْ مَا مَلَكَتْ أَيْمَانُكُمْ ذَٰلِكَ أَدْنَىٰ أَلَّا تَعُولُوا ﴿٣﴾

3 If you are afraid of not behaving justly towards orphans, then marry other permissible women, two, three or four. But if you are afraid of not treating them equally, then only one, or those you own as slaves. That makes it more likely that you will not be unfair.

If you are afraid of not behaving justly towards orphans,

If you are afraid that you will not be fair in respect of their dowries and in spending on them, then marry other women. The Imāms agree that 'Urwah ibn az-Zubayr reported that 'Ā'ishah said about this *āyah*, 'Nephew, this refers to an orphan girl who is in the care of her guardian and is his partner in his property; he likes both her property and her beauty and so he wants to marry her without being fair with respect to her bride-price, not giving her the like of what someone else would give her. They were forbidden to marry them unless they were fair to them and gave them the highest customary bride-price. They were commanded to marry women other than them who were lawful to them.'

Ibn Khuwayzimandād said, 'This is why it is permitted for an executor to buy and sell using the property of the orphan as long as it does not entail gifts. A person can examine what his guardian buys or sells for him, and the ruler can oversee that. No one can oversee a father as long as there is not gift giving in which case, that should be overseen by the ruler.' This was discussed in *al-Baqarah*.

Aḍ-Ḍaḥḥāk, al-Ḥasan and others say that the *āyah* abrogates what existed in the Jāhiliyyah and the beginning of Islam, when a man would marry however many free women he wished. This *āyah* restricts him to four. Ibn 'Abbās, Ibn Jubayr and others said that it means: if you fear you will not be fair to orphans, then also fear about women, because they used to refrain from injustice to orphans, but not women.

Khawf (fear) is one of the words that can have opposite meanings. 'Be afraid' can mean 'feel certain' or 'think it probable'. For that reason scholars disagree about the meaning of 'fear' in this context. Abū 'Ubaydah said that it means if you are certain. Others say that it means you think it probable, and Ibn 'Aṭiyyah said that this is what skilled scholars prefer, and so it has the normal meaning of thinking probable rather than of being certain. So it means if someone thinks it probable he will not be fair to the orphan girl, he should turn away from marrying her.

The verb *aqsaṭa* means 'to be fair'. *Qasaṭa* means to act unjustly and wrong someone. The Almighty says: *'The unjust* (qāsiṭūn) *will be fuel for the Fire.'* (72:15) The Prophet ﷺ said, 'Those who are just (*muqsiṭūn*) in the *dīn* will be on minbars of light on the Day of Rising.' Ibn Waththāb and an-Nakha'ī recited *'taqsiṭū'* from *qasaṭa* with the implied additional '*lā*'. It is as if Allah were saying, 'If you do, you will be unfair.'

then marry other permissible women, two, three or four.

How can *mā* be used for human beings when it is normally used for non-sentient things? There are five answers to this objection. One is that *man* and *mā* are interchangeable as we see in other *āyahs* like 91:5 and 24:45. Here it is used for women, who are sentient beings. Ibn Abī 'Ablah recited '*man*'. The second is the view of the Basrans that *mā* can be used in an adjectival way for anything. So it means to marry lawful women. What Allah forbade is not good (*ṭayyib*). The third is the idea that *mā* here is adverbial, meaning 'as long as you think it good to marry.' Ibn 'Aṭiyyah says that this is weak. The fourth is al-Farrā's view that it is used as a verbal noun, but an-Naḥḥās said, 'This is very unlikely indeed. It is not sound. Marry a good woman.' Al-Jawharī said, 'The verb for to be good is *ṭāba, yaṭību, ṭaybah, taṭyāb.* The fifth is that what is meant here is the contract, i.e. 'marry in a wholesome manner.' The reading of Ibn Abī 'Ablah rejects these three latter views.

Abū 'Amr ibn al-'Alā' related that when the people of Makkah heard thunder, they would say, 'Glory be to the One (*mā*) whom the clouds glorify!' using *mā*. This is also seen in other similar expressions. All of those concerned with knowledge agree that Allah's words: *'If you are afraid of not behaving justly towards orphans'* does not convey the idea that someone who does not fear being unfair towards orphans should marry more than someone who is afraid of being unfair. It indicates that the *āyah* was revealed in response to those who feared that and that its ruling is more universal than that.

Abū Ḥanīfah connects this *āyah* to the permission to marry an orphan girl before she comes of age. He says that she is only an orphan before she comes of age since, once she was of age, she would be able to agree to a lowering of her dowry and is no longer called 'orphan'. There is no consensus on this. Mālik, ash-Shāfi'ī and the main body of scholars believe that marriage is not permitted until she comes of age and gives her consent, as Allah says: *'They will ask you for a fatwā about women.'* (4:127). The word 'women' *(nisā')* is used for adult women as *'rijāl'* is used for adult men. Neither 'man' nor 'woman' is used of a child. 'Women' is used with 'orphans' in that *āyah* and means 'orphans' is in this *āyah* as 'Ā'ishah said. Adult women orphans are included in the *āyah*. An adult orphan woman may only be married with her permission and a child may not be married because she cannot give her permission.

This is like what is related from by ad-Dāraquṭnī from Muḥammad ibn Isḥāq from Nāfi' that Ibn 'Umar said, 'My uncle, Qudāmah ibn Maz'ūn, married me to his niece, the daughter of his brother, 'Uthmān ibn Maz'ūn. Al-Mughīrah ibn Shu'bah went to her mother and desired her on account of her wealth and proposed to her. The case was presented to the Prophet ﷺ. Qudāmah said, "Messenger of Allah, she is my niece and I am her father's executor and I have not short-changed her. I gave her in marriage to one whose excellence and kinship I know." The Messenger of Allah ﷺ said to him, "She is an orphan, and an orphan is more entitled to dispose of her own affair." She was removed from me and al-Mughīrah ibn Shu'bah married her.' Ad-Dāraquṭnī said, 'Muḥammad ibn Isḥāq did not hear it from Nāfi', but heard it from 'Umar ibn Ḥusayn from Nāfi'.'

Ibn Abī Dhi'b related from 'Umar ibn Ḥusayn from Nāfi' from 'Abdullāh ibn 'Umar that he married the daughter of his maternal uncle, 'Uthmān ibn Maz'ūn, and her mother went to the Messenger of Allah ﷺ and said, 'My daughter dislikes that,' and the Messenger of Allah ﷺ commanded that she be separated from him. He said, 'Do not give an orphan in marriage until you ask for her consent. If she is silent, that constitutes her permission.' After 'Abdullāh she was married to al-Mughīrah ibn Shu'bah.

This refutes the position of Abū Ḥanīfah that a girl does not require a *walī* when she reaches adulthood, based on his position that a *walī* is not a precondition for a valid marriage. This was already discussed in *al-Baqarah*. There is no sense in their claim that this hadith is based on her not being an adult since he said, 'with her permission' without mentioning her being an orphan. Allah knows best.

'Ā'ishah's explanation of this the *āyah* provides understanding of what Mālik said about appropriate dowries and his referring to it when the dowry is disordered and cheating occurs regarding its amount. The appropriate dowry must be known for every group of people according to their circumstances. Mālik said, 'People have marriage customs which they know and recognise,' referring to dowries and equivalence.

Mālik was asked about a man who gave his wealthy daughter in marriage to a poor cousin of his despite her mother's objection. He said, 'I do not think that she has any say regarding that. She can argue about it until it is evident that that is the view that the father has taken and then the mother's objection is ignored.' It is permitted for a girl who is not an orphan to be married with the minimum dowry for a woman of her class because the *āyah* is about orphans. This leads us to understand that it is different for those who are not orphans.

When an orphan girl comes of age and her guardian is fair in respect of her dowry, he can marry her as was explained by 'Ā'ishah. Abū Ḥanīfah, al-Awzā'ī, ath-Thawrī and Abū Thawr said that, and among the Tābi'ūn, al-Ḥasan and Rabī'a said it as did al-Layth. Zafar and ash-Shāfi'ī said, 'It is not permitted to marry her without the permission of the ruler or unless the marriage is authorised by another relative who is closer to her or has the same level of kinship. As for him being both the husband and the one who gives in marriage, that is not allowed. Evidence for this is found in the hadith of the Prophet ﷺ, "There is no marriage without a *wālī* and two just witnesses." So there are necessarily a certain number of people: the one who marries, the one who gives in marriage and the witnesses. If someone combines two roles, then one of the number is lacking.' A third view is that she entrusts her affair to a man to give her in marriage. This is related from al-Mughīrah ibn Shu'bah. It is the position of Aḥmad, and Ibn al-Mundhir mentioned it.

'Permissible women' means those who are lawful for you, as al-Ḥasan, Ibn Jubayr and others said. It is sufficient in this respect to mention those whom one is permitted to marry because there are many categories of women who are forbidden. Ibn Abī Isḥāq, al-Jaḥdarī and Ḥamzah recited *'ṭāba'* with *imālaha*. We find in the Qur'an of Ubayy *'ṭība'* with *yā'*. This is evidence of *imālah*.

Using the word 'women' indicates that it is adult women who are meant. The root of *nisā'* is *niswah* and *niswah* has no singular. The noun for one woman is *'imra'ah'*. *'Two, three or four'* is an appositive for *mā*. It is indefinite and undeclined and so it is an equivalent in description as Abū 'Alī said. Aṭ-Ṭabarī said that they are definite like a noun because the *alif-lām* is added. It is in the position of 'Umar in being definite. Al-Kūfī said that. Az-Zajjāj said that this is an error.

It is said that it is not inflected because it diverts from the expression. *Uḥād* diverts from *wāḥid wāḥid*, *mathnā* from *ithnayn ithnayn*, *thulāth* from *thalāthah, thalātah, rubā'* from *arba'ah arba'ah*. There are two dialectical forms of each: *fu'*āl and *maf'al*. It is said: *uḥād* and *mawḥad, thunā- and mathnā, thulāth* and *mathlath*, and *rubā'* and *marba'*. That continues to *ma'shar* and *'ushār*. Abū Isḥāq ath-Tha'labī related a third dialectical possibility: *uḥud, thunā, thuluth* and *ruba'*, like 'Umar and Zufar. That is how an-Nakha'ī recites it in this *āyah*. Al-Mahdawī related from an-Nakha'ī and Ibn Waththāb *'thulāth* and *ruba'* without *alif* in *ruba'*. It is shortened from *rubā'*. [POEM] Ath-Tha'labī said, 'This form does not go beyond four except in a verse of al-Kumayt where he uses *"'ushār"* for *"ashrah."*'

Ibn ad-Dahhān said, 'Some of them stop on what is heard, which is *uḥād* to *rubā'*. The verse is not considered since it is aberrant. Abū 'Amr ibn al-Ḥājib said, 'It is said: *uḥād* and *mawḥad, thunā- and mathnā, thulāth* and *mathlath*, and *rubā'* and *marba'*. Is it said going up to nine or not? There is disagreement about that, and the soundest view is that it is not confirmed.' Al-Bukhārī has a text about that in the *Ṣaḥīḥ*.

That diverts from its meaning. It is not used in a place where the numbers are used unless it is diverted. You say, 'Two and three came to me' as *'ithnān* and *thalāthah'* and it is not permitted to say, *'mathnā* and *thulāth'* unless it is preceded by a plural. Where that happens it is used as a *ḥāl* as here in the *āyah*. It is an adjective. These numbers being used adjectivally is clear in His words in 35:1 which describe wings. It is in the indefinite. [POEM+BIT MORE ON THIS]

Know that this does not indicate that nine is permissible as is said by someone with little grasp of the Book and the *Sunnah*. He turns away from the position of the early members of this Community. If someone says that the *'wāw'* is used to add the numbers up and supports that by saying that the Prophet ﷺ had nine wives and was married to all of them, this amounts to ignorance. The Rāfiḍites and some of the literalists take this position and make *mathnā* the same as 'two' (*ithnayn*) and do the same with *thulāth* and *rubā'*. Some of the literalists have an even more repugnant position and say that it is permitted to have eighteen, taking the view that the form gives repetition and the *wāw* addition. So *mathnā* is two-two, and the same with the rest of the numbers. This is all ignorance of the language and the *Sunnah* and is contrary to the consensus of the community since it is not heard that any of the Companions or Tābi'ūn married more than four.

It is transmitted by Mālik in the *Muwaṭṭā'* and by an-Nasā'ī and ad-Dāraquṭnī that the Prophet ﷺ said to Ghaylān ibn Umayyah ath-Thaqafī, when he became Muslim and had eleven wives, 'Choose four of them and divorce the rest.' Abū Dāwud reported that al-Ḥārith ibn Qays said, 'I became Muslim and had eight wives. I mentioned that to the Prophet ﷺ and he said, "Choose four of them."' Muqātil said, 'Al-Ḥārith ibn Qays had eight free wives. When this *āyah* was revealed, the Messenger of Allah ﷺ commanded him to divorce four and keep four.' He is sometimes called Qays ibn al-Ḥārith, but what is correct is that he was al-Ḥārith ibn Qays al-Asadī as Abū Dāwud said. That is also how it is related by Muḥammad ibn al-Ḥasan in his *as-Siyar al-Kabīr*: it is Ḥārith ibn Qays. He is known by the *fuqahā'*. As for what the Prophet ﷺ was permitted in that regard, that was one of his special prerogatives and will be dealt with in *Sūrat al-Aḥzāb*.

We have already mentioned their statement that the *wāw* is combining and what was said about that. Allah Almighty addressed the Arabs with the most eloquent language. The Arabs would not abandon saying 'nine' for saying 'two and three and four.' So it is ugly for someone to say, 'Give him four, six, eight' rather than 'eighteen'. The *wāw* in this place is an appositive which means: 'marry three rather than two' and 'four rather than three'. That is why they are joined with *wāw* and not '*aw*' (or). If He had said '*aw*', it would be permitted for the one with two not to have three or the one with three not to have four.

As for their statement that *mathnā* demands *ithnān*, *thulāth* demands *thalāthah* and *rabā'* demands *arba'ah*, this is arbitrary and scholars of language do not agree with them. It is ignorance on their part. Others are also ignorant of the fact that *mathnā* demands two-two, *thulāth* three-three, and *rubā'* four-four. They do not know that *ithnayn-ithnayn*, *thalāth-thalāth*, and *arba'ah-arba'ah* is confined to numbers, and *mathnā, thulāth* and *rubā'* are different. For Arabs, the diverted numbers have a further meaning that is not in the root. That is because when one says, 'The horses came *mathnā*' by that you mean two by two, in other words that they came in pairs. Al-Jawharī said, 'The same is true of all diverted numbers.'

Someone else said that if you describe people coming *mathnā*, *thulāth* or *uḥād* or '*ushār*, it means they came to you, two by two, three by three, one by one or ten by ten. This meaning is not in the root because when you say that people came to me three (*thalāthah*) by three or ten ('*ashrah*) by ten, you count the number of the people with your words, *thalāthah* and '*ashrah*. When you say *rubā'* and *thunā'*, you do not count their number. You mean that they came to you four by four or two by two. The numbers, large or small, make no difference in this context. So their confining each form to less than what it demands is arbitrary.

Muslim scholars disagree about someone who marries a fifth wife when already married to four. Mālik and ash-Shāfi'ī said that the *ḥadd* is inflicted on him if he did it knowingly. That is the position of Abū Thawr. Az-Zuhrī said that he is stoned if he did that knowingly, but if he was ignorant of the prohibition, he receives the lesser *ḥadd*, which is flogging. The woman receives her dowry and they are divorced and may not ever re-marry. One group said that there is no *ḥadd* punishment in respect of any of that. That is the view of An-Nu'mān.

Ya'qūb and Muḥammad said that there is a *ḥadd* for a forbidden woman, but no other marriage: that is like when someone marries a Magian, marries five women in one contract, contracts a *mut'ah* (temporary marriage), marries without witnesses, or marries a slave-girl without the permission of her owner. Abū Thawr said, 'When he knows that that it is not lawful, he receives the *ḥadd* punishment for any of those things, except for a marriage without witnesses [and marrying a Magian].'

A third view is that of an-Nakha'ī who said that if someone marries a fifth woman deliberately before the end of the *'iddah* of one of his four wives, he is given a hundred lashes, but not exiled. These are the fatwas of our scholars about marrying a fifth wife according to what Ibn al-Mundhir mentioned. The same holds true for more than that.

Az-Zubayr ibn Bakkār related from Ibrāhīm al-Ḥizāmī that Muḥammad ibn Ma'n al-Ghifārī said, 'A woman came to 'Umar ibn al-Khaṭṭāb and said, "Amīr al-Mu'minīn, my husband fasts in the day and prays at night and I do not like to complain when he is obeying Allah." He said to her, "Your husband is an excellent husband." She kept repeating it and he gave the same reply. Ka'b al-Asadī said to him, "Amīr al-Mu'minīn, this woman is complaining about her husband's distancing her from his bed." 'Umar said, "As you have understood her words, decide between them." Ka'b said, "Bring your husband." He was brought and told that his wife had complained about him. He asked, "Is it about food or drink?" "No," he said. The woman said:

"O Qāḍī who is wisely guided,
the mosque has diverted my friend from my bed.

His worship has made him ascetic regarding my bed.
Therefore, Ka'b, make a decision and do not hesitate.

He does not sleep day or night,
so I do not praise him respecting women."

Her husband said:

"I have been made ascetic in her bed and cavorting.
I am a man who has been distracted by what has been revealed

in *Sūrat an-Naḥl* and the Seven Long Ones.
The Book of Allah contains that which alarms and causes fear."

Ka'b said:

"O man, she has a right which you owe her.
Her share is one fourth for the person who understands.

Give her that and abandon your defects."

Then he said, "Allah Almighty has made two, three and four women lawful for you. So that would be three nights and days in which you can worship your Lord." 'Umar said, "By Allah, I do not know which of the things you did is more extraordinary! Is it your grasp of their situation or your ruling regarding them? Go – I have appointed you Qāḍī of Basra."'

Abū Hudbah Ibrāhīm ibn Hudbah related that Anas ibn Mālik said, 'A woman went to the Prophet ﷺ to ask for help with her husband. She said, "I do not have what women normally have. My husband fasts constantly." He said, "You have a day and he has a day. One day for worship and one day for the wife."'

But if you are afraid of not treating them equally, then only one,

Aḍ-Ḍaḥḥāk and others said that this refers to inclination, love, sexual intercourse, company and division between multiple wives. So more than one is forbidden if that will lead to loss of fairness in division and keeping company. That indicates the mandatory nature of good company, and Allah knows best.

It is recited as *'wāḥidatun'* in the nominative which implies, 'One is enough.' It is also recited in the accusative which implies the verb: 'marry one'.

or those you own as slaves.

This means slave-girls. It indicates that if a man fears that he will not be fair to one, then he should have slave-girls. This provides evidence that the right to sexual intercourse with the slave-girl is by virtue of ownership and is not part of marital division because the words of the *āyah* makes all ownership the same. That negates any right of a slave-girl to sexual intercourse or to a share in the division of time. Nonetheless, it is a duty for the owner to be a good owner and to be kind to slaves.

Allah ascribes ownership to the right hand (literally 'what your right hands own') for praise. The right hand is singled out for good qualities. Do you not see that it is the spending hand? It is as the Prophet ﷺ said, 'until his left hand does not know what his right hand spends.' It is the hand used for making contracts. The right hand receives the banners of glory as he says:

When a banner for glory is raised,
the Arabs take it with the right hand.

That makes it more likely that you will not be unfair.

That is closer to not inclining away from the truth and being unfair, as Ibn 'Abbās, Mujāhid and others said. The verb *'āla* is used of someone who is unfair and biased. They say that the arrow deviated (*'āla*) from the target. Ibn 'Umar said that it is used for being unfair in weight or measure. A poet said:

They said, 'We have followed the Messenger of Allah."
Then they discard the Messenger's words and are unfair (*'ālū*) in the balance.

Abū Ṭālib said:

A true balance does not cheat a single grain.
It itself bears witness that it is not unfair (*'ā'il*).

The verb can also mean 'to become poor' as Allah says, *'If you fear impoverishment* ('aylah).' (9:27) A poet says:

A poor man does not know when he will become wealthy
and the wealthy does not know when he will become indigent (*ya'īlu*).

The singular for indigent is *'ā'il* and the plural is *'aylah. 'Aylah* and *'ālah* mean poverty. The verb can also mean to impose a burden and to make something momentous.

Ash-Shāfi'ī said that the *āyah* means: 'it is more likely that you will not have a large number of dependants,' which is another meaning of the verb, but ath-Tha'labī says that no one else says this. The verb for that *a'āla* (Form IV).

Ibn al-'Arabī claims that there are only seven meanings for *'āla* and no more. It can mean: to incline towards, to increase, to be unjust, to become poor, to burden (as Ibn Darīd says), to undertake the burden of dependants, as the Prophet ﷺ says, 'begin with dependants', and to overpower, as one says, "*īla ṣabrihi*", 'his patience was overcome'. One uses the verb *a'āla* to describe a man with many dependants. Using *'āla* to describe having many dependants is not sound.

As for the statement of ath-Tha'labī that no one else says that, ad-Dāraquṭnī reported it in his *Sunan* from Zayd ibn Aslam. It is the position of Jābir ibn Zayd. These are two imams from among the Muslim scholars and imams who preceded ash-Shāfi'ī. As for what Ibn al-'Arabī mentioned about their number and lack of soundness, that itself is not sound. We mentioned that a matter can be 'momentous' (*'āla*), and al-Jawharī related that. Al-Harawī said in *Gharīb*: 'Abū Bakr said, 'It is said that a man acts unjustly in the land.' Al-Aḥmar said that the verb can mean that something renders a person powerless. Al-Kisā'ī, Abū 'Umar ad-Dūrī and Ibn al-A'rābī mentioned the meaning of having numerous dependants. Abu-l-Ḥasan 'Alī ibn Ḥamzah al-Kisā'ī said that the Arabs used *'āla* and *a'lā* for having numerous dependants. Abū Ḥātim said, 'Ash-Shāfi'ī had greater knowledge of the Arabic language than us. Perhaps it is a dialect.' Ath-Tha'labī the commentator related that his teacher Abu-l-Qāsim ibn Ḥabīb said, 'I asked Abū 'Umar ad-Dūrī about this. He is an unimpeachable master of language. He said that it is a dialect of Ḥimyar and quoted a verse for evidence.' [POEM] Abū 'Amr ibn al-'Alā' said, 'There are so many prominent Arabs that I fear to take ungrammatical Arabic.' Ṭalḥab ibn Muṣarrif recited *'allā ta'īlū'* which is the evidence of ash-Shāfi'ī.

Ibn 'Aṭiyyah said, 'Az-Zajjāj and others rejected the interpretation that *'āla* is from *'iyāl* since Allah Almighty allowed many concubines and that entails many dependants. So how can it be closer to not having many dependants?' This objection is not valid because concubines are part of property which can be disposed of by selling. Those dependants (*'iyāl*) which diminish are free women with obligatory rights. Ibn al-A'rābī related that the Arabs use the verb *'āla* of a man with many dependants.

This *āyah* is connected to someone who permits a slave to marry four wives since Allah did not specify in the *āyah* whether the stipulation applies to slaves or just free men. This is the position of Dāwud and aṭ-Ṭabarī, and it is known from Mālik, and his final position is what is in the *Muwaṭṭā'*. It is also related from Ibn al-Qāsim and Ashhab. Ibn al-Mawwāz mentioned that Ibn Wahb reported that Mālik said that a slave may only marry two wives, and that is position of al-Layth.

Abū 'Umar said, 'Ash-Shāfi'ī, Abū Ḥanīfah and their people, ath-Thawrī and al-Layth ibn Sa'd said that a slave may not marry more than two wives. Aḥmad and Isḥāq said that. It is related that 'Umar ibn al-Khaṭṭāb, 'Alī ibn Abī Ṭālib and 'Abd ar-Raḥmān ibn 'Awf said that a slave may not marry more than two. I do not know of anyone among the Companions who disagreed with that. It is the position of ash-Sha'bī, 'Aṭā', Ibn Sīrīn, al-Ḥakam, Ibrāhīm and Ḥammād.' The argument for this position is a sound analogy with divorce and *ḥadd* punishment. All say that his *ḥadd* is half that of a free man, his divorce is twice, his īlā' is two months and the like of similar rulings. Therefore it is not unlikely for there to be a reduction in respect of marrying four wives. Allah knows best.

وَءَاتُوا۟ ٱلنِّسَآءَ صَدُقَـٰتِهِنَّ نِحْلَةً ۚ فَإِن طِبْنَ لَكُمْ عَن شَىْءٍ مِّنْهُ
نَفْسًا فَكُلُوهُ هَنِيٓـًٔا مَّرِيٓـًٔا ﴿٤﴾

4 Give women their dowries as an outright gift. But if they are happy to give you some of it, consume it with pleasure and goodwill.

Give women their dowries as an outright gift.

Ṣaduqāt (dowries) is the plural of *ṣaduqah*. Al-Akhfash said, 'The Banū Tamīm say "*ṣudqah*" and "*ṣudqāt*". The *dāl* can have a *fatḥah* or a *sukūn*.' Al-Māzinī said that it is called *ṣidāq*, not *ṣadāq*. Ya'qūb and Aḥmad ibn Yaḥyā said that an-Naḥḥās said that it is *ṣadāq*.

Husbands are addressed in this *āyah*, according to Qatādah, Ibn Zayd and Ibn Jurayj. Allah commanded them to give their dowries as gifts to their spouses. It is said that it is addressed to guardians, according to Abū Ṣāliḥ. The guardian would take the woman's dowry and not give her any of it. They were forbidden to do that and commanded to hand it over to them. We find in the transmission of al-Kalbī: 'In the Jāhiliyyah, when a guardian gave a woman in marriage and she was with him in the same clan, he would not give her any of her dowry. If she was outside it, he would take her on a camel to her husband and not give her anything except that camel and so this *āyah* was revealed: *"Give women their dowries as an outright gift."*' Al-Mu'tamir ibn Sulaymān reported that his father said, 'A Ḥaḍramawtī claimed that what was meant by the *āyah* was those who practised the *shighār* marriage (exchanging women without dowries) and they were commanded to give them dowries. The first view is the more likely. The pronouns are the same and refer to husbands. They are those who are meant in these *āyahs*. It is mandatory for the pronouns to be in harmony.

This *āyah* indicates that a dowry is mandatory for a woman, and it is agreed upon and there is no disagreement except for what is related from one of the people of knowledge among the people of Iraq, that when a master marries his slave to his slave-girl, then there is no dowry obliged. This is not right because this *āyah* is not restricted in its command here and elsewhere (4:25). Scholars agree that there is no maximum to the dowry and disagree about its minimum, as will be dealt with later. (4:20)

Most recite '*ṣaduqātihinna*'. Qatādah recited '*ṣudqātihinna*' and an-Nakha'ī and Ibn Waththāb recited '*ṣuduqatahunna*'.

'*An outright gift*' is *niḥlah* or *nuḥlah*. They are two dialectical forms. Its root means a gift. *Ṣadāq* is a gift from Allah to the woman and it is said that *nihlah* is given willingly with no dispute on the part of the husband. Qatādah said that '*niḥlah*' means 'mandatory'. Ibn Jurayj and Ibn Zayd said, 'a specified obligation'. Abū 'Ubayd said that it must be known and specified. Az-Zajjāj said, 'a religious obligation'. *Niḥlah* also means a religion. You say, 'This is his religion (*niḥlah*).' This is good inasmuch as it is addressed to the guardians who used to take it in the Jāhiliyyah so that a woman said about her husband:

He does not take the gift from his daughters.

She meant that he did not do what others did. Allah wrested it from them and commanded that it be given to women.

'*Niḥlah*' is in the accusative as a *ḥāl* modifying an implied verb. It implies: 'Give them a gift.' It is said that it is in the accusative for explanation, and it is said that it is a verbal noun in the position of a *ḥāl*.

But if they are happy to give you some of it,

This is addressed to husbands. The fact that it is general is evidence that it is permitted for a woman, virgin or non-virgin, to give her dowry to her husband, and that is the position of the majority of the *fuqaha'*. Mālik forbids a gift from a virgin to her husband and assigns that to the guardian even though she is the owner.

Al-Farrā' claimed that it is addressed to the guardians because they would take the dowry and not give the woman any of it. They are not permitted to do that unless the woman is happy about it. The first position is sounder because the guardians were not mentioned.

The pronoun 'it' refers to the dowry. That is what 'Ikrimah and others said. The reason that the *āyah* was revealed was that it was mentioned that some people avoided taking any of what they had given their wives. Then this was revealed.

Scholars agree that when a woman who has charge of herself gives her dowry to husband, that is carried out and she cannot take it back – except for Shurayh who thinks she can. He used this *āyah* as evidence and said that if she asks for it back, then she is not happy about it. Ibn 'Arabī says that this is baseless because she was happy when it happened and it is like consuming something. Once it is consumed, it is gone. 'Make use of' is literally 'eat', but does not mean actual 'eating', but alludes to making something lawful. This is clear.

If a woman stipulates as a condition in the marriage contract that her husband may not marry another wife and for that provision she reduces some of her dowry, and then he does marry another wife, according to Ibn al-Qāsim she has nothing because it was an unacceptable condition, as occurred when the owners of Barīrah stipulated that they would have her *walā'* if 'Ā'ishah bought and freed her. The Prophet ﷺ validated the contract but not the condition. Here the reduction of the dowry is sound but not it being connected to not marrying another wife. Ibn 'Abd al-Ḥakam said if the proper dowry for a woman of her class, or more than that, remains, then she does not demand anything from him. If she reduces something of her proper dowry and he marries another wife, then she can demand the full dowry of a woman of her class from him because he agreed to the stipulation and took recompense for it. Therefore, it is mandatory for it to be taken from him and he must fulfill it since the Prophet ﷺ said, 'Believers abide by their conditions.'

This *āyah* is evidence that emancipation is not considered to be a dowry because it is not wealth since the wife cannot give it nor the husband consume it. This is the position of Mālik, Abū Ḥanīfah, Zafar, ash-Shaybānī and ash-Shāfi'ī. Aḥmad ibn Ḥanbal, Ishaq and Ya'qub say that it can be a dowry, based on the hadith related by the imams about Ṣafiyyah when the Prophet ﷺ freed her and made her being freed her dowry. It is related from Anas that he did that. He is also the one who relates the hadith about Ṣafiyyah. The first group say that there is no argument in the hadith about Ṣafiyyah because the Prophet ﷺ had the prerogative to marry without a dowry. He wanted to marry Zaynab and she was unlawful to Zayd. He married her without a *walī* or a dowry. Therefore, this is not evidence. Allah knows best.

It is said that the word '*nafsan*' is in the accusative for clarification. Sībawayh and the Kufans do not permit putting something that is in the accusative for clarification first. Al-Māzinī and Abu-l-'Abbās al-Mubarrad permit that when the regent is a verb. [POEM] An example of this in the Revelation is the phrase: '*with downcast eyes, emerging*' (54:7). The people of Sībawayh said that '*nafsan*' is in the accusative by an implied verb. It implies: 'I mean personally.' It is not in the accusative for distinction. If that is the case, there is no argument regarding it. [POEM] All agree that it is not permitted to put that which is distinguishing first when the regent is not inflected.

consume it with pleasure and goodwill.

What is meant by the verb '*kulū*' here is not literally 'eating', but permission for whatever manner it is consumed. That is what is meant by His words in the following *āyah*: *'People who consume the property or orphans wrongfully'* (4:10). What is meant is not actually eating, although eating is the most complete form of enjoyment of wealth which can be designated by the word 'eating'. It is similar to Allah's words: *'When you are called to the prayer on the Day of Jumu'ah, hasten to the remembrance of Allah and abandon trade.'* (62:9) It is not just trade that is being indicated here; what is meant is anything that distracts one from remembering Allah, such as marriage and other things. Trade is mentioned because it is the principal thing that distracts one from remembering Allah in this context.

The words *'pleasure and goodwill'* are in the accusative as an adverbial *ḥāl* describing '*it*'. It is said that it describes something elided, such as a pleasant consumption with goodwill. *Hana'a, yahna'u* is used for food and drink delighting a person. Something agreeable is described as *hanī'*. *Han'ua* is used for being wholesome The verbal noun is *han'* or *hin'*. All that is consumed without difficulty or toil is with pleasure (*hanī'*). *Hanī'* is an active participle from *hanu'a* like *ẓarīf* from *ẓarf*. The verb is *hani'a, yahna'u* with the noun *hani'*. One says of food being enjoyed and digested, '*hana'a* and *mara'a*'. If *hana'a* is not mentioned but *amrā'a* is, then it means 'digested'. Abu-l-'Abbās said that Ibn al-A'rābī had the verb with a middle *kasrah*, but it is uncommon. It is said that *hanī'* means with no sin and *marī'* means with no illness. Kuthayyir said:

May you enjoy it (*hanī'an marī'an*) without an illness mixed in,
for a might which does not make our honour fair game.

A man visited 'Alqamah while he was eating something which his wife had given him from her dowry. He said to him, 'Eat from that which is pleasure and good will.'

It is said that *hanī'* means that which good and allowed and which does not disturb anything and *marī'* is that which has a praised outcome and will not injure or harm. It is also said: 'they do not fear any demand for it in this world or come-back in the Next World.' This is indicated by what Ibn 'Abbās reported that the Prophet ﷺ said about this: 'It is when she gives her husband a gift voluntarily without compulsion. It does not imply any power over you and Allah will not take you to task for it in the Next World.' It is related that 'Alī ibn Abī Ṭālib said, 'When one of you has an illness, he should ask his wife for a dirham of her dowry and buy honey with it and drink it with rainwater and by that Allah will join for him what is pleasure and goodwill with blessed water.' Allah knows best.

وَلَا تُؤْتُوا۟ ٱلسُّفَهَآءَ أَمْوَٰلَكُمُ ٱلَّتِى جَعَلَ ٱللَّهُ لَكُمْ قِيَـٰمًا وَٱرْزُقُوهُمْ
فِيهَا وَٱكْسُوهُمْ وَقُولُوا۟ لَهُمْ قَوْلًا مَّعْرُوفًا ۝

5 Do not hand over to the incompetent any property of theirs for which Allah has made you responsible, but provide for them and clothe them out of it, and speak to them correctly and courteously.

Do not hand over to the incompetent any property of theirs

When Allah commanded that orphans be given their property, and dowries be given to wives, He made it clear that it is not permitted to give minors or the incompetent their property. The *āyah* indicates affirmation of the need to have an executor, guardian, and custodian for orphans.

The people of knowledge agree that it is permitted to give the role of guardianship to a free, trustworthy, upright Muslim. They disagree about free women, but most say that it is permitted. Aḥmad deduces evidence in the fact that 'Umar made Ḥafṣah an executrix. It is related that 'Aṭā' ibn Abī Rabāḥ said about a man who made his wife his executrix, 'A woman may not be an executrix. If someone does that, the duty is transferred to a man of her people.'

They also disagree about slaves having the right of guardianship. Ash-Shāfi'ī, Abū Thawr, Muḥammad and Ya'qūb forbade it, and Mālik, al-Awzā'ī and Ibn 'Abd al-Ḥakam allowed it. It is the position of an-Nakha'ī who made his slave an executor. This was already adequately discussed in *al-Baqarah.*

The linguistic meaning of *'incompetent'* was mentioned in *al-Baqarah.* Scholars disagree about who the incompetent are. Sālim al-Afṭas reported from Sa'īd ibn Jubayr that they are orphans who are not given their property. An-Naḥḥās said that this is the best of what has been said about this *āyah.* Ismā'īl ibn Abī Khālid related that Abū Mālik said that they are young children who are not given their wealth lest they waste it and remain penniless. Sufyān related from Ḥumayd al-A'raj that Mujāhid said that they are women. An-Naḥḥās and others said that this is not sound, even linguistically, as the word *sufahā'* is used and the Arabs use *safā'ih* or *safīhāt* for women. It is said: 'Do not give your wealth in a *qirāḍ* or to an agent who is not good in commerce.' It is related that 'Umar said, 'Whoever does not understand should not trade in our market.' This is based on Allah's words: *'Do not hand over to the incompetent any property of theirs.'* This means those who are ignorant of rulings, and it is said that means the unbelievers, which is why scholars dislike Muslims entrusting a *dhimmī* with buying and selling or giving him a *qirāḍ* investment.

Abū Mūsā al-Ash'arī said, 'The incompetent are those who must be declared legally incompetent.' This is general. Ibn Khuwayzimandād said, 'As for debarring the incompetent from competence, there are different cases. Some are debarred because of youth, some due to lack of good sense owing to insanity or something else, and some because of poor management of property. As for someone who is unconscious, Mālik recommended that he not be declared incompetent because that quickly departs.'

Legal incompetence is sometimes for the sake of a person himself and sometimes for the rights of others. We have mentioned those under debarment for their own sake. Those debarred for the sake of others are slaves, those in debt, those who are ill, in respect of two-thirds of their property, bankrupts, wives in respect of their husbands' entitlements, and a virgin in respect of herself. As for children and the insane, there is no disagreement about their limitation. As for an adult, in their case it is because they do not manage their property well and are not safe from ruining their property and so they resemble a child. There is a disagreement about this that will be dealt with. There is no difference between someone destroying his property through acts of disobedience, pious deeds or permitted ones. Our people disagree if they consume their property through pious deeds. Some debar them and some do not. There is no disagreement about slaves.

What a debtor has is taken from him and given to his creditors by the consensus of the Companions. 'Umar did that to Usayfi' of Juhaynah and Mālik mentioned it in the *Muwaṭṭā'*.

As long as a virgin is secluded she is limited in her ability to transact because she is not considered good at overseeing her affairs until she marries, mixes with people and goes out, so that she is able to discern what is harmful from what is beneficial. As for someone ignorant of legal rulings, even he is not restricted with regard to making his property grow or lack of management, he is not given his property because of his ignorance of what constitutes valid and invalid sales and what is lawful and unlawful. In the case of a woman with a husband, the Messenger of Allah ﷺ said, 'A wife is only permitted to dispose of a third of her property.'

In the case of someone who is ignorant of legal rulings, even if he is competent with regard to growing his wealth and managing it, property is not given to him since he is ignorant of what is sound and unsound in transactions or what is unlawful and unlawful. The same applies to a *dhimmī* both on account of his ignorance of correct sales and because it is feared that he will engage in usury, and Allah knows best.

Scholars disagree about the reason for the ascription of property to 'you' when it actually belongs to the incompetent. [The Arabic is literally 'your property'.] It is said that it is ascribed to them because it is in their possession and they oversee it and so the ascription is expanded, as when Allah says: *'greet one another'* (24:61) [The Arabic is literally 'yourselves'] and: *'kill yourselves'* (2:54).

It is said that it is ascribed to them because it is the same sort of property as theirs. Property is shared between creatures and moves from one hand to another and from one owner to another, meaning that it is theirs when they need it, like your property which guards your honour, protects you and exalts your worth and by which you support yourselves.

A second position is articulated by Abū Mūsā al-Ash'arī, Ibn 'Abbās, al-Ḥasan and Qatādah. It is that what is meant by the property of those addressed is actual. Ibn 'Abbās said, 'Do not give the property on which your livelihood depends to your wife and child and thus remain poor, waiting for them and what they have. You should be the one who spends on them.' According to this, the 'incompetent' are women and young children. This is transmitted along with the position of Mujāhid and Abū Mālik about the incompetent.

The *āyah* indicates that it is permitted to limit the competence of the incompetent by the command of Allah to do that here. Allah also says: *'If the person incurring the debt is incompetent or weak.'* (2:282) So guardianship is confirmed for the incompetent as it is for the weak. Weakness refers to children and lack of competence to adults. That is because 'incompetent' is a word entailing blame, and there is no blame for what someone has not earned. The pen does not record against someone who is not an adult, so they have no blame. Al-Khaṭṭābī said that.

Scholars disagree about the actions of the incompetent when they are considered to be legally incompetent. Mālik and all his people except for Ibn al-Qāsim say that the dealings and commands of the incompetent are permitted until the ruler stops them. That is the position of ash-Shāfi'ī and Abū Yūsuf. Ibn al-Qāsim said that their dealings are not permitted, even if the ruler does not stop them. Asbagh says that if someone's incompetence is clear, his dealings are rejected, but if it is not evident, then his dealings are not rejected until the ruler bars him. Saḥnūn uses as evidence Mālik words, 'If the dealings of the incompetent had been rejected before they were deemed incompetent, there would be no need for the ruler to do that to anyone.'

There is disagreement about limiting the competence of an adult. Mālik and the majority of *fuqahā'* say that it may be done but Abū Ḥanīfah said that a sane adult cannot be declared legally incompetent unless he ruins his property. If that is the case, he is not given his property until he is twenty-five. When he is twenty-five, it is given to him in any case, whether he spoils it or not because it was kept from him for twelve years. Then he could have had a child six months later and become a father and a grandfather. He said, 'I am embarrassed to debar someone who might be a grandfather.' It is said that he said about the period of debarring property, that it is when it reaches the point of being spoiled, in which case it can be forbidden to hand over property out of caution.

All of this is weak both in terms of reason and tradition. Ad-Dāraquṭnī related from Muḥammad ibn Aḥmad ibn al-Ḥasan aṣ-Ṣawwāf from Ḥāmid ibn Shu'ayb from Shurayḥ ibn Yūnus from Ya'qūb ibn Ibrāhīm, who is Qāḍī Abū Yūsuf, from Hishām ibn 'Urwah from his father that 'Abdullāh ibn Ja'far went to az-Zubayr and said, 'I have purchased such-and–such goods. 'Alī wants to go to the Amīr al-Mu'minīn to ask him to debar me with respect to it!' Az-Zubayr said, 'I am your partner in the transaction.' 'Alī went to 'Uthmān and said, 'Ibn Ja'far purchased such-and-such goods. Debar him with respect to them.' Az-Zubayr said, 'I am his partner in the transaction.' 'Uthmān said, 'How can I debar a man in a sale when az-Zubayr is his partner in it?' Ya'qūb said, 'I adopt debarring and think it is correct. I invalidate the sale and purchase of someone debarred. I allow what he bought or sold before he was debarred.' Ya'qūb ibn Ibrāhīm said, 'Abū Ḥanīfah does not debar or adopt limitation.' The statement of 'Uthmān, 'How can I debar a man', is evidence that it is permitted to debar an adult. 'Abdullāh ibn Ja'far was born in Abyssinia and was the first child born in Islam. He came to the Prophet ﷺ with his father in the year of Khaybar and listened to him and memorised from him. Khaybar was in 5 AH. This refutes the view of Abū Ḥanīfah. His argument will be dealt with, Allah willing.

for which Allah has made you responsible,

This means your livelihood and good state of your *dīn*. There are three dialectical forms of 'which': *allatī*, *allati* (with *kasrah*) and *allat* (wih *sukūn*). There are also three dialectical forms of the dual: *allatāna*, *allatā* (with the *nūn* elided), and *allatānni*. The plural will be dealt with in its place in this *sūrah*, Allah willing.

'*Qiyām*' and '*qiwām*' both mean to attend to the best interests of someone. It is said that *qiyām* is attending to the family and *qiwām* is attending to the house. He is he one who puts it right. It is *qiwām*, the *wāw* has replaced the *yā'*. The people of Madīnah read it as '*qiyam*' without *alif*. Al-Kisā'ī and al-Farrā' said that '*qiyam*' and '*qiwām*' both mean '*qiyām*'. They believe that it is in the accusative through being a verbal noun. It means: 'Do not hand over to the incompetent their property which you put in order and are responsible for putting in order.' Al-Akhfash says that it means to manage their affairs, believing that it is plural. The Basrans say that *qiyam* is a plural of *qīmah*, like *dīmah* and *diyam*, meaning that Allah has acquainted you with the value of things.' Abū 'Alī said that this view is wrong and said that it is a verbal noun like *qiyām* and *qiwām*. Its root is *qiwam*, but it is irregular in becoming a *yā'* as we see in *jiyād* as the plural of *jawād*, and the like. *Qiwam*, *qiwām* an *qiyām* mean being in firm is rectifying the state of something and being constant in that.

Al-Ḥasan and an-Nakha'ī recited '*allātī*' as the plural of '*allatī*'. The common reading is '*allatī*'. Al-Farrā' said that in Arabic one usually uses *allawātī* for women and *allatī* for property as well as other things than property. An-Naḥḥās mentioned it.

but provide for them and clothe them out of it.

This means: 'Appoint for them out of it or allot them out of it.' This is about those that a man is obliged to support and clothe: his wife or young children. It is evidence that it is mandatory for a father to maintain his child and a husband to maintain his wife. Al-Bukhārī reports from Abū Hurayrah that the Prophet ﷺ said, 'The best *ṣadaqah* is that given by the wealthy. The upper hand is better than the lower hand. Begin with your immediate dependents. A woman says, "Either feed me or divorce me." A slave says, "Feed me and employ me." A child says, "Feed me. Who will you leave me to?"' They said, 'Abū Hurayrah, did you hear this from the Messenger of Allah ﷺ?' 'No,' he said, 'this is from the bag of Abū Hurayrah!' Al-Muhallab said, 'Maintenance of one's wife and children is mandatory by consensus. This hadith is evidence for that.'

Ibn al-Mundhir said that there is disagreement about the age at which the maintenance of children ends when they have no money or work. One group say that a father should support male children until they reach puberty and girls until they marry and the marriage has been consummated. If a daughter is divorced after consummation or she is widowed, the father does not have to support her. If she is divorced before consummation, he must continue to support her.

Maintenance of grandchildren is not obligatory. This is the position of Mālik. One group say that a grandfather should maintain his grandchildren until puberty or menstruation and then does not have to maintain them after that unless they are chronically ill, and that male and female are the same in that respect if they have no property. That also applies to great grandchildren and so on, if they do not have a father who is able to provide for them. This is the position of ash-Shāfi'ī.

One group oblige maintenance for all children, including adult men and women, when they do not have adequate maintenance. This is based on the literal meaning of the words of the Prophet ﷺ to Hind: 'Take what is sufficient for you and your children in a reasonable manner.' We also find a hadith reported by Abū Hurayrah in which a child says, 'Feed me. Who will you leave me to?' It indicates that anyone who has no ability or profession may say that. However, someone who has reached puberty should not say that because they can work for themselves and earn, as indicated by the words of the Almighty: *'until they reach a marriageable age'* (4:6), and He set the age of marriage as a limit for that.

The words, 'A woman says, "Either feed me or divorce me"' refute those who say that there is no divorce on account of poverty and that the woman should be patient. Maintenance is a husband's responsibility by the ruling of a judge. This is the position of 'Aṭā' and az-Zuhrī. The Kufans believe that, holding to the words of the Almighty: *'If someone is in difficult circumstances, there should be a deferral until things are easier.'* (2:280) They said, 'Therefore it is obliged for her to wait until her husband is wealthier.' Allah says: *'Marry off those among you who are unmarried.'* (24:22) They said, 'Here the Almighty recommends marrying off the poor, and so poverty cannot be considered a reason for divorce, since it does not forbid marriage.' They have no proof in this *āyah* as will be explained in the proper place. The hadith is the text for the dispute.

It is said that this is addressed to the guardians of orphans, authorising them to spend some of their wealth which is under their supervision as we already mentioned concerning the ascription of wealth. A guardian spends on the orphan according to his wealth and circumstances. If he is young and has much wealth, he procures a wet-nurse and carers for him and spends generously on him. If he is old, he allots him fine clothes, delicious food and servants. If he is less well off than that, he spends accordingly. If he has still less than that, he must provide basic food and clothing according to need. If orphans are poor without any wealth, then the ruler must support them from the Treasury. If the ruler does not do it, then the

Muslims must do it based on whoever is closer to to the orphan concerned. His mother is closest to him and she must nurse him and support him. Neither she nor anyone else can demand to be paid back for that. This was already mentioned in *al-Baqarah* (2:233).

speak to them correctly and courteously.

This means with gentle words and promises of care. There is disagreement about *ma'rūf.* It is said that it means to pray for them, using such words as: 'May Allah bless you and protect you,' or saying, 'I will look after you,' and similar things. It is said that it means to promise them good, telling them, 'When you are mature, we will give you your property' or a parent telling his child, 'My wealth will go to you and you, Allah willing, will own it when you are mature and know how to deal with it.'

وَابْتَلُوا الْيَتَامَىٰ حَتَّىٰ إِذَا بَلَغُوا النِّكَاحَ فَإِنْ آنَسْتُم مِّنْهُمْ
رُشْدًا فَادْفَعُوا إِلَيْهِمْ أَمْوَالَهُمْ ۖ وَلَا تَأْكُلُوهَا إِسْرَافًا وَبِدَارًا
أَن يَكْبَرُوا ۚ وَمَن كَانَ غَنِيًّا فَلْيَسْتَعْفِفْ ۖ وَمَن كَانَ فَقِيرًا
فَلْيَأْكُلْ بِالْمَعْرُوفِ ۚ فَإِذَا دَفَعْتُمْ إِلَيْهِمْ أَمْوَالَهُمْ فَأَشْهِدُوا عَلَيْهِمْ ۚ
وَكَفَىٰ بِاللَّهِ حَسِيبًا ﴿٦﴾

6 Keep a close check on orphans until they reach a marriageable age, then if you perceive that they have sound judgment hand over their property to them. Do not consume it extravagantly and precipitately before they come of age. Those who are wealthy should abstain from it altogether. Those who are poor should use it sensibly and correctly. When you hand over their property to them ensure that there are witnesses on their behalf. Allah suffices as a Reckoner.

Keep a close check on orphans until they reach a marriageable age,

This means to test and ascertain their state. This is addressed to everyone in explaining how to give them their property. It is said that it was revealed about Thābit ibn Rifā'ah and his uncle. Rifā'ah died leaving a child who was a minor. His uncle Thābit went to the Prophet ﷺ and said, 'My nephew is an orphan in my care. What is lawful for me of his property and when should I hand it over to him?' So Allah revealed this *āyah*.

Scholars disagree about the meaning of 'keeping a close check'. It is said that a guardian should assess the character of the orphan in his care and listen to his desires, thereby obtaining knowledge of his excellence and of his ability or inability to deal with his his property in his own best interests. If he is good in this respect, scholars and others say that there is no harm in giving him some of his money which he can dispose of. If it grows and he attends to it well, he passes the test and then the guardian must hand over all of his property to him. If he is a poor manager, then the guardian should keep hold of his property. No one says that if the child is tested and found to have good judgment, guardianship is automatically removed and his guardian must give him his money and allow him to deal with it since the Almighty says: *'until they reach a marriageable age.'*

A group of *fuqahā'* say that the child must either be a boy or girl. If it is a boy, he is tested by being allowed to spend on the household for a month, or is given a small amount to deal with to see if he can manage it well. Nonetheless, he is overseen while doing that to ensure he does not misspend it. If he does misspend it, his guardian is not liable. When the guardian sees that he is able to act correctly, he should hand over his property to him in the presence of witnesses. If it is a girl, her guardian should give her what would normally be given to the lady of the house to manage, for instance, the spinning process and oversee the spinners in terms of buying and paying for cotton and completing the spinning process in full. If he sees that she has sound judgment, he should give her her property. Otherwise orphans should remain in care until their good judgment is ascertained. Al-Ḥasan, Mujāhid and others said that they should be tested in respect of their minds, their *dīn* and their ability to make their property grow.

The term '*marriageable age*' means puberty since Allah says: *'Once your children have reached puberty.'* (24:59) It means the age of puberty and marriage. There are five signs of puberty. Three are common to men and women and two apply to women alone, namely, menstruation and pregnancy. Scholars do not disagree that menstruation or pregnancy indicates puberty and then the obligations and rulings dependent on that are obliged for her. They disagree about the other three. As for growth of hair and age, al-Awzā'ī, ash-Shāfi'ī and Ibn Ḥanbal say that for a boy it is the age is fifteen if he has not had a wet dream. That is the position of Ibn Wahb, Asbagh, 'Abd al-Malik ibn Mājishūn, 'Umar ibn 'Abd al-'Azīz and a group of the people of Madīnah. Ibn al-'Arabī also preferred that. The *ḥudūd* and obligations are obliged in their view on someone of this age. Aṣbagh ibn al-Faraj says, 'What we say is that the age at which the *ḥudūd* and obligations of the *dīn* are imposed is fifteen. I prefer that and recommended it because it is the age at which one can participate in *jihād*.' His evidence is the account of Ibn 'Umar when he presented himself for the Battle of the Ditch. He was fifteen and was allowed to participate but he had not been allowed to participate at Uḥud when he was fourteen. Muslim transmitted it.

Abū 'Umar ibn 'Abd al-Barr said, 'This is when the date of someone's birth is known. If his time of birth and age is unknown, or he denies it, then one acts according to what Nāfi' related from Aslam from 'Umar ibn al-Khaṭṭāb. He wrote to his generals: "Only impose the *jizyah* on those who have started to shave."' 'Uthmān said about a boy who had stolen: 'See if his pubic hair has begun to grow. If it has, then cut off his hand.' 'Aṭiyyah al-Quraẓī said, 'The Messenger of Allah ﷺ dealt with the Banū Qurayẓah and, going by the judgment of Sa'd ibn Mu'ādh, killed all of them who had pubic hair and excused those whose pubic hair had not yet begun to grow. I was one of those in that category and he left me.'

Mālik, Abū Ḥanīfah and others said that there is no judgment against anyone who has not had a wet dream until they reach the age at which someone must have reached puberty. That is considered to be seventeen. Then the *hadd* punishment is imposed on them. Mālik once said that it is when the voice breaks and the nose is fully formed. In another variant from Abū Ḥanīfah, the age is nineteen, and that is what is best known. He said about a girl that she reaches puberty at seventeen, but there is some debate about this. Al-Lu'lu'ī said that the age is eighteen. Dāwud said that he does not reach the age of puberty if he does not have a wet dream, even if he is forty.

As for the growth of pubic hair, some say that that indicates puberty. That is related from Ibn al-Qāsim and Sālim. Mālik said that once and it is one of the positions of ash-Shāfi'ī. Aḥmad, Isḥāq and Abū Thawr also said that. It is said that it denotes puberty and it was a judgment used in regard to the unbelievers: those with pubic hair were killed and those without made captives. Ash-Shāfi'ī said this in another position which is based on the hadith of 'Aṭiyyah al-Quraẓī. A little fluff is not considered sufficient, proper hair growth is needed. Ibn al-Qāsim said, 'I heard Mālik say, "What is acted on with us is based on the hadith of 'Umar ibn al-Khaṭṭāb, who said: 'If the razor has been passed over him, I will impose the *ḥadd* punishment on him.'"' Asbagh said, 'Ibn al-Qāsim said to me, "I prefer that the *ḥadd* punishment should only be carried out on someone when there is both hair growth and puberty."' Abū Ḥanīfah said that the growth of hair is means nothing and is not a sign of puberty nor proof of it.

Az-Zuhrī and 'Aṭā' said that no *ḥadd* punishment can be imposed on anyone who has not reached puberty, and that is the position of ash-Shāfi'ī. Mālik inclined to that view once and it is held by some of his followers. Its literal meaning implies not paying attention to hair growth or age. Ibn al-'Arabī said, 'If the hadith of Ibn 'Umar is not a proof of age, then every age they mention is a false claim. The age at which the Messenger of Allah ﷺ allowed him to go is more appropriate than the age that he considered insufficient and for which there is no evidence in the Sharī'ah. Similarly the Messenger of Allah ﷺ considered hair growth in respect of the Banū Qurayẓah. Who will excuse someone for abandoning two matters which the Messenger of Allah ﷺ took into consideration and consider what the Messenger of Allah ﷺ did not consider and Allah did not appoint in the Sharī'ah.'

Ibn al-'Arabi says this in the context of this ayah, but the reverse in *Sūrat al-Anfāl* since he does not base himself on the hadith of Ibn 'Umar, but interprets it as our scholars do. What differentiates between those who are able to fight and receive a share and those who cannot and do not receive a share is the age of fifteen. Those younger are dependents. That is what 'Umar ibn 'Abd al-'Azīz understood from the hadith. Allah knows best.

then if you perceive that they have sound judgment hand over their property to them

Ānasa means to see, perceive and know. It is also used in 28:29 with that meaning. Az-Zuhrī said, 'The Arabs say, 'Go and look *(asta'nis)* if you see anyone.' [POEM] One says *ānastu*, *aḥsastu* and *wajadtu* mean the same. The root is to perceive.

Most recite *'rushd'* *(sound judgment)* while as-Sulamī, 'Īsā, ath-Thaqafī and Ibn Mas'ūd recited *'rashad'*. They are two dialectical possibilities. Scholars disagree about the interpretation of *'rushd'*. Al-Ḥasan, Qatādah and others said that it refers to soundness in both mind and *dīn*. Ibn 'Abbās, as-Suddī, and ath-Thawrī said that it is about soundness of mind and preservation of property. Sa'īd ibn Jubayr and ash-Sha'bī said, 'It is when a man trims his beard and shows his good sense. One does not give an orphan his property, even if he is an old man, until one is discerns his good sense.' That is like what aḍ-Ḍaḥḥāk said: 'An orphan is not given his property, even if he is a hundred years old, until it is known that he can deal properly with it.' Mujāhid said that *rushd* only applies to soundness of mind.

Most scholars believe that *rushd* only exists after puberty and if an orphan still shows no sound judgment after puberty, even if they are old, the status of legal incompetence is not removed from them. That is the position of Mālik and others. Abū Ḥanīfah says that an adult free man cannot be declared legally incompetent after reaching puberty, even if he is the most impious and spendthrift of people, as long as he is sane. Zufar ibn al-Hudhayl also said that, and it is the position of an-Nakhā'ī. Their evidence for that is what Qatādah related from Anas about Ḥabbān ibn Munqidh. He used to sell and he was unguarded in his contracts: It was asked, 'Messenger of Allah, should he be debarred? There is weakness in his contracts.' The Prophet ﷺ summoned him and said, 'Do not sell.' He said, 'I cannot bear not to.' He told him, 'Then when you sell, say, "No cheating," and you have an option to retract for three days.' They said that because people asked for him to be declared legally incompetent due to the way he was being cheated in transactions and the Prophet ﷺ did not do that, that it confirms that making adult people legally incompetent is not permitted. There is no proof in that because it was a special case as we explained in *al-Baqarah*. Other people are not subject to it.

Ash-Shāfi'ī says that if someone ruins his property and his *dīn*, or his property but not his *dīn*, he should be declared legally incompetent. If he ruins his *dīn* and puts his property in order, there are two possibilities. One is that he is declared legally incompetent, which is what is preferred by al-'Abbās ibn Shurayḥ. The other is that he is not, and that is preferred by Isḥāq al-Marwazī, and it is the most apparent position of the school of ash-Shāfi'ī. Ath-Tha'labī said, 'What we mentioned about making a simpleton legally incompetent was the position of 'Uthmān, 'Alī, az-Zubayr, 'Ā'ishah, Ibn 'Abbās, and 'Abdullāh ibn Ja'far among the Companions, and Shurayḥ among the Tābi'ūn. Among the *fuqahā'*, it is the position of Mālik and the people of Madīnah, al-Awzā'ī and the people of Syria, Abū Yūsuf, Muḥammad, Aḥmad, Ishāq and Abū Thawr. Ath-Tha'labī said, 'Our fellows claim that there is consensus in respect of it.'

The upshot of all this is that you should know that there are two preconditions for handing over property: ascertainment of good judgment and puberty. If there is one but not the other, it is not permitted to hand property over. That is the testing ordered by the *āyah*. It is transmitted by Ibn al-Qāsim, Ashhab, and Ibn Wahb from Mālik. It is the position of the *fuqahā'* with the exception of Abū Ḥanīfah, Zafar and an-Nakha'ī, who remove this stipulation when the person concerned reaches the age of twenty-five. Abū Ḥanīfah said that that is because he might be a grandfather. This indicates the weakness of his position, and the argument of Abū Bakr ar-Rāzī in *Aḥkām al-Qur'ān*, which makes use of it, is weak regarding the two *āyah*s, as was already mentioned. It comes under the principle of the unrestricted (*muṭlaq*) and restricted (*muqayyad*), and the people of *uṣūl* agree that the unrestricted returns to what is restricted. What is the point of saying he might be a grandfather when he is not one? However, in the case of a girl, our scholars stipulate consummation of marriage as well as puberty.

Then there is the test of good judgment. Abū Ḥanīfah and ash-Shāfi'ī thought that both male and female should be tested, whereas our scholars differentiate between them and say that girls differ from boys since they are confined and not concerned with business and do not go out because they are unmarried. That is why one waits for a girl to be married and so all the goals are focused in that. A male is different in that he deals with matters and meets with people from the beginning of his development until he reaches puberty and so he has experience and his mind is completely formed at puberty. Therefore, the goal is achieved in his respect. What ash-Shāfi'ī said is more correct. Sexual intercourse with actual penetration cannot be said to increase her good judgment when she is already aware of all her affairs and goals and does not squander her money.

Then our scholars continue and add, 'Her marriage with her husband must be consummated and followed by a lapse of time in which in which she gains practical experience.' Ibn al-'Arabī said, 'Our scholars have many positions about how long that should be. Some say five, six or seven years for a woman with a father. They set one year after consummation for an orphan girl without a father or guardian and make it perpetual for one with a guardian until her good judgment is confirmed. There is no evidence for any of this. The stipulation of years in respect of a woman with a father is harsh and, even harsher than it, is a year for an orphan. And as for the continuation of denial of legal competence for a woman with a guardian until her good judgment is clear, the guardian brings her out of it or a judge does so. So it goes by the literal text of the Qur'an. It is all subject to this *āyah*.' *'Good judgment'* is considered, but ascertainment of it varies according to different circumstances of the one ascertaining it. He recognises it and avoids being arbitrary when there is no evidence for it.

They disagree about the actions of a woman with a father during that period. It is said that what she does can be revoked as long as she is considered legally incompetent but that what she does after that is allowed. Some say that what she does in that period is subject to being revoked unless it is clear that it is correct, and what she does after that is assumed to be carried out unless it is clearly a matter of incompetence.

They disagree about giving property to a person who is legally incompetent and whether that requires the permission of the ruler. One group say that the case must be presented to the ruler and the person's good judgment confirmed with him, and then they may be given their property. Another group say that the matter is left to the discretion of the guardian without having to be taken before the ruler. Ibn 'Aṭiyyah said that the correct position is that the guardians of our time must present the case to the ruler and confirm the person's good judgment in his presence. That is because guardians may contrive to have a child deemed to be competent when someone who is incompetent would not be responsible for his dealings because of his incompetence and lack of good judgment at that time.

When property is handed over on the basis of a person having good judgment and then they revert to incompetence by displaying extravagance and lack of management, we think that they are again deemed to be legally incompetent. That is one of two positions of ash-Shāfi'ī. Abū Ḥanīfah disagrees on the basis that the person concerned is an adult, and his responsibility in cases of retaliation and *ḥudūd* is accepted. Our evidence is the words in the *āyah*: *'Do not hand over to the incompetent any property of theirs for which Allah has made you responsible'* (4:5) and *'If the person incurring the debt is incompetent or weak or unable to dictate, then his guardian should dictate to him justly.'* (2:282) Allah did not make a distinction between the person who is legally incompetent being incompetent or having that happen to him in general.

It is permitted for guardians to deal with an orphan's property as a father would – with respect to trade and buying and selling. He must pay the *zakāt* due on their property, be it on money, crops, livestock or *fiṭrah*, and any fines for damages, maintenance of parents and all statutory rights. They are permitted to arrange a marriage for them, pay the dowry for them, buy them a slavegirl and attend to what is generally considered their best interests. If they settle some of their debts and leave others, that is permitted. If the remainder of their property is used up, the remaining creditors can do nothing against the guardian or those whose debts have been settled. If the creditors take all of an orphan's property and then other creditors come and he knew about that debt, or the deceased had acknowledged the debt, then the guardian is liable and he can go back to the first creditors to demand a redistribution. If he did not know about that, and the deceased had not acknowledged it, then the guardian owes nothing. If he pays a creditor without witnesses, he is liable. If there were witnesses and a long time has passed and the witnesses have died, he owes nothing. This was already discussed in *al-Baqarah* (2:220) in the rulings concerning the executor with respect to spending and other things.

Do not consume it extravagantly and precipitately before they come of age.

This does not mean that consuming it without extravagance is permitted. What is meant is: 'Do not consume it. That is extravagance.' Allah forbade guardians to consume orphans' property other than what is permissible and necessary as will be explained. *Isrāf* is extravagance and excessiveness. It was already mentioned in *Āl 'Imrān*. *Saraf* is error in spending as the poet said:

They gave a hundred camels, eight men driving them.
Their gift contained no favour requiring recompense nor error in the gift.

It means that they did not miss the proper amount for the gift. Another said:

Their speaker spoke when the horses trampled them,
'You overdid it.' We answered, 'We are extravagant.'

An-Naḍr ibn Shumayl said that *saraf* is squandering and negligence. *Isrāf* will be further explained in *al-An'ām*, Allah willing.

'Precipitately' means before they grow up and become adult. It means to rush to something. It means: 'Do not avail yourself of the property of the one who is legally incompetent and in your care and consume it, saying, "I will take it before he is an adult so that he will not have sound judgment and take it."' Ibn 'Abbās and others said that.

Those who are wealthy should abstain from it altogether.

Allah makes it clear what is lawful for them of this property and commanded that someone who is wealthy should refrain from it while He permits a poor guardian to consume from the property of the charge in a correct manner. *'Iffah* (the root of *ista'ffa*) means to abstain from what is not lawful or proper. To abstain from something is to abandon doing it. Allah says: *'Those who cannot find the means to marry should be abstinent (la-yasta'fif).'* (24:33) *'Iffah* is to refrain from everything that is not lawful and which one should not do. Abū Dāwud related from Ḥusayn al-Mu'allim from 'Amr ibn Shu'ayb from his father from his grandfather that a man went to the Prophet ﷺ and said, 'I am poor and have nothing and I am also the guardian of an orphan.' He said, 'Use your orphan's property but not extravagantly or precipitately or in an attempt to enrich yourself.'

Those who are poor should use it sensibly and correctly.

Scholars disagree about who is addressed by this *āyah*. We find in *Ṣaḥīḥ Muslim* that 'Ā'ishah said about the phrase *'Those who are poor should use it sensibly and correctly'*: 'It was revealed about an orphan's guardian who maintains him and attends him. When he is in need, he can use some of it.' One variant has, 'Correctly according to the amount of his property.'

Some say that what is meant is the orphan himself – when he is wealthy, he is generous to his guardian and refrains from his property. If he is poor, he spends on him accordingly. That was stated by Rabī'ah and Yaḥyā ibn Sa'īd. The first is the sound position of the majority because the orphan is not instructed to spend because he is a child and legally incompetent. Allah knows best.

Most disagree about what consuming correctly is. Some say that it is borrowing when in need and settling the debt when wealthy. That was stated by 'Umar ibn al-Khaṭṭāb, Ibn 'Abbās, 'Abīdah, Ibn Jubayr, Ash-Sha'bī, Mujāhid and Abu-l-'Āliyah. It is the position of al-Awzā'ī. A guardian should not borrow more than he needs. 'Umar said, 'In relation to the property of Allah I put myself in the position of a guardian in relation to an orphan's property. If I am wealthy, I abstain. If I am in need, I consume correctly. Then when I am wealthy again, I repay it.' 'Abdullāh ibn al-Mubārak related from Abu-l-'Āliyah that the words *'those who are poor should use it sensibly and correctly'* refer to taking a loan. Then he recited the rest of the *āyah*.

A second position related by Ibrāhīm, 'Aṭā', al-Ḥasan al-Baṣrī, an-Nakha'ī, and Qatādah is that a poor guardian does not have to pay back what he uses when it is consumed correctly because that is the right of supervision. The *fuqahā'* take that position. Al-Ḥasan said, 'It is food from Allah for him.' That consists of consuming what will satisfy his hunger and wearing what will clothe his nakedness. He may not wear fine cotton or robes. The proof of the soundness of this position is the consensus of the Community that a ruler who oversees the Muslims is not indebted for what he consumes correctly because Allah Almighty has allotted him his share in the property of Allah. They have no argument in the words of 'Umar, 'When I am wealthy, I repay it,' even if it is sound.

It is related from Ibn 'Abbās, Abu-l-'Āliyah, and ash-Sha'bī that consuming correctly refers to things like using milk from herds, employing slaves and riding animals when the capital is not harmed, applying tar to mangy animals, looking for lost animals, plastering water-basins and harvesting dates. As for the sources of wealth and capital, a guardian may not take that. This is all transmitted with the position of the *fuqahā'* that a guardian may take a wage for his work. A group said that and that that is what is correct and he does not have to pay it back. Taking more than that is forbidden.

Al-Ḥasan ibn Ṣāliḥ ibn Ḥayy made a distinction between a guardian appointed by the father and a guardian appointed by a judge. A guardian appointed by the father can consume correctly while one appointed by a judge is not permitted to touch the property in any way. This is a third position.

There is a fourth position related from Mujāhid who said that a guardian may not take a loan or anything else and he believes that the *āyah* is abrogated by the words of Allah: *'O you who believe, do not consume one another's property by false means, but only by means of mutually agreed trade.'* (4:29) This is not commerce. Zayd ibn Aslam said that the *āyah* is abrogated by Allah's words: *'People who consume the property of orphans wrongfully'* (4:10). Bishr ibn al-Walīd reported that Abū Yūsuf said, 'I do not know. Perhaps *this āyah* was abrogated by: *"O you who believe, do not consume one another's property by false means, but only by means of mutually agreed trade."* (4:29)'

A fifth position distinguishes between being at home and being on a journey. On this understanding a guardian is barred from using an orphan's property when he is resident within in a city, but when he needs to travel for the orphan's sake, he can take what he needs but should not trade. Abū Ḥanīfah and his people said that.

A sixth position espoused by Abū Qilābah is that he may consume in a correct manner from any income. As for the capital, he may not take any of it, as a loan or otherwise.

A seventh position, related by 'Ikrimah from Ibn 'Abbās, is that he may use the property when he is compelled by dire need. Ash-Sha'bī said, 'Then it is like blood and pork which someone in dire need may consume.' An-Naḥḥās said that this makes no sense because in extreme need the same ruling applies to all property, not just the orphan's.

Ibn 'Abbās and an-Nakha'ī also said that what is meant is the guardian consuming correctly from his own property so that he has no need of the orphan's property. Someone wealthy refrains because of his wealth and someone poor stints himself so that he has no need of the orphan's property. This is the best of what is related about the commentary on the *āyah* because other people's property is sacrosanct. None of it is open to use unless there is an absolute pressing need.

Aṭ-Ṭabarī preferred this position in *Aḥkām al-Qur'ān*. He said, 'Some of the early people imagined that the ruling of this *āyah* is that a guardian has general permission to consume the property of a child to an extent which does not reach extravagance. That is contrary to what Allah Almighty commands when He says: *"Do not consume one another's property by false means, but only by means of mutually agreed trade."* This is not possible in respect of an orphan's property. Allah's words: "*Those who are wealthy should abstain from it altogether,*" refer to consuming his own property rather than that of the orphan. It means: "Do not consume orphans' property together with your own property," in other words confine yourself to using your own property. This is indicated by the words of Allah: *"Do not assimilate their property into your own. Doing that is a serious crime."* (4:2) And it is made clear by His words: "*Those who are wealthy should abstain from it altogether. Those who are poor should use it sensibly and correctly.*" It is confined to sufficiency so that he does not need to consume the orphan's property. This is the full meaning of the *āyah*.'

We found that *āyah*s of judgment forbid the consumption of another person's property without their consent, especially that of an orphan. We found that this *āyah* is susceptible to various interpretations. It can make specific what is obliged by the *āyah*s of judgment. Those who support the position of the early people say that *qāḍī*s take a wage because of their work for the Muslims. Is not a guardian in the same position when he works for an orphan? So why would he not take a wage for the work he does? They should be told that they must know that none of the early people permitted a guardian to take any of a child's property when the guardian is wealthy. This is not the case with a *qāḍī*. That is the difference between the two cases. Furthermore, the position taken by the *fuqahā'*, *qāḍī*s and caliphs was that attending to the affairs of Islam does not entitle them to your property. Allah assigned unclaimed lost property to various categories, one of which are *qāḍīs*. A guardian would be taking for his work some of the property of a particular person without their consent. His work is unknown and his wage unknown. That is far from constituting entitlement.

Our Shaykh, Imām Abu-l-'Abbās said, 'If the estate of the orphan is very large and requires a lot of attention on the part of the guardian, which distracts him from his needs and concerns, then a wage for his work is allotted to him. If it is insignificant and does not distract him from his needs and concerns, he should not consume any of it, although it is recommended for him to have a small drink of milk and eat a little food and ghee, without causing harm or taking a lot of it. That is according to custom.' Our Shaykh said, 'The mention of a wage and taking a small amount of dates and milk is confined to an appropriate amount. That is a correct application of the *āyah*.' Allah knows best. It is better, however, to be cautious.

As for what a *qāḍī* takes for dividing inheritance and is called a fee, I do not know of any justification for it and it is not lawful. That falls under the generality of Allah's words: *'People who consume the property of orphans wrongfully consume nothing in their bellies except fire.'* (4:10)

When you hand over their property to them ensure that there are witnesses on their behalf.

Allah commands the presence of witnesses to ensure the preservation of the property and remove any suspicion. A group of scholars say that this testimony is recommended and that the statement of a guardian is accepted because he is a trustee. Another group say that it is obligatory, which conforms with the literal meaning of the *āyah*, and that the guardian is not a trustee, making his statement accepted on that basis. He is in the position of an agent (*wakīl*) when he claims that he has returned what he was given or entrusted with and he is a trustee of the father: his statement is not accepted against another's. Do you not see that if an agent claims that he gave Zayd what he was commanded to, based on his integrity, his statement requires confirmatory evidence? The same applies to guardians.

'Umar ibn al-Khaṭṭāb and Ibn Jubayr said that there should be witnesses to an affluent guardian repaying what he borrowed of an orphan's property in a state of need. 'Abīdah said, 'The *āyah* is evidence that it is obligatory for a guardian to repay what he consumes. It means: when you borrow or consume, call witnesses to confirm your debt.'

The sound position is that the expression is general and includes this and other things. What is meant is having witnesses to anything you spend so that if there is a dispute, there can then be clear evidence. Any property which is taken on trust with witnesses is only discharged when there are witnesses to its return, based on the words of Allah. When it was given without witnesses, then there is no need for witnesses as to its return. Allah knows best.

As a guardian must preserve an orphan's property and make it productive, so he must also care for the child physically. Property is preserved by keeping safe and the body is cared for by teaching. This was discussed in *al-Baqarah*. It is related that a man asked the Prophet ﷺ, 'I have an orphan in my care. Can I consume some of his property?' He answered, 'Yes, but not in order to enrich yourself or to protect your property with his.' He said, 'Messenger of Allah, can I beat him?' He answered, 'Only as you would your own child.' Ibn al-'Arabī said, 'It has no confirmed *isnād*, but there is no one who inclines away from it.'

Allah suffices as a Reckoner.

Allah is a sufficient reckoner of our actions and repays us for them. This is a threat to anyone who refuses to discharge a right. The *bā'* is redundant and is in the position of the nominative.

لِّلرِّجَالِ نَصِيبٌ مِّمَّا تَرَكَ الْوَالِدَانِ وَالْأَقْرَبُونَ وَلِلنِّسَاءِ نَصِيبٌ مِّمَّا تَرَكَ
الْوَالِدَانِ وَالْأَقْرَبُونَ مِمَّا قَلَّ مِنْهُ أَوْ كَثُرَ نَصِيبًا مَّفْرُوضًا ﴿٧﴾

7 Men receive a share of what their parents and relatives leave and women receive a share of what their parents and relatives leave, a fixed share, no matter whether it is a little or a lot.

After mentioning orphans, Allah then deals with inheritance. The *āyah* was revealed about Aws ibn Thābit al-Anṣārī. He died and left a wife called Umm Kuḥḥah and three daughters by her. Two men, Suwayd and 'Arfajah, who were the sons of the uncle of the deceased and his executors, came and took his property without giving his wife and daughters anything. In the Jāhiliyyah women and children, even boys, did not inherit. They said, 'It is only given when someone can fight on horseback, use a spear or a sword and get booty.' Umm Kuḥḥah mentioned that to the Messenger of Allah ﷺ and he summoned them. They said, 'Messenger of Allah, her children do not ride a horse, carry a sword nor wound the enemy.' He said, 'Leave me until I see what Allah tells me about them.' Then this was revealed to refute them, invalidate their statement and remove their ignorance. Young heirs are more entitled to the property than adults since they are unable to transact and attend to their own affairs and so the ruling was reversed and the assumptions of the two men refuted. They erred in their ideas and conduct.

Our scholars say that there are three benefits in this *āyah*. One is clarification of the cause of inheritance, which is kinship. The second is the general nature of kinship, close and distant. The third is the general statement about the obligatory shares, which is further clarified in the *Āyat* of Inheritance. This *āyah* prepares the way for the ruling and nullifies the false view.

It is confirmed that when Abū Talḥah gave his property at Bayruḥā' as *ṣadaqah* and mentioned that to the Prophet ﷺ, he told him, 'Give it to your poor relatives,' and he gave it to Ḥassān and Ubayy. Anas said, 'They were closer to him than me.' Abū Dāwud said that he heard Muḥammad ibn 'Abdullāh al-Anṣārī say, 'Abū Talḥah al-Anṣārī was Zayd ibn Sahl ibn al-Aswad ibn Ḥarām ibn 'Amr ibn Zayd Manāh ibn 'Amr ibn Mālik ibn an-Najjār. He and Ḥassān ibn Thābit ibn al-Mundhir ibn Ḥarām shared a common great-grandfather: Ḥarām. Ubayy was Ubayy ibn Ka'b ibn Ways ibn 'Ubayd ibn Zayd ibn Mu'āwiyah ibn 'Amr ibn Mālik ibn an-Najjār.' Al-Anṣārī said, 'There were six ancestors between Abū Talḥah and Ubayy.' He said that 'Amr ibn Mālik was a common ancestor of

Ḥassān, Ubayy ibn Ka'b and Abū Talḥah. Abū 'Umar said, 'This demands that kinship goes as far as this level. What is closer than that is even more properly referred to as kinship.

a fixed share, no matter whether it is a little or a lot.

Allah affirmed that daughters have a share in inheritance but did not specify how much. So the Prophet ﷺ sent word to Suwayd and 'Arfajah not to divide up the property of Aws. Allah had allotted Aws's daughters a share but had not revealed the amount. So they were to wait until Allah revealed that. When *āyah*s 11-13 were revealed, he told them, 'Give Umm Kuḥḥah an eighth of what Aws left and give his daughters two-thirds and you have the rest.'

Our scholars use this as evidence for including in the division things which would be altered by the shares such as bath-houses, threshing floors and houses, whose benefits would be nullified if the shares in them were confirmed. Mālik said, 'They are divided, even if none of them has a useful share since Allah says: "*a fixed share, no matter whether it is a little or a lot.*"' That is the position of Ibn Kinānah, and ash-Shāfi'ī states that and it is similar to the position of Abu Ḥanīfah. Abu Ḥanīfah said about a small house shared between two people, when one of them asks for the division and his fellow inheritor refuses, that it is divided.'

Ibn Abī Laylā said, 'If there are those whose share is not useful, there is no division.' Any division which causes harm to one person rather than another is not executed. That is the position of Abū Thawr. Ibn al-Mundhir said that is the sounder of the two views. Ibn al-'Arabī mentioned this as being related by Ibn al-Qāsim from Mālik. Ibn al-Qāsim said, 'I think that houses, dwellings and bath-houses that cannot be divided up, and other things whose division would cause harm and are not used when divided, should be sold and there is no pre-emption in it since the Prophet ﷺ said, "There is pre-emption in all undemarcated property. When there are clear boundaries, there is no pre-emption."' This is the evidence provided by the hadith.

Part of the argument for this position is what ad-Dāraquṭnī reports from Ibn Jurayj from Siddīq ibn Mūsā from Muḥammad ibn Abī Bakr from his father, Abū Bakr, that the Prophet ﷺ said, 'There is no division for the people of inheritance except in respect of things that will support division.' Abū 'Ubayd said, 'This is when a man dies and leaves something which, if divided among his heirs, will entail harm to all or some.' He said that such things are not divided. Examples might be a gem, a bath-house, a shawl and similar things. Allah says: '*...making sure that no one's rights are prejudiced.*' (4:12) So He rejects causing harm. Similarly the

Prophet ﷺ said, 'There is no harm nor repayment of harm.'

While the *āyah* does not specify division, it does insist on the obligation of the share and portion to both adult and child, whether it is a little or a lot, to refute the practice of the Jāhiliyyah. Allah says: *'Men have a portion'* and *'women have a portion'* (4:32), and this is very clear. Extracting the portion is based on another argument, and that is that the heir says, 'I am entitled to a share by the words of Allah, so give it to me.' His co-inheritor says, 'As for it belonging only to you, that is not possible because that would lead to harm to both you and me by destroying the property, changing its condition and lowering its value.' So something else is preferred [in this instance]. What is most apparent is that the [physical division to obtain the] share is cancelled when doing so would invalidate benefit and depreciate the value of property. Allah is the One Who grants success.

'A fixed share' is similar to the words, 'a mandatory portion' and 'necessary right'. It is a noun with the meaning of a verbal noun which is why it is in the accusative. Az-Zajjāj said that it is in the accusative for the *ḥāl* and means: 'Those have shares in the obligatory dividing up.' Al-Akhfash said, 'Allah appoints that as a share for them.' *Mafrūḍ* is decreed and mandatory.

وَإِذَا حَضَرَ ٱلْقِسْمَةَ أُوْلُوا۟ ٱلْقُرْبَىٰ وَٱلْيَتَـٰمَىٰ وَٱلْمَسَـٰكِينُ فَٱرْزُقُوهُم
مِّنْهُ وَقُولُوا۟ لَهُمْ قَوْلًا مَّعْرُوفًا ۝٨

8 If other relatives or orphans or poor people attend the sharing-out, provide for them out of it and speak to them correctly and courteously.

Allah makes it clear here that if someone not entitled to any inheritance attends the division, and is a relative, orphan, or poor person who does not inherit, they should be honoured and not deprived if there is a lot of wealth, and given an apology if it is land or only a little which does not allow for gifts. There is, however, a great reward for a gift from a little, one dirham takes precedence over 100,000.

The *āyah,* according to this position, is one of judgment. Ibn 'Abbās said that, and a group of the Tābi'ūn followed his opinion: 'Urwah ibn az-Zubayr and others. Abū Mūsā al-Ash'arī commanded it. It is related from Ibn 'Abbās that it is abrogated by the words of Allah: *'Allah instructs you regarding your children: A male receives the same as the share of two females.'* (4:11) Sa'īd ibn al-Musayyab said that it was abrogated by the *Āyat* of Inheritance and bequest. Among those who said that it was abrogated were Abū Mālik, 'Ikrimah and aḍ-Ḍaḥḥāk.

The first is sounder. It explains the entitlement of heirs to their shares and recommends sharing with those who are present who have no share. Ibn Jubayr said, 'People waste this *āyah*.' Al-Ḥasan said, 'Rather people are avaricious.' In *al-Bukhārī* Ibn 'Abbās says about this *āyah*: 'It is one of judgment and not abrogated.' One variant has: 'Some people claim that this *āyah* is abrogated. No, by Allah, its not abrogated! But it is one of the things that are made light of.'

There are two categories of guardians (*walī*): those who inherit, and those are the ones who give, and those who do not, and this is the one who speaks correctly and says, 'I do not have anything to give you.'

Ibn 'Abbās said, 'During the division to heirs, the believers are commanded to give to relatives, orphans and poor from the bequest. If there is no bequest, they are given to from the inheritance.' An-Naḥḥās said, 'This is the best of what is said about the *āyah*: that it is recommendation and encouragement to do good and to thank Allah.'

One group said, 'This giving is mandatory as an obligation. The heirs should give to these categories what they are happy to give, such as tools, used garments and small things.' Ibn 'Aṭiyyah and al-Qushayrī related this position. The sound position is, however, that it is recommended because, if it had been an obligation, it would be an entitlement to what is left and the sharing out of the legacy would be by one aspect that is known and another that is unknown, and that is contrary to wisdom and would cause division and dissension.

One party believes that those addressed by the *āyah* are those who divide their property in a will, not the heirs. That is related from Ibn 'Abbās, Sa'īd ibn al-Musayyab and Ibn Zayd. If a sick person wants to divide his property by a will, and there are those present who do not inherit, he should not deprive them. This, and Allah knows best, was revealed when a will was obligatory and the *āyah* of inheritance had not yet been revealed. The sound view is the first one. It is relied on.

When the heir is a child who is not able to dispose of his property, one group say that the guardian of the child should give some of the property as is fitting. It is said that he should not give but should say to those who are present, 'I cannot do anything with this property. It belongs to an orphan. When he comes of age, inform him of your right.' This is the commonly accepted position, and this is also when the testator does not make any bequest to him. If he does make a bequest, then he is given what he left him.

'Abīdah and Muhammad ibn Sirin thought that the providing referred to in this *āyah* means to prepare food for them to eat, and they did that by slaughtering a sheep from the estate. 'Abīdah said, 'If it had not been for this *āyah*, I would have done this from my own property.' Qatādah reported that Yaḥyā ibn Ya'mar said, 'Three verses of judgment have been abandoned by people. This *āyah*, the *āyah* of asking permission before entering: *"O you who believe! Those you own as slaves should ask your permission…"* (24:58), and the instruction in: *"O mankind! We created you from a male and female…"*(49:13)'

The pronoun in *'out of it (minhu)'* refers to the division (*qismah*) since it has the meaning of property and inheritance. We also see it in the phrase *'produced it (hā) from his brother's bag'* (12:76), in reference to *ṣuwā'* (goblet) which is masculine. Another example of that usage is seen in the words of the Prophet ﷺ, 'Fear the supplication (*da'wah*) of the wronged. There is no veil between it (*baynahu*) and Allah.' So it is in the masculine with the meaning of *'du'*ā". That is also like his words ﷺ to Suwayd ibn Ṭāriq al-Ju'fī when he asked him about wine, 'It is not a remedy, but rather an illness,' and he repeated the pronoun meaning an alcoholic drink. There are many examples of this.

The verb for 'share out' is *qāsama*, *taqāsama* and *iqtasama*. The noun is *qismah* which is feminine, and *qasm* is the verbal noun. 'I divided (*qasamtu*) and the thing was divided (*inqasama*). The place is *maqsim*, like *majlis*. Time divided them (*taqassama*) and so they were divided (*taqassamū*). *Taqsīm* is separation. Allah knows best.

Speak to them correctly and courteously.

Sa'īd ibn Jubayr said that what should be said is, 'Take, may you be blessed in it.' It is said to be that a person says when they give, 'I wish it could be more.' It is said that there is no need for an excuse when giving, but if the distributor does not give anything to them, he should speak courteously and offer some excuse.

وَلْيَخْشَ ٱلَّذِينَ لَوْ تَرَكُوا۟ مِنْ خَلْفِهِمْ ذُرِّيَّةً ضِعَٰفًا خَافُوا۟ عَلَيْهِمْ فَلْيَتَّقُوا۟
ٱللَّهَ وَلْيَقُولُوا۟ قَوْلًا سَدِيدًا ﴿٩﴾

9 People should show concern in the same way that they would fear for small children if they were to die leaving them behind. They should have *taqwā* of Allah and say words that are appropriate.

People should show concern in the same way that they would fear for small children if they were to die leaving them behind.

The *alif* is omitted from *'show concern'* (*wa-l-yakhsha*) to indicate the imperative.

Sībawayh said that it is not permitted to imply the imperative *lām*, based on analogy with the genitive particles except for the demands of poetry. The Kufans permit it. [POEM] The object of *yakhsha* is elided since the words indicate it. 'Fear' is the apodosis of '*law*' and implies: 'If they would leave them behind, they would fear.' It is permitted to elide the *lām* in the apodosis of '*law*'.

Scholars disagree about the interpretation of this *āyah*. One group say that this is admonition to guardians, meaning 'Behave towards orphans as you would want your children to be treated after your death.' Ibn 'Abbās said that. This is why Allah says: '*People who consume the property of orphans wrongfully...*' (4:10)

Another group say that what is meant is all people. They are commanded to fear Allah in dealing with orphans and other people's children, even if they are not in their care. This instruction is reinforced by calling their attention to the way each of them would want his child to be treated after his death. Related to this is what ash-Shaybānī said: 'We were at Constantinople with the army of Maslamah ibn 'Abd al-Malik, and one day we sat in a group of the people of knowledge, including Ibn ad-Daylamī. We discussed the terrors at the end of time and I said to him, "Abū Bishr! I do not want to have a child." He said to me, "It is not up to you. There is no soul which Allah has decreed will emerge from a man but that it will emerge, whether he wants that or not. But if you want to be reassured about them, fear Allah in the way you treat others."' Then he recited the *āyah*. One variant has: 'Shall I direct you to something by doing which Allah will deliver you from it, and if you leave a child or children, Allah will preserve them for you?' 'Yes, indeed!' was the reply, and he recited this *āyah*.

This understanding is related by Muḥammad ibn Ka'b al-Quraẓī from Abū Hurayrah who said that the Prophet ﷺ said, 'Whoever gives good *ṣadaqah* will cross the Sirāṭ. If anyone looks after the needs of a widow, Allah will replace him in those he leaves behind.'

A third position is taken by a group of commentators. This is when those present with a man who is dying at the time he is making his will say, 'Allah will provide for your child. Look to yourself. Bequeath your property in the Way of Allah. Give *ṣadaqah* and set slaves free,' until he has given the bulk of his property away, and that harms his heirs. People were forbidden to do that. So it is as if the *āyah* was saying to them, 'As you would fear for your heirs and descendants after you, so fear for the heirs of others and do not impel someone to squander his property.' Ibn 'Abbās, Qatādah, as-Suddī, Ibn Jubayr, aḍ-Ḍaḥḥak and Jubayr said this. Sa'īd ibn Jubayr related that Ibn 'Abbās said, 'When a man attends the making of a will, he should not say, "Will away your property. Allah will provide for your child." Rather he should say, "Advance for yourself and leave something for your child." That is the import of Allah's words: *"They should have taqwā of Allah."'*

Miqsam and Ḥaḍramī said, 'It was revealed about the opposite of this. It is that those present tell the dying person, "Keep it for your heirs and leave it to your children. There is no one more entitled to your property than your children." They prevent him from making bequests, and that harms relatives and those entitled to a bequest. They are told, "As you fear for your descendants and want people to be good to them, so speak correctly to the poor and orphans and fear Allah in respect of harming them."'

Both these last two views are based on the time when making a will was obligatory before the *Āyat* of Inheritance was revealed, as Sa'īd ibn Jubayr and Ibn al-Musayyab said. Ibn 'Aṭiyyah said, 'These two views are not mutually exclusive. Rather people fall into two categories. One view is proper for one of them and the other view for the second category. That is that if a man is leaving his heirs independently wealthy, then it is good to recommend him to make bequests and it is possible for him to send ahead [as *sadaqa*] something for himself. But if he is leaving weak, neglected, poor heirs, then it is good to recommend that he leave what he has to them and be cautious. His reward in doing that is like his reward in respect of giving to the poor. What one takes account of is weakness and one must make it one's guiding principle.'

This distinction is sound since the Prophet ﷺ said to Sa'd, 'It is better for you to leave your heirs wealthy than to leave them poor and dependent on people.' If someone has no children, or he is independently wealthy, inheriting his wealth from his father, then he is its trustee. In such a case, when a person has old wealth in his possession such that he will not spend it on those after him in a proper manner, then it is a burden for him.

and say words that are appropriate.

'Appropriate' (*sadīd*) means 'just and correct words.' This means: 'Direct the ill person to pay the obligatory dues from his property and then to will to his relatives an amount which will not harm his young heirs.' It is said that it means: Speak fair words to the dying, which entails instructing them to say, 'There is no god but Allah.' You do not command him to say that, but say it yourself in such a way that the person can hear it. The Prophet ﷺ said, 'Encourage your dying to say: "There is no god but Allah."' He did not say, 'Command them' because such a command might anger the person, making him refuse. It is said that what is meant is the orphan: 'Do not chide him or make light of him.'

إِنَّ ٱلَّذِينَ يَأْكُلُونَ أَمْوَٰلَ ٱلْيَتَـٰمَىٰ ظُلْمًا إِنَّمَا يَأْكُلُونَ فِى بُطُونِهِمْ
نَارًا ۖ وَسَيَصْلَوْنَ سَعِيرًا ١٠

10 People who consume the property of orphans wrongfully consume nothing in their bellies except fire. They will roast in a Searing Blaze.

People who consume the property of orphans wrongfully

It is related that this was revealed about a man of Ghaṭafān called Mirthad ibn Zayd. He was in charge of the property of his nephew, who was an orphan, and consumed it. Then Allah revealed this about him. Muqātal ibn Ḥayyān said that. That is why a group said that what is meant here are trustees who consume what they are not permitted to consume of the property of orphans in their care. Ibn Zayd said, 'It was revealed about the unbelievers who did not allow women or children to inherit.'

Consuming in all its aspects is called 'eating' because it uses property up, and 'bellies' are mentioned to make their wrongdoing clear and show the ugliness of doing this which is contrary to noble character. What is consumed is called fire because that is what it leads to. That usage is the same as that found in Allah's words: *'I dreamt that I was pressing wine'* (12:36) which means, in this context, grapes. It is said that '*fire*' means 'the unlawful' here because the unlawful makes the Fire mandatory. That is why Allah called it this.

Abū Sa'īd al-Khudrī said, 'The Prophet ﷺ related about his Night Journey, "I saw some people with lips like those of camels. Someone would take hold of their lips and put a rock of fire in their mouths which then emerged from their rear. I asked, 'Jibrīl, who are they?' He replied, 'They are those who wrongfullly consumed the property of orphans.'"'

The Book and *Sunnah* indicate that consuming the property of orphans is one of the major wrong actions. The Prophet ﷺ said, 'Avoid the seven deadly ones,' and he mentioned consuming orphans' property among them.

They will roast in a Searing Blaze.

Ibn 'Āmir and 'Āṣim in the transmission of Ibn 'Abbās recited *'sa-yuṣlana'* in the passive instead of *'sa-yaṣlana'* from the verb *aṣlā*, to roast. Allah says: *'I will roast* (sa-uṣlīhi) *him in Saqar.*' (74:26) Abū Ḥaywah recited *'sa-yuṣallawna'* in Form II as we see in 69:31. That can mean time after time. *Taṣallā* is to warm with fire. A poet said:

> You warmed the heat of their war
>   as someone chilled is warmed from the cold

The rest recite *'sa-yaslana'* from *ṣalā* with the nouns *ṣallā* and *ṣilā'*. Allah says: *'in which only the most wretched will roast.'* (92:15) *Ṣalā'* is to heat by proximity to the fire or actually bring in direct contact with it. *Sa'īr* are burning coals.

This is one of the *āyahs* of threat but there is no evidence in it for anyone who says that wrong actions make someone an unbeliever. What the people of the *Sunnah* believe is that the threat will be carried out on some rebellious Muslims who will be burned and die, as opposed to the people of the Fire who do not die and do not live. This seems to be an attempt to combine the Book and the *Sunnah* since there is some disparity. By His will Allah will remove from the Fire whomever He wills. Allah says: *'Allah does not forgive partners being attributed to Him but He forgives whomever He wills for anything apart from that.'* (4:47) That is the upshot with everything said to you on this theme.

Muslim related in his *Ṣaḥīḥ* from Abū Hurayrah that the Messenger of Allah ﷺ said, 'As for the people of the Fire who are truly its people, they will not die in it or live, but some people will be burned by the Fire for their wrong actions (or errors). Allah will make them die until they are charcoal and then permission for intercession will be granted. They will be brought in groups and cast up on the banks of the rivers of the Garden. Then it will be said, "People of the Garden, pour on them!" They will pour [water] on them and they will grow like seeds grow in what is carried by the flood." A man from among the people said, 'It seems that the Messenger of Allah ﷺ has herded animals in the desert.'

يُوصِيكُمُ ٱللَّهُ فِىٓ أَوْلَٰدِكُمْ لِلذَّكَرِ مِثْلُ حَظِّ ٱلْأُنثَيَيْنِ فَإِن كُنَّ نِسَآءً فَوْقَ ٱثْنَتَيْنِ فَلَهُنَّ ثُلُثَا مَا تَرَكَ وَإِن كَانَتْ وَٰحِدَةً فَلَهَا ٱلنِّصْفُ وَلِأَبَوَيْهِ لِكُلِّ وَٰحِدٍ مِّنْهُمَا ٱلسُّدُسُ مِمَّا تَرَكَ إِن كَانَ لَهُۥ وَلَدٌ فَإِن لَّمْ يَكُن لَّهُۥ وَلَدٌ وَوَرِثَهُۥٓ أَبَوَاهُ فَلِأُمِّهِ ٱلثُّلُثُ فَإِن كَانَ لَهُۥٓ إِخْوَةٌ فَلِأُمِّهِ ٱلسُّدُسُ مِنۢ بَعْدِ وَصِيَّةٍ يُوصِى بِهَآ أَوْ دَيْنٍ ءَابَآؤُكُمْ وَأَبْنَآؤُكُمْ لَا تَدْرُونَ أَيُّهُمْ أَقْرَبُ لَكُمْ نَفْعًا فَرِيضَةً مِّنَ ٱللَّهِ إِنَّ ٱللَّهَ كَانَ عَلِيمًا حَكِيمًا ۝

وَلَكُمْ نِصْفُ مَا تَرَكَ أَزْوَٰجُكُمْ إِن لَّمْ يَكُن لَّهُنَّ وَلَدٌ فَإِن كَانَ لَهُنَّ وَلَدٌ فَلَكُمُ ٱلرُّبُعُ مِمَّا تَرَكْنَ مِنۢ بَعْدِ وَصِيَّةٍ يُوصِينَ بِهَآ أَوْ دَيْنٍ وَلَهُنَّ ٱلرُّبُعُ مِمَّا تَرَكْتُمْ إِن لَّمْ يَكُن لَّكُمْ

وَلَدٌ فَإِن كَانَ لَكُمْ وَلَدٌ فَلَهُنَّ ٱلثُّمُنُ مِمَّا تَرَكْتُم مِّنۢ بَعْدِ
وَصِيَّةٍ تُوصُونَ بِهَآ أَوْ دَيْنٍ وَإِن كَانَ رَجُلٌ يُورَثُ كَلَٰلَةً
أَوِ ٱمْرَأَةٌ وَلَهُۥٓ أَخٌ أَوْ أُخْتٌ فَلِكُلِّ وَٰحِدٍ مِّنْهُمَا ٱلسُّدُسُ
فَإِن كَانُوٓا۟ أَكْثَرَ مِن ذَٰلِكَ فَهُمْ شُرَكَآءُ فِى ٱلثُّلُثِ
مِنۢ بَعْدِ وَصِيَّةٍ يُوصِى بِهَآ أَوْ دَيْنٍ غَيْرَ مُضَآرٍّ وَصِيَّةً
مِّنَ ٱللَّهِ وَٱللَّهُ عَلِيمٌ حَلِيمٌ ﴿١٢﴾ تِلْكَ حُدُودُ ٱللَّهِ وَمَن يُطِعِ
ٱللَّهَ وَرَسُولَهُۥ نُدْخِلْهُ جَنَّٰتٍ تَجْرِى مِن تَحْتِهَا ٱلْأَنْهَٰرُ
خَٰلِدِينَ فِيهَا وَذَٰلِكَ ٱلْفَوْزُ ٱلْعَظِيمُ ﴿١٣﴾ وَمَن يَعْصِ ٱللَّهَ
وَرَسُولَهُۥ وَيَتَعَدَّ حُدُودَهُۥ نُدْخِلْهُ نَارًا خَٰلِدًا فِيهَا وَلَهُۥ
عَذَابٌ مُّهِينٌ ﴿١٤﴾

11 Allah instructs you regarding your children: A male receives the same as the share of two females. If there are more than two daughters they receive two-thirds of what you leave. If she is one on her own she receives a half. Each of your parents receives a sixth of what you leave if you have children. If you are childless and your heirs are your parents your mother receives a third. If you have brothers or sisters your mother receives a sixth, after any bequest you make or any debts. With regard to your fathers and your sons, you do not know which of them is going to benefit you more. These are obligatory shares from Allah. Allah is All-Knowing, All-Wise. 12 You receive half of what your wives leave if they are childless. If they have children you receive a quarter of what they leave after any bequest they make or any debts. They receive a quarter of what you leave if you are childless. If you have children they receive an eighth of what you leave after any bequest you make or any debts. If a man or woman has no direct heirs, but has a brother or sister, each of them receives a sixth. If there are more than that they share in a third after any bequest you make or any debts, making sure that no one's rights are prejudiced. This is an instruction from Allah. Allah is All-Knowing, All-Forbearing. 13 These are Allah's limits. As for those who obey Allah and His Messenger, We will admit

them into Gardens with rivers flowing under them, remaining in them timelessly, for ever. That is the Great Victory. 14 As for those who disobey Allah and His Messenger and overstep His limits, We will admit them into a Fire, remaining in it timelessly, for ever. They will have a humiliating punishment.

Allah instructs you regarding your children:

In this *āyah* Allah clarifies what is undefined in His words: *'Men have a portion...'* (4:32) This indicates that it is permitted to delay clarification of a matter beyond the moment of the question about it. This *āyah* is one of the pillars of the *dīn* and underpinnings of judgments and one of the matrix *āyah*s of the Qur'an. Shares of inheritance are so important that they constitute a third or a half of knowledge. It is the first knowledge which will be taken from people and forgotten. Ad-Dāraquṭnī reported from Abū Hurayrah that the Prophet ﷺ said, 'Learn the shares of inheritance and teach them to people. It is half of knowledge and the first thing which will be forgotten. It is the first thing which will be removed from my community.' He also related from 'Abdullāh ibn Mas'ūd that the Messenger of Allah ﷺ said, 'Learn the Qur'an and teach it to people. Learn the shares of inheritance and teach them to people. Learn knowledge and teach it to people. I am a man who will be taken. Knowledge will be taken and seditions will appear. It will be such that two will dispute their share and not find anyone to decide between them.'

This being confirmed, know that the knowledge of shares of inheritance constituted the bulk of the knowledge of the Companions and was an important topic of discussion, but people have lost it. Muṭarrif related from Mālik that 'Abdullāh ibn Mas'ūd said, 'If someone does not learn the shares, divorce and *ḥajj*, how does he differ from the people of the desert?' Ibn Wahb reported that Mālik said, 'I heard Rabī'ah say, "If someone learns the shares of inheritance without learning them from the Qur'an, he is quick to forget them."' Mālik added, 'He spoke the truth.' Abū Dāwūd and ad-Dāraquṭnī related from 'Abdullāh ibn 'Amr ibn al-'Āṣ that the Messenger of Allah ﷺ said, 'Knowledge consists of three things, and what is other than them is extra: an *āyah* of judgment, a confirmed *sunnah* and a just share.' Abū Sulaymān al-Khaṭṭābī said, 'The *āyah* of judgment is the Book of Allah, and mastery is stipulated in it because some *āyah*s are abrogated and not acted on and one must act on what supersedes them. A confirmed *sunnah* is what is established as coming from the Messenger of Allah ﷺ. A just share can be interpreted in two ways. One is that someone is just in the division and fair in the portions and shares mentioned in the Book and *Sunnah*. The other is that it is derived from the Book and *Sunnah* and what is like them.'

'Ikrimah related: 'Ibn 'Abbās sent to Zayd ibn Thābit to ask him about a woman who died leaving a husband and parents. He said, "The husband receives half, and the mother has a third of what is left." He asked, "Do you find it in the Book or is that your opinion?" He replied, "It is my opinion. I do not prefer a mother to a father."' Abū Sulaymān said, 'This is part of balancing the share when there is no text concerning it. It is based on the interpretation of the text: *"If your heirs are your parents, your mother receives a third."* When the share of a mother is a third, the rest, which is two-thirds, goes to the father. The half left of the property after the husband's share is analogous to property when there is no child or anyone with a share along with the parents. So the remaining half is divided into three: one share for the mother and two shares for the father. This is a fairer division than giving the mother a third of all the property and the father what remains, which is a sixth, thereby preferring her to him, which is not the basic rule in inheritance. It is fairer than what Ibn 'Abbās believed about giving a full third to the mother and thereby diminishing the right of the father to a sixth. Most *fuqahā'* abandon his position for that of Zayd.'

Abū 'Umar said, "Abdullāh ibn 'Abbās said about a case when there is a husband and both parents that the husband receives a half, the mother a third of the total and the father receives the rest. He said that in the case where there is a wife and both parents that the wife receives a quarter, the mother a third of the total and the father receives the rest. This was the position of Qāḍī Shurayḥ, Muḥammad ibn Sīrīn and Dāwud ibn 'Alī, and a group, including Abu-l-Ḥasan Muḥammad ibn 'Abdullāh al-Faraḍī al-Miṣrī, known as Ibn al-Labbān, about both cases. He claimed that it is analogous to the view of 'Alī about a *mushtarikah* case. He said elsewhere that he related it from 'Alī.'

Abū 'Umar said, 'What is well known and famous from 'Alī, Zayd, 'Abdullāh and the rest of the Companions and most scholars is what Mālik wrote. Part of their argument against Ibn 'Abbās is that when the parents are among the heirs, others do not share with them. The mother has a third and the father two-thirds. That is the same when they share in the half left by a husband: she has a third and he has two-thirds of it. This is sound in investigation and analogy.'

There are various transmissions about the reason for the revelation of the *Āyah* of Shares of Inheritance. At-Tirmidhī, Abū Dāwūd, Ibn Mājah, and ad-Dāraquṭnī reported from Jābir ibn 'Abdullāh that the wife of Sa'd ibn ar-Rabī' said, 'Messenger of Allah, Sa'd has died and left two daughters and a brother. His brother came and took what Sa'd left. Women are married on account of their property.' He did not answer her in that gathering. Then she came to him and said,

'Messenger of Allah, what about the daughters of Sa'd?' He said, 'Summon his brother to me.' He came to him and the Prophet ﷺ told him, 'Give his daughters two-thirds, his wife an eighth, and you have the rest.' That is how Abū Dāwud has it. At-Tirmidhī and others have: 'The *Āyah* of Inheritance was revealed,' and he said that this is a sound hadith.

Jābir also reports, 'The Messenger of Allah ﷺ and Abū Bakr came walking to visit me among the Banū Salimah when I was ill and unconscious. He ﷺ performed *wuḍū'* and then poured his *wuḍū'* water over me. I regained consciousness and said, "Messenger of Allah, who will inherit from me as I have no direct heirs?" Then the *Āyah*s of the Shares of Inheritance were revealed.' It is in the *Ṣaḥīḥ* Collections. At-Tirmidhī transmitted it and has in it: 'I said, "Prophet of Allah, how should I distribute my wealth among my children?" He did not give me any answer at all. Then it was revealed: *"Allah instructs you regarding your children…"*' He said that it is a sound *ḥasan* hadith.

We find in al-Bukhārī from Ibn 'Abbās that the *āyah* was revealed concerning the property of children and the bequest to the parents. That was abrogated by these *āyah*s. Muqātil and al-Kalbī said that it was revealed about Umm Kuḥḥah, as we mentioned earlier. As-Suddī said that it was revealed because of the daughter of 'Abd ar-Raḥmān ibn Thābit, the brother of Ḥassān ibn Thābit. It is said that in the Jāhiliyyah they only allowed those who could fight in battle to inherit and then this was revealed to make it clear that every child and old person had a share. It may have been an answer to all the cases mentioned which is why its revelation was delayed. Allah knows best.

Aṭ-Ṭabarī said, 'There are some traditions related about not allowing children to inherit, which remained at the beginning of Islam until they were abrogated by this *āyah*. We do not believe that that was part of the Sharī'ah. Indeed, the opposite is established. This *āyah* was revealed about the heirs of Sa'd ibn ar-Rabī' or the heirs of Thābit ibn Qays ibn Shammās. The first is sounder according to the people of transmission. The Messenger of Allah ﷺ cancelled inheritance for the paternal uncle. If that had been confirmed before in our Sharī'ah, he would not have cancelled it. It was also not confirmed in our Sharīah that a child was not given a share until he could fight on horseback and defend the tribe.'

That is what Qāḍī Abū Bakr ibn al-'Arabī said: 'The revelation of this *āyah* indicates that it was based on something new. In the beginning of Islam, there was no law based on how property was inherited in the Jāhiliyyah. It was silent about it which amounts to affirmation because if there had been a confirmed law about it, then the Prophet ﷺ would not have judged that the uncle of the two girls had to return any of their property because, when rulings have been delivered and then abrogation comes afterwards, that has an effect in the future and does not undo what happened in the past. Injustice was removed.'

The Shāfi'īs say that the words of Allah: *'Allah instructs you regarding your children…'* is literally about children. As for the grandchildren, they are included by extension. When someone swears that he has no children and he does have a grandchild, he does not break his oath. When he makes a bequest to a certain child, that does not include that child's child. Abū Ḥanīfah said that the grandchild is included when the child no longer exists.

Ibn al-Mundhir said that according to the literal meaning of the *āyah*, it would give obligatory inheritance rights to all children, believers or unbelievers. It is confirmed that the Messenger of Allah ﷺ said, 'An unbeliever does not inherit from a Muslim.' It is known that it means only some children because a Muslim does not inherit from an unbeliever or vice versa based on the literal meaning of the hadith.

When Allah says: *'your children,'* He includes in that captives in the hands of the unbelievers. They inherit as long as they are known to be Muslim and alive. That is the position of all the people of knowledge except an-Nakha'ī who says that captives do not inherit. If someone is not known to be alive, their ruling is that of someone absent. The legacy of the Prophet ﷺ is not included in the generality because he said, 'We do not leave inheritance. What we leave is *ṣadaqah*.' That will be explained in *Sūrat Maryam*, Allah willing. Similarly, the ruling does not include someone who murders his father, grandfather, brother or uncle by the consensus of the Community. A murderer does not inherit anything from the property of the one he killed nor any of his blood-money as was explained in *al-Baqarah*.

If the killing is accidental, the killer does not inherit from the blood-money, but does inherit from the estate, according to Mālik, but not according to ash-Shāfi'ī, Aḥmad, Sufyān and the People of Opinion as already explained in *al-Baqarah*. The position of Mālik is sounder. That is the position of Isḥāq and Abū Thawr as well as Sa'īd ibn al-Musayyab, 'Aṭā' ibn Rabāḥ, Mujāhid, az-Zuhrī, al-Awzā'ī, and Ibn al-Mundhir, because the inheritance of the heir is confirmed by Allah in His Book and there is no exception to it except by *Sunnah* or consensus. Any disagreement regarding it is referred to the apparent meaning of the *āyah*s which deal with inheritance.

Know that in the beginning of Islam entitlement to inheritance came by various means, among them alliance, emigration and treaty. Then all that was abrogated in this *sūrah* when Allah says: *'We have appointed heirs for everything.'* (4:33)

Scholars agree that when there is someone who has a fixed share along with the children of the deceased person, he is given it. In respect of the rest of the property a male has the portion of two females since the Prophet ﷺ said, 'Give the shares to their people.' This means the shares designated in the Book of Allah, which are six: a half, a quarter, an eighth, two-thirds, a third and a sixth. Five have a half share: the daughter, son's daughter, full sister, paternal sister and husband. All of that is when they have no one to exclude them. A quarter is for the husband when there is exclusion, and for wives when there is no exclusion. An eighth is for wives when there is exclusion. Four have two-thirds: two or more daughters, a son's daughters, full sisters or paternal sisters. All of that is when there is no exclusion.

A third is for the mother when there are no children or the children of the son, and fewer than two or more brothers and sisters, and for two or more the mother's children. This is a third of the total property. As for the third of what remains, that is for the mother in the case of a spouse and both parents. The mother has a third of what remains, as has already been explained. In the case of a grandfather when there are brothers, when there is someone with a share with them, he has a third of what remains. Seven have a sixth: parents and a grandfather when there is a child and grandchild, grandmother, or grandmothers when there are more than one, granddaughters by a son when there is a daughter, paternal sisters when there are full sisters, and a child, male or female, of the mother. All these shares are taken from the Book of Allah except for the grandmother which is taken from the *Sunnah*.

There are three things which make these shares obligatory: established lineage, contracted marriage, and the *walā'* of emancipation. The three can be combined, as when someone is the husband of a woman, her emancipator (*mawlā*) and a son of her paternal uncle. There can also be only two of them, as when someone is a woman's husband and her emancipator (*mawlā*), or her husband and the son of her paternal uncle. Then he inherits by two paths and has all the property if he is the only heir: half by being her husband and half on the basis of the *walā'* or by lineage. A similar case is when a woman is a man's daughter and his emancipator (*mawlā*); she also receives all of the estate when she is the only heir: half by lineage and half by the *walā'*.

Inheritance only takes place after any debts have been paid and any bequests made. When someone dies, specific rights are paid from his estate, then what is needed for his shroud and burial, then his debts in order, then the third for bequests and what is like that in order, and the rest is inheritance for the heirs, who are seventeen in total. Ten are men: son, grandson – however far removed – father, grandfather – however far removed – brother, brother's son, paternal uncle, and his son, husband, and male *mawla*. The seven women are: daughter, son's daughter – however far removed – mother, grandmother – however far removed – sister, wife, and female *mawla*. An excellent man put them in order, saying:

If you want to count all the heirs, both male and female,
They are ten men and seven women.

I have counted them in order: the son, the son's son, the paternal uncle's son,
The father who is in the rank, the grandfather, before the close brother,

The son of the closest brother, indeed, the uncle, the husband,
the *mawla* and then the mother.

The son's daughter after her, the daughter, the wife, the grandmother
and the sister.
And the female *mawla*. Take that number exactly.

'*Your children*' includes all your children, whether present or in the womb, near or far removed, male and female, except for unbelievers. Some say that it is actually about the near, and by extension about the far removed. Some say that it is actually about all of them because it comes from 'birth', although they inherit according to nearness. Allah says: '*O sons of* Ādam' (7:26) and the Prophet ﷺ said, 'I am the master of the sons of Ādam.' He ﷺ also said, 'Sons of Ismā'īl, shoot! Your father was an archer.'

However, it is generally applied to those who are specifically close to one in reality. If there is a direct male child, then the son's son gets nothing. This is agreed on by the people of knowledge. If there is no male child, but there are male grandchildren, one begins with the actual daughters and they are given the two-thirds and then the remaining third is given to the grandchildren if they are equal in closeness to the deceased, or if the male is further removed than the daughters, since the male has the share of two females. This is the position of Mālik, ash-Shāfi'ī, and the People of Opinion. It is stated by the majority of the people of knowledge among the Companions, Tābi'ūn and those after them except for something which is related from Ibn Mas'ūd who said that if there is a male grandchild opposite a granddaughter, he precludes her. If he is further away in lineage, he does not. In that he took account of the words of Allah: '*If there are more than two daughters they receive two-thirds of what you leave.*' Even if there are many, He did not assign them more than two-thirds.

Ibn al-'Arabī also gave an opinion based on this distinction from Ibn Mas'ūd. Ibn al-Mundhir and al-Bājī mentioned that he said that what is left after the daughters inherit goes to the sons of the son rather than the daughters of the son, and there is no distinction. Ibn al-Mundhir related it from Abū Thawr. Abū 'Umar related the like of it and said, 'Ibn Mas'ūd disagreed with that and said, 'When daughters take the two-thirds, the remaining third goes to the sons of the son rather than their sisters and rather than those closer and further than them of the daughters of the son.' This is the position of Abū Thawr and Dāwud ibn 'Alī. The like of it is related from 'Alqamah. The argument of those who take this position is found in the hadith of Ibn 'Abbās who reported that the Prophet ﷺ said, 'Divide the property between the people of obligatory shares according to the Book of Allah. What remains of the shares goes to the closest male relative.' Al-Bukhārī, Muslim and others transmitted it.

Part of the majority argument are the words of Allah: *'Allah instructs you regarding your children: a male receives the same as the share of two females'* because the child of a child is also considered a child. From the standpoint of reflection and analogy, whoever is deemed to be *'aṣabah* in his degree in respect of the entire property must also be *'aṣabah* in any excess property, like immediate children. Therefore, it is mandatory that the son's son shares with the son of his sister, as the direct son shares with his sister. As for the argument of Abū Thawr and Dāwud that as the son's daughter does not inherit anything of the excess after the two-thirds, she is alone and so her brother does not make her one of the *'aṣabah,* the answer is that when her brother is with her, she is strengthened by him and becomes one of the *'aṣabah* with him. The apparent meaning of: *'Allah instructs you regarding your children'* is that she is one of the children.

If there are more than two daughters they receive two-thirds of what you leave.

Allah obliged a half share for one daughter, and two-thirds for more than two, and so, if there are just two, they are not given a specified share in the Book. Scholars discussed the evidence about whether they are given two-thirds. It is said that this is the consensus but that is rejected because the sound view from Ibn 'Abbās is that two daughters are given a half because of this *āyah.* It is said that they are given two-thirds by analogy with two sisters as Allah says at the end of the *sūrah*: *'...he has a sister and she has a half of what he leaves'* (4:186) and *'...if they are two, they have two-thirds of what he leaves.'* So two daughters are connected to two sisters in sharing in two-thirds, and if there are more sisters than two, they are connected to the daughters and share in two-thirds. This is countered by the fact that it is a text about sisters.

It is said that the *āyah* indicates that two daughters receive two-thirds. That is since when there is one with her brother, she has a third when she is alone, we know that two have two-thirds. This is the position of Qāḍī Ismā'īl and Abu-l-'Abbās al-Mubarrad. An-Naḥḥās says that this argument is erroneous because the disagreement is about two daughters, not one. His opponents would say, 'Then if there are daughters and a son, the daughters receive a half.' This is evidence that this is their share.

It is said that the word '*fawq*' (more) is redundant, and the actual meaning is 'if they are two.' Grammatically, this is like Allah's words: *'Strike (above) the necks'* (6:12), which actually means 'the necks' themselves. This position is refuted by an-Naḥḥās and Ibn 'Aṭiyyah because it is not permitted for prepositions and nouns to be meaningless in Arabic. Ibn 'Aṭiyyah said, 'That is because His words, "*Strike (above) the necks*" is a matter of eloquence and "*fawq*" here is not redundant. Rather it makes the meaning precise because striking the neck must be above the neck joint and below the brain as Darīd ibn aṣ-Ṣimah said, "Lower than the brain and above the joint. That is how I strike the necks of heroes."'

The strongest argument for two daughters receiving two-thirds is the sound hadith related about the reason for its revelation. The dialect of the people of the Hijaz and the Banū Asad is *thuluth* and *rubu'* up to ten. The dialect of the Banū Tamīm and Rabī'ah is *thulth*, and so on up to ten. [BIT MORE]

If she is one on her own she receives a half.

Nāfi' and the people of Madīnah read the word '*one*' (*wāḥidatun*) in the nominative meaning 'it has happened and occurred' and so it is a full *kāna*. [POEM] The rest read it as '*wāḥidatan*' in the accusative. An-Naḥḥās said that it is a good reading, meaning if she is left [as a sole daughter] or born [as a sole daughter].

If there are daughters of the son with daughters and the daughters are two or more, they exclude the daughters of the son from inheriting because they have no access to inheritance by any share other than that of the two-thirds. If there is no daughter, then the daughter or daughters of the son inherit with the daughter to complete the two-thirds. They take the place of the other daughters, just as the sons of son take the place of the sons in exclusion and inheritance. In the absence of any of them who are entitled to the sixth, it then goes to the son's daughter. She is more entitled to the sixth than the full sister according to the majority of *fuqahā'* among the Companions and Tābi'ūn, except for what is related from Abū Mūsā and Sulaymān ibn Abī Rabī'ah that the daughter has a half, the sister the other half, and the son's daughter nothing.

There is a sound transmission from Abū Mūsā that he retracted that. We find in al-Bukhārī from Ādam from Shu'bah from Abū Qays that Huzayl ibn Shuraḥbīl said, 'Abū Mūsā was asked about a daughter, a son's daughter and a sister. He said, "A daughter receives a half. A sister receives a half. If you go to Ibn Mas'ūd, he will corroborate me." Ibn Mas'ūd was asked and was told of what Abū Mūsā said. He said, "I would then be misguided and not one of the guided. I give the decision which the Prophet ﷺ gave. A daughter has a half and a daughter of a son has a sixth which completes two-thirds, and what is left is for the sister." Then I went to Abū Mūsā and told him what Ibn Mas'ud had said, and he said, "Do not ask me as long as this scholar is among you."'

If there is a son with the son's daughter or daughters who is at the same level as them or less in the *'aṣabah*, then the second half is shared between them, the male having the share of two females, differing from Ibn Mas'ūd. Then the immediate daughters, or immediate daughters and sons' daughters take the full two-thirds. The same is said about full sisters and paternal siblings: the paternal sister and mother have a half, and the rest goes to the brothers and sisters as long as the individual share is not more than a sixth. If it is more than a sixth, then they are given the full two-thirds, but no more than that. Abū Thawr said that.

If a man dies and leaves a pregnant wife, the property is held in hand until the sex of the child is clear. The people of knowledge agree that when a man dies while his wife is pregnant, the child in her womb inherits and is inherited from if it is born alive and cries. They all say that if it is born dead, it does not inherit. If it is born alive and does not cry, one group say that it has no inheritance, even if it moves or sneezes. This is the position of Mālik, al-Qāsim ibn Muḥammad, Ibn Sīrīn, ash-Sha'bī, az-Zuhrī and Qatādah. Another group said, 'If life is recognised by movement, crying, suckling, or breathing, then the rulings concerning it follow those of the living.' That is the view of ash-Shāfi'ī, Sufyan ath-Thawrī and al-Awzā'ī. Ibn al-Mundhir said, 'What ash-Shāfi'ī said is open to debate although the report in fact precludes it. The Prophet ﷺ said, "There is no child born but that Shayṭān pricks it and so it cries at the prick of Shayṭān except for the son of Maryam and his mother."' This is a report, and there is no abrogation in respect of a report.

If one of the children is a hermaphrodite, scholars agree that the inheritance is determined by how the child urinates. If it is like a male, then he receives the inheritance of a male. If it is like a female, then it is the inheritance of a female. Ibn al-Mundhir said that he did not record anything about this from Mālik. Ibn al-Qāsim said that he was too in awe of Mālik to ask him about it. If the individual urinates in both ways, then one considers how urination begins. Sa'īd ibn al-Musayyab, Aḥmad and Isḥāq said that. That is also related from the People of Opinion. Qatādah related that Sa'īd ibn al-Musayyab said that a hermaphrodite inherits according to how they urinate, and that if they urinate in both ways, it is according to which manner is first.

If they urinate in both ways at the same time, then it is half that of a male and half that of a female. Ya'qūb and Muḥammad said that they inherit according to which manner produces the most urine. That is related from al-Awzā'ī. An-Nu'mān said, 'When a baby urinates in both ways together, it is problematic. I do not know which of them predominates.' It is related that he hesitated about a person when they are like that. It is related that he said, 'When things are unclear, they are given the smaller of the two shares.'

Yaḥyā ibn Ādam said, 'When someone urinates like a man and menstruates like a woman, they inherit according to their manner of urination because we find in a tradition, "He inherits according to his urination."' Ash-Shāfi'ī said, 'When someone urinates from both places and one has no precedence over the other, then they are problematic and receive the inheritance of a female. The rest is held between them and the other heirs until the business is clear or they come to an agreement.' Abū Thawr said that. Ash-Sha'bī said, 'Such a person is given half the inheritance of a male and half that of a female.' Al-Awzā'ī said that, and it is the position of the Māliki school.

Ibn Shās said in *Jawāhir ath-Thamīnah 'alā madhhab Mālik 'ālim al-Madīnah*: 'Someone is considered to be a hermaphrodite when they have two sets of genitals – those of a female and those of a male – and urinate from both. Ruling about them is given on the basis of how they urinate. If they urinate in both ways, then it is more frequent of them. When they are both equal, one considers which starts first. If they both start at the same time, one considers the growth of a beard or size of breasts and whether they are like a woman's breasts. If someone has both, then one considers their state at puberty. If they menstruate, then the ruling is given based on that. If they only have a wet dream, then the ruling is given based on that. If both exist, then they are problematic. The same is true if someone has no genitalia and nothing specific designating either a male or a female but has a site by which they urinate. In that case one waits until puberty to see if any distinguishing sign appears. If it does not, they are problematic. Then we judge by that and they inherit half the share of a male and half that of a female.'

This is what has been mentioned about the signs of a problematic hermaphrodite. We indicated the sign in *al-Baqarah* and the beginning of this *sūrah*: one considers the ribs. That is related from 'Alī and judgment is given on that basis. One of the excellent scholars wrote some verses on the ruling of the hermaphrodite. They begin:

One considers circumstances: breasts, beard and urination.

He says in it:

If his circumstances are equal and unclear, and signs are ambivalent,
Then his share of the inheritance of a relative is six-eighths of a share.

This is what he is entitled to because of the lack of clarity,
and there is the abstention that is in it.

He should not marry as long as he lives in this world nor be given in marriage.
Then he does not have dependants nor bringing up young as men do.

All that I have mentioned in poetry was stated by the leaders of scholars.
Some people refuse to speak about it, and there is no blame in that,

Because of atrocities that may arise in discussion, and clear repulsiveness.
The ruling of the pleasing imam, 'Alī, was already given on it

About if the person is lacking a rib. Men must follow that
In inheritance, marriage, *iḥrām* in *ḥajj*, prayer and rulings.

If she has a rib more than men, then she is female
Because women have a rib more than men. So take advantage of that.

It was missing from Ādam before on account of the creation of Ḥawwā'.

This is a true statement.
There is evidence for that in what the Messenger, peace be upon him, said.

Abu-l-Walīd ibn Rushd said, 'Someone problematic in this way may be neither a husband nor a wife, nor a mother nor a father. It is said that they may have children from the womb and children from the back [i.e. sperm].' Ibn Rushd said, 'If this is sound, then the person inherits from their son by sperm with the full share of a father and from their son by the womb with the full share of a mother. This is unlikely, and Allah knows best.' We find in the *Sunan* of ad-Dāraquṭnī that

Abū Hāni' 'Umar ibn Bashīr said, "Āmir ash-Sha'bī was asked about a child who is neither male nor female who did not have what either a male or female have, and urine and faeces came from his navel. He was asked about its inheritance and 'Āmir said that it is half the share of a male and half the share of a female.'

Each of your parents receives a sixth of what you leave if you have children.

'Parents' here means the parents of the deceased. This alludes to something not mentioned which is permitted linguistically. 'Sixth' is in the nominative by the inceptive and what is before it is its predicate. The same is true of 'third,' 'half', fourth, etc.

The word *'parents'* is dual: the father and mother (*ābah*). The expression *umm* spares the need for *ābah*. Some Arabs prefer one to the other since it is easy and famous. That is heard in sound names, like calling the parents *al-abwān*, calling the sun and moon 'two moons' and night and day *al-malawān*. 'The two 'Umars' is used for Abū Bakr and 'Umar. They make the moon dominate the sun because it is easy to remember and 'Umar dominate Abū Bakr because 'Umar ruled for a long time and his time was famous. Whoever claims that it means 'Umar ibn al-Khaṭṭāb and 'Umar ibn 'Abd al-'Azīz has nothing to stand on because they spoke of 'the two 'Umars' before they saw 'Umar ibn 'Abd al-'Azīz. Ash-Shajarī said that.

The word *'parents'* does not include grandparents here, however distant, since it is in the dual whereas further descendants are included in the word *'children'*. The fact that the word *'parents'* is dual means cannot be universal and plural. This is not the case with *'children'*. This is proven by Allah's words: *'If you are childless and your heirs are your parents your mother receives a third.'* The grandmother does not receive a third by consensus and so she is definitely not part of this.

There is, however, disagreement about the grandfather. Among those who said that he is a father and excludes the brothers was Abū Bakr aṣ-Ṣiddīq. While he was alive, none of the Companions disagreed with him regarding that. They did disagree after his death. Among those who said that the grandfather was included under the word 'father' were Ibn 'Abbās, 'Abdullāh ibn az-Zubayr, 'Ā'ishah, Mu'ādh ibn Jabal, Ubayy ibn Ka'b, Abu-d-Dardā' and Abū Hurayrah. All of them made the grandfather like the father in the father's absence and made him exclude all brothers who do not inherit anything when he is present. That was the view of 'Aṭā', Ṭāwus, al-Ḥasan and Qatādah. Abū Ḥanīfah, Abū Thawr and Isḥāq also believed that. Their argument is found in the words of the Almighty: *'the religion of your father Ibrāhīm'* (22:78) and *'O sons of* Ādam' (7:26) as well as the words of the Prophet ﷺ, 'Shoot, sons of Ismā'īl. Your father was an archer.'

'Alī ibn Abī Ṭālib, Zayd and Ibn Mas'ūd believed that the grandfather inherits with the brothers and there is no decrease in the third with the full brothers or the father except with those with stipulated shares. That is the position of Mālik, al-Awzā'ī, Abū Yūsuf and ash-Shāfi'ī. 'Alī made the brothers and grandfather share in a sixth and the sixth did not reduce any of the obligatory shares of others. That is the position of Ibn Abī Laylā and a group. Scholars agree that the grandfather does not inherit when the father is alive, and the son does not exclude his father. They put the grandfather in the same position as the father in respect of exclusion and inheritance when the deceased does not have a father closer than him.

Most believe that the grandfather cancels brothers in inheritance, except for what is related from ash-Sha'bī from 'Alī that he is treated like the sons of the brothers in the division. The argument of the majority is that he is a male who does not make his sister one of the *'aṣabah* and so the grandfather does not have a share like the paternal uncle and son of the paternal uncle.

Ash-Sha'bī said that the first grandfather to inherit in Islam was 'Umar ibn al-Khaṭṭāb. A son of 'Āṣim ibn 'Umar died, leaving two brothers. 'Umar wanted to claim his property and consulted 'Alī and Zayd about that. They told him a parable about it and he said, 'Were it not that I see that you two agree, I would not think that he was my son nor I was his father.' Ad-Dāraquṭnī related from Zayd ibn Thābit that 'Umar ibn al-Khaṭṭāb asked permission to visit him one day and he gave it. His head was in the hand of a girl of his who was combing it. He removed his head and 'Umar told him, 'Let her comb you.' I said, 'Amīr al-Mu'minīn, if you were to send for me, I would come to you.' 'Umar said, 'I have need of you. I came to you to look into the position of a grandfather.' Zayd said, 'No, by Allah! What do you say about it?' 'Umar said, 'There is no revelation so that we could modify it one way or another. It is something based on opinion. If your opinion agrees with me I will follow it. Otherwise there is no going against you in it.'

Zayd refused to give an opinion and 'Umar left angry, exclaiming, 'I came to you thinking that you would relieve me!' Then he went to him again at the same time that he had come to him the first time and kept at him until he said, 'I will write something for you.' So he wrote it for him on a piece of hide and he made a parable for him. The parable was a tree which grows on one trunk and branches issue from it. Then the branches produce other branches. The trunk waters the branch. If the first branch is cut off, the water reverts to another branch. If the second branch is cut off, the water reverts to the first. He took it and 'Umar addressed the people and then read what was written on the piece of hide to them. Then he said, 'Zayd ibn Thābit has stated a position about the grandfather and I have carried it out.' He said that 'Umar was the first grandfather and wanted to take all the property of his son's son rather than his brothers. So 'Umar ibn al-Khaṭṭāb divided that.

The people of knowledge agree that the grandmother has a sixth if the deceased has no mother. They agree that a mother excludes both her mother and the father's mother. They agree that the father does not exclude the mother's mother. They disagree about the inheritance of the grandmother when her son is alive. Some say that the grandmother does not inherit when her son is alive. That is related from Zayd ibn Thābit, 'Uthmān and 'Alī. It was the position of Mālik, ath-Thawrī, al-Awzā'ī, Abū Thawr and the People of Opinion. One group said, 'The grandmother inherits with her son.' That is related from 'Umar, Ibn Mas'ūd, 'Uthmān, 'Alī and Abū Mūsā al-Ash'arī, and is the position of Shurayḥ, Jābir ibn Zayd, 'Ubaydullāh ibn al-Hasan, Shurayk, Aḥmad, Isḥāq and Ibn al-Mundhir. He said, 'As the grandfather is only excluded by the father, so the grandmother is only excluded by the mother.' At-Tirmidhī related from 'Abdullāh about the grandmother with the son that she was the first grandmother to whom the Messenger of Allah ﷺ gave a sixth with her son while her son was alive. Allah knows best.

Scholars disagree about the inheritance of grandmothers. Mālik said only two grandmothers inherit: the mother's mother and the father's mother and their mothers. That is what is related by Abū Thawr from ash-Shāfi'ī, and a group of Tābi'ūn said that. If there is only one, she has a sixth. If there are more and have the same closeness, the sixth is shared between them. All of this is agreed upon. If the one on the mother's side is closer, she alone has a sixth. If the one on the father's side is closer, it is shared between her and the one on the side of the mother, however far removed. Only one grandmother inherits on the mother's side and the grandmother of the mother of the father does not inherit. This is the position of Zayd ibn Thābit. It is the most confirmed of what is related on that. It is the position of Mālik and the people of Madīnah.

It is said that the grandmothers are also mothers. If there are several, the sixth is for the closer of them, as is the case when there are several fathers [including grandfathers]. The closest of them is the one most entitled to the inheritance. The same hold true for sons, brothers, sons of brothers and sons of uncles when there are several: the closest of them is the most entitled to inherit. Ibn al-Mundhir said, 'This is the sounder view, and is my position.'

Al-Awzā'ī makes three grandmothers inherit: one from the mother's side and two from the father's side. That is the position of Aḥmad ibn Ḥanbal. Ad-Dāraquṭnī related it from the Prophet ﷺ as *mursal*. The opposite of that is related from Zayd ibn Thābit: three grandmothers inherit: two from the side of the mother and one from the father. 'Alī has the same position as Zayd. They both give the sixth to the closest of them, on the side of the mother or father and no one shares with her in it unless they are of the same level of closeness. That is the position of ath-Thawrī, Abū Ḥanīfah and his people, and Abū Thawr.

'Abdullāh ibn Mas'ūd and Ibn 'Abbās, however, make the four grandmothers inherit. That is the position of al-Ḥasan al-Baṣrī, Muḥammad ibn Sīrīn and Jābir ibn Zayd. Ibn al-Mundhir said, 'Any grandmother connected to the deceased who has a father in her lineage between two mothers does not inherit.' The position of each of them by the people of knowledge.

Allah allotted a sixth to each of the parents of someone with children, and the male and female child are the same in that respect. If a man dies leaving a son and both parents, each of the parents has a sixth and the rest goes to the son. If he leaves a daughter and two parents, the daughter has half and the parents two-sixths and what remains goes to the *'aṣabah*, the paternal relations, since the Messenger of Allah ﷺ said, 'What is left of the shares is for the male relatives of a man.' The father has rights on two sides: paternal lineage and obligatory share.

If you are childless and your heirs are your parents your mother receives a third.

When the parents are the heirs, the mother takes a third, as is indicated by Allah's words, and the rest, which is two-thirds, goes to the father. It is as when you tell two men, 'This property is shared between you,' and then you tell one of them, 'You have a third of it.' Your words have stipulated that the other has two-thirds. The strength of His words indicate that that the two are alone among people entitled to shares. There is no disagreement about this. According to this, two-thirds is a share prescribed for the father and not inasmuch as he is *'aṣabah*. Ibn al-'Arabī mentioned that the point is to prefer the mother with a third in the absence of male children. The mother is confirmed over the share because of kinship.

This is contradictory. That exists when he is alive, so why is he denied the sixth? That which is clear is that a father is denied the sixth while he is alive out of kindness to the child and guarding his property since part of his property may be removed unjustly or that is an act of worship. That is the most appropriate thing to say. Allah is the One Who gives success.

The addition of the *wāw* in *'and your heirs'* makes it clear that this is a continuing firm command. The position of the parents when they are the only heirs is like the position of two children: the male receives twice the share of a female. The father has two shares: the normal share and that of *'aṣabah* when he excludes the brothers as the child does. This is a balanced rulings and its wisdom is clear. Allah knows best.

The people of Kufa recite *'li-immihi'* which is a dialect related by Sībawayh. Al-Kisā'ī said that it is a dialect of many of Hawāzin and Hudhayl. That is because when there is a *lām* with a *kasrah* and it is connected to a letter, they dislike having a *ḍammah* after a *kasrah* because there is no *fi'ula* in words. If someone has a *ḍammah*, he takes the root. It is also because the *lām* is separate and added to the noun. An-Naḥḥās said all of that.

If you have brothers or sisters your mother receives a sixth,

Brothers reduce the share of the mother from a third to a sixth. This is partial exclusion, whether the brothers are full or half brothers. They have no share. It is related from Ibn 'Abbās that the sixth which the brothers exclude the mother from is for the brothers. He also related the like of the position of the people that it is for the father. Qatādah said that the father takes it rather than them because he provides for them and attends to their marriage and maintenance.

The people of knowledge agree that two or more siblings, male or female, full or half, reduce a mother from a third to a sixth except what is related from Ibn 'Abbās that two brothers have the same ruling as one and less than three do not exclude the mother.

Some people believe that sisters do not reduce a mother from a third to a sixth because the Book of Allah speaks about brothers, and the strength of the inheritance of the female is not like the strength of the inheritance of the male. Aṭ-Ṭabarī says that what their position would mean is that the sisters are not included with the brothers, as sons do not include daughters. That would necessitate that a mother with one brother and a sister is not reduced from a third to a sixth, which is counter to the consensus of the Muslims. If they are meant by the *āyah* with the brothers, they are also meant when they are on their own.

All of them deduce that the minimum plural is two because it is adding one to another like it. Therefore, it must be a plural. Furthermore, the Prophet ﷺ said, 'Two or more is a group.' It is related that Sībawayh said, 'I asked al-Khalīl about what is the best way to take the words in the dual and he said, "Two is a plural."' The words of the poet are sound:

Two distant barren deserts
like the backs [plural] of two shields.

Al-Akhfash said:

When the two women brought us the news
They [plural] said, 'The business is famous among us.'

Another said:

They give the greeting to wealthy people
and are miserly with greeting the poor.

Is not death the same between them [dual]
when they die [plural] and go to the graves?

There was a disagreement about that between 'Uthmān and Ibn 'Abbās. 'Uthmān said to him, 'Your people (meaning Quraysh) exclude her, and they are the people of eloquence and fine rhetoric.'

Some say that the minimum is three: Ibn Mas'ūd, ash-Shāfi'ī, Abū Ḥanīfah and others. Allah knows best.

After any bequest you make or any debts.

Ibn Kathīr, Abū 'Amr, Ibn 'Āmir and 'Āṣim recite *yuṣā* and the rest have it as *yuṣī*. The readings from 'Āṣim vary. Abū 'Ubayd and Abū Ḥātim prefer the *kasrah* because the deceased was mentioned before this. Al-Akhfash said: 'The confirmation of that is His words "*yūṣīna*" and "*tūṣūna*".'

It may be asked, 'What is the wisdom in mentioning bequests before debts when debts take priority by consensus?' At-Tirmidhī related from al-Ḥārith that someone said to 'Alī, 'The Prophet ﷺ paid debts before bequests and confirmed bequests after debts while this mentions bequests before debts.' He said, 'The action regarding this according to most of the people of knowledge is that one begins with debts before bequests.' Ad-Dāraquṭnī reported from 'Āṣim ibn Ḍamrah from 'Alī that the Messenger of Allah ﷺ said, 'Debts come before bequests, and an heir receives no bequest.' Abū Isḥāq al-Hamdānī related it from both of them.

There are five aspects to the answer to this. The first is that what is intended is to put these two categories before the shares of inheritance and no particular order is proposed by it. That is why bequests are put first. The second is that since a bequest is less necessary than a debt, it is put first out of concern for it, as the Almighty said about His Book: *'which does not pass over any action, small or great.'*

(18:49) The third is that bequests are put first because they often exist and so it is like it is necessary for every dead person as the Sharī'ah has a text on it, and debts are mentioned afterwards because they are rarer and may or may not exist. So Allah begins first with what is necessary. This is strengthened by 'or'. If there had been an order involved, He would have used the conjunction 'and'. The fourth is that bequests are put first because they are the portion of the wretched and weak, and debts last because it is the portion of the creditor who will seek it with strength and force. The fifth is that it is because a bequest is from himself that it is put first, while a debt is confirmed, whether mentioned or not.

Since this is confirmed, ash-Shāfi'ī added as a corollary to that the putting of debts of *zakāt* and *ḥajj* before the inheritance. He said, 'When a man has been lax about his *zakāt*, that must be taken from his capital.' This is evident because it is one of the religious rights and must be paid after death, like the rights of human beings, especially since *zakāt* is given to human beings. Abū Ḥanīfah and Mālik said, 'If someone puts it in the will, it is paid from the third. If they are silent about it, nothing is paid.' They said, 'Because that might entail leaving heirs poor since the entire estate could be used up, leaving the heirs with nothing.'

With regard to your fathers and your sons, you do not know which of them is going to benefit you more.

This is in the nominative by the inceptive whose predicate is elided. *'Your'* implies: 'They are the ones who are given shares.' It is said that the benefit is in this world through supplication and *ṣadaqah*, as is the tradition, 'A man is elevated by the supplication of his child after him.' We find in a sound hadith: 'When a man dies, his actions are cut off except for three.' Among them he mentioned a righteous child who makes supplication for him. It is said that it is in the Next World and the son may be better and can intercede for his father, as Ibn 'Abbās and al-Ḥasan stated. Some commentators say that if the son has a higher degree than his father in the Hereafter, he asks Allah to raise him to him, and the same applies to the father. This will be explained in *aṭ-Ṭūr*. It is said that it is in both this world and the Next. Ibn Zayd said that the expression implies that.

These are the obligatory shares from Allah.

'Obligatory shares' is the object of 'instructs you' or it is in the accusative because it is a verbal noun. This informs people that they are spared the effort of making bequests to relatives when they are joined in lineage, meaning that fathers and sons benefit one another in this world by means of mutual help and solace and in

the Next World by means of intercession. As that is confirmed about fathers and sons, it is confirmed about all relatives.

If the division had been entrusted to individual discretion, that would oblige investigating the wealth of each and then there would no precision since the matter varies. Therefore, the Lord makes it clear that what is best for the person is that the amounts of inheritance are not left to their discretion. So Allah clarified legal amounts.

'Allah is All-Knowing' of the division of the shares and *'All-Wise'* in judging their division and making it clear to people. Az-Zajjāj said, 'He knows things before He created them and is wise in what He decrees for them and decides about them.' Some said that Allah was and is. The report in the past regarding Him is the same as that in the future tense. The school of Sībuwayh is that they saw wisdom and knowledge and so they were told that Allah was like that and remains like that.

You receive half of what your wives leave if they are childless.

This is addressed to men. Here the word 'childless' refers to not having children themselves or, therefore, grandchildren, however far removed, male or female, one or more, by consensus. Scholars agree that the husband receives a half when there are no children or grandchildren. If there are children, then he receives a quarter. When there are no children, the wife inherits a quarter from her husband, and an eighth if there are children. They agree that the ruling of one, two, three or four wives is out of the quarter if there are no children and the eighth if there are. They share in that because Allah did not distinguish between one or all as He did between one daughter and one sister and the ruling of all of them.

If a man or woman has no direct heirs

The word *kalālah* (tr. 'has no direct heirs') is a verbal noun derived from *takallala* in reference to lineage, meaning encompassed. Crown (*iklīl*) comes from it as it encompasses the head. *Iklīl* is also one of the stations of the moon which is encompassed by the moon. The technical term *kalālah* is used when a man dies and has no children or parents, as is said by Abū Bakr, 'Umar, 'Alī and most of the people of knowledge.

Yaḥyā ibn Ādam mentioned from Sharīk, and Zuhayr and Abu-l-Aḥwaṣ from Abū Isḥāq that Sulaymān ibn 'Ubayd said, 'I have not seen anyone who did not agree that the person who dies without father or child is *kalālah*.' That is what was stated by the author of *Kitāb al-'Ayn*, Abū Manṣūr al-Lughawī, Ibn 'Arafah, al-Qutabī, Abū 'Ubayd and Ibn al-Anbārī. The father and child are the two ends of lineage and 'surround' him. A meadow is 'crowned' (*mukallalah*) when it is surrounded in blossoms. They said:

His dwelling is a crowned meadow
Covered in Ayhuqān and sweet trefoil.

He means two plants. Imru 'l-Qays said:

Companion! you see lightning and I will show you its flash
like the clap of hands in the surrounding (*mukallalah*) clouds.

Relatives are called '*kalālah*' because they 'surround' him on all sides, they not being from him nor him from them. Their surrounding him is that they are connected to him, as a desert Arab would say, 'My wealth is great and the *kalālah* with loose relationship will inherit from me. Al-Farazdaq said:

You did not inherit the staff of majesty through *kalālah*,
but from the two sons of Manāf, 'Abd Shams and Hāshim.

Another said:

A man's father gives him protection,
but the client of *kalālah* is not roused to anger.

It is also said that *kalālah* (not having direct heirs) is derived from *kalāl*, which is fatigue. So it is as inheritance goes to the heir from a distance and with toil. Al-A'shā uses it to mean exhaustion

Abū Ḥātim and al-Athram reported that Abū 'Abīdah said, '*Kalālah* refers to the one who dies with no father, son or brother. The Arabs called him *kalālah.'* Abū 'Umar says that mentioning the brother is a mistake on his part. No one else mentions him as part of *kalālah.* It is also reported from 'Umar ibn al-Khaṭṭāb that it only applies to someone with no children. That was also related from Abū Bakr, and then they both retracted it. Ibn Zayd said, '*Kalālah* describes both the living and the dead.' 'Aṭā' said that *kalālah* is property. Ibn al-'Arabī said that that is an unusual view with no sense whatsoever. I say that it has a meaning which was already explained by the syntax. It is reported from Ibn al-A'rabī that *kalālah* are the distant sons of the paternal uncle. As-Suddī said that it is the deceased. He also mentioned the view of the majority.

These statements make its aspects clear through the syntax. Some Kufans recite '*yūrrithu kalālatan*'. Al-Ḥasan and Ayyūb recite '*yūrithu'* while there is disagreement from the two of them. According to these two readings, the *kalālah* is only the heirs or the property. That is what is related by the people who deal with meanings.

The first is from *warratha* and the second from *awratha* and *kalālah* is the object and '*kāna*' means 'occurred'.

If someone recites '*yūrithu*', he makes *kalālah* mean property. It implies: 'He inherits the legacy of the *kalālah*, and so it is an adjective of an elided verbal noun. *Kalālah* can also be a name for the heirs and the predicate of *kāna*. So it would imply: 'with *kalālah*'. It can also be complete with the meaning of 'occurred' and '*yūrithu*' is an adjective of '*man*' and '*man*' is in the nominative by '*kāna*', and *kalālah* is in the accusative for explanation or for the *ḥāl* on the basis that the *kalālah* is the deceased. It implies: a man allows the relatives surrounding the deceased to inherit.

Allah mentions *kalālah* in His Book in two places: here and at the end of the *sūrah*, and in neither place does He mention any heirs except brothers. As for this *āyah*, scholars agree that the brothers in it are the mother's brothers since the Almighty says: *'If there are more than that they share in a third.'* Sa'd ibn Abī Waqqāṣ recited, 'and he has a brother or sister by his mother.' There is no disagreement among the people of knowledge that the brothers of the father or mother are not the heirs. There is consensus that the brothers mentioned at the end of the *sūrah* are the siblings of the deceased by both the father and mother or by just the father going by Allah's words: *'If there are brothers and sisters, the males receive the share of two females.'* (2:176) There is no disagreement that the inheritance of maternal siblings is not like that. So the two *āyah*s together indicate that all siblings are *kalālah*. Ash-Sha'bī said, '*Kalālah* designates heirs other than children and parents: siblings and others of the *'aṣabah*.' That is like what 'Alī, Ibn Mas'ūd, Zayd and Ibn 'Abbās said. It is the first view with which we began.

Aṭ-Ṭabarī said, 'What is correct is that *kalālah* are those other than parents and children who inherit from the deceased based on the sound report of Jābir who said, "I said, 'Messenger of Allah, the *kalālah* inherit from me. Shall I will away all of my property?' 'No,' he answered."'

Linguists say that a male is described as *kalālah* and a female also as *kalālah* and there is no plural or dual because it is a verbal noun like *wakālah*, *dalālah*, *samāḥah* and *shajā'ah*. In '*lahu akh*' the singular pronoun is repeated and not '*lahumā*' in the dual. It was already mentioned that the custom in Arabic about men and women is that when the two names have been mentioned and then they are reported about and both have the same ruling, sometimes it is attributed to one of them and sometimes to both of them. You say, 'Whoever has a slave and slavegirl should be good to him, to her, to both and to them,' using any of the four pronouns. Allah says: '*Seek help in steadfastness and the prayer. It* (innahā) *is very hard.*' (2:45) Allah also says: *'Whether rich or poor, Allah is well able to look after them* (bihimā)' (4:135) in the dual. Al-Farrā; and others said that it would be permitted to say *'bihim'* [in the plural].

A woman is called *'imra'ah'* which is the root. The root of *akh* (brother) is *akhw* as is indicated in the dual, *akhwān*. It is elided from it and changed. Al-Farrā' said that the beginning of *ukht* (sister) has a *ḍammah* because of the elision of the *wāw* and there is a *kasrah* at the beginning of *bint* (daughter) because of the elision of the *yā'*. This elision and weakness are not based on any reference.

If there are more than that they share in a third.

This sharing demands equality between a male and female, even if they are many. When they take via the mother, there is no preference for male over female. This is consensus of the scholars. There is no place in the shares in which men and women are equal except in the inheritance of the siblings of the mother.

If a woman dies and leaves a husband, mother and brother by her mother, the husband has a half, the mother a third, and the brother a sixth. If she leaves two brothers and sisters, then the husband has a half, the mother a sixth, and brothers and sisters a third and that completes the sharing out. This is the position of most of the Companions because they reduce the mother by the brother and sister from a third to a sixth. Ibn 'Abbās does not think that there is adjustment, even if the mother is given a third. Adjustment (*'awl*) is mentioned elsewhere rather than here. If she leaves a husband and brothers by the mother and a brother by the father and mother, the husband gets a half and the brothers by the mother a third, and the rest goes to the full brothers.

This is in the case of those who do not have a named share. The rest goes to the paternal relatives (*'aṣabah*). If she leaves six brothers, this is the Ḥimāriyyah case and it is also called the shared case (*mushtarikah*). Some people said that the maternal brothers have a third, the husband half, and the mother a sixth, and the full siblings and paternal siblings are dropped. That is related from 'Alī, Ibn Mas'ūd, Abū Mūsā, ash-Sha'bī, Shurayk, and Yaḥyā ibn Ādam. That is the position of Aḥmad ibn Ḥanbal, and Ibn al-Mundhir preferred it, because the husband, mother and maternal brothers have named shares and nothing remains for the *'aṣabah*. Some people said that the mother is one and that leaves their father like a donkey! They made them share the third. That is why this case is called the *mushtarikah* or Ḥimāriyyah. This is related from 'Umar, 'Uthmān, Ibn Mas'ūd, Zayd ibn Thābit, Masrūq and Shurayḥ. It was stated by Mālik, ash-Shāfi'ī and Isḥāq. This case is not right when the deceased is a man.

This is the sum of the knowledge of obligatory shares which the *āyah* contains. Allah is the One Who gives success to guidance.

In the Jāhiliyyah, inheritance was based on maleness and strength. Men rather women inherited, and then Allah nullified this by His words: *'men have a portion'* and *'women have a portion'* (4:32) as was already mentioned. Also in the Jāhiliyyah and at the beginning of Islam, inheritance was by alliance. Allah says: *'If you have a bond with people'* (4:33). Then after alliance, there was alliance by *hijrah.* Allah says: *'As those who believe but have not made hijrah, you are not in any way responsible for their protection until they make hijrah.'* (8:72)

Then there was the position about relatives and their inheritance. In *Sūrat an-Nūr* we will discuss the inheritance of the child of a *li'ān*, a bastard and a *mukātib.* Most scholars say that if someone who has been captured by the enemy is known to be alive, his inheritance is confirmed because he is part of the sum of Muslims subject to the rulings of Islam, although it is related that Sa'īd ibn al-Musayyab said that someone held by the enemy does not inherit. The inheritance of an apostate was mentioned in *Sūrat al-Baqarah.*

making sure that no one's rights are prejudiced.

This is in respect of the bequests, in other words without that harming the heirs. For instance, it is not appropriate for someone to put a debt in the will, that he does not owe, in order to harm the heirs. Causing harm refers to bequests and debts. In bequests, it is to make bequests of more than a third or to make a bequest to an heir. If it is more than a third, it is rejected unless the heirs allow it because it is denying them their rights, not a right of Allah. A bequest to an heir reverts to the general inheritance. Scholars agree that a bequest to an heir is not permitted. This was already mentioned in *al-Baqarah.* As for claiming a debt, it is affirmation in a situation in which it is not permitted, as when someone affirms in his final illness that he owes it to his heirs or a close friend. We do not think that that is permitted.

It is related that al-Ḥasan recited *'ghayra muḍārri waṣīyatin'* based on *iḍāfah.* An-Naḥḥās said, 'Some linguistic scholars claim that this is ungrammatical because the noun of the active participle is not put into *iḍāfah* with a verbal noun. The reading is good based on an elision. It means: not prejudicing the one with a will,' i.e. not harming his heirs in their inheritance by it.

Scholars agree that affirming a debt to other than a relative in a final illness is allowed when someone did not have the debt while healthy. If there is clear evidence of a debt being incurred while he was healthy and he affirms a debt owed to a non-relative, one group say that one begins with debts incurred while he was healthy. This is the view of an-Nakha'ī and the Kufans. They said, 'When the person settles them, the people who have been confirmed while he was ill take shares. Another group says that they are both the same when the creditor is not an heir. This is the position of ash-Shāfi'ī, Abū Thawr, and Abū 'Ubayd. Abū 'Ubayd mentioned that it is the position of the people of Madīnah. He related that from al-Ḥasan.

The different aspects of harm in respect of bequests were already discussed in *al-Baqarah*. It is reported by Abū Dāwud from Sahr ibn Ḥawshab (who is attacked) from Abū Hurayrah that the Messenger of Allah ﷺ said, 'A man or woman may obey Allah for sixty years and then they are dying and they cause harm in their will and so the Fire becomes mandatory from them.' Then Abū Hurayrah would recite this *āyah*.

Ibn 'Abbās said that causing harm by one's will is one of the great wrong actions, and he related that from the Prophet ﷺ. The well-known position of the school of Mālik and Ibn al-Qāsim is that the harm of someone who makes a will cannot exceed the third because that is his right to dispose of as he wishes. There is also a position in the school which is that harm is rejected. Success is by Allah.

Allah is All-Knowing, All-Forbearing.

He knows the people of inheritance and is forbearing to the people of ignorance among you. Some people recite *Ḥakīm* (wise) instead of *Ḥalīm* (All-Forbearing), meaning that He is wise regarding the division of the legacy and wills.

These are Allah's limits.

'Those' means 'these', i.e. these are the rulings of Allah which He has made clear to you so that you know them and act by them.

As for those who obey Allah and His Messenger

They obey Him in respect of the division of inheritance and affirm it as Allah has commanded them. The sentence: *'We will admit them into Gardens with rivers flowing under them'* is in the position of the accusative as an adjective of 'Gardens'.

As for those who disobey Allah and His Messenger and overstep His limits,

They disobey Him in respect of the division of inheritance and do not distribute it and do not act by it. They *'overstep His limits'* by opposing His command. If disobedience here means disbelief, then it is in the Fire forever. If it means a major wrong action and exceeding Allah's commands, then it is a metaphor for a certain period, and that is a usage of *khalada* as one might say, 'May Allah make his kingdom endure forever!' Zuhayr said:

> Nothing is forever except the firm mountains.

This has been discussed elsewhere.

Nāfi' reads this as '*We will admit*' (*nudkhilhu*) with the Divine 'We' in the two places while the rest read it as '*He will admit*' (*yudkhilhu*) because Allah was already mentioned. It means: Allah will admit him.

وَٱلَّٰتِي يَأۡتِينَ ٱلۡفَٰحِشَةَ مِن نِّسَآئِكُمۡ فَٱسۡتَشۡهِدُواْ عَلَيۡهِنَّ أَرۡبَعَةٗ
مِّنكُمۡۖ فَإِن شَهِدُواْ فَأَمۡسِكُوهُنَّ فِي ٱلۡبُيُوتِ حَتَّىٰ يَتَوَفَّىٰهُنَّ
ٱلۡمَوۡتُ أَوۡ يَجۡعَلَ ٱللَّهُ لَهُنَّ سَبِيلٗا ١٥

15 If any of your women commit fornication, four of you must be witnesses against them. If they bear witness, detain them in their homes until death releases them or Allah ordains another procedure for their case.

In this *sūrah*, Allah mentions being good to women and giving them their dowries and He also mentions their inheritance together with that of the men. Then He mentions being harsh to them in the case of any fornication they may commit of so that it might not be imagined that a woman be allowed to be lax where chasteness is concerned.

Allātī is the plural of *allatī* and it is an undefined feminine noun which is definite. It is not permitted to remove the *alif-lām* from it to make it indefinite and it is only complete when connected. As we already mentioned, it has three dialectical forms and a plural: *allāti* without the *yā'* but with the *kasrah*, *allā'ī* with a *hamzah* and keeping the *yā'*, and *allā* with the *hamzah* elided. When you make the plural plural, you use *allawātī* for *allāti*, *allawā'ī* for *allā'ī*. It is related from them as *allawāti* without the *yā'* but with the *kasrah*. Ibn ash-Shajarī said that. [POEMS WITH FURTHER GRAMMATICAL EXAMPLES] *Fāḥishah* here means fornication. *Faḥishah* is an ugly action, and it is a verbal noun like *'āqibah* and *'āfīyah*. Ibn Mas'ūd recited '*bi-l-fāḥishati*'.

'Your women' means Muslim women, not those related by lineage. It explains the state of the believing women. The same usage is seen in 2:282. That is because an

unbelieving woman might be connected to women of the Muslims by lineage but would not not be subject to this ruling.

four of you must be witnesses against them.

This means four Muslims. Allah requires four witnesses to fornication in order to make it hard for the claimant and to veil people. Requiring four reputable witnesses to fornication is a firm ruling in both the Gospel and the Qur'an. Allah says: *'But those who make accusations against chaste women and then do not produce four witnesses: flog them with eighty lashes.'* (24:4) Here He mentions four.

Abū Dāwūd reports from Jābir ibn 'Abdullāh: 'The Jews brought a man and woman of theirs who had committed fornication. The Prophet ﷺ said, "Fetch me the most knowledgeable two men among you." They brought him the sons of Ṣūriyā and he asked, "What do you find in the Torah about the business of these two?" They said, "We find in the Torah that if four testify that they saw his penis in her vagina like a stick in a kohl bottle, then they are stoned." He asked, "What keeps you from stoning them?" They replied, "Our authority has gone and we dislike killing." So the Messenger of Allah ﷺ summoned the witnesses and they came and testified that they saw his penis in her vagina like a stick in a kohl bottle, and the Messenger of Allah ﷺ commanded that they be stoned.'

Some people say, 'The witnesses in fornication are four so that there are two witnesses against each of the two parties, as is the case in all rights, since a right is taken from each of them.' This is weak. The oath deals with property and suspicion in the *qasamah*, and it does not apply here. The witnesses must be male since He says, '*minkum*', and there is no disagreement in the Community about that, and they must be of good character because Allah stipulates good character in sales and retraction, and this is a greater matter so it is more fitting here. This is part of applying the general to the restricted in evidence as mentioned in the fundamental principles of *fiqh*. They cannot be *dhimmīs*, although judgment can be made against *dhimmīs*. That will be discussed in *al-Mā'idah*. Abū Ḥanīfah added that *'four of you'* is about the husband when he is one of the witnesses in slander and does not carry out the *li'ān*. This will be explained in *an-Nūr*.

If they bear witness, detain them in their homes

This was the first of the punishments for fornication. It was at the beginning of Islam. 'Ubādah ibn aṣ-Ṣāmit, al-Ḥasan and Mujāhid said that. That lasted until it was abrogated by the punishment after it and then that was abrogated by the *āyah* in *an-Nūr* and stoning for someone previously married. One group said that the corporal punishment was first and then was abrogated by detaining but the order in recitation is different. Ibn Fūrak mentioned that. Detaining used to be in houses at the beginning of Islam before there were a lot of criminals. When they were a lot and their strength was feared, a prison was constructed for them. Ibn al-'Arabī said that.

Scholars disagree about whether prison is a *ḥadd* punishment or threatening with a *ḥadd*. One position is that it is threatening a *ḥadd* and the second that that is an actual *hadd*. Ibn 'Abbās and al-Ḥasan said that. Ibn Zayd said that they were forbidden to marry until they died as a punishment for them when they had unlawful sexual intercourse. This indicates that it was a *ḥadd* punishment and indeed more severe. However, that ruling ended with the punishment prescribed in the other *āyah*, according to the difference in the two interpretations about which was first. Both had a term in the words of the Prophet ﷺ in the hadith of 'Ubādah ibn aṣ-Ṣāmit: 'Take from me. Take from me. Allah has made a way for them: a hundred lashes and exile for a year for a virgin and a hundred lashes and stoning for someone previously married.' This is like Allah's words: *'Fulfil the fast until the night appears.'* (2:187) When night comes, the ruling of fasting is removed; it is not abrogated. This is what is stated by accurate later scholars from among those who study fundamentals. Abrogation occurs when there are two contradictory positions which cannot be combined. It is possible to combine imprisonment and ignominy, and flogging and stoning.

Some scholars said that abuse and ignominy remain with flogging because they are not contradictory and can both be combined against the same person. There is consensus that imprisonment is abrogated. It is permissible to apply abrogation to the like of it. Allah knows best.

وَٱلَّذَانِ يَأْتِيَـٰنِهَا مِنكُمْ فَـَٔاذُوهُمَا ۖ فَإِن تَابَا وَأَصْلَحَا فَأَعْرِضُوا۟
عَنْهُمَآ ۗ إِنَّ ٱللَّهَ كَانَ تَوَّابًا رَّحِيمًا ﴿١٦﴾

16 If two men commit a like abomination, punish them. If they repent and reform, leave them alone. Allah is Ever-Returning, Most Merciful.

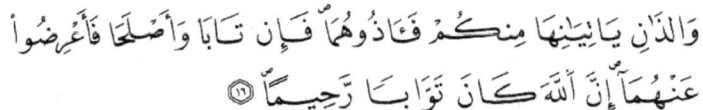

'Two' (*alladhāni*): it is the dual of *alladhī*. By analogy, one would say, *'alladhayāni'* like *raḥayāni*, *muṣṭafayāni* and *shajayāni*. Sībawayh said that the *yā'* is elided in order to differentiate between declinable nouns with nunnation and demonstrative pronouns. Abū 'Alī said that the *yā'* is elided for lightening when one is safe from confusion in *alladhānī* because the *nūn* is not elided, although the *nūn* of the dual in declinable nouns is elide when it is in *iḍāfah* in *raḥayā*, and *muṣṭafayā*. If the *yā'* had been elided, it would have resembled the singular with two.

Ibn Kathīr recited *'alladhānni'* with a doubled *nūn* which is the dialect of Quraysh. The reason is that the doubling takes the place of the *alif* of *dhā* as will be explained in *al-Qaṣaṣ*. (28:32) There is another dialect which has *'alladhā'* with the *nūn* elided. This is the view of the Kufans. The Basrans said that the *nūn* is elided because of the length of the word when connected. Similar is the reading of *'hadhānni'* and *'fa-dhānnaka burhānāni'*. The rest have *'alladhāni'*. Abū 'Amr has the aberrant *'fa-dhānnika'*.

'Two' is in the nominative for the inceptive. Sībawayh says that it means: 'in what is recited to you: if two men among you commit it (meaning fornication).' The *fā'* is added to 'punish them' because the words have the meaning of a command because when *'alladhī'* is connected to a verb, it is possible for it to have the meaning of a precondition when nothing specific is applied to it. When a precondition is possible and nothing is defined, then it acts as a precondition and the *fā'* is added, and what is implied before it does not act on it, as the precondition is not affected by [what is implied or clearly stated before it. Then it is unlikely that what is implied before it acts on 'those', then the implication is not good.] The accusative is permitted when a verb is implied, and that is preferred when the words convey the meaning of a command or prohibition, like: 'Those who are with you: honour them.'

punish them.

Qatādah and as-Suddī said that it means to rebuke and reproach. A group said that it is castigation and being harsh without reproach. Ibn 'Abbās said, 'It is attacking with the tongue and hitting with sandals.' An-Naḥḥās said that some people claim it is abrogated. Ibn Abī Najīḥ related that Mujāhid said that this and the previous *āyah* existed at the beginning and then were abrogated by the *āyah* in *an-Nūr*. An-Naḥḥās said that it more fitting that it is not abrogated and it is obliged to punish them with rebuke, saying, 'You committed this, sinned and opposed Allah's command.'

Scholars disagree about the interpretation of the prepositions 'they' (fem.) in the previous *āyah* and 'two' here. Mujāhid and others said that the first *āyah* is about women in general, *muḥṣanāt* or not. The second is about men in particular, and the dual makes the category of men clear, *muḥṣan* or not. The punishment of women is imprisonment and that of men is castigation. This is what the words demand and the words deal in full with the types of fornication. That is reinforced by what His words in the first, *'your women'* and *'you'* in the second. An-Naḥḥās preferred that and related it from Ibn 'Abbās.

As-Suddī, Qatādah and others said, 'The first is about *muḥṣanāt* women, and so includes men who are *muḥṣan*, and the second is about men and women who are virgins.' Ibn 'Aṭiyyah said, 'According to this, the meaning is complete, although the expression of the *āyah* is unsettled about it.' Aṭ-Ṭabarī preferred that but an-Naḥḥās rejected it, saying that it is unlikely that the feminine preposition would dominate the masculine.

It is said that a fornicatress is imprisoned rather than the man, but they are both castigated. Qatādah said, 'A woman is imprisoned and both are castigated. This is because a man needs to earn and work.' Scholars disagree about the position according to the hadith of 'Ubādah which clarifies the rulings of fornication as we made clear. 'Alī ibn Abī Ṭālib's position, in which there is no dispute, was in agreement with it. He flogged Shurāḥah al-Hamdāniyyah with a hundred lashes and stoned her afterwards. He said, 'I flogged her by the Book of Allah and stoned her by the *sunnah* of the Messenger of Allah ﷺ.' Al-Ḥasan al-Baṣrī, al-Ḥasan ibn Ṣāliḥ ibn Ḥayy and Isḥāq said that.

A group of scholars said, 'Someone previously married is stoned without being flogged.' This is related from 'Umar and is the position of az-Zuhrī, an-Nakha'ī, Mālik, ath-Thawrī, al-Awzā'ī, ash-Shāfi'ī, the People of Opinion, Aḥmad and Abū Thawr, holding to the fact that the Prophet ﷺ stoned Mā'iz and the Ghāmidiyyah woman without flogging them, and to what the Prophet ﷺ said to Unays, 'Go to this woman and if she confesses, stone her.' He did not mention flogging. If it had been prescribed, he would not have been silent about it. The response to that was that he was silent about it because it is confirmed by the Book of Allah. It is not impossible for him to have been silent about it since it was well known and there is a text on it in the Qur'an since Allah says: *'A woman and a man who commit fornication: flog both of them with a hundred lashes.'* (24:2) This includes all fornicators. Allah knows best. This explains what 'Alī did by adopting it from the caliphs and no one objected to it. The answer to this is that he acted by the abrogated and left the abrogating. This is clear.

They disagree about the exile of unmarried people in addition to flogging. The position of the majority is that they are exiled as well. The *Rāshidūn* caliphs, Abū Bakr, 'Umar, 'Uthmān and 'Alī, said that. It is the position of 'Aṭā' Ṭāwus, Sufyān, Mālik, Ibn Abī Laylā, ash-Shāfi'ī, Aḥmad, Isḥāq and Abū Thawr. Ḥammād ibn Abī Sulaymān, Abū Ḥanīfah and Muḥammad ibn al-Ḥasan ash-Shaybānī said that it is abandoned. The evidence of the majority is the hadith of 'Ubādah and that of Abū Hurayrah and Zayd ibn Khālid in which the Prophet ﷺ said, 'By the One who has my soul in His hand, I will decide between you two by the Book of Allah. Your sheep and slave-girl should be returned to you.' He flogged his son with a hundred and exiled him for a year. The imams transmitted it.

Those who do not think that there should be exile use the hadith of Abū Hurayrah about the slave-girl in which flogging rather than exile is mentioned. 'Abd ar-Razzāq mentioned from Ma'mar from az-Zuhrī that Sa'īd ibn al-Musayyab said, "Umar exiled Rabī'ah ibn Abī Umayyah ibn Khalaf to Khaybar for drinking wine where he joined Heraclius and became a Christian. 'Umar said, "I will not exile a Muslim after this."' They said, 'If exile had been a *hadd* punishment of Allah, 'Umar would never have abandoned it. The text which is in the Book is flogging and increase beyond the text is abrogated.'

In reply to this, the hadith of Abū Hurayrah is about slave-girls, not free people. There is a sound report that 'Abdullāh ibn 'Umar beat his slave-girl for fornication and exiled her. As for the hadith of 'Umar, he meant for wine, and Allah knows best, since Nāfi' related from Ibn 'Umar that the Prophet ﷺ flogged and exiled as did Abū Bakr and 'Umar. At-Tirmidhī in the *Jāmi'* and an-Nasā'ī in the *Sunan* transmitted it from Abū Kurayb Muḥammad ibn al-'Alā' al-Hamdānī from 'Abdullāh ibn Idrīs from 'Ubaydullāh ibn 'Umar from Nāfi'. Ad-Dāraquṭnī said that 'Abdullāh ibn Idrīs alone had it and the only reliable person who has it from him is Abū Kurayb. Exile is reported in a sound transmission from the Prophet ﷺ, so no one can debate its validity. Whoever differs from the Sunnah argues with it. Success is by Allah.

What they said about increase over the text being abrogated is not sound. There can be an additional ruling to the basic one. There are many instances of this about things which are not in the Qur'an. This was discussed in *al-Baqarah.*

Those who disagree about exile do not do so about exiling free males. They disagree about exiling slaves or slave-girls. Ibn 'Umar was one of those who thought that they should be exiled: he flogged a slave-girl for fornication and exiled her to Fadak. It is the position of ash-Shāfi'ī, Abū Thawr, ath-Thawrī, aṭ-Ṭabarī and Dāwud. They disagree about ash-Shāfi'ī's position about exiling slaves. Sometimes he said that exiling slaves is subject to doing an *istikhārah,* sometimes he said that it is for half a year, and sometimes he said that it is a year to a different town, as aṭ-Ṭabarī said.

They have two positions about exiling slave-girls. Mālik said that men should be exiled but not women or slaves. The one who is exiled is detained in the place to which they are exiled, as from Egypt to the Hijaz, Shaghb, Aswan and the like, and from Madīnah to Khaybar and Fadak. That is what 'Umar ibn 'Abd al-'Azīz did, and 'Ali exiled people from Kufa to Basra. Ash-Shāfi'ī said that the minimum is the journey of a day and a night.

Ibn al-'Arabī said, 'The basis of exile is that the tribe of Ismā'īl agreed that someone who committed something wrong in the Ḥaram should be exiled from it and so that became a *sunnah* in their *dīn*. That is why the *sunnah* of the people was that when someone committed something wrong, they were exiled. That continued in the Jāhiliyyah until Islam came and then it was confirmed only in the case of fornication.'

Those who did not think that exile applied to slaves used the hadith of Abū Hurayrah as evidence. That is also because exile then becomes a punishment for the owner who is denied the use of the slave during the period of exile. That is not in keeping with the usage of the Sharī'ah. None but the perpetrator should be punished. Allah knows best. Furthermore, *Jumu'ah*, *ḥajj* and jihad which are Allah's right are cancelled for him because of his master. The same is true of exile. Allah knows best.

When a woman is exiled, that could be a cause for her falling into the very thing she was expelled for, which is fornication. Exile might act as a cause of her being exposed and possibly ruin her. That was the reason for not letting her leave her house and for her praying in it being better. This restricts the generality of the hadith about exile to the aspect of welfare that is witnessed in it. It is a topic of disagreement among those who deal with *uṣūl* and thinkers. One group took an aberrant view and said that flogging and stoning are combined in the case of an old man while a young man is flogged. This is based on holding to the word 'old man' in the hadith of Zayd ibn Thābit who heard the Messenger of Allah ﷺ say, 'When an old man and old woman fornicate, stone them completely.' An-Nasā'ī transmitted it. This is unsound because in another hadith he called him 'previously married (*thayyib*).'

If they repent and reform, leave them alone.

'If they repent' of fornication and *'reform'* with respect to what they do afterwards, *'leave them alone,'* meaning do not castigate them. That was before the revelation of the *ḥadd* punishments. When the *ḥudūd* were revealed, this *āyah* was abrogated. What is meant by '*leave them alone*' is not emigration but being shunned and left alone. That is abasement for them because of their disobedience and because of the ignorance in the other *āyah*. Allah is Ever-Turning means that He makes His slaves turn back from acts of disobedience.

إِنَّمَا ٱلتَّوْبَةُ عَلَى ٱللَّهِ لِلَّذِينَ يَعْمَلُونَ ٱلسُّوٓءَ بِجَهَٰلَةٍ ثُمَّ يَتُوبُونَ مِن
قَرِيبٍ فَأُوْلَٰٓئِكَ يَتُوبُ ٱللَّهُ عَلَيْهِمْ وَكَانَ ٱللَّهُ عَلِيمًا حَكِيمًا ﴿١٧﴾
وَلَيْسَتِ ٱلتَّوْبَةُ لِلَّذِينَ يَعْمَلُونَ ٱلسَّيِّـَٔاتِ حَتَّىٰٓ إِذَا حَضَرَ أَحَدَهُمُ
ٱلْمَوْتُ قَالَ إِنِّى تُبْتُ ٱلْـَٰٔنَ وَلَا ٱلَّذِينَ يَمُوتُونَ وَهُمْ كُفَّارٌ أُوْلَٰٓئِكَ
أَعْتَدْنَا لَهُمْ عَذَابًا أَلِيمًا ﴿١٨﴾

17 Allah only accepts the repentance of those who do evil in ignorance and then quickly repent after doing it. Allah turns towards such people. Allah is All-Knowing, All-Wise. 18 There is no repentance for people who persist in doing evil until death comes to them and who then say, 'Now I repent,' nor for people who die unbelievers. We have prepared for them a painful punishment.

Allah only accepts the repentance of those who do evil in ignorance

This *āyah* is general to all who commit a wrong action. It is also said that it only applies to those who commit do evil in ignorance. *Tawbah* (repentance), however, is for everyone who does a wrong action. The Community agree that *tawbah* is obligatory for the believers since the Almighty says: *'Turn to Allah, every one of you, O believers.'* (24:31) It rectifies a wrong action even if he does another one of a different type, which differs from the Mu'tazilites who say that someone who does any other wrong action has not truly repented. There is no difference between one act of disobedience and another. This is the school of the people of the *Sunnah.*

When a person repents, Allah can accept it if he wishes or not accept it. It is not logically obligatory for Allah to accept repentance, as opponents state, because a precondition of an obligator is that it is necessarily higher than the rank of the object of the obligation. Allah created creation and is its King and the One who imposes responsibility and so cannot be described as there being anything obligatory on Him. He is exalted above that. Nonetheless He states that He fulfils His promise to accept repentance from those of His slaves who disobey when He says: *'It is He Who accepts repentance from His slaves and pardons evil acts'* (42:25) and: *'Do they not know that Allah accepts repentance from His slaves'* (9:104) and: *'But I am Ever-Forgiving to anyone who repents.'* (20:82).

So He speaks about things which He makes obligatory on Himself while the belief is that nothing is logically obliged for him. As for what the words say, their literal expression indicates that He accepts the repentance of the one who repents. Abu-l-Ma'ālī and others said that the literal accords probability; it is not an absolute statement that Allah will accept repentance. Ibn 'Aṭiyyah said, 'Abū 'l-Ma'ālī and others were opposed in their espousal of this meaning. If we assume that someone repents with sincerity and with all the preconditions necessary for it, according to Abu-l-Ma'ālī, it is only probable that his repentance be accepted. Others say that it is certain that Allah will accept it since He has reported this about Himself.' Ibn 'Aṭiyyah said, 'My father inclined to this position and gave it predominance. It is also my position. Allah is too merciful to His slaves to break this promise to the one who repents, as He says: "*It is He Who accepts repentance from His slaves*" (42:25) and: "*But I am Ever-Forgiving*" (20:82).'

Since this is confirmed, know that this means that there is elision here and it is not taken literally. It means: 'It is from the bounty and mercy of Allah to His slaves.' This is similar to what the Prophet ﷺ said to Mu'ādh, 'Do you know the right that Allah's slaves have over Him?' He replied, 'Allah and His Messenger know best.' He said, 'That He admits them to the Garden.' This all means 'by His favour and mercy,' and it is a promise. The evidence is in His words: *'Allah has prescribed for himself mercy'* (6:12), meaning He has promised it.

It is also said that the preposition *'alā* here means 'with'. The meaning is the same. It means that Allah does not fail in His promise to accept repentance when four conditions are fulfilled: regret in the heart, immediately abandoning the action, resolve not to return to the like of it, and that it arises from shame before Allah, not other people. If one of these conditions is lacking, then repentance is not sound. It is said that another of its conditions is admission of the wrong action and a lot of asking forgiveness. Many of the ideas and rulings about repentance were mentioned in *Āl 'Imrān.*

There is no disagreement that repentance does not rescind a *ḥadd* punishment. That is why our scholars said that if a male or female thief or slanderer repent but evidence against them is established, then the *ḥadd* punishment must still be carried out on them.

It is also said that the preposition *'alā* here means 'from', meaning that *tawbah* comes from Allah to those. Abū Bakr ibn 'Abdūs said that. Allah knows best. Sincere repentance and the things for which repentance should be made will be discussed in *at-Taḥrīm.*

In the phrases *'of those who do evil in ignorance'* and in *'If anyone among you does evil out of ignorance'* (6:54) the word *'evil'* includes both disbelief and disobedience. Anyone who disobeys his Lord is ignorant until he ceases his disobedience. Qatādah said, 'The Companions of the Prophet ﷺ agreed that every act of disobedience is ignorance, whether intentional or out of ignorance.' Ibn 'Abbās, Qatādah, aḍ-Ḍaḥḥāk, Mujāhid and as-Suddī said that. It is related that aḍ-Ḍaḥḥāk and Mujāhid said that the ignorance meant here is intentional. 'Ikrimah said, 'All the matters of this world are ignorance,' meaning in particular what is not obedience to Allah. This refers to the worlds of the Almighty: *'The life of this world is merely a game and diversion.'* (47:36) Az-Zajjāj said that 'ignorance' here is their choosing passing pleasure over the lasting pleasure. It is said that 'ignorance' means not knowing the manner of punishment. Ibn Fūrak mentioned that, but Ibn 'Aṭiyyah said it is weak and refuted.

and then quickly repent after doing it.

Ibn 'Abbās and as-Suddī said that this means before a person's final illness. It is related that aḍ-Ḍaḥḥāk said, 'All that occurs before death is quick.' Abū Miljaz, aḍ-Ḍaḥḥāk, 'Ikrimah, Ibn Zayd and others said that it means before seeing the angels and drivers and before a person is overpowered. Maḥmūd al-Warrāq said some excellent verses on this:

Before you die and before tongues are stopped,
send ahead hopeful repentance.

Hasten with it before breath is stopped.
It is a treasure and booty for the penitent good-doer.

Our scholars say that repentance is sound at this moment because hope still remains, and regret and resolve to reform is sound. At-Tirmidhī related from Ibn 'Umar from the Prophet ﷺ, 'Allah accepts the repentance of a person as long it is before the death rattle.' He said that this is a *ḥasan gharīb* hadith. That is as long as his spirit has not reached his throat. So the position is where the rattle or gargling takes place as al-Harawī said.

It is also said that it means people should repent soon after the wrong action without persisting in it. It is better to do so when one is still healthy since there is then hope of performing righteous actions. The furthest distance is death. It is as is said:

[They say, 'You are not far away' as they are burying me.]
Where is distance except where I am.

Ṣāliḥ al-Murrī related that al-Ḥasan said, 'Whoever faults his brother for a wrong action for which he repents to Allah, Allah will test him by it.' Al-Ḥasan said, 'When he fell Iblīs said, "By Your might, I will not leave the son of Ādam as long as his spirit is in his body." Allah replied, "By My might, I will not veil repentance from the son of Ādam as long as he has not made his death rattle."'

There is no repentance for people who persist in doing evil until death comes to them

Allah precludes those who are dying and despairing of life from being included under the judgment of repentance, as, for instance, was the case of Pharaoh when he was drowning. The faith he displayed did not help him. Repentance at that moment is of no use because it takes place after the removal of responsibility. That is what Ibn 'Abbās, Ibn Zayd and the majority of commentators say.

As for the unbelievers who die in their disbelief, there is no possibility of repentance for them in the Next World, as Allah indicates to them when he says: *'We have prepared for them a painful punishment,'* meaning for all eternity. Although the words indicate everyone, the punishment for the disobedient Muslim is not eternal. The same applies to all wrong actions short of disbelief. It means that repentance is possible for anyone who does evil deeds short of unbelief and then repents at death, but not for someone who is an unbeliever who repents on the Day of Rising. It is said that the evil here is unbelief and so it means: 'There is no repentance for the unbelievers who repent at the time of death nor for those who die while they are unbelievers.'

Abu-l-'Ālīyah said, 'The first *āyah* was revealed about the believers: *"Allah only accepts the repentance,"* and the second is about the hypocrites: *"There is no repentance..."*, meaning there is no acceptance of repentance from those who persist in their actions until they are dying and see the Angel of Death.' Then his words, *'Now I repent'* do not constitute repentance. The unbelievers will have a painful abiding punishment.

يَـٰٓأَيُّهَا ٱلَّذِينَ ءَامَنُوا۟ لَا يَحِلُّ لَكُمْ أَن تَرِثُوا۟ ٱلنِّسَآءَ كَرْهًا
وَلَا تَعْضُلُوهُنَّ لِتَذْهَبُوا۟ بِبَعْضِ مَآ ءَاتَيْتُمُوهُنَّ إِلَّآ أَن يَأْتِينَ بِفَـٰحِشَةٍ
مُّبَيِّنَةٍ ۚ وَعَاشِرُوهُنَّ بِٱلْمَعْرُوفِ ۚ فَإِن كَرِهْتُمُوهُنَّ فَعَسَىٰٓ أَن تَكْرَهُوا۟
شَيْـًٔا وَيَجْعَلَ ٱللَّهُ فِيهِ خَيْرًا كَثِيرًا ﴿١٩﴾

19 You who believe! it is not lawful for you to inherit women by force. Nor may you treat them harshly so that you can make off with part of what you have given them, unless they commit an

act of flagrant indecency. Live together with them correctly and courteously. If you dislike them, it may well be that you dislike something in which Allah has placed a lot of good.

it is not lawful for you to inherit women by force.

This is connected to what was already mentioned about wives. What is meant is to prevent any injustice or harm to them. It is addressed to guardians. *'An'* is in the nominative by 'not lawful', in other words, 'it is not lawful for you to inherit women.' *'Karh'* is a verbal noun in the position of a *ḥāl.*

Various things are said about the reason for the revelation of this *āyah*. Al-Bukhārī reported about it from Ibn 'Abbās: 'When a man died, his guardians were entitled to his wife. If one of them wished, he could marry her, or give her in marriage or not give her in marriage. They were more entitled to her than her own family and so this *āyah* was revealed about that.' Abū Dāwud transmitted it. Az-Zuhrī and Abū Mijlaz said, 'Their custom when a man died was that when his son by another woman or the closest of his paternal relatives cast his garment on the wife, he became more entitled to her than herself and her guardians. He could marry her without any dowry other than the one she had been given by the deceased or marry her to another and take her dowry and not give her anything. If he wished, he could leave her in limbo until she ransomed herself with what she had inherited or until she died. So Allah revealed this.' It means: 'It is not lawful for you to inherit women from their husbands and become their husbands.' It is said that if the heir arrived first and threw a garment on her, he was more entitled to her. If she reached her family first, then she was entitled to herself. As-Suddī said that.

It is said that if an old woman was married to a man and he desired a young woman and disliked leaving the old one because of her wealth, he would keep her and not go near her until she ransomed herself from him by her property or died so that he would inherit her wealth. This *āyah* was revealed and the husband ordered to divorce her if he disliked her company and not to keep her forcibly. That is the meaning of this *āyah*. What is meant by the *āyah* is to annul what they did in the Jāhiliyyah and not to treat women like property which could be inherited by men.

'Force' is read as *karh* by all except Ḥamzah and al-Kisā'ī who read it '*kurh*'. They are two dialectical forms. Al-Qutabī said that *karh* means force and *kurh* means hardship. It is said that it means doing that willingly or unwillingly.

The *āyah* is addressed to guardians. It is also said that it is addressed to the husbands of women when they retain them while at the same time treating them badly out of desire for their inheritance or wanting them to ransom themselves with some of their dowries. This is sounder, and preferred by Ibn 'Aṭiyyah. The proof of that is: *'unless they commit an act of flagrant indecency.'* If they do that, then the guardian cannot keep them in order to exhaust their property: that is the consensus in the community. That is for the husband as will be explained further on.

nor may you treat them harshly

The meaning of *'aḍl*, which is prevention, was explained in *al-Baqarah.*

unless they commit an act of flagrant indecency.

People disagree about what is meant by this. Al-Ḥasan said, 'It refers to fornication. If a virgin commits fornication, she is given a hundred lashes and exiled for a year and returns to her husband what she took from him.' Abū Qilābah said, 'If a man's wife commits fornication, there is nothing wrong in harming her and constricting her until she ransoms herself.' As-Suddī said, 'If they do that, take their dowries.' Ibn Sīrīn and Abū Qilābah said, 'It is not lawful to take ransom from her unless he finds a man on her belly. Allah says: *"unless they commit an act of flagrant indecency."'"* Ibn Mas'ūd, Ibn 'Abbās, aḍ-Ḍaḥḥāk and Qatādah said a flagrant act of indecency in this *āyah* means hatred and recalcitrance. They said, 'When she refuses to fulfil her duties, her husband can take her property, and this is the school of Mālik.' Ibn 'Aṭiyyah said, 'I do not have any text from him about the "*act of flagrant indecency*" referred to in the *āyah*.'

Some people said that *fāḥishah* here means foul language and bad company in respect of word and action. This is recalcitrance (*nushūz*). Some of the people of knowledge permit taking money from a disobedient wife in a *khul'* although he cannot exceed what he gave her since Allah says: *'to make off with part of what you have given them.'* Mālik and another group of the people of knowledge said that a husband can take everything that a disobedient wife owns. Ibn 'Aṭiyyah said, 'Fornication is harder for the husband than disobedience and harm. Every *fāḥishah* renders taking property lawful.'

Abū 'Umar said, 'I consider the statement of Ibn Sīrīn and Abū Qilābah to be nothing because *fāḥishah* can be foul language and harm. Someone who uses foul language is called *fāḥish*. If an act of *fāḥishah* is committed, the husband can pronounce a *li'ān* or simply divorce her. But he is not allowed to harm her to make her ransom herself from him with her money. I do not know of anyone who says that he can harm her and be bad to her so that she demands a *khul'* if he finds that she has fornicated – other than Abā Qilābah. Allah knows best.'

Allah says in *Surah al-Baqarah*: *'If you fear that they will not remain within Allah's limits'* (2:229). This means that in the event that there is no likelihood of the the couple maintaining good companionship and the husband respecting his wife's rights over him and the wife respecting her husband's rights over her: *'There is nothing wrong in the wife ransoming herself.'* Allah also says: *'If they are happy to give you some of it, make use of it with pleasure and goodwill.'* (4:4) These *āyahs* give us the basic principles underlying this matter. Ibn 'Aṭā' al-Khurāsānī said, 'It used to be that if a man's wife committed adultery, he would take from her what he had given her and throw her out. That was abrogated by the *ḥudūd*.' A fourth position is that this means: 'unless they fornicate. If they do so, they are detained in their houses.' So this refers to the time before the abrogation and this is the same idea as the position of Ibn 'Aṭiyyah. It is weak.

If we take the position that it is guardians who are addressed, then its *fiqh* is that, if it is proven that the guardian is unduly harsh, the Qāḍī investigates the business of a woman and her husband and he should only look at her as a father would at his daughters. If there is benefit in his preventing her marriage, he is not opposed in doing that. That is in relation to one or more marriage proposals. If it is proven that he is simply preventing her from marrying, there are two positions on it in the school of Mālik. One is that he is like all guardians and the Qāḍī can marry off any of his daughters he wishes to, and the other is that he is not opposed in what he does.

The words *'Nor treat them harshly'* can be jussive as a prohibition, and the *wāw* is then conjunctive, adding a sentence composed of words disconnected from the first sentence. It can also be in the accusative as joined to '*inherit* and so the *wāw* is shared, adding one verb to another. Ibn Mas'ūd recited *'walā ta'ḍulūhunna'*, a reading which strengthens the possibility of the accusative and the fact that it is a statement about *'aḍl* not being permitted.

Nāfi' and Abū 'Amr read 'clear' as *'mubayyinah'* and *'mubayyanāt'* in 24:34 and 46. Ibn 'Abbās reads *'mubīnah'* from Form IV which is used for the thing being clear itself and for making it clear. All of these are eloquent dialectical usages.

Live together with them correctly and courteously

This means according to what Allah has commanded in terms of keeping good company. It is addressed to everyone since all keep company, whether they are husbands or guardians. The command, however, is directed particularly to husbands, as in Allah's words: *'retain them with correctness and courtesy.'* (2:229) It means to give a wife full rights of dowry and maintenance and not to frown at her for no reason and to be cheerful in speech, not rude or harsh or showing inclination for another woman. 'Living together' refers to mixing together and socialising. Illustrating that are the words of Ṭarafah:

> If the tract she travels in is sometimes far,
> Perhaps the promise of the lover will be intimate.

He makes the lover like an associate and company. *'Āshara, mu'āsharah,* is to consort with as *ta'āshara* describes people mixing together as does *a'tashara.*

Allah commands people to keep good company with women when a contract is made with them so that there is familiarity between them and perfect companionship. It is more calming for the self and better for life. This is a duty for the husband, but he is not obliged to make it up. One of them said, 'He should beautify himself for her as she does for him.' Yaḥyā ibn 'Abd ar-Raḥmān al-Ḥanẓalī said, 'I went to Muḥammad ibn al-Ḥanafiyyah and he came out to me wearing a red mantle with perfume dripping from his beard. "What is this?" I asked. He replied, "This is a cloak which my wife put on me and she put perfume on me as well. They want of us what we want of them."' Ibn 'Abbās said, 'I want to adorn myself for my wife as I want my wife to adorn herself for me.' Ibn 'Aṭiyyah said, 'For the meaning of the *āyah,* look at the words of the Prophet ﷺ, "Enjoy her even if there is some crookedness in her," meaning do not show bad companionship towards her even if she is crooked. That will produce opposition and end in a split. It is the reason for *khul'.*'

Scholars use the words as evidence that when one servant is not enough for a woman, her husband should provide her with servants commensurate with her social standing, as, for instance, in the case of the daughter of a caliph or king and those like them for whom one servant is not enough. That is living together correctly. Ash-Shāfi'ī and Abū Ḥanīfah said, 'He is only obliged to provide one servant. That will spare her serving herself. There is no woman in the world for whom one servant is not adequate. This is like someone who has a number of horses. He only gets the share of one horse because he can only fight on one horse.' Our scholars said, 'This is wrong because daughters of kings, who have many servants, are not satisfied by one servant because they need to have their clothes washed, their beds made and others things which require more than one.' This is clear and Allah knows best.

If you dislike them, it may well be that you dislike something in which Allah has placed a lot of good.

This dislike may come about because of ugliness or bad character that did not involve their committing an act of indecency or disobedience. In that case putting up with it is recommended. Perhaps the reason for that is that through her Allah will provide him with righteous children. This is indicated by something in *Ṣaḥīḥ Muslim* from Abū Hurayrah who reported that the Messenger of Allah ﷺ said, 'A believing man should not hate a believing woman. If he dislikes something in her character, he should be pleased with some other – or another – trait of hers.' It is said that it means that he should not hate her completely which might move him to divorce her. He should forgive her bad because of her good and overlook what he dislikes on account of what he likes. Makḥūl said, 'I heard Ibn 'Umar say, "A man does the *istikhārah*, asking for good from Allah and He chooses for him, and then he is angry with his Lord. It is not long before he sees that in the end it is better for him."'

Ibn al-'Arabī mentioned from Abu-l-Qāsim in Mahdia from Abu-l-Qāsim as-Sayūrī that Abū Bakr ibn 'Abd ar-Raḥmān said, 'Shaykh Abū Muḥammad ibn Abī Zayd had position and recognition with regard to knowledge and the *dīn*. He had a wife who was a bad companion and she was lax with respect to his rights and injured him with her tongue. People spoke to him about her and he was criticised for being patient with her. He used to say, "I am a man to whom Allah has given full blessing in the health of my body, recognition and what I own. Perhaps she was sent as a punishment for my wrong actions and I fear that if I divorce her a worse punishment may descend on me."'

Our scholars said, 'This is evidence for the dislike of divorce even though it is permitted.' It is related that the Prophet ﷺ said, 'Allah does not dislike anything He has allowed except for divorce and eating. Allah dislikes full intestines.'

وَإِنْ أَرَدتُّمُ ٱسْتِبْدَالَ زَوْجٍ مَّكَانَ زَوْجٍ وَءَاتَيْتُمْ إِحْدَىٰهُنَّ
قِنطَارًا فَلَا تَأْخُذُوا۟ مِنْهُ شَيْـًٔا أَتَأْخُذُونَهُۥ بُهْتَٰنًا وَإِثْمًا مُّبِينًا ﴿٢٠﴾
وَكَيْفَ تَأْخُذُونَهُۥ وَقَدْ أَفْضَىٰ بَعْضُكُمْ إِلَىٰ بَعْضٍ وَأَخَذْنَ
مِنكُم مِّيثَٰقًا غَلِيظًا ﴿٢١﴾

20 If you desire to exchange one wife for another and have given your original wife a large amount, do not take any of it. Would you take it by means of slander and outright crime? 21 How could you take it when you have been intimate with one another and they have made a binding contract with you?

Since the previous *āyah* dealt with the ruling of divorce instigated by the wife, and the husband taking property from her, Allah follows that by mentioning divorce instigated by the man. It is clear that He means divorce without there being disobedience or bad companionship and so he cannot ask her for any property.

Scholars disagree about what happens when a couple want to divorce and one of them displays bad companionship and disobedience. Mālik said that the husband can take from his wife if she instigates the divorce but does not mention [whether he can] when he instigates it. Most scholars say that that is not permitted to take money unless the disobedience is hers alone and she asks him for divorce.

and have given your original wife a large amount,

This *āyah* indicates the permission to give a large amount as a dowry because Allah would only use something permissible as an example. 'Umar said in a speech, 'Do not be excessive in the amount of a woman's dowry. If she is noble in this world or in *taqwā* of Allah, the Messenger of Allah ﷺ would have been more entitled to that than you, and none of his wives or daughters was given a dowry of more than twelve *ūqiyyahs*.' A woman got up and said, "Umar! Allah gives to us and you forbid us! Does not Allah say: "*...and have given your original wife a large amount do not take any of it*"?' 'Umar said, 'The woman is right and 'Umar was wrong.' In one variant, "Umar bowed his head and said, "Everyone has more understanding of *fiqh* than you, 'Umar!"' Another has, 'The woman is right and the man is wrong. Allah is the One from whom help is sought.' He dropped his objection.

Abū Ḥātim al-Bustī transmitted with a sound *isnād* that Abu-l-'Ajfā' as-Sulamī said, "Umar said in a speech to the people...' as far as 'more than twelve *ūqiyyahs*.' He did not mention the woman standing up to address him. Ibn Mājah transmitted it in his *Sunan* from Abu-l-'Ajfā' and added after mentioning the *ūqiyyahs* continued, 'A man may feel so burdened by his wife's dowry that this engenders his animosity towards her and he says, "You cost me everything I own (lit. the strap of the water-skin or the sweat of the water-skin)!" I was an Arab man and did not know what was meant by the strap of the water-skin or the sweat of the water-skin.' Al-Jawharī said that 'strap (*'alaq*) of a water-skin' is a dialectical form of the sweat (*'araq*) of a waterskin'.' Someone else said that *'alaq* is the string which ties a water-skin. So he is saying, 'You have cost me everything, even the string that ties the water-skin.' *'Araq* is the liquid in a waterskin. One uses the expression in saying, 'I tired myself out for us and imposed on myself until I sweated like a water-skin,' meaning its flow. It is said that they used to provision themselves with water and tied it to camels to carry, and it was heavy on their backs. This explains both expressions.

Al-Aṣma'ī said, 'The sweat of a water-skin is an expression which conveys hardship. I do not know its origin.' Al-Aṣma'ī further said, 'I heard Ibn Abī Ṭarafah, one of the most eloquent men I have seen, say, "I heard our shaykhs say, 'I have met the sweat of the water-skin from so-and-so,' and he meant hardship." He quoted to me from Ibn Aḥmar:

It is not counted an insult, when her pardon
Is the sweat of the water-skin on a tired camel.

Abū 'Ubayd said, 'He means that he hears a word which angers him and is not an insult and the person is punished by it and for him it is like the sweat of a water-skin. He uses a different word for water-skin for the sake of the poem. Then he said 'a tired camel'. It is as if it means that the water-skins are hung on the camel in their journeys. This idea is like what al-Farrā' related. He claimed that in the desert on their journeys they stocked themselves with water and they would hand it on the camels and take it in turns. That entailed toil and hardship on the back. Al-Farrā' used this explanation in hanging water-skins with *lām*.

Some people say that it does not give permission to have excessive dowries because Allah uses the amount of a '*qinṭār*' simply as an example, as if he saying, 'Even if you were to give this large amount which no one is given.' This is like the words of the Prophet ﷺ, 'Anyone who builds a mosque, even one the size of the nest of a sand grouse, Allah will build a house for him in the Garden.' It is known that there is no mosque the size of the nest of a sand grouse.

When Ibn Abī Ḥadrad came to the Prophet ﷺ to ask for his help with paying a dowry, the Prophet ﷺ asked him about it and he said that it was two hundred. The Prophet ﷺ became angry and said, 'It is as if you are cutting gold and silver from surface of al-Ḥarrah or a mountain.' Certain people deduced from this that it is forbidden to give excessive dowries. This is not necessary. The Prophet ﷺ objected to this man, not as an objection to a large amount of dowry, but because he was poor in that state and needed to beg and ask for help. This is agreed to be disliked. 'Umar gave Umm Kulthūm bint 'Alī, the daughter of Fāṭimah, a dowry of 40,000 dirhams.

Abū Dāwud reported from 'Uqbah ibn 'Amr that the Prophet ﷺ asked a man, 'Do you want me to marry you to so-and-so?' 'Yes,' he replied. He said to the woman, 'Do you want me to marry you to so-and-so?' 'Yes,' she replied. So he married them to one another. The man consummated the marriage without allotting her a dowry and did not give her anything. He was one of those who had been at al-Ḥudaybīyah and had a share at Khaybar. When he died, he said, 'The Messenger of Allah ﷺ married me to so-and-so and I did not allot her a dowry or give her anything. I testify that I have given her my share at Khaybar as her dowry.' She took his share and sold it for 100,000.

Scholars agree that there is no limit on the maximum amount for a dowry because of this *āyah*. They disagree about its minimum. That will be discussed in *āyah* 24. The definition of *qinṭār* was mentioned in *Āl 'Imrān*.

Ibn Muḥayṣin recited *'ātaytumu-ḥdāhunna'* with the *alif* connected to '*iḥdāhunna*'. It is a dialectical usage. [POEMS]

do not take any of it.

Bakr ibn 'Abdullāh al-Muzanī said, 'The husband used not to take anything from the wife divorced by a *khul'* according to the words of Allah: *"do not take."* Then it was abrogated by the *āyah* in *al-Baqarah*.' Ibn Zayd and others said that it is abrogated by the words in *al-Baqarah*: *'It is not lawful for you to keep anything you have given them.'* (2:229)

The sound position is that these *āyah*s are both *āyah*s of judgment and there is no abrogation or abrogated in them. They support one another. Aṭ-Ṭabarī says that it is an *āyah* of judgment and there is no sense to the words of Bakr. If you wish, it is about gifts, and the Prophet ﷺ allowed Thābit to take from his wife what he had given her.

How could you take it when you have been intimate with one another?

The reason for the prohibition against taking it back is that they have been intimate together. Someone said that '*ifḍa"* (being intimate) is being with her under the same blanket, whether or not sexual intercourse took place. Al-Harawī related that and that is the position of al-Kalbī. Al-Farrā' said that it refers to when a man has been alone with his wife and has had sexual intercourse with her. Ibn 'Abbās, Mujāhid, as-Suddī and others said that in this *āyah* it means sexual intercourse. Ibn 'Abbās said that Allah is noble and uses an allusion. The linguistic root of *ifḍā'* is mixing together. A mixture is called '*faḍā*'. A poet said:

I said to her, 'My aunt, you can have my she-camel.
It makes a mixture (*faḍā*) in my bag with raisins.

People who described as *fawḍā* are mixed together without a leader.

Taking the meaning to be 'being alone together', even if there is no sexual intercourse, does that mean that the dowry is confirmed by that or not? Our scholars disagree about it, taking four positions: that it is confirmed by the simple fact of being alone together; that it is only confirmed by sexual intercourse; that it is confirmed by being alone in the house where a wife is given to her husband; and that there is a difference between her room and his room.

The sound position is that it is confirmed by simply being alone together. That is the position of Abū Ḥanīfah and his people. They say, 'When he has been properly alone with her, the full dowry is obliged as well as *'iddah*, whether or not he consummates the marriage.' That is based on what ad-Dāraquṭnī related from Thawbān that the Messenger of Allah ﷺ said, 'Anyone who removes the veil of a woman and looks at her must pay the dowry.' 'Umar said, 'When he closes the door, lowers the curtain and sees her private parts, payment of the dowry is obliged, she must observe *'iddah* and she inherits.' 'Alī said, 'When he closes the door, lowers the curtain and sees her private parts, the payment of the dowry is obliged.' Mālik said, 'When he stays a long time with her, like a year, and they agree that there was no touching, and she asks for her full dowry, she has it.' Ash-Shāfi'ī said, 'She has no *'iddah* and receives half the dowry.' This was discussed in *al-Baqarah*.

they have made a binding contract with you

There are three things said about this. It is said that it is what is meant by the words of the Prophet ﷺ, 'Fear Allah regarding women. You take them as a trust of Allah and you are allowed access to their private parts by the Word of Allah.' 'Ikrimah and ar-Rabī' said that. The second is that it refers to the words of the Almighty: '*Wives may be retained with correctness and courtesy or released with good will.*' (2:229). Al-Ḥasan, Ibn Sīrīn, Qatādah, aḍ-Ḍaḥḥāk and as-Suddī said that. The third is that what is meant is a verbal contract of marriage where a man says, 'I have married' and 'I have the marriage contract.' Mujāhid and Ibn Zayd said that. Some people said that it is a child. Allah knows best.

وَلَا تَنكِحُوا۟ مَا نَكَحَ ءَابَآؤُكُم مِّنَ ٱلنِّسَآءِ إِلَّا مَا قَدْ سَلَفَ
إِنَّهُۥ كَانَ فَٰحِشَةً وَمَقْتًا وَسَآءَ سَبِيلًا ٢٢

22 Do not marry any women whom your fathers married – except for what may have already taken place. That is an indecent act, a loathsome thing and an evil path.

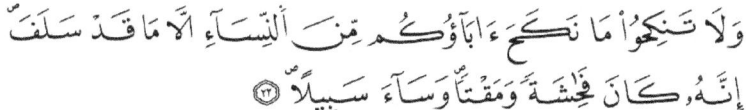

Do not marry any women whom your fathers married

It is said that people used to marry their father's wife with her permission after Allah revealed: *'it is not lawful for you to inherit women by force.'* When this was revealed, it became unlawful in all cases, whether or not the marriage had been consummated, as the meaning of the term *nikāḥ* includes both the contract and sexual intercourse. When a father marries a woman or, indeed, has sexual intercourse with her outside marriage, she is unlawful to his son as will be explained.

In the words *'whom your fathers married'*, it said that *'mā'* (tr. *'whom'*) here means women. It is said that it means the contract, in other words that such a marriage is void and contrary to the *dīn* of Allah since Allah has given judgment regarding the manner of marriage and detailed its preconditions. That is what aṭ-Ṭabarī prefers. *'Min'* is connected to 'marry' and *'mā nakaḥa'* is a verbal noun. He said that if it had meant 'Do not marry women whom your fathers have married,' it would be obliged to have "who" (*man*) and not "what" (*mā*). According to this, the prohibition is about marriage in the unsound manner of your fathers. The first is sounder, because *'mā'* (what) can mean *'man'* (who), and the Companions took it to mean that. From it is deduced the prohibition against sons marrying their fathers' wives.

The custom of some Arab tribes was that a man's son would marry his father's wife. That was a binding practice among the Anṣār and permitted among Quraysh with mutual consent. 'Amr ibn Umayyah married his father's wife after his death and she bore him Musāfir and Abū Mu'ayṭ, and she had Abu-l-'Īṣ and others from Umayyah. The sons of Umayyah were both the brothers and uncles of Musāfir and Abū Mu'ayṭ.

Another example of it is Ṣafwān ibn Umayyah ibn Khalaf who married his father's wife, Fākhitah bint al-Aswad ibn al-Muṭṭallib ibn Asad. Umayyah was killed while married to her. Another example was Manẓūr ibn Zabbān who married Mulaykah bint Khārijah who had been married to his father, Zabbān ibn Zayyār. Another example is Ḥiṣn ibn Abī Qays who married his father's wife, Kubaysha bint Ma'n and al-Aswad ibn Khalaf who also married his father's wife.

Al-Ash'at ibn Sawwār said, 'Abū Qays died. He was one of the righteous men of the Anṣār. His son Qays proposed to his father's wife. She said, "I think of you as a son. I will go to the Messenger of Allah ﷺ to consult him about it," and she went to him and told him and Allah revealed this *āyah*.'

Some Arabs used to marry their daughters. One of them was Ḥājib ibn Zurārah who became a Magian and did this. That was mentioned by an-Naḍr ibn Shumayl in *Kitāb al-Mathālib.* Allah forbade the believers to follow this custom of their fathers.

except for what may have already taken place.

This is what has passed and gone. *Salaf* are your forefathers and relatives. This is an absolute exception, meaning 'avoid and leave what happened before.' It is said that 'except' means 'after', i.e. after what already happened. This usage is seen in Allah's words: *'They will not taste any death there – other* (illā) *than the first one.'* (44:56) This means 'after the first death'. It is said that it means 'not what has already taken place' as in the words: *'A believer should never kill another believer unless* (illā) *it is by mistake,'* (4:92) meaning not by mistake either. It is said that there is a change of order in the *āyah* and it means: 'Do not marry women your fathers married. It is indecent and an evil path, except for what already happened.'

It is said that the *āyah* contains an implication which means: if you do that, you will be punished for it, except for what was in the past.

That is an indecent act, a loathsome thing and an evil path.

This is a resulting grave censure which indicates that the forbidden action is very foul indeed. Abu-l-'Abbās said, 'I asked Ibn al-A'rabī about what a 'loathsome marriage' is. He answered, "It is that a man marries his father's wife when he divorces her or leaves her a widow. Such a man is called *'ḍayzan'*."'

Ibn 'Arafah said, 'When a man married his father's wife and she bore him a child, the child was called *maqtiyy*.' The root of *maqt* means to be hateful from the verb, *maqata*, to hate. So the Arabs called a man who marries his father's wife *'maqīt'* (hated). Allah called this marriage *'maqt'* (hateful and loathsome) since hatred is attached to the one who does it.

It is said that the meaning of the prohibition is forbidding a man from having sexual intercourse with any woman with whom his father had sexual intercourse, except for what happened in the past in the Jāhiliyyah in respect of women their fathers had fornicated with and were not actually married to. A son is permitted to marry a woman with whom his father fornicated and to have lawful sex in marriage with her. Ibn Zayd said that. He believes that the exception is connected and that it is a basic principle that fornication does not make someone unlawful as will be explained. Allah knows best.

Table of Contents for *Āyats*

96-97 The first House established for mankind was that at Bakka... 1
98-99 Say, 'People of the Book, why do you reject Allah's Signs... 17
100 You who believe! if you obey a group of those given the Book... 18
101 How can you disbelieve, when Allah's Signs are recited to you... 19
102 You who believe! have *taqwā* of Allah with the *taqwā* due to Him... 20
103 Hold fast to the rope of Allah all together, and do not separate... 21
104 Let there be a community among you who call to the good... 28
105 Do not be like those who split up and differed after the Clear Signs... 28
106-7 on the Day when faces are whitened and faces are blackened... 29
108-9 These are Allah's Signs which We recite to you with truth... 32
110 You are the best nation ever to be produced before mankind... 32
111 They will not harm you except with abusive words... 36
112-5 They will be plunged into abasement wherever they are found... 37
116 As for those who disbelieve, their wealth and children will not help... 40
117 The metaphor of what they spend in their life in this world... 40
118 You who believe, do not take any outside yourselves as intimate... 41
119 There you are, loving them when they do not love you... 44
120 If something good happens to you, it galls them... 46
121 Remember when you left your family early in the day... 47
122 And remember when two of your clans were on the point of losing heart...48
123-5 Allah helped you at Badr when you were weak so have *taqwā*... 53
126-7 Allah only did this for it to be good news for you... 60
128-9 You have no part in the affair. Either He will turn towards them... 61
130-2 You who believe, do not feed on usury, multiplied... 64
133 Race each other to forgiveness from your Lord and a Garden... 66
134 those who give in times of both ease and hardship... 68
135 those who, when they act indecently or wrong themselves... 71
136 Their recompense is forgiveness from their Lord, and Gardens... 78
137 Whole societies have passed away before your time, so travel about... 79
138 This is a clear explanation for all mankind, and guidance... 80
139 Do not give up and do not be downhearted. You shall be uppermost... 80
140 If you have received a wound, they have already received a similar... 81

141 and so that Allah can purge those who believe... 83
142 Or did you imagine that you were going to enter the Garden... 83
143 You were longing for death before you met it. Now you have seen it... 84
144 Muḥammad is only a Messenger and he has been preceded... 85
145 No self can die except with Allah's permission... 90
146-7 Many a Prophet has been killed, when there were many... 91
148 So Allah gave them the reward of this world... 94
149-150 You who believe! if you obey those who disbelieve... 94
151 We will cast terror into the hearts of those who disbelieve... 95
152 Allah fulfilled His promise to you... 96
153 Remember when you were scrambling up the slope... 101
154 Then He sent down to you, after the distress, security... 104
155 Those of you who turned their backs on the day... 106
156 You who believe! do not be like those who disbelieve... 109
157-8 If you are killed in the Way of Allah or if you die... 110
159 It is a mercy from Allah that you were gentle with them... 111
160 If Allah helps you, no one can vanquish you. If He forsakes you... 116
161 No Prophet would ever be guilty of misappropriation... 117
162 Is someone who pursues the pleasure of Allah the same as... 124
164 Allah showed great kindness to the believers... 125
165 Why is it that when a calamity happens to you... 126
166-7 What assailed you on the day the two armies met... 128
168 They are those who said of their brothers... 130
169 Do not suppose that those killed in the Way of Allah are dead... 130
171 rejoicing in blessings and favour from Allah... 137
172 Those who did good and were godfearing... 138
173 those to whom people said, 'The people have gathered against you... 141
174 So they returned with blessings and bounty from Allah... 144
175 It was only Shayṭān frightening you through his friends... 144
176 Do not let those who rush headlong into unbelief sadden you... 145
177 Those who sell belief for unbelief do not harm Allah in any way. 147
178 Those who disbelieve should not imagine... 148
179 Allah will only leave the believers in the position you now are in... 150
180 Those who are tight-fisted with the bounty Allah has given them... 152
181-2 Allah has heard the words of those who say, 'Allah is poor... 155
183-4 Those who say, 'Allah has made a contract with us... 157
185 Every self will taste death. You will be paid your wages in full... 159
186 You will be tested in your wealth and in yourselves... 164
187 Allah made a covenant with those given the Book... 165

188 Those who exult in what they have done... 167
189 The kingdom of the heavens and earth belongs to Allah... 169
190-200 In the creation of the heavens and the earth... 170

Sūrat an-Nisā'

1 O mankind, have *taqwā* of your Lord who created you... 188
2 Give orphans their property, and do not substitute bad things for good... 193
3 If you are afraid of not behaving justly towards orphans... 196
4 Give women their dowries as an outright gift... 206
5 Do not hand over to the incompetent any property of theirs... 210
6 Keep a close check on orphans until they reach a marriageable age... 216
7 Men receive a share of what their parents and relatives leave... 228
8 If other relatives or orphans or poor people attend the sharing-out... 230
9 People should show concern in the same way that they would fear... 232
10 People who consume the property of orphans wrongfully... 235
11-14 Allah instructs you regarding your children... 237
15 If any of your women commit fornication, four of you must be witnesses... 262
16 If two men commit a like abomination, punish them... 264
17-18 Allah only accepts the repentance of those who do evil in ignorance... 269
19 You who believe! it is not lawful for you to inherit women by force.... 272
20-21 If you desire to exchange one wife for another... 277
22 Do not marry any women whom your fathers married... 281

Glossary

Abū Ḥātim: Sahl ibn Muḥammad al-Jushanī as-Sijistānī, d. 255/869, a prominent Basran philologist.
Abū Isḥāq: Ibrāhīm ibn as-Sarī az-Zajjāj, author of *I'rab al-Qur'ān.*
Abū Ja'far: aṭ-Ṭabarī.
Abū 'Ubayd: al-Qāsim ibn Sallām al-Harawī or al-Baghdādī, d. 224/838.
Abū 'Ubaydah: Ma'mar ibn al-Muthanna at-Taymī, d. 209/824, author of *Majāz al-Qur'ān*, the first book on the linguistic analysis of the Qur'an.
adhān: the call to prayer.
'Adn: Eden, part of Paradise.
Amīr al-Mu'minīn: 'the Commander of the Believers', the caliph.
Anṣār: the "Helpers", the people of Madīnah who welcomed and aided the Prophet ﷺ.
'Arafah: a plain 15 miles to the east of Makkah. One of the essential rites of the *ḥajj* is to stand on 'Arafah on the 9th of Dhu-l-Ḥijjah.
'aṣabah: male relatives on the father's side.
'Aṣr: the mid-afternoon prayer.
'awl: adjustment, accommodation by reducing inheritance shares when the percentage due to shares exceeds the total estate.
Aws: along with Khazraj, one of the two major tribes of Madīnah.
āyah: a verse of the Qur'an.
Ayyūb: the Prophet Job.
Badr: a place near the coast, about 95 miles south of Madīnah where, in 2 AH in the first battle fought by the newly established Muslim community, the 313 outnumbered Muslims led by the Messenger of Allah overwhelmingly defeated 1000 Makkan idolaters.
Banū: lit. sons, meaning a tribe or clan.
Baqī' al-Gharqad: the cemetery of Madīnah.
Bi'r Ma'ūnah: site of an expedition four months after the Battle of Uḥud where a delegation of Muslims were attacked and killed.
Burāq: the mount on which the Prophet ﷺ made the Night Journey.
Buwāṭ: a place near Mt. Juhaynah near Raḍwā on the caravan route to Syria. The Prophet ﷺ led a raid there in 2/623.

Dajjāl: the false Messiah whose appearance marks the imminent end of the world. The root in Arabic means 'to deceive, cheat, take in'.
ḍammah: the Arabic vowel 'u'.
Ḍamrah: a tribe who lived about eighty miles from Madīnah. They entered into a treaty with the Prophet in 2/632. They were a clan of the Banū Kinānah.
Dāwud: the Prophet David.
dhimmah: obligation or contract, in particular a treaty of protection for non-Muslims living in Muslim territory.
dhimmī: a non-Muslim living under the protection of Muslim rule.
Dhu-l-Ḥijjah: the twelfth month of the Muslim calendar, the month of the hajj.
Dhu-l-Qa'dah: the eleventh month of the Muslim calendar.
dīn: the life-transaction, lit. the debt between two parties, in this usage between the Creator and created.
Ditch: the Battle of the Ditch (or Trench), which took place in 5/627 in which the combined forces of Quraysh and their allies unsuccessfully laid siege to Madīnah for thirty days.
Fajr: the dawn prayer.
farḍ: an obligatory act of worship or practice of the *dīn* as defined by the Sharī'ah.
farḍ kifāyah: a collective obligation, something which is obligatory for the community as a whole and is satisfied if one adult performs it.
Fadak: a small, rich oasis in the north of the Hijaz near Khaybar.
al-Fārūq: a name for the second caliph, 'Umar ibn al-Khaṭṭāb, It means someone who makes a distinction between truth and falsehood, or between cases.
faqīh: pl. *fuqahā'*, a man learned in knowledge of fiqh who by virtue of his knowledge can give a legal judgment.
fāsiq: someone not meeting the legal requirements of righteousness. The evidence of such a person is inadmissible in the court.
fatḥah: the Arabic vowel 'a'.
Fātiḥah: "the Opener," the first *sūrah* of the Qur'an.
fatwā: an authoritative statement on a point of law.
fiqh: the science of the application of the Sharī'ah. A practitioner or expert in *fiqh* is called a *faqīh.*
Firdaws: Paradise.
fitnah: civil strife, sedition, schism, trial, temptation, also shirk see below.
fiṭrah: the natural form on which man was created.

fuqahā': plural of *faqīh*.
al-Ghābah: a plain a few miles outside of Madīnah in the direction of Syria where an expedition took place in in 6/627.
gharīb: a hadith which has a single reporter at some stage of the *isnād*.
Ghaṭafān: a very large tribal grouping who lived east of Madīnah and Makkah in the land between the Hijaz and the Shammar mountains.
ghazwah: a military expedition.
ghulūl: stealing from the war booty before it has been distributed.
ghusl: major ablution of the whole body with water required to regain purity after menstruation, lochia and sexual intercourse.
ḥadd: pl. *ḥudūd*, Allah's boundary limits for the lawful and unlawful. The *ḥadd* punishments are specific fixed penalties laid down by Allah for specified crimes.
hadith: reported speech of the Prophet ﷺ.
ḥāfiẓ: pl. *ḥuffāẓ*, someone who has memorised the Qur'an. In the sciences of hadith it is someone who has memorised 100,000 hadith both in their texts and their *isnād*s.
hajj: the annual pilgrimage to Makkah which is one of the five pillars of Islam.
ḥāl: In Arabic grammar, a circumstantial adverb in the accusative case which describes something happening at the same time as the action or event mentioned in the main clause.
Hamrā' al-Asad: an expedition in 3/625 when the Muslims were returning to Madīnah from Uḥud. It is eight miles from Madīnah.
Ḥanīfiyyah: the religion of the Prophet Ibrāhīm, the primordial religion of *tawḥīd* and sincerity to Allah.
Ḥaram: Sacred Precinct, a protected area in which certain behavior is forbidden and other behaviour necessary. The area around the Ka'bah in Makkah is a Ḥaram, and the area around the Prophet's Mosque in Madīnah is a Ḥaram. They are referred to together as al-Ḥaramayn, 'the two Ḥarams'.
Hārūn: the Prophet Aaron, the brother of Mūsā.
Ḥarūriyyah: the first Khārijites who separated themselves from 'Alī and based themselves at Ḥarūrā', a town two miles from Kufa.
ḥasan: good, excellent, often used to describe a hadith which is reliable, but which is not as well authenticated as one which is *ṣaḥīḥ*.
Ḥāṭim: the Hijr of the Ka'bah, or the wall of the Ḥijr over which is the spout (Mīzāb).
Hawāzin: one of the large Arab tribes in the Hijaz who were part of the

Qays tribal grouping.
Ḥawwā': Eve, the first woman.
Hijaz: the region along the western seaboard of Arabia in which Makkah, Madīnah, Jidda and Ta'if are situated.
al-Ḥijr: the unroofed portion of the Ka'bah which at present is in the form of a semi-circular compound towards the north of the Ka'bah.
Hijrah: emigration in the way of Allah. Islamic dating begins with the Hijrah of the Prophet Muḥammad ﷺ from Makkah to Madīnah in 622 AD.
Ḥimāriyyah: see *mushtarikah.*
Hubal: pre-Islamic idol worshipped by Quraysh at the Ka'bah.
Hūd: the Prophet sent to the people of 'Ād.
Ḥudaybīyah: a well-known place ten miles from Makkah on the way to Jiddah where the Homage of ar-Riḍwān took place.
Hudhayl: a tribe which lived in the hills between Makka and Ṭā'if and were linked genealogically with Quraysh.
ḥudūd: plural of *ḥadd.*
Ḥunayn: a valley between Makkah and Ta'if where the battle took place between the Prophet ﷺ and Thaqīf pagans in 8/630.
Iblīs: the personal name of the Devil. He is also called Shayṭān or the 'enemy of Allah'.
Ibrāhīm: the Prophet Abraham.
'Īd: a festival, either the festival at the end of Ramadan or at the time of the Hajj.
iḍāfah: a possessive construction in Arabic in which the first noun is indefinite and the second usually definite. It is used to indicate possession. The first word is called '*muḍāf*' and the second is '*muḍāf ilayhi*'.
'iddah: a period after divorce or the death of her husband for which a woman must wait before re-marrying.
idhkhīr: a kind of sweet rush well known for its good smell and found in the Hijaz.
Idrīs: a Prophet, possibly Enoch.
iḥrām: the conditions of clothing and behaviour adopted by someone on *ḥajj* or *'umrah.*
ijtihād: to exercise personal judgment in legal matters.
īlā': a vow by a husband to abstain from sexual relations with his wife. If four months pass, it is considered a divorce.
imam: Muslim religious or political leader; leader of Muslim congregational worship.
īmān: belief, faith.

'Īsā: the Prophet Jesus.
'Ishā': the obligatory evening prayer.
Isḥāq: the Prophet Isaac.
isnād: a hadith's chain of transmission from individual to individual.
Isrāfīl: the archangel who will blow the Trumpet which announces the end of the world.
istikhārah: a prayer performed by someone who has not decided what to do in a matter hoping to be inspired to do the right thing.
Jabriyyah: pre-determinism, the name given to those who, in opposition to the Qadariyyah, deny the freedom of the will, and on this point make no distinction between man and inanimate nature, inasmuch as his actions are subordinate to the compulsion (*jabr*) of God. Thus everything has been pre-determined and man has no responsibility whatsoever for his actions.
Jāhiliyyah: the Time of Ignorance before the coming of Islam.
Jahmites: followers of Jahm ibn Ṣafwān who claimed, among other things, that human beings are forced to do what they do without any volition on their part.
Jamā'ah: the main body of the Muslim community; also the Group Prayer.
jamrah: lit. a small walled place, but in this usage a stone-built pillar. There are three *jamra*hs at Minā. One of the rites of *ḥajj* is to stone them.
janābah: major ritual impurity requiring a *ghusl*: brought about by sexual intercourse, sexual discharge, menstruation, childbirth.
Jibrīl: the angel Gabriel.
jihad: struggle, particularly fighting in the way of Allah to establish Islam.
jinn: inhabitants of the heavens and the earth made of smokeless fire who are usually invisible.
jizyah: a protection tax payable by non-Muslims living under Muslim rule as a tribute to the Muslim ruler.
Juhaynah: a large nomadic tribe from the Hijaz whose territory covered the routes between Syria and Makkah.
Jumāda-l-Ākhir: the sixth month of the Muslim calendar.
Jumāda-l-Ulā: the fifth month of the Muslim calendar.
Jumu'ah: the day of gathering, Friday, and particularly the Jumu'ah prayer which is performed instead of Ẓuhr by those who attend it.
Ka'bah: the cube-shaped building at the centre of the Ḥaram in Makkah, originally built by the Prophet Ibrāhīm. Also known as the House of Allah.
kalālah: someone who dies without direct heirs.
kasrah: the Arabic vowel (i).
khalifāh: caliphate.

Khandaq: Arabic for Ditch, Battle of, see above.
Khārijites: the earliest sect, who separated themselves from the body of the Muslims and declared war on all those who disagreed with them, stating that a wrong action turns a Muslim into an unbeliever.
Khaybar: Jewish colony to the north of Madina which was laid siege to and captured by the Muslims in the seventh year after the Hijra.
Khazraj: along with Aws, one of the two major tribes of Madīnah.
khaṭīb: an orator, someone who delivers the *khuṭbah.*
Khorasan: Persian province southeast of the Caspian Sea; a centre of many dissident movements in early Islamic history.
khul': a form of divorce initiated by the wife from her husband by giving him a certain compensation, or by returning back the dowry (*mahr*) which he gave her.
khuṭbah: a speech, and in particular a standing speech given by the imam before the Jumu'ah prayer and after the two 'Īd prayers.
Khuzā'ah: an Azdī tribe who were concentrated around Makkah.
kufr: disbelief, to cover up the truth, to reject Allah and refuse to believe that Muhammad ﷺ is His Messenger.
kunyah: a respectful but intimate way of addressing people as "the father of so-and-so" or "the mother of so-and-so."
li'ān: mutual cursing, a form of divorce in which the husband and wife take oaths when he accuses her of adultery and she denies it.
Maghrib: the sunset prayer; also the western part of Muslim lands. Today it means Morocco.
maḥram: a male relative with whom marriage is forbidden.
Maqām of Ibrāhịm: the place of the stone on which the Prophet Ibrāhīm stood while he and Ismā'īl were building the Ka'bah, which marks the place of the two *rak'ah* prayer following *ṭawāf* of the Ka'bah.
maqāsid: the goals or higher objectives of the Sharī'ah: preservation of the *dīn*, life, lineage, intellect and property.
marfū': 'elevated' , a narration from the Prophet ﷺ mentioned by a Companion, e.g. "The Messenger of Allah ﷺ said..."
Maryam: Mary, the mother of 'Īsā.
Mash'ar al-Ḥarām: a venerated place in the valley of Muzdalifah where it is a sunnah to stop.
Masjid al-Ḥarām: the great mosque in Makkah.
mawlā: a person with whom a tie of *walā'* has been established, usually by having been a slave and then set free.

mawqūf: 'stopped', a narration from a Companion without mentioning the Prophet ﷺ.
mu'adhdhin: someone who calls the *adhān* or call to prayer.
muḍāf: see *iḍāfah.*
mu'ḍal: 'perplexing', in hadith, one missing one or two links in the *isnād.*
mudd: a measure of volume. approximately a double-handed scoop.
Mudlij: an Arab tribe which was a branch of Kinānah.
mufti: someone qualified to give a legal opinion or *fatwā.*
Muhājirūn: Companions of the Messenger of Allah ﷺ who accepted Islam in Makkah and made hijrah to Madīnah.
Muḥarram: the first month of the Muslim lunar year.
muḥṣan: someone who has been in a valid marriage. The feminine is *muḥṣanah.*
munkar: "denounced", a narration reported by a weak reporter which goes against another authentic hadith.
muqayyad: a term used in fiqh meaning restricted, qualified, conditional in respect of a ruling.
murābiṭ: one who is garrisoned defending the frontier, someone living in a *ribāṭ.*
Al-Muraysī': a battle between the Prophet and the Banu-l-Muṣṭaliq in 6/627.
Murji'ites: the opponents of the Kharijites. They held that it is faith and not actions which are important. They also had a political position which suspends judgment on a person guilty of major sins.
mursal: a hadith where a man in the generation after the Companions quotes directly from the Prophet without mentioning the Companion from whom he got it.
Mūsā: the Prophet Moses.
Musaylimah: the false prophet of the Banū Ḥanīfah in Najd.
mushtarikah: 'shared', also called Ḥimāriyyah, a case in inheritance where male and female siblings have equal shares and the husband a half and mother a sixth.
musnad: a collection of hadiths arranged according to the first authority in its *isnād*; also a hadith which can be traced back through an unbroken *isnād* to the Prophet.
mutakallimūn: those who study the science of *kalām,* the science of investigating theological doctrine.
Mu'tazilite: someone who adheres to the school of the Mu'tazilah which is rationalist in its approach to existence. Originally they held that anyone

who commits a sin is neither a believer nor an unbeliever. They also held the Qur'an to be created.

muṭlaq: in *fiqh*, unrestricted, qualified or limited in its application. When it is qualified, it becomes *muqayyad*.

An-Naḍīr: a Jewish tribe in Madīnah.

nāfilah: (plural *nawāfil*): supererogatory act of worship.

Nūḥ: the Prophet Noah.

People of the Book: principally the Jews and Christians whose religions are based on the Divine Books revealed to Mūsā and 'Īsā; a term also used to refer to any other group who claim to be following a Book revealed prior to the Qur'an.

People of Hadith: 'the adherents of Hadith', the movement who considered only the Qur'an and hadith to be valid sources of *fiqh*.

People of Opinion (ra'y): a term used to describe those who use personal opinion to deduce judgment. It was a term used particularly to describe the early Ḥanafīs.

Qadariyyah: sect who said that people have power (*qadar*) over their actions and hence free will.

qāḍī: a judge, qualified to judge all matters in accordance with the Sharī'ah and to dispense and enforce legal punishments.

Qādisīyah: a decisive four day battle fought against the Persians in Iraq in 15/636.

Qārūn: the Biblical Korah who was famed for his incredible wealth and became arrogant on account of it. The earth swallowed him up.

qiblah: the direction faced in the prayer which is towards the Ka'bah in Makkah.

qinṭār: plural *qanāṭīr*, a relatively large measure for food grains, approx. 45 kgs.

qirāḍ: wealth put by an investor in the trust of an agent for use for commercial purposes, the agent receiving no wage, but taking a designated share of the profits after the capital has been repaid.

qunūt: a supplication said in the prayer.

Quraysh: one of the great tribes of Arabia. The Prophet Muḥammad ﷺ belonged to this tribe, which had great powers spiritually and financially both before and after Islam came. Someone from this tribe is called a Qurayshī.

Qurayẓah: one of the Jewish tribes of Madīnah.

Rabī' al-Awwal: the third month of the Muslim calendar.

Rabī' al-Ākhir: the fourth month of the Muslim calendar.

Raḍwā: a mountain to the west of Madīnah.
Rāfiḍites: the Rawāfiḍ, a group of the Shi'ah known for rejecting Abū Bakr and 'Umar as well as 'Uthmān. It is a nickname, meaning "deserters".
Rajab: the seventh month of the Muslim calendar.
rak'ah: a unit of the prayer consisting of a series of standings, bowing, prostrations and sittings.
Ramadan: the month of fasting, the ninth month in the Muslim lunar calendar.
Rāshidūn: 'Rightly Guided', the title given to the first four caliphs in Islam: Abū Bakr, 'Umar, 'Uthmān and 'Alī.
ribāṭ: the stronghold traditionally used by the Muslims to prepare for jihad against their enemy, situated on exposed points on the frontier.
Riddah: the defection of various Arab tribes after the death of the Prophet ﷺ which brought about the Riddah War.
Ridwān: the Homage of Riḍwān was a pledge which the Muslims took at Ḥudaybīyah to avenge 'Uthmān when they thought that Quraysh had murdered him in 6/628.
rukū': the bowing position in the prayer.
ṣā': a measure of volume equal to four mudds.
ṣadaqah: charitable giving in the Cause of Allah.
Ṣafā and Marwah: two hills close to the Ka'bah.
Ṣafar: the second month of the Muslim lunar calendar.
ṣaḥīḥ: healthy and sound with no defects, used to describe an authentic hadith.
Ṣaḥīḥ: "the Sound", the title of the hadith collections of al-Bukhārī and Muslim.
Salaf: the early generations of the Muslims.
Ṣāliḥ: the Prophet sent to the people of Thamūd.
Saḥūlī: pure white cotton cloth from Saḥūl in Yemen.
sariyyah: an expedition sent by the Prophet ﷺ in which he did not participate.
Sha'bān: the eighth month in the Muslim calendar
shādhdh: an 'irregular' hadith which is reported by a trustworthy person but which goes against the narration of someone who is more reliable than him.
shahādah: bearing witness, particularly bearing witness that there is no god but Allah and that Muhammad is the Messenger of Allah. It is one of the pillars of Islam. It is also used to describe legal testimony in a court of law.

Sharī'ah: The legal modality of a people based on the revelation of their Prophet. The final Sharī'ah is that of Islam.
Shawwāl: the tenth month of the Muslim calendar.
Shayṭān: devil, particularly Iblīs, one of the jinn.
shighār: a forbidden form of marriage agreement whereby a man gave his daughter in marriage to a man who in return gave his daughter in marriage to him, without either of them paying any dowry to their respective brides.
Aṣ-Ṣiḥāḥ: the famous dictionary *Tāj al-'Arūs wa-ṣ-Ṣiḥāh al-'Arabīyah*, by Ismā'īl ibn Ḥammād al-Jawharī.
shirk: the unforgiveable wrong action of worshipping something or someone other than Allah or associating something or someone as a partner with Him.
Shu'ayb: the Prophet Jethro.
shūrā: consultation, especially used for the council of six Companions who met after the death of 'Umar to choose the next Caliph.
Sīrah: biography, particularly biography of the Prophet ﷺ.
Ṣirāṭ: the narrow bridge which spans the Fire and must be crossed to enter the Garden. It is described as sharper than a sword and thinner than a hair. It will have hooks over it to catch people as they cross it.
Ṣubḥ: dawn prayer
sujūd: prostration.
sukūn: a diacritic mark that means that there is no sound after a consonant.
Sulaymān: the Prophet Solomon.
sunan: plural of sunnah.
Sunnah: the customary practice of a person or group of people. It has come to refer almost exclusively to the practice of the Messenger of Allah ﷺ.
sūrah: a chapter of the Qur'an.
Tābi'ūn: the second generation of the early Muslims who did not meet the Prophet Muhammad ﷺ but learned the *dīn* of Islam from his Companions.
Tabūk: a town in northern Arabia close to Jordan.
Ṭā'if: a walled town south of Makkah known for its fertility. It was the home of the tribe of Thaqīf.
takbīr: saying 'Allāhu Akbar,' 'Allah is greater'.
takbīr al-iḥrām: the *takbīr* which begins the prayer.
talbīyah: saying '*Labbayk*' ('At Your service') during the hajj.
tanwīn: nunation.
taqwā: awe or fear of Allah, which inspires a person to be on guard against wrong action and eager for actions which please Him.
ṭawāf: circumambulation of the Ka'bah, done in sets of seven circuits.

tawḥīd: the doctrine of Divine Unity.
tawakkul: reliance, unshakeable trust in Allah.
Thaqīf: a tribe based in the town of Ta'if, a branch of the tribe of Hawāzin.
Tihāmah: the Red Sea coastal plain of Arabia.
Uḥud: a mountain just outside of Madīnah where five years after the Hijrah, the Muslims lost a battle against the Makkan idolaters. Many great Companions, and in particular Ḥamzah, the uncle of the Prophet, were killed in this battle.
Umm al-Mu'minīn: literally 'Mother of the Believers', an honorary title given to the wives of the Prophet.
'umrah: the lesser pilgrimage to the Ka'bah in Makkah performed at any time of the year.
ūqiyyah: unit of measurement equal to 40 dirhams in weight or 118.80 gs.
Al-'Ushayrah: a place between Makkah and Madīnah in the direction of Yanbū'. It was the site of an early expedition.
uṣūl: plural of *aṣl*, the basic principles of any source used in *fiqh*.
'Uzayr: Ezra.
Al-'Uzzā: a female idol worshipped by the pagan Arabs in the Hijaz in the Jāhiliyyah.
Waddān: a settlement about eight miles from al-Abwā' where an expedition took place in 2/623.
Wādī al-Qurā: located near the Gulf of 'Aqabah north of the Red Sea where a Jewish settlement was located in the time of the Prophet ﷺ.
walā': the tie of clientage established between a freed slave and the person who frees him, whereby the freed slave becomes integrated into the family of that person as a client (*mawlā*).
walī: (plural *awliyā'*) someone who is a 'friend' of Allah, thus possessing the quality of *wilāyah*. Also a relative who acts as a guardian.
wakīl: a person who is an authorized representative, agent or proxy.
wuḍū': ritual washing to be pure for the prayer.
Yaḥyā: the Prophet John the Baptist, the son of Zakariyyā.
Yamāmah, Battle of: also known as the Battle of 'Aqraba, the major battle of the Riddah War in which the Muslims defeated the forces of the false Prophet Musaylimah in 12/633.
Yanbū': a sea port near Riḍwā, between Makkah and Madīnah.
Ya'qūb: the Prophet Jacob, also called Isrā'īl (Israel).
Yūnus: the Prophet Jonah.
Yūsuf: the Prophet Joseph.
Zabūr: the Psalms of Dāwud.

Zakariyyā: the Prophet Zachariah, the father of Yaḥyā, John the Baptist, and guardian of Maryam.
zakat: a wealth tax, one of the five pillars of Islam.
zakat al-fiṭr: a small obligatory head-tax imposed on every Muslim who has the means for himself and his dependants. It is paid at the end of Ramadan.
Zamzam: the well in the Ḥaram of Makka.
ẓihār: an oath by a husband that his wife is like his mother's back to him, meaning she is unlawful for him. It was a form of divorce in the Jāhiliyyah.
Ẓuhr: the midday prayer.

www.ingramcontent.com/pod-product-compliance
Lightning Source LLC
Chambersburg PA
CBHW080424230426
43662CB00015B/2204
* 9 7 8 1 9 0 8 8 9 2 9 6 6 *